The Philosopher Responds

Letter from the General Editor

The Library of Arabic Literature makes available Arabic editions and English translations of significant works of Arabic literature, with an emphasis on the seventh to nineteenth centuries. The Library of Arabic Literature thus includes texts from the pre-Islamic era to the cusp of the modern period, and encompasses a wide range of genres, including poetry, poetics, fiction, religion, philosophy, law, science, travel writing, history, and historiography.

Books in the series are edited and translated by internationally recognized scholars. They are published in parallel-text and English-only editions in both print and electronic formats. PDFs of Arabic editions are available for free download. The Library of Arabic Literature also publishes distinct scholarly editions with critical apparatus and a separate Arabic-only series aimed at young readers.

The Library encourages scholars to produce authoritative Arabic editions, accompanied by modern, lucid English translations, with the ultimate goal of introducing Arabic's rich literary heritage to a general audience of readers as well as to scholars and students.

The publications of the Library of Arabic Literature are generously supported by Tamkeen under the NYU Abu Dhabi Research Institute Award G1003 and are published by NYU Press.

Philip F. Kennedy
General Editor, Library of Arabic Literature

About this Paperback

This paperback edition differs in a few respects from its dual-language hardcover predecessor. Because of the compact trim size the pagination has changed. Material that referred to the Arabic edition has been updated to reflect the English-only format, and other material has been corrected and updated where appropriate. For information about the Arabic edition on which this English translation is based and about how the LAL Arabic text was established, readers are referred to the hardcover.

The Philosopher Responds

An Intellectual Correspondence from the Tenth Century

BY

Abū Ḥayyān al-Tawḥīdī

Abū ʿAlī Miskawayh

TRANSLATED BY

Sophia Vasalou and James E. Montgomery

FOREWORD BY

Jonathan Rée

VOLUME EDITOR

Devin J. Stewart

NEW YORK UNIVERSITY PRESS

New York

NEW YORK UNIVERSITY PRESS
New York

Library of Congress Cataloging-in-Publication Control Number: 2020051554

Series design and composition by Nicole Hayward
Typeset in Adobe Text

Manufactured in the United States of America

10 9 8 7 6 5 4 3 2 1

Contents

Foreword

JONATHAN RÉE

The first history of philosophy was written in Greek around 200 CE by the Greek historian Diogenes Laertius, who offered sketches of the lives and works of more than eighty philosophers, every one of whom was Greek, or at least taught and wrote in the Greek language. The obvious implication—that philosophy is innately and essentially Greek—will no doubt strike most modern readers as outdated and absurd, and probably offensive too. Nowadays we can all claim the right to philosophize, regardless of who we are, where we come from, or what language we speak. Diogenes's Grecocentrism has placed him, it would seem, on the wrong side of history.

Or perhaps not. We all recognize some things as inherently Greek, both in origin and in nature: the *Iliad* and the *Odyssey*, for example, or classical Comedy and Tragedy, or the ancient Olympic games. Perhaps Diogenes was simply saying that philosophy—which, by the way, he did not hold in very high esteem—was just one more of the peculiarities of the Greeks. He must in any case have been aware that several works of philosophy had been circulating in Latin translations for at least two centuries. But a cursory glance would have revealed that the translators had often been lost for words: there were dozens of philosophical terms for which they could not find Latin equivalents, and they were reduced to coining Greek-rooted transliterations such as *ethica, logica, physica*, and of course *philosophia*. "It was from the Greeks that philosophy (φιλοσοφία) took its rise," as Diogenes observed, "and its very name refuses to be translated into other languages."

But how exactly does translation work? We tend to think of it as the linguistic equivalent of digging a canal between two oceans, in order to allow intellectual traffic to pass back and forth. Sometimes, however, it may be more like building a replica of some foreign structure, using local materials and techniques—as with the Colosseum in Las Vegas, the Nashville Parthenon, or perhaps the mock-Athenian columns of ancient Rome. Experience suggests, moreover, that even the most perfect replicas tend to lack the vitality and charm of their originals: they are liable to look too regular and too smooth, and as a rule they will not age well. When the corpus of Greek philosophy got its makeover into Latin, the effect was somewhat similar. What had appeared to the Greeks—for example to Diogenes Laertius—as an open-ended miscellany of doctrines whose lapses and inconsistencies reflected the idiosyncrasies of some of their headier fellow-citizens, was reconstructed in Latin as an immaculate temple of exotic wisdom, which readers were expected to approach in hushed reverence.

When Greek philosophy was translated into Arabic—a systematic undertaking carried out mainly in the eighth and ninth centuries, largely by Iraqi Christians—the effect was much the same. Diverse works on logic, metaphysics, physics, politics, ethics, medicine, and astrology, by many different authors, were transformed into a self-contained and homogeneous sector of Arabic literature, known by the Greek-derived term *falsafah*.

In *The Philosopher Responds*, the celebrated scholar Abū ʿAlī Miskawayh offers us a fascinating tour of the wonderful world of *falsafah* as it was in the tenth century. Philosophy for Miskawayh was a treasury of perfect knowledge and, after years of assiduous study, he knew it like the back of his hand. He never attempted, however, to discriminate between the voices of different authors or the textures of different works, and he showed no interest in the Greek words lurking behind the Arabic. (Most likely he did not know any Greek.) He simply took it for granted that philosophy originated in the work of Plato, and that Plato had a pupil called Aristotle who brought it to such a pitch of perfection that his successors were left with nothing to do apart from expounding his doctrines and applying them to new topics. The correct method in philosophy, as far as Miskawayh was concerned, was to start by consulting the works of Aristotle, and if "the Philosopher" (as Miskawayh liked to call him), had expressed an opinion on any matter then there was "no need to look further." Failing that you should find out "the view of the philosophers," or what "has been established by philosophical inquiries." In this way you would eventually arrive at an impersonal doctrine with an authority from which there could be no appeal.

Philosophy, as Miskawayh saw it, has several memorable lessons to teach us. The first is that there are *four causes,* or four types of explanation: material, formal, efficient, and best of all "final," meaning those that refer to the purposes things serve. Philosophy also tells us that bodily health depends on maintaining a balance between the *four humors,* which in turn arise from the *four elements* which compose the natural world, namely earth, air, fire, and water. But the most important lesson is that our existence comprises *two elements*: in addition to our body, which is multiple and mortal, we have a soul, which is essentially "one" and "above time." Our body belongs to the same ignoble natural order as animal life, and while we should not neglect it we owe a far higher duty to our soul. And our soul turns out, despite its unity, to have *three powers*—animal, irascible, and rational—which are in constant tension with each other. It is of course self-evident that we ought to take the side of reason, which involves raising ourselves above the natural world and cultivating both virtue (defined as choosing the midpoint between two extremes) and knowledge (defined as the perception of forms). In other words—to clinch the argument—we must devote ourselves to studying the supreme intellectual discipline, which is of course philosophy.

If Miskawayh had written a treatise summarising these well-worn doctrines, it would probably have been rather dry, and might have sunk like a stone. But *The Philosopher Responds* is not a treatise but a dialogue, in which Miskawayh confronts a motley assortment of questions submitted to him by a fellow scholar, Abū Ḥayyān al-Tawḥīdī. They were however no kindred spirits: al-Tawḥīdī was more interested in life's little ironies than in the stately wisdom of the philosophers, and he likened his questions to a herd of wild camels, challenging Miskawayh to try and round them up. Miskawayh was sometimes riled by al-Tawḥīdī's questions ("I feared that you would trip yourself up in the swell of your volubility" as he exclaims at one point), and instead of quoting them in full he trimmed and paraphrased them to suit his own purposes. But he did not always remove their sharp edges. Why, for example, are people such hypocrites that they rail against greed, while seizing every opportunity to turn a profit? Could a habitual liar become truthful? And why do languages contain so many different words that mean more or less the same thing?

Miskawayh always had an answer at his fingertips. Philosophy has shown, he explains, that human existence is essentially a site of struggle, in which the timeless excellences of the soul are pitted against the temptations of the flesh: hence hypocrisy. As for lying, books on ethics concur in presenting it as a symptom of spiritual disease, while truthfulness is an expression of good health; moreover, physical health is an attribute of the body as a whole, whereas diseases only affect particular parts, and can usually be overcome; and the analogy implies that a chronic liar can be cured. Miskawayh then turns to the phenomenon of linguistic proliferation, using it to illustrate what seems to have been his favorite philosophical theme: that none of us can provide for all our own needs, and hence that our lives overlap and our existence is essentially political: "human beings are unable to act in isolation," as he put it, and "most human affairs can only be accomplished through mutual help and partnership."

These were all good and interesting responses, but al-Tawḥīdī did not get the chance to follow them up, so it is impossible to tell whether he was satisfied. In some cases, he may have been, but in others it seems unlikely that he was. How, he had asked, can friendship flourish between people who have little or nothing in common? An intriguing question, one might have thought, but Miskawayh dodged it by affirming, dogmatically and at great length, that friendship always rests on likeness or affinity. He was equally obtuse when faced with questions involving theology, such as "what is the proof that angels exist?" His answer—that angels must exist, in the first place because they are mentioned in the Qur'an, and secondly because philosophy informs us that denying their existence is self-contradictory—will surely have left al-Tawḥīdī wondering what Miskawayh would have said of the possibility that philosophy and the Qur'an might sometimes point in opposite directions.

On top of that, some of al-Tawḥīdī's questions were simply weird, and readers may well suspect that they were not quite serious: "Why do tall people tend to be foolish?" for instance, or "why is seawater salty?" As always Miskawayh had his answers at the ready—tallness places the brain too far from the heart, and the sea lies so near the sun that it gets cooked—but one wonders if he was falling into a trap. The same applies when al-Tawḥīdī poses questions which sound rather insulting, such as "why are men of knowledge given to conceit?" and "why do some people claim to have knowledge when they know they do not?" Could he by any chance have been trying to raise a laugh at the expense of a philosophical know-it-all?

This is of course mere speculation, based on a twenty-first-century translation of a medieval Arabic classic. But those of us who come to it with some background in modern philosophy are bound to feel as if we have entered an inverted world, with a guide who keeps promising us what he calls "the pleasure of certainty," when we are probably more attached to the pleasures of doubt. Such a reaction may of course be anachronistic (whatever that means), but then again it may not. At one point al-Tawḥīdī himself posed a question that seems to anticipate the bewilderment that envelops the modern reader: "why is it," he asks, "that when certainty obtains, it does not last long enough to take root, whereas when doubt assails, it drops anchor and stays put?" True to form, Miskawayh dismissed his opponent's premise, asserting that "the person who has attained certainty is tranquil and at ease and utterly immune to being moved by doubt." But some of us may permit ourselves—like al-Tawḥīdī, it would seem—to wonder if Miskawayh got it right.

Jonathan Rée
Wolvercote, near Oxford
Europe

Acknowledgments

Sophia Vasalou would like to express her thanks to Devin Stewart and James Montgomery for invaluable feedback. James Montgomery would like to thank Sophia Vasalou for so graciously acknowledging his contribution to the translation; Stuart Brown for producing yet another gorgeous book; Keith Miller for his copy-editing panache; and Chip Rossetti and Lucie Taylor, without whose dedication the Library of Arabic Literature could not function. Peter Adamson and members of his group at the University of Munich scrutinized parts of the translation with great care and provided very helpful suggestions at the last stage of this work, while Wadad Kadi's attentive reading of the introduction helped pull out several weeds.

Introduction

The present book is unusual in having not one, but two authors. It is the result of a collaboration between two figures, both of whom were outstanding contributors to that remarkable flowering of cultural and intellectual life that took place in the Islamic world during the fourth/tenth century under the Buyid dynasty.

Military men of Persian extraction and Shiʿi sympathies, the Buyids rose to power with the collapse of the Abbasid Caliphate and ruled over large parts of the eastern Islamic lands for over a century (320–454/932–1062). A time of economic distress and social insecurity, of religious and ideological rivalries, this period nevertheless saw an outpouring of creative energy that would shape Islamic intellectual history for centuries to come. Intellectual possibilities that had already dawned crystallized and solidified. The engagement with the legacy of classical antiquity, already begun in Abbasid times, intensified, and the concerted efforts to translate and study the works of major philosophical and scientific thinkers of the ancient world—Aristotle and Plato, Euclid and Ptolemy, Hippocrates and Galen—ministered to a climate of rationalistic inquiry that is one of the hallmarks of that period. The distinctive form of literary refinement known as *adab*, whose standard-bearers were the secretaries, scribes, and other members of the administrative apparatus of the state, blossomed alongside this philosophical culture.

The ruling class had a large hand in galvanizing this activity, not only through active patronage but also through the spirit of tolerance they nurtured in the face of new ideas and existing antagonisms. During the heyday of Buyid rule, the courts of princes and viziers in key cities across Iraq and western Iran—notably Baghdad, Rayy, Isfahan, and Shiraz—became nerve centers of intellectual activity, lodestones for philosophers, scientists, and literati competing for recognition and support. Many of the luminaries from this period who have become household names for students of Islamic intellectual history, including our own two authors, were shaped and fostered by this social milieu.

This book forms part of the rich legacy left behind by that historical moment—a moment in which many have read the contours of an Islamic "Renaissance" or humanistic Enlightenment. Taken simply, the book consists of a series of wide-ranging questions posed by the litterateur Abū Ḥayyān al-Tawḥīdī to the philosopher and historian Abū ʿAlī Miskawayh. The Arabic title of the book, *al-Hawāmil wa-l-shawāmil,* makes this dual character somewhat clearer than its English rendering. *Hawāmil* are camels that have been left free to wander without bridle or burden—such are al-Tawḥīdī's questions. In answering them, Miskawayh seeks to contain (*shamila*) these wandering questions and bring them home as a good "herder" and "steward" would.

Al-Tawḥīdī and Miskawayh: Life and Works

How did this collaborative work come about, and what is its precise character? A brief overview of the careers of both men will provide some context for answering these questions. Abū ʿAlī Aḥmad ibn Muḥammad ibn Yaʿqūb Miskawayh was born in Rayy around 320–35/932–47, with one biographical report placing his death in 421/1030. He served as a secretary (which was his training) and a librarian under a series of ruling figures in the Buyid courts. His first appointment to the service of the vizier al-Muhallabī (d. 352/963) in Baghdad was followed by appointments at the court in Rayy under the vizier Abū l-Faḍl Ibn al-ʿAmīd (d. 360/970), his son Abū l-Fatḥ (d. 366/976), and the emir ʿAḍud al-Dawlah (d. 372/983). Many of his patrons were men of great cultural accomplishment whose courts served as lodestones of intellectual activity. The galvanizing effect of this environment would register clearly in Miskawayh's own output. As a historian, Miskawayh is best known for his multivolume work *The Experiences of the Nations* (*Tajārib al-umam*), which includes important first-person accounts of events that took place within his own lifetime. Yet it is to his philosophical work that he no doubt owes the greatest part of his reputation. His philosophical output includes *The Degrees of Happiness and the Classification of the Sciences* (*Tartīb al-saʿādāt wa-manāzil al-ʿulūm*) and *The Minor Triumph* (*al-Fawz al-aṣghar*), and tackles key philosophical questions about the nature of God, the nature of the soul, and prophecy. His most celebrated work, however, is *The Refinement of Character* (*Tahdhīb al-akhlāq*), in which the ethical focus that forms the hallmark of his intellectual orientation comes into full fruition. Synthesizing Aristotelian, Platonic, Neoplatonic, and Galenic ideas that had become available to Arabic readers through translation from Greek and Syriac sources over the preceding two centuries, this work offers an account of virtuous character, its relation to happiness, and the means of educating it, an account that would prove widely influential to later writers in ethics. In developing his philosophical ideas, Miskawayh builds on the work of his predecessors, notably Abū Yūsuf al-Kindī (d. between 247–52 and 861–66), and refines it in new ways.

Miskawayh's elder by a few years, Abū Ḥayyān ʿAlī ibn Muḥammad ibn ʿAbbās al-Tawḥīdī is thought to have been born between 310/922 and 322/934, either in Iraq or in Fars; the date of his death is given as 414/1023. After a traditional education, which included instruction in the philological and religious sciences in Baghdad, he worked as a copyist before launching a series of concerted attempts to find patronage in courtly circles. He would spend several years between Baghdad and Rayy pursuing this quest without success, first approaching the elder Ibn al-ʿAmīd, then his son, and finally the vizier al-Ṣāḥib Ibn ʿAbbād (d. 385/995), in whose service he spent three discontented years before finding temporary patronage in Baghdad with the vizier Ibn Saʿdān (d. 374/984–85). His inability to attain the worldly success he felt he merited—which many have attributed to his difficult character—left him impoverished and produced a lasting embitterment that is reflected in much of his work, tinging it with a pessimism and "tragic sense of life" that makes for its distinctive voice and personal immediacy.

His literary output is shaped by the philosophical interests he acquired through interaction with leading philosophers of his time, including Yaḥyā ibn ʿAdī (d. 363/974) and, more notably, Abū Sulaymān al-Sijistānī (d. ca. 375/985), whose study sessions he assiduously attended. It is also shaped by, and shines a brilliant light on, the social context in which learned exchange took place in his time. One of his best-known works, *The Book of Enjoyment and Conviviality* (*Kitāb al-Imtāʿ wa-l-muʾānasah*), is a lively, stylized account of the evening conversations between al-Tawḥīdī and Ibn Saʿdān, covering philosophical, literary, scientific, and other topics. Another work, *Conversations* (*al-Muqābasāt*), documents a number of exchanges featuring the philosophers Yaḥyā ibn ʿAdī and al-Sijistānī, among other figures. Other well-known works include the literary compilation *Insights and Treasures* (*al-Baṣāʾir wa-l-dhakhāʾir*), the treatise *On Friendship and Friends* (*al-Ṣadāqah wa-l-ṣadīq*), a work lampooning the two viziers Ibn al-ʿAmīd and Ibn ʿAbbād (*Dhamm akhlāq al-wazīrayn*), and the mystical work *Divine Intimations* (*al-Ishārāt al-ilāhiyyah*).

The Philosopher Responds in Context

How can we locate the present book in the work and life of these two thinkers? Even this brief outline of their respective biographies has suggested convergences of social context and intellectual interests that would not make such a collaboration improbable. Although we do not know for certain where the two men first met, whether in Rayy or Baghdad, the learned and courtly circles in which they both moved provided ample opportunity. It has been speculated that they may have met as early as the 340s/950s during the period of Miskawayh's first appointment in Baghdad.[1] A learned exchange within the pages of a book, similarly, seems fully at home in the dialogic spirit of the intellectual culture they shared in, so vividly portrayed in al-Tawḥīdī's work.

Taken as a philosophical exchange in particular—and, as we will see in a moment, the book has a distinct philosophical focus—there was even more specific precedent available. The Aristotelian *Problemata* literature, at least partly translated into Arabic by that time, had offered a clear model for the way philosophical topics might be explored in a question-and-answer format.[2] Even more directly, other eminent philosophers had appropriated this format in initiating learned correspondence of different kinds. A good example is the correspondence that took place between Yaḥyā ibn ʿAdī and the Jewish scholar Ibn Abī Saʿīd al-Mawṣilī, in which the former offered his response to fourteen questions on logic, physics, and metaphysics put to him by the latter.[3] The philosopher-historian Miskawayh and al-Tawḥīḍī, that wide-ranging intellectual whom one biographer, Yāqūt al-Ḥawamī (d. 626/1229), memorably called the "philosopher of the litterateurs and the litterateur of the philosophers," had a number of well-marked tracks in which to tread in opening their conversation.[4]

There will be something more to say about the nature of this exchange and its peculiar type of conversation in a moment. Yet, certainly, when it comes to anchoring the work chronologically within the careers of the two writers, forming a clear view of its genesis is not an entirely straightforward task. It seems reasonable to suppose, as many of those approaching the question have done, that the work belongs to a relatively early stage in the writing career of both thinkers, predating their major writings. As has been aptly pointed out, for example, Miskawayh—ever the academic in his hearty appetite for citing his own past work—only makes reference to a single existing work, the *Minor Triumph,* which was likely written at the behest of ʿAḍud al-Dawlah (r. 338–72/949–83). One of the strongest hypotheses, advanced by Mohammed Arkoun, would locate the composition of the book during the time of Miskawayh's service to the latter, in the period between 367/977 and 372/983, when al-Tawḥīdī would have also been in Rayy at the court of Ibn ʿAbbād. Arkoun speculates that al-Tawḥīdī may have composed his questions during his sojourn in Rayy between 367/977 and 370/980 and that Miskawayh may have responded to them between 370/980 and 372/982. It is during his service to an emir who was himself a philosopher and patron of the intellectual elite, he suggests, that Miskawayh was most likely confirmed in his philosophical vocation and would have felt especially motivated to compose a work that would help cement his philosophical credentials. Al-Tawḥīdī, on his end, would have hoped to extract some benefit through the support of his well-positioned interlocutor.[5] This chronological hypothesis has not gone uncontested. Arkoun himself would later revise his view, framing the more open-ended hypothesis that the whole work was composed after 375/985, when al-Tawḥīdī would have left Rayy for Baghdad.[6] Erez Naaman dismisses this proposal, pointing out that nowhere in the book does al-Tawḥīdī refer to his revered teacher al-Sijistānī, whom he would already have met by that time. His own view is that the work was composed earlier, in the late 350s/960s or 360s/970s.[7]

Taken on its own, the debate about the chronology of the work might seem of relatively narrow interest. What makes it both especially intriguing and elusive is its enmeshment with the way we understand the relations between the two thinkers, the motivations that drove them, and thus the spirit and nature of the exchange. These questions contribute to the somewhat enigmatic character of the book as a whole.

One of the principal interpretive levers used for approaching the relations between the two men is the remarks made by al-Tawḥīdī about Miskawayh in a number of works, notably *Enjoyment and Conviviality*. Many of these remarks bear the unmistakable mark of al-Tawḥīdī's barbed tongue. In a well-known passage, he characterizes Miskawayh as "a pauper among the affluent and a stutterer among the eloquent" who only has a smattering of knowledge, having wasted many opportunities to learn and having been overly obsessed with the study of alchemy. He's covetous, a miser, and a hypocrite, naturally vicious in character.[8] In introducing the 1951 edition of the present book, Ṣalāḥ Raslān must have had these disparaging comments in mind when he suggested that al-Tawḥīdī's aim in initiating this exchange was to taunt Miskawayh and to reveal his intellectual inadequacy by confronting him with a barrage of challenging questions—not unlike what al-Jāḥiẓ, one of al-Tawḥīdī's idols, had done in a work entitled *The Square and the Round* (*al-Tarbīʿ wa-l-tadwīr*) that was addressed to one Aḥmad ibn ʿAbd al-Wahhāb.[9]

In arguing for his later chronological hypothesis, Arkoun takes an explicit stance against this view of the book's spirit. This view, he suggests, conflicts with the "serenity and even affectionate tone" of Miskawayh's responses. In the preface to the book, he points out, we hear Miskawayh seeking to console his ever-lamenting interlocutor, who must have opened his correspondence with an all-too-familiar complaint. "You began your letter with a lament about the sorry times we live in." You are not alone in your suffering, Miskawayh rejoins: "Your lament falls on the ears of one who himself laments, and your tears are shed before one who is equally tearful. There is a lump in every man's throat, and a mote in every man's eye." And in Arkoun's revised view, we can make the greatest biographical sense of this spirit of fellowship through shared suffering after 375/985.[10] Naaman, likewise, draws on a specific reading of the book's spirit and what it reveals about the relations between the two men in framing his own chronological hypothesis. He comments on the "admiring" tone of the book—"you are a storehouse of arcane learning and recondite wisdom," al-Tawḥīdī tells his respondent at one place as he lays a challenging question at his feet, and I have "fixed my hopes on seeing it answered by you" (§147.1)—and on the "unequal scholarly authority" and "student-teacher relationship" the work evokes. This deferential attitude, he suggests, conflicts with the negative view of Miskawayh voiced in *Enjoyment and Conviviality*, and argues for an earlier composition date when al-Tawḥīdī's view of the philosopher was still rose tinted.[11]

Yet, to the extent that these chronological conjectures pivot implicitly or explicitly around specific readings of the tone of the book and what it reveals about the state of the relations between the two men, no conjecture seems immune to questioning. For one, even al-Tawḥīdī's characterization of Miskawayh elsewhere does not provide unequivocal witness, which might be bookmarked to track his changing view and used as a cast-iron basis for definitive chronologies. As some have pointed out, this characterization, in *Enjoyment* and elsewhere, is riddled with ambiguities, and even within the boundaries of a single work offers contradictory testimony. In one place al-Tawḥīdī derides Miskawayh's eloquence and knowledge, and in another he praises him for his intelligence and poetic compositions. A desire to shine before his audience, and jealousy of Miskawayh's worldly successes, certainly did not make al-Tawḥīdī a stable or impartial witness here.[12] Turning to the evidence of the present book, what one reader will hear as al-Tawḥīdī's admiring tone, a reader more impressed by his acerbic remarks in *Enjoyment* may hear as ironic. What one reader will hear as the affectionate tone of Miskawayh's consolation, another will hear as so much rebuking or haranguing.

This last reading, or hearing, in fact dovetails with impressions generated by other parts of the book, where we find Miskawayh reacting to the content and form of al-Tawḥīdī's questions with an asperity that borders on condescension, sometimes going so far as to land a few sharp ad hominem blows on the ethical character of his questioner as expressed in his flawed questions. A good example appears in §§4.1–14. In his question, al-Tawḥīdī opens with a query about renunciation (*zuhd*), which might be paraphrased most simply as follows. Why do people praise renunciation of the world, yet still we see them running headlong after worldly things? It is an interrogative pattern—"Why x, yet/when y?"—that can be seen at work in many of al-Tawḥīdī's questions, which are often structured by a quest for reasons twinned to an observation of paradox.

Yet, rather than confining himself to this particular question, al-Tawḥīdī begins to pull a new question out of the end of the first. The request for causes and reasons suddenly makes him think of causes and reasons generally, and makes him want to ask what these are. Another turn of phrase sparks a question about the nature of time and place, and about the difference between different concepts of time. Having hurtled breathlessly from one grand question to another, he finally throws up his hands in ecstatic wonderment at the grandeur of these matters, at the chastening limits of human power and understanding, and at the majesty of God. "Good God! This is a topic to make your mouth dry, to press your cheek to the ground, to plunge the soul into a state of ferment, to make the glutton choke on his next bite, to reveal the emptiness of claims to knowledge, and to make one confess the limits of one's adequacy and power. It is a topic that proves the unity of Him who encompasses these mysteries and truths" (§4.2). Taking the podium, Miskawayh begins by dryly objecting to this irresponsible heaping of questions, and proceeds to diagnose it as a manifestation of ethical malaise, no less—of al-Tawḥīdī's "vanity" and "conceit"—completing the point with an image calculated to deliver a poisonous sting. In putting this question, he tells al-Tawḥīdī, you went about "like a proud stallion . . . lustily swishing your tail back and forth, running sidelong across fields, swaggering in your pride and pressing ahead with your extravagance until I feared you would trip yourself up in the swell of your volubility" (§4.4).

Even without this pathologizing tenor, we often find Miskawayh taking issue with the form and content of al-Tawḥīdī's questions and sparing al-Tawḥīdī little of his own barbed tongue in conveying his dissatisfaction. In numerous places, he rejects or corrects the premises of al-Tawḥīdī's questions. In others, he declares them vulgar and unworthy of consideration, as when al-Tawḥīdī asks him about the meaning of certain popular sayings (§157.1) or about the origins of different human customs (§44.1). This is a question to which "I cannot offer a response," Miskawayh replies, and then grandly continues: "I would not want it should someone offer to provide it for me, nor would I consider it real knowledge" for there "would be no advantage to be gained from it" (§44.2). In other questions, he objects to al-Tawḥīdī's manner of expressing himself. The author of these questions, he remarks in one place, "follows a rhetorical style, and does not proceed the way the logicians do in investigating a question" (§86.2). In making these criticisms, he often switches from addressing al-Tawḥīdī in the second person to addressing him in the third, as if he were no longer in the room.

The last point raises a question about Miskawayh's understanding of his audience to which we will be returning. Might it have been this superior tone and bare-knuckle treatment that *later* seeded al-Tawḥīdī's own truculent comments about the philosopher? One may only speculate. Yet this kind of exchange illustrates the reasons why, even though the overall tone or spirit of the work is difficult to determine and offers a shaky foundation for factual conjectures about its genesis, it is difficult to keep it from occupying a central place in one's engagement with the book. As Arkoun remarked, the interest of the book does not lie simply or exclusively in the intellectual content of the questions, but also, at least in part, in the spirit or perspective in which these questions are posed and answered—and thus in the often striking contrast between the two spirits or perspectives we find juxtaposed as question and answer.[13]

Al-Tawḥīdī's Questions

This is by no means to deny the interest of the intellectual content as such. The best way of getting at the spirit of the exchange, in fact, is to start by considering its content, and by taking a closer look at the nature of al-Tawḥīdī's questions. His questions, true to their name (*hawāmil*, "the wandering herd"), do not appear to follow any particular order, and wander freely across a wide array of topics. Several questions relate to topics that fall solidly within the philosophical curriculum broadly conceived. There are questions of natural science, about why mountains exist (§165.1) and why the sea is located on one side of the earth and not another (§167.1). There are questions of medicine or physiology, such as why epilepsy is so hard to treat (§37.1). There are questions of philosophical psychology, such as why the souls are three in number (§166.1). There are questions about the methods of philosophical inquiry, about why we inquire into objects by asking four types of questions—whether, what, which, and why (§159.1). There are questions about practices or crafts allied to the philosophical domain, about what physiognomy is (§63.1), what alchemy is, and why people pursue it (§151.1). There are also broad questions about the nature of key concepts or entities whose interest transcends philosophical boundaries, about what knowledge is (§50.1), what injustice is (§29.1), and what dreams are (§48.1). Many of these questions were hot topics among intellectuals of al-Tawḥīdī's day, and were discussed not only by philosophers but also by dialectical theologians (*mutakallimūn*) and by members of other disciplines. Several of the questions al-Tawḥīdī brings up were staples of debate in different intellectual circles, such as his question about the possibility of conflict between reason and the religious Law (§147.1) or about the relative merits of prose and poetry (§142.1). The latter is one of many that attest to al-Tawḥīdī's literary and philological interests. A further set of questions that focus on the meanings of words, and on the distinctions between closely related words, flag these philological interests even more systematically. It is all the questions just enumerated that make this book a kind of *Wunderkammer* showcasing not only the remarkable diversity of al-Tawḥīdī's interests, but the intellectual interests of his age more broadly.

Yet these kinds of erudite questions are joined to another, larger, family of questions that is rather harder to categorize, and harder to read in a spirit of mere detached "erudition." If we insisted on categorizing them, we might label many of them as questions of an ethical kind, particularly if we connect this term to its root—*ethos*: custom, character—and take it in a sense sufficiently broad to include psychological or social phenomena.[14] Several of them share in the "Why . . . yet/despite" paradoxical structure picked out above. Why do people extol discretion and the keeping of secrets—and yet broadcast secrets for all to hear? (§2.1) Why are men of knowledge prone to conceit, even though knowledge naturally begets humility? (§7.1) Why are men of quality prone to envy, even though they know envy to be vile? (§23.1) Why do people disparage avarice, even though they're avaricious? (§42.1) Many of these questions derive their edge from an observation of the chasm between moral ideals and actual practice in human life.

Things are different with another group of questions, which target aspects of human behavior that do not carry obvious moral significance, and in which the question "Why?" is more open. Why do people long for the past, even when the past was filled with suffering? (§6.1) Why is it that when a person sees a beautiful picture or hears a pleasing tune, he says, "By God, I've never seen or heard anything like that before," even though he knows he has heard and seen better things? (§51.1) Why do people experience fear in the absence of anything fearful? (§70.1) Why do we find it easier to spontaneously conjure extreme hideousness in the eye of our imagination than to conjure exquisite beauty? (§98.1) Why is laughter contagious? (§101.1) Why do some people prefer company when they are anxious and aggrieved, and others prefer solitude and remote places? (§121.1) Why do we feel embarrassed when we see someone embarrass himself? (§145.1) Why do we hate hearing the same thing twice? (§146.1) Here we see al-Tawḥīdī as a sharp-eyed observer of human life with an instinct not only for outright curiosities but also for those everyday phenomena that seem so ordinary we would normally be little inclined to question or remark them. Al-Tawḥīdī remarks them, and is plunged into wonder: "There are things about human beings . . . that carry us to the ends of wonder and plunge our hearts into perplexity" (§98.1).

The same flair for surprise at the ordinary is exhibited in many of al-Tawḥīdī's questions. It is this surprise—this constant ability to step back from what is familiar and no longer take it for granted—that gives many of his questions their special savor, and makes the questions an experience in their own right for the reader. The surprise itself, the remarking of the hitherto-unnoticed fact, is already an offering, regardless of the way it may or may not then be resolved. A masterpiece of this kind of programmatic surprise—of what we may call al-Tawḥīdī's practice of defamiliarization—is the question he poses about the human response to music. Why is it, he asks (§155.1), that "people in a transport at singing and delighted by a musical performance stretch out their hands, move their heads, and sometimes get up and drift about—dancing, making impassioned sounds, crying out, and sometimes even running and wandering here and there distractedly?" Al-Tawḥīdī observes the human response to music with the eyes of someone who might have just landed from the moon and was seeing it for the first time. His questions go to the heart of even more central social practices elsewhere, as when he picks out the practice of honoring the sons of illustrious fathers or grandfathers and not the reverse—why *must* it work that way? (§80.1).

The questions that issue from this defamiliarizing perspective are often profound, as when al-Tawḥīdī asks about the reasons why we take pleasure in beauty (§52.1), why we feel the state of ill-being and not the state of well-being (§100.1), or why it is easier for doubt rather than certainty to take root in our minds (§128.1). At other times they seem so maddeningly strange as to verge on the trivial or nonsensical, as when he asks why people need to acquire knowledge but not ignorance (§15.1), or why people don't grow young again after they've grown old (§45.1).

The curiosity or surprise at work in al-Tawḥīdī's questions is of different kinds, as the above suggests. The surprise that is built on an observation of the gap between real and ideal—*is* and *ought*—is not of the same kind as the surprise provoked by many of the other phenomena listed above. In the latter set, as Elias Muhanna notes, the surprise seems more genuine and less rhetorical.[15] It also seems freer, in the sense of not carrying the obvious marks of a personal investment.

This investment is easier to pick out in the first type of questions, aligning itself far more closely with what we know of al-Tawḥīdī's character and standing concerns—above all, the attitude of "moral protestation" that suffuses his work, his condemnation of hypocrisy in all its forms, and his penchant for delving into the darkest nooks and crannies of human behavior to sleuth out ethical foibles. This biographical link is emblazoned even more strongly elsewhere, where it is impossible to hear the questions in impersonal accents and not to hear, only flimsily veiled under the sophisticated literary style, the visceral concerns of al-Tawḥīdī the living and breathing man. On no less than four occasions, he poses the question of suicide in different formulations. "What causes a person to take his own life when failures crowd him, when poverty besieges him, when circumstances defy his power and capacity, when his demands and desires meet with closed doors, when passionate love oppresses him and shows itself recalcitrant to cure?" (§56.1; see §§24.1, 57.1, 74.1). It is hard to miss the passionate undertone of this lyrical phrasing, with its rising crescendo of successive restatements, and inevitably a rhetorical air clings to it. It is also hard to miss in another question, particularly as al-Tawḥīdī explicitly points us to its importance by announcing it as the "queen of all questions" (§88.1). Put pithily: Why do the worthy fail, and the unworthy succeed? Taken bookishly, it is the theological question of theodicy, or one of its strands—the age-old question of why virtue and happiness do not coincide. Taken viscerally, it is the question of al-Tawḥīdī's life. Al-Tawḥīdī's saturnine temper and personal anxieties seep through his lyrical, complex prose.

It is all the features outlined above—the passionate element and personal undertone of many of the questions, the ethical (in the broad sense) focus of many, their orientation to familiar everyday phenomena—that set al-Tawḥīdī's questions off from the types of questions that feature in other instances of question-and-answer works or forms of learned correspondence with which we might think to align them. Their content sets them apart, for example, from the Greco-Arabic genre of *Problemata physica*, which is dominated by questions of a scientific nature. Their lack of specialization sets them apart from the type of exchange we find in a model of learned correspondence mentioned earlier, that between Yaḥyā ibn ʿAdī and Ibn Abī Saʿīd al-Mawṣilī, insofar as the latter's questions range over points of physics, metaphysics, and logic, raising subtle problems that presuppose a shared grasp of key philosophical texts.[16] It also sets them apart from the questions put to Miskawayh himself by another (unidentified) correspondent in a different work, the *Epistle on the Soul and the Intellect* (*Risālah fī l-Nafs wa-l-ʿaql*), many of which again have the aspect of *aporias* or *shukūk*, presupposing some philosophical foundations.[17] Al-Tawḥīdī is not raising philosophical doubts of this kind. And if his questions seem far from the *dialectical* usage of the question-and-answer genre, they also have an uncertain relationship to its *didactic* usage, in which questions straightforwardly reflect a position of ignorance and answers aim to bring enlightenment.[18]

Miskawayh's Responses

One of the most striking aspects of the transition that occurs as Miskawayh rises to the podium, in this respect, is the rather more definite terms in which he reconfigures this relationship, assimilating the exchange more recognizably to a didactic format. Arkoun rightly picks up on Miskawayh's teacherly tone,[19] and if there is any truth in what Naaman says about the unequal student-teacher relation the work evokes, it is from Miskawayh's answers that this most strongly derives.

Miskawayh approaches al-Tawḥīdī's questions as an opportunity to inform and instruct. The voice he speaks in is very much that of the well-schooled philosopher representing his discipline and seeking to convey the solid results of its investigations. In many ways, his view of his task and the spirit in which he pursues it is well captured by the title of his half of the book (*al-shawāmil*, "the ones that contain"). To al-Tawḥīdī's rhapsodic and wandering questions, Miskawayh proposes to bring order and containment. The sense of order registers stylistically in the first instance, as al-Tawḥīdī's flowery prose cedes to Miskawayh's more direct, sedate, and austere mode of expression. This style in turn reflects a deeper attitude of intellectual confidence and a robust trust in the ability to provide the answers. It is the confidence of a philosopher aware of standing with his back against centuries of venerable philosophical inquiry. "Philosophical inquiries have shown" is one of Miskawayh's favorite ways of opening a reply.

In responding to al-Tawḥīdī's questions, Miskawayh thus unveils for his readers, in bite-sized segments, large parts of the edifice of philosophical knowledge as he understood it to stand in his day. The brevity of the replies seems to have been a condition stipulated by al-Tawḥīdī, and Miskawayh often refers to this condition when justifying his reluctance to probe topics at greater length.[20] Many of the philosophical ideas he presents synoptically in the book can be found developed more fully in other works, such as the *Minor Triumph* and the *Refinement of Character*. This includes, above all, his understanding of philosophical psychology, which pivots around a Platonic conception of the soul as consisting of three parts or powers—the irascible, the appetitive, and the rational—and of the ethical task as a matter of ordering these powers or faculties correctly, that is, with reason in the ruling seat. The virtues or excellences that arise from the proper ordering of these powers are understood, in an Aristotelian fashion, as means between extremes. The realization of the specifically human perfection is tied to the perfection of reason in both its practical and, above all, its intellectual aspects. This understanding is anchored in a Galenic physiology that views the human body as depending on a mixture of four humors that need to be constantly maintained in balance, and whose precise configuration is reflected in the ethical and psychological characteristics of different individuals.

These are some of the chief aspects of the philosophical understanding that Miskawayh unfolds in response to al-Tawḥīdī's questions. Yet, given the very particular spirit in which many of the latter are posed, one of the most interesting questions for the reader is how fully or directly these responses meet them not only in their content, but also in their spirit. To the extent that this spirit is one of wonder, it is clear that Miskawayh, as a true Aristotelian, sees his task not as that of meeting it, but indeed of dislodging it. Wonder, as Aristotle indicated at the opening of the *Metaphysics*, is the result of ignorance, and more specifically ignorance of the cause of something (982b–983a)—a definition that Miskawayh echoes in one of his responses (§16.5). Once knowledge has been acquired, wonder loses its purpose and place. In responding to al-Tawḥīdī's questions, Miskawayh thus aims to supply the knowledge that will function as the natural solvent of al-Tawḥīdī's wonder, as he signals directly in many places. The contagious effect of laughter will no longer seem wondrous or surprising (*laysa bi-ʿajab*) once a person realizes that the soul is in reality one (§101.2). Once al-Tawḥīdī has grasped the right account of "interpretive effort" (*ijtihād*) in the religious law, he "will no longer be amazed" by the differences between juridical opinions (*lam yaʿriḍ laka al-ʿajab*, §153.6).

Yet, even if the philosopher may legitimately regard wonder as something to be eliminated by explanation, one is sometimes inclined to question whether Miskawayh has put his finger on the precise quality of al-Tawḥīdī's motivating passion. "What does the soul seek in this world?" al-Tawḥīdī asks in one place. He continues with pathos: "Man is a mystery to man" (§68.1). It is this sighing remark that Joel Kraemer had in mind when he described al-Tawḥīdī's humanism as "a sober acceptance of man's ambiguity" rather than a "joyful celebration of man's grandeur."[21] The term "man," Miskawayh expounds in replying, "has been appointed to designate the entity composed of a rational soul and a natural body." The philosopher who has properly assimilated the fruit of his predecessors' labors and confidently grasped the nature of human beings can dispel any appearance of mystery in the topic. Yet those who have felt the personal angst and existential concerns seeping through al-Tawḥīdī's questions will wonder whether this was a response quite calibrated to meet the spirit in which they were posed.[22]

A sense of tension between the spirit of the questions and the spirit of the replies is more sharply felt on other occasions. In places, for example, Miskawayh seems unable to take al-Tawḥīdī's questions seriously, and appears more disposed to criticize their actuating wonder than to take active steps to dispel it. This is particularly the case faced with those of al-Tawḥīdī's questions that focus on self-evident or familiar aspects of human life, which are harder to treat as straightforward cases of "ignorance" that can be removed through an informative account. (Here we may also see the root of the temptation some readers may feel to hear al-Tawḥīdī's questions as ironic, and his intention as one to taunt—though not by inquiring after abstruse matters, but after insultingly simplistic ones.) Why do people who have something to hide become anxious, so much that they virtually give themselves away? (§104.1) Your question, Miskawayh tersely replies, "only provokes perplexity (*ḥayrah*) in people who do not acknowledge the reality of the soul" (§104.2); nobody who knows the first thing about the topic could be surprised by this fact. Why do people grow more hopeful the older they grow? (§94.1). Rather than respond directly, Miskawayh gives a deconstructive genealogy of the wonder that drove it (apparently ignorant of the fact that Aristotle himself had dignified the topic with a discussion in the *Rhetoric*).[23] "This question took an act of the soul and connected it with an act of nature, of the sort that depends on the body and the bodily mixture, and then a comparison was struck between the two, though they are distinct and do not resemble each other. This is why it provoked a sense of astonishment" (§94.2). Why do those who die young outnumber those who die old? "There is little to wonder at" in this, as "it would indeed be worthy of wonder if the opposite obtained" (§96.2). Elsewhere, his impatience becomes clearer. "The merest reflection suffices to answer this question," he says in one place (§80.2), after the briefest of replies. "Your question answers itself," he curtly says elsewhere (§76.2). Several times he describes al-Tawḥīdī's questions as "too obvious" to be worth the toil of serious response (e.g., §§1.11, 4.11, 38.2). Sometimes his only way of dealing with an almost absurd or trivial-sounding question about self-evident things is by converting it into a different question. A good example is Question 15, where al-Tawḥīdī asks—and here we translate as literally as possible—why people need to "learn knowledge" (*yataʿallama l-ʿilm*) rather than "learn ignorance" (*yataʿallama l-jahl*). Miskawayh deals with this extraordinary question by hearing it as an invitation to provide a philosophical overview of the nature of knowledge.

Yet the sharpest contrast probably emerges in those questions broadly called "ethical," particularly those paradoxical "Why . . . yet . . . ?" questions, which reveal al-Tawḥīdī's preoccupation with the gap between the real and the ideal in human life. Arkoun has aptly spoken of the "passion for teaching in which all of Miskawayh's works abound."[24] In Miskawayh's responses to these questions, we see this passion take a powerful moral form that gives us a clear glimpse of the future author of the *Refinement*. Asked why people behave one way or another, Miskawayh's response is often to simply state that they shouldn't. Asked why the real and the ideal diverge, Miskawayh often responds by correcting al-Tawḥīdī's notion of the real to tip it more firmly into the domain of the ideal. The *really* learned man will never be conceited. *Real* men of quality are not prone to envy. If one tells secrets or breaks promises or displays avarice even though one shouldn't—well, all that can be done is to simply reassert that one shouldn't, and to explain why one nevertheless does through a closer analysis of the soul, which reveals the existence of different powers that compete for supremacy, the highest often losing out to the lowest. Miskawayh's response is thus to reassert the idealistic viewpoint that al-Tawḥīdī interrogates by referring to the observed facts. It is this dimension of the exchange that has prompted Arkoun to state that a "misunderstanding" runs through the entire book.[25]

The difference between the spirit or perspective of the questions and responses can be overstated. As Arkoun himself emphasizes, for example, it would be wrong to write this up as a contrast between a passionate, experiential, personal perspective and a dispassionate, abstract, impersonal one. The ethical views Miskawayh outlines here and elsewhere also carried lived or experiential significance for him: They were ideals meant to guide his *own* conduct. This is a personal dimension he makes crystal clear in the *Refinement*, and is also evident in the so-called "oath" or "covenant" (*ʿahd*) with which he announced his philosophical conversion.[26] Even more basically, both questioner and respondent are united in at least one set of fundamental values—an aspiration to uncover rational answers, and a belief in the possibility of obtaining them. Yet the differences in intellectual temper that divide the two thinkers remain real, and they form an integral part of the reader's experience of the book and of the interest with which one approaches it. If we want to read on even after we discover our authors in a state of "misunderstanding," it is not only because the questions and the answers as such engage us, but also because this misunderstanding is interesting.

Audience and Method of Composition

So much for the content of the work. What can we say about its method of composition? This question is in fact closely connected to a question (and indeed puzzle) about its intended audience. The book opens with a preface in which Miskawayh, addressing al-Tawḥīdī in the second person, acknowledges the questions he has sent to him and outlines the method he will follow in responding to them. His replies will be brief, and for further detail, he will refer his reader to books where they can be found more fully elaborated. Taking this preface at face value, it seems plausible that al-Tawḥīdī sent all of his questions to Miskawayh at a single stroke, though in places Miskawayh expresses his readiness to receive new ones (e.g., §16.6). The body of Miskawayh's responses suggests that he likewise delivered them all together. He occasionally refers back to his earlier responses, particularly when he wishes to avoid repetition. Unlike other forms of learned correspondence we are familiar with—such as the famous exchange between Avicenna (d. 428/1037) and al-Bīrūnī (d. ca. 440/1048)—there is no evidence that any follow-up took place between the two men after the initial answers were given. There is only one instance in the entire work that provides the tantalizing suggestion of a counter-response having been offered by al-Tawḥīdī.[27]

One aspect of Miskawayh's preface that is so obvious it may not strike us immediately is that we have no independent access to al-Tawḥīdī's initial letter, which Miskawayh responds to in the preface, except through the summary Miskawayh provides. The point applies, in fact, to al-Tawḥīdī's questions as a whole, and reflects an important aspect of the book's composition that enters the reader's experience repeatedly throughout the book. While in many places it seems clear that al-Tawḥīdī's questions have been quoted verbatim, in many other places it is equally evident that Miskawayh has intervened in that section of the text that is marked out in the translation as al-Tawḥīdī's speaking part. Sometimes, instead of quoting a question in full, he reports it in truncated form, paraphrases it, or summarizes parts of it (see, e.g., §§4.3, 68.1, 165.1, 173.1). Often, this reflects an overt dismissal of the value of the remarks summarized or left unreported. On occasion, the interventions are so drastic that the reader is only allowed the barest access to al-Tawḥīdī's question. An example is §157.1, which Miskawayh expresses so much disdain for that not only does he refuse to answer it; he doesn't even fully quote it.

One challenging consequence of this practice is that it is sometimes difficult to disentangle al-Tawḥīdī's remarks from Miskawayh's interventions and determine whose voice we are hearing. A particularly acute example of this is §149.1, though there are many others. In several cases, the editorial work makes the logical flow of the question harder to follow, though Miskawayh's responses are usually a good guide for identifying the core thread of questioning. Such heavy-handed editorializing has a bearing on how we understand Miskawayh's view of the audience of this written exchange. On the one hand, as already mentioned, there was a sufficiently established precedent of question-and-answer works of different types—and even more broadly, of composing works at the behest of particular individuals while offering them to the wider public—that it is reasonable to suppose Miskawayh likewise intended this work for wider consumption. On at least one occasion, he refers to it as a "book" (§151.4).[28] In a passage that is of special importance for reconstructing his understanding of his audience, he apologizes for his brevity in answering a particular question and remarks: "I pray that the statements to which I have confined myself will suffice for those perusing [*al-nāẓir*] the present questions; for I have been addressing my answers to a reader who [*man*] already has a purchase on these subjects and so commands respect. Whoever is not at this level must school himself well in these subjects first, and only then, God willing, peruse these answers" (§146.2).

While it could be debated whether the terms that feature in the first part of this passage ("those perusing," "a reader") should be translated in the singular or the plural, the last statement makes it clear that Miskawayh expected the work to find readers beyond the single questioner he is most immediately addressing. This remark also illuminates Miskawayh's conception of his audience on another level, suggesting that despite the book's synoptic character, he thinks of his reader not as the beginner, the young disciple, or the amateur (as Arkoun, for one, proposes), but as a person with a certain degree of intellectual accomplishment.[29] The fact that he is not addressing himself exclusively to al-Tawḥīdī but speaking beyond him to a wider audience appears to find confirmation at several junctures of the text where one sees Miskawayh abandoning the second-person pronoun ("you") and referring to al-Tawḥīdī in the third person (e.g., §§57.3, 86.2, 128.2). The fact that in many of these cases Miskawayh is implicitly conveying a negative view of al-Tawḥīdī's questioning (giving this grammatical shift an expressive significance) leaves the point untouched.

At the same time, this widened conception of Miskawayh's intended audience is hard to square with some of his editorial interventions. In several places, these interventions leave the question opaque in ways that seem to presuppose that the reader would have independent means of access to al-Tawḥīdī's questions beyond the access Miskawayh provides.[30] On those occasions, it is as if Miskawayh had lost sight of his wider audience and was addressing himself more narrowly to al-Tawḥīdī. One possible conjecture, more compatible with the broader view of his audience, is that Miskawayh indeed expected that al-Tawḥīdī's questions would circulate separately.

Labeling the Questions

These puzzles about the book's audience and method of composition bring us to a related issue. Readers will notice that several of the questions—particularly early on in the book—carry labels of different kinds. Some are very specific, e.g., on the meaning and origin of injustice (§29.1) or on why some dreams are true and other false (§47.1). Most of them, however, speak to broad categories. The main categories are: "ethical" (*khuluqiyyah*), "relating to (voluntary) choice" (*ikhtiyāriyyah*), "natural" (*ṭabīʿiyyah*), "voluntary" (*irādiyyah*), and "linguistic" or "lexical" (*lughawiyyah*). Occasionally we see these labels being combined, e.g., "natural-ethical" or "natural-linguistic." What is the function and significance of these labels? And to which of our two authors may we ascribe the initiative of affixing them to the questions? The function of these labels, in fact, is not entirely transparent. With the exception of the questions tagged as "linguistic"—which predictably focus on issues of a philological kind—a closer examination of the labels of the questions against their content does not enable one to confidently assign a clear meaning to each label and demarcate it sharply from the others.

Certainly, there are broad patterns to be observed. The questions labeled "ethical" tend to focus on aspects of human behavior that carry ethical significance, and sometimes straightforwardly relate to excellences or defects (virtues or vices) of character.[31] (Examples: on why men of knowledge tend to be conceited [§7.1] and on why men of virtue and reason feel envious toward their equals even though they know envy is blameworthy [§23.1].) The questions labeled "natural"—contrary to what we might anticipate—also tend to focus on human behavior, with the perhaps discernible distinction that this behavior usually does not carry apparent ethical significance. (Examples: on why people long for the past [§6.1]; on why people want to know what other say about them in their absence [§12.1]; and on why people end up loving particular months or days and why they form different conceptions of different days [§28.1].) Those labeled as "questions of voluntary choice" often seem to revolve around value judgments or responses of approval/disapproval to different kinds of things. (Examples: on why it is bad to praise people in their presence [§11.1]; on why people disapprove of young people who act as if they were older [§13.1]; and on why it is unseemly to eulogize long-term friends and acquaintances [§17.1].) The paucity of questions labeled "volitional" makes it harder to speak of distinct patterns.

Yet all of the patterns one discerns are shot through with exceptions. The category of "natural questions" is probably the best example, incorporating a number of questions that fit a little more predictably under that heading, such as ones relating to medicine or physiology. (Examples: on why blind people are often endowed with unusual powers [§18.1] and on why epilepsy is so hard to treat [§37.1].) It will also be clear that the content of many of these variously labeled questions is remarkably similar, with most focusing on human behavior. The seams between topics seem thin, and sometimes the label settled on one question may not strike the reader as the most suitable one based on its apparent semantic pattern. Moreover, the pattern is made harder to discern by the ricocheting style of al-Tawḥīdī's questioning, which sometimes leaves in doubt which of the multiple strands of his questions the label is intended to reflect. No less puzzlingly, nearly a third of the way into the list of questions (after §§49.1–6), the labels come to an abrupt end.

What to make of all this? It might help if we could say with greater definiteness who was responsible for assigning these labels in the first place, even if it would not entirely resolve the conundrum. Most of those who have reflected on the issue have credited the labels to al-Tawḥīdī. One of the strongest arguments in favor of this hypothesis is the one offered by Elias Muhanna, who suggests that had the labels been added by the hand of a copyist, he might have taken greater care to ensure the adequacy of a given label to its multilayered question.[32] Yet one must wonder whether there is *any* single label that would be capacious enough to reflect and encompass all the threads of al-Tawḥīdī's thinking.

My own sense is that the labels should be ascribed either to a copyist or to Miskawayh himself. The desire to order, systematize, and categorize certainly seems far more of a piece with what we see of Miskawayh's intellectual temper, and his evident interest to situate his enterprise against recognizable rubrics and intellectual formats. Besides this psychological evidence, there is also the evidence of the questions and answers themselves. It is striking that in a number of cases, the labels do not reflect the content of the questions nearly as well as they reflect the answers. In the label for §3.1, for example, literally rendered as "A composite question about the secrets of nature and the letters of the language," the term "letters" (*ḥurūf*) does not appear in the question itself, and appears for the first time in the reply. §33.1 carries the label "A psychological (*nafsāniyyah*) question," a label that seems mystifying if one looks only at the question, which asks for an explanation of certain kinds of coincidence. ("Why does a person who is the subject of conversation unexpectedly appear at the very moment he is being mentioned?") Miskawayh, however, builds his reply precisely on considerations about the nature of the soul (*nafs*). Likewise, it is noteworthy that some of the questions labeled "ethical" are given a distinct ethical inflection, and connected more directly to the excellences or defects of character, in Miskawayh's reply rather than in al-Tawḥīdī's question (§§27.1–3 is an example).

This hypothesis doesn't rule out the possibility that it was a copyist, rather than Miskawayh himself, who assigned the labels; it only argues against their being the work of al-Tawḥīdī. Why the abrupt stop? Did the meticulous categorizer, toiling over the wild garden of al-Tawḥīdī's questions, reach a point where he threw up his hands at their untamable profusion and simply gave up? Short of clinching evidence, one may only speculate. But for the reader of the present questions, there could be no greater commendation than such a defeat.

Sophia Vasalou

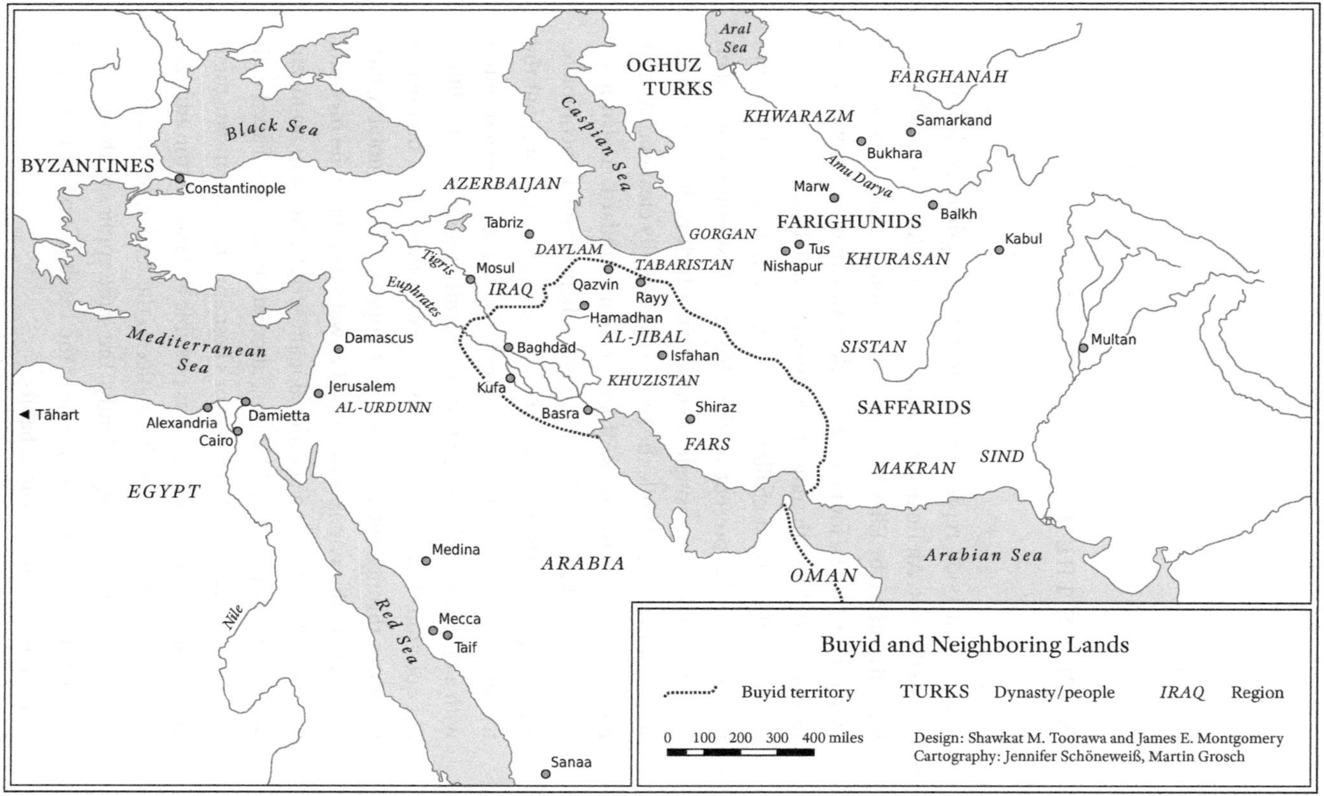

Buyid and Neighboring Lands

Note on the Text

The present book represents the first full-length English translation of the text. An English translation of al-Tawḥīdī's questions was recently offered by Elias Muhanna and a French translation of select extracts can also be found in the work of Mohammed Arkoun. More recently, a full-length translation appeared in Italian.[33]

One of the largest challenges of translating the text stems from the fact that the present edition, like the first edition published in 1951, is based on a single manuscript, which is the only manuscript known to us. While the script is beautifully clear and in most respects the manuscript is of an excellent standard, it also has a number of weaknesses, the most obvious being that it is incomplete. The first page of the manuscript announces 180 questions, but the text breaks off in the middle of the response at §175.2, and it resumes with a disconnected passage that is evidently a response to a different question.[34] Besides this obvious lacuna, there are a number of junctures throughout where the text appears flawed, notably passages where the syntax is disturbed in ways that make the meaning hard to follow. Lacking additional manuscripts, we have no means of correcting the text and locating alternative readings. Faced with passages of this kind, the translator's best option is to translate them as faithfully and conservatively as possible and pass on the ambiguity and breadth of interpretive choice to the reader, so that she can make up her mind independently. The same applies to those cases where the opacity is less obviously the result of textual flaws, and more a reflection of stylistic habits.

A more interesting, and somewhat more tractable, challenge is posed by the simple yet important fact that the present book is an exchange between two thinkers, each of whom is interpreting the words of the other no less than the reader is interpreting theirs. Both because al-Tawḥīdī's questions are written in a highly distinctive literary style and because they are the expression of an intellectual temper that is unlike Miskawayh's in many respects, it is not a foregone conclusion that Miskawayh will always interpret them in the way that seems (to us, as interpreting readers) correct or most natural—or that, even if he interprets them "correctly," he will answer them in the way al-Tawḥīdī's question most readily invited. This creates a challenge for the translation, which needs to preserve enough continuity between the language of question and answer to enable the reader to track their relationship, while adapting the language to reflect the fact that its meaning has changed between question and answer. An example of this shifting meaning can be seen in §119.1, which quotes a remark made by the caliph al-Ma'mūn on the difficulty of chess. "I wonder at myself," the caliph says. "I have the ends of the earth under my power [*udabbiru āfāq al-arḍ*], yet I cannot master a small square." Miskawayh replies by offering some general remarks on the nature of crafts and the need for practice. "Since chess is a craft that conforms to this pattern," he concludes, "neither deliberative power [*tadbīr*], nor good imagination, nor excellent judgment suffices without the addition of active engagement and practice." The term *tadbīr*, exercise of power, is the lexical link that holds the entire question-and-answer sequence together; yet in answering the question, Miskawayh has effected a not insignificant shift in its meaning.

Besides these local challenges, the most demanding aspect of the translation has been deciding how to negotiate the subset of questions—and they are no small number—that center on the meanings of Arabic terms. This type of discussion is a key focus in two long questions (§§1.1 and 34.1) and forms an element of a number of others. Already a first challenge, in fact, is deciding whether to read these questions as philological questions about the meaning of words, or to read them as ontological questions about the nature of things. Is al-Tawḥīdī asking what the Arabic word *quwwah means*, for example, or about what capacity or power *is* (§34.1)? Is he asking what the word *ʿillah means*, or what a cause *is* (§4.1)? The seams between the linguistic and the ontological parsings of the question are not always easy to mark—after all, the seams are in themselves porous—but in many places it seems clear that al-Tawḥīdī's questions are best understood in the first sense. That being granted, the challenge is then how to convey in English a discussion that is essentially lexicographical in kind.

One approach entertained was to retain the target words in Arabic. A strong argument in favor of this approach was that in the majority of cases, it is impossible to locate English equivalents whose meanings dovetail with the explanations Miskawayh provides for the Arabic terms, enough indeed to be used for every single appearance of the relevant term. Insofar as semantic correspondence fails, translating the Arabic means a discussion that has the form of an English lexicographical exercise without its proper content. The sense of paradox is perhaps heightened by the fact that many of the terms Miskawayh is asked to define (distinguishing between ostensibly synonymous expressions in the process) are not technical terms but words that belong to ordinary language—words like "to give" or "to seek," to be "joyful" or "lucky." The alternative, however, was long tracts of English translation dominated by transliterated Arabic terms, which would be alienating to the general reader. The decision was thus taken to translate the terms, in the hope that this will put the general reader in the best position to follow the discussion and appreciate its character. Therefore Arabic is rarely introduced into the translation, where the discussion involves an appeal to the morphology or etymology of the terms.

Among the decisions taken regarding the translation of specific terms, one that is perhaps worth a brief comment concerns the translation of the key philosophical term *quwwah*, which may strike some readers as lying slightly off the beaten track. "Power"—the translation adopted throughout this book—is a natural choice for many uses of the term, but not the most common translation for its usage in the context of philosophical psychology, where it is usually translated as "faculty" (e.g., *al-quwwah al-ghaḍabiyyah*, the irascible faculty, *al-quwwah al-shahwiyyah*, the appetitive faculty). Yet the decisions that might appear most natural in the context of an open discussion of ideas may not be the ones that appear most appropriate in the context of the translation of complete texts. In approaching the latter, one is forced to pay closer heed to the overall linguistic environment and the different ways in which particular terms are deployed within it. Having taken this overall environment into account, part of the reason "faculty" seems dissatisfying is that it forces one to draw uncomfortably sharp distinctions between different uses of the term—ones that sometimes stand only a stone's throw apart in the text—on the basis that one of them enjoys a place in Miskawayh's philosophical psychology that is sufficiently serious or systematic for it to be dignified with a more technical translation, whereas another doesn't. When *quwwah* refers to the core aspects of the human soul as tabulated in the Platonic tradition—anger, appetite, reason—"faculty" comes naturally. Yet what about those cases where Miskawayh refers to other, rather more expansive, aspects or capacities of the soul, such as the *quwwah* of giving and the *quwwah* of receiving (§2.2)? What about the case in which the term is used to refer to the soul itself, and indeed also to the body (§4.5)? What if the mention of the *quwwah* of anger is succeeded, moments later, by a reference to the *quwwah* of jealousy (§§95.3–4)? Is jealousy a "faculty" in a sense sufficiently similar to anger? The choice of "power" as a translation reflects the translator's discomfort with the necessity of drawing such sharp distinctions, and her sense that it is the more inclusive term that best passes on the full gamut of semantic possibilities to the readers and allows them to take their own decisions about how to "hear" particular terms—just as Miskawayh's reader, confronted with a single Arabic term, would have had to.

No doubt other translators would approach such challenges differently. Be that as it may, our hope is that the present translation will help open up this distinctive intellectual exchange for English-speaking readers and allow them to look as lucidly as possible into the mirror it holds to the minds of two great thinkers of their time—and indeed, to the entire cultural era they represent.

Note that, throughout the text the translators have added descriptive titles to each of the topics addressed in the correspondence between al-Tawḥīdī and Miskawayh; and pious phrases have been omitted after their first occurrence, with an exception made for pious phrases addressed by one author to the other. Renderings of Qur'anic passages generally follow the translation by A. J. Arberry.

Notes to the Introduction

1 See Naaman, *Literature and the Islamic Court*, 268n37.

2 For more on the reception of this literature, see Filius, "The Genre *Problemata* in Arabic," and "La tradition orientale des *Problemata Physica*."

3 For a helpful survey of the different types of question-and-answer works, see Daiber, "Masā'il wa-Adjwiba."

4 *Muʿjam al-udabāʾ*, 5:1924.

5 See the discussion in Arkoun, "L'humanisme arabe (part I)," 75–78.

6 Arkoun, *L'humanisme arabe*, 110–12.

7 Naaman, *Literature and the Islamic Court*, 267–69n37. Naaman provides a very helpful overview of the competing chronological hypotheses offered by different scholars.

8 See al-Tawḥīdī, *Al-Imtāʿ wa-l-muʾānasah*, 1:35–36, and see also Arkoun, *L'humanisme arabe*, 39–48, for a more exhaustive documentation and analysis of al-Tawḥīdī's remarks about Miskawayh.

9 *Al-Hawāmil wa-l-shawāmil*, ed. Amīn and Ṣaqr, Introduction, 29.

10 Arkoun, *L'humanisme arabe*, 110–11.

11 The quote is from Naaman, *Literature and the Islamic Court*, 240, read against the remarks at 267–69n37.

12 For discussion of these points, see Arkoun, *L'humanisme arabe*, 39–48.

13 Arkoun, "L'humanisme arabe (part I)," 78–79.

14 The book as we have it in fact assigns its own set of labels to some of the questions. We will come back to this point.

15 See his comments in "The Scattered and the Gathered," 255–56; and see generally 251–58 for a more detailed overview of the different types of questions.

16 See the discussion of this exchange in Pines, "A Tenth Century Philosophical Correspondence."

17 In his edition of the epistle—"Deux épîtres de Miskawayh"—Arkoun entertains the possibility that this correspondent may also have been al-Tawḥīdī (12n6), but the stark stylistic differences alone make that seem highly unlikely.

18 For the distinction between these uses, see Daiber, "Masāʾil wa-Adjwiba," though Daiber also brings out its porousness. Many of the above features also make it hard to speak of a substantial affinity to al-Jāḥiẓ's *The Square and the Round* in either content or intention, despite the thematic breadth they share. Many of the questions that feature in the latter appear to have a deliberately recondite or "unanswerable" character, as Robert Irwin notes (*Penguin Anthology of Classical Arabic Literature*, 100; though see Montgomery, "Al-Ǧāḥiẓ and Hellenizing Philosophy," for a very different reading of the nature and aims of the book). It is perhaps worth noting, nevertheless, that a number of al-Tawḥīdī's questions overlap with al-Jāḥiẓ's; see, e.g., the more general questions at *Al-Tarbīʿ wa-l-tadwīr*, 39 (§68).

19 Arkoun, "L'humanisme arabe (part II)," 74.

20 See the Preface and Conclusion of the book, and also, e.g., the remarks at §§29.3, 88.3.

21 Kraemer, *Humanism in the Renaissance of Islam*, 222.

22 For another discussion of Miskawayh's relationship to the passions of inquiry and an attempt at a more positive characterization of the curiosity or wonder at work in his thought, see also Arkoun's thoughtful remarks in *L'humanisme arabe*, 216–21.

23 We have in mind the remarks in *Rhetoric* Book 2, chapters 12–13, where Aristotle discusses the character of the young and the old; their diverging relationship to hope is a central theme of that discussion. Compare the remarks in the extant Arabic version: *Aristotle's Ars Rhetorica*, 120.18–125.7.

24 Arkoun, *L'humanisme arabe*, 206.

25 Arkoun, "L'humanisme arabe (part I)," 84.

26 See the remarks in *Tahdhīb al-akhlāq*, 50. Cf. Arkoun, *L'humanisme arabe*, 34–35, and see 81ff. for a translation and discussion of the oath.

27 That single instance is §162.6, where Miskawayh refers to (without quoting verbatim) a subsequent question asked by al-Tawḥīdī, which appears to *challenge* the account Miskawayh has just provided, and more specifically his claim that the ratio for currency conversions must be ten to one. Another instance that seems to breathe the faintest whiff of responsiveness into the composition process is found in §§96.4 and 97.1. In replying to the first question, Miskawayh employs a comparison or analogy (*mithāl*) (§96.4), and it then seems like a curious coincidence that the next question focuses precisely on the attraction of seeking analogies or likeness.

28 See §110.1, though it is ambiguous whether this particular remark is in Miskawayh's or al-Tawḥīdī's voice; and see also §153.1, in al-Tawḥīdī's voice this time.

29 Arkoun, *L'humanisme arabe*, 208–10.

30 §89.1 is a striking example of this, but far from being the only one.

31 The translators take a somewhat different view of this category than the one followed by Muhanna in his otherwise very helpful discussion of the problem in "The Scattered and the Gathered," 251ff.

32 Muhanna, "The Scattered and the Gathered," 252n10. Cf. Aḥmad Amīn's remarks in the first edition of the *Hawāmil*, p. *ṭā'*.

33 See the work by Muhanna and Arkoun already cited. The book has been translated into Italian by Lidia Bettini as *Il libro dei cammelli errabondi e di quelli che li radunano.*

34 One interesting question, of course, is whether the announced number takes into account Miskawayh's editorial manipulations, which sometimes involve deleting entire questions or amalgamating them with others.

The Philosopher Responds

In the name of God, the Merciful. I ask God for assistance.

May God help you attain the truth and open your heart to it. May He preserve you from the folly of false views and help you avoid them. May He give you knowledge as you deserve and grant you a generous portion of learning. May He grant you happiness in the efforts you take and guide you to the good. May He make you appreciate the beauty of decent conduct and conceding truths, and may He rouse your repugnance to unjust conduct and disputing untruths. May He help you unearth treasure troves of wisdom and shine a beacon for you into the darker reaches of knowledge. May He inspire you to just words, that you may choose them in all your affairs and concerns, and make them your custom in all you say and do. 0.1

I have read the questions you have asked me to answer. You began your letter with a lament about the sorry times we live in, and about the unintelligent people who surround us, harping on an old complaint and a malady without chance of cure. God bless you! Look at all the people weeping around you and take comfort; look at those suffering with you and find solace. I assure you in the strongest terms that your lament falls on the ears of one who himself laments, and your tears are shed before one who is equally tearful. There is a lump in every man's throat, and a mote in every man's eye. We all seek from our fellow men things we can never hope to receive. The philosophers have defined a "friend" by saying: A friend is another person who is you but is not you by being a separate individual.[1] Alas, if that is so, then I believe it will be easier to find a pregnant stallion, a phoenix, or red sulfur on this earth. 0.2

My advice to you is that if you wish to live among people and be part of their mix, and if you would like to lead a pleasant and agreeable life, you would do well to be forbearing toward your 0.3

fellow men and prepared to put yourself in the wrong, so that you disregard every claim you have on them and instead grant them the sort of rights over you that they do not expect for themselves. You should take to heart the rule of conduct spelled out by the poet Bashshār—for it is an excellent rule of conduct—and the admonition given by the poet al-Nābighah—for it is an excellent admonition.[2] And you should not accustom those who share your company and your dinner table to listen to your complaints so that they grow so used to them that they no longer seek to assuage them, and you should not reproach them so frequently that they grow so familiar with them as to no longer seek to reproach you.

0.4 This assumes that he does not have more complaints and reproaches against you than you have against him, and that you are not launching an attack against a breast already filled with resentment and a heart festering with spite. For in that case you will stir up and arouse his pent-up anger, by reminding him of things he had chosen to forget, be it out of good grace or in an attempt to be gracious, things that he had swept under the carpet, be it out of clemency or in an attempt to be clement. That is if he treats you fairly, and does not rush to do you some evil, and if he is truthful and does not tell you barefaced lies. Anyone who understands the nature of this age and its people, and the character of this time and its children, will not aspire to what is in itself unreasonable and will not set out to achieve what is unattainable, and he will not expect to find clarity in turbid waters or bliss in a world of tribulation.

0.5 If your own soul does not help you achieve contentment, even though the soul is what is most properly your own, and if the humors of your own body are not in harmony with your wishes, even though they lie closest to you, how can you seek such things from someone else, and solicit them from your fellow? Seek refuge in God from Satan's wiles and from the impurities and confusions of ignorance. Ask for God's help and He will help you; ask Him to meet your needs and He will do so—strength comes from God alone. This is the sum total of the counsels and admonitions I can offer you, and I hope they meet with your acceptance and assent as I trust they will, God willing.

Now I turn to answer your questions. You call them a "Wandering Herd." Therefore, I have striven to return them to you in the care of attentive herders and watchful stewards, unhobbled and with their hides branded. My hope is that herein you will find the wisdom you are searching for and the knowledge you are seeking, so that through their acquisition you may savor the pleasure of certainty, if God so wills it. 0.6

The procedure we will adopt in this work is as follows. In the discussion of a given question, we will aim to clarify what is abstruse and explain what is obscure. If that happens to touch on matters that have already been discussed and firmly established, or on recognized and reliably known principles that have been explained and clarified by others, especially when these others have a solid, established reputation for wisdom, we will point to these principles and indicate where they can be found, while providing brief synopses. I think this is preferable to the bother of copying and reproducing them and going on at length. God alone gives success. 0.7

In the name of God, the merciful.

On the differences between a number of similar words—a linguistic question

1.1 You asked, may God show you favor: What is the difference between the terms *swiftness* and *haste*? When two words share a single meaning and converge on a single import, should there always necessarily be a difference between them? For we say "he was delighted" and "was glad," and "he was exuberant" and "was merry." Again, one says "he was distant" and "went far away," "he jested" and "joked," "he blocked" and "thwarted," "he restrained" and "drove off." We also say "he gave" and "handed over," "he sought" and "strived," "he applied himself to something" and "occupied himself with something," "he went" and "left." We say "he judged" and "ruled," "he came" and "arrived," "he approached" and "advanced," "he talked" and "spoke," "he was accurate" and "was right." We say "he sat down" and "took a seat," "he kept away" and "kept at a distance," "he was present" and "attended" something, "he was uninterested" and "was indifferent." Do the terms "delight," "joy," "happiness," "rapture," "gaiety," "cheerfulness," "gladness," "pleasure," and "rejoicing" have exactly the same meaning, or do their meanings differ? Use this as your model for dealing with all the other cases, because the subject is substantial—its topics are tied up in endless knots and it has numerous interrelated instances. And if between each such pair of similar things there *is* a difference that separates one meaning from another, distinguishes one signification from another, and demarcates one import from another, then why isn't this difference common knowledge, the way the basic notion is? Building on that: What is the distinction between the terms "aim," "meaning," and "intention" I just used? Why is it that the difference between "to speak" and "to be silent" is obvious, whereas the difference between "to speak" and "to talk," and "to be silent" and "to be mute," is so elusive?

Miskawayh's response

In order to answer this question, we must say something about the 1.2
reason why a linguistic convention is required, about why people are driven to posit names that signify through common accord, and about why people are impelled to conjoin letters so as to produce nouns, verbs, and particles by way of agreement and convention. We must also say something about the logical categories that are imposed on us through the necessity of reason. We thus begin by offering a few words on this subject by way of preface, to make our task easier and to serve as clarification in itself and as assistance for obscurer points.

The reason why speech is needed is that individual human beings 1.3
are not self-sufficient in their lives and cannot satisfy what they need to survive over the determinate time that has been allocated to them. They thus need to solicit their vital necessities from others during the span of their continued existence, and justice demands that they give others something in exchange for what they obtain from them, which they do through mutual assistance. This is why the philosophers said: Human beings are political by nature. The ways people offer each other assistance, the vital necessities they share—which make it possible for them to survive, to stay alive, and to live well—are particulars and concrete individuals of several different kinds, and circumstances of a disparate sort, and they are many in number—in fact, they are infinite. Sometimes they are physically present, and it is possible to point to them; sometimes they are physically absent, and it will not be possible to point to them. It will then be necessary to have recourse to sonic movements that

signify those things by way of convention, so that people can solicit them from one another and provide mutual assistance, enabling humankind to survive and human life to be perfected.

1.4 In the subtlety of His wisdom, and through His prior knowledge and power, God equipped human beings with an organ that surpasses all other bodily members in its agility and the range of its powers, positioning it, in terms of how sound is produced, at a location that allows it to break up the sound that emerges with the breath, one consistent with all the other organs that contribute to the production of speech. This organ is the bodily member best suited to apply a variety of movements in order to produce the different kinds of sounds that signify the things we have mentioned above. In the Arabic language, the number of individual sounds broken up by these movements—which we call "letters"—comes to twenty-eight, which are then organized in clusters of two, three, and four. These clusters constitute a calculable number of finite groups, because the basic ingredients and simple elements out of which they are formed are circumscribed in number, and so the things that are formed from them must also be circumscribed in number.

1.5 When reason considers these words from the perspective of how they signify meanings, it decrees that only five situations are logically possible, and accordingly words fall into one of the following five categories: Word and meaning converge; word and meaning diverge; the words converge and the meanings diverge; the words diverge and the meanings converge; the word is a composite, and the letters and meaning converge to a certain extent, but diverge in the remainder. These are the five types of terms that the Philosopher enumerated at the beginning of his logical books and that commentators have discussed, designating them in turn as "homonyms," "heteronyms," "synonyms," "polyonyms," and "paronyms." A fuller account of them can be found in those sources.[3] But only one of these categories is required for the purpose for which speech was needed, which is that words should vary with the meaning, which corresponds to "heteronymous" terms. The other categories arose out of particular constraints and specific needs, and did not arise from the primary purpose, as we will show with God's help.

We have established that the things and situations the soul represents to itself are very many in number—that in fact they are infinite. By contrast, the posited letters that signify by common accord and the composites that are formed out of them are finite, limited, and circumscribed in number. It is crystal clear and intuitively obvious that when a large number of things are distributed over a smaller number of things, several will end up being shared by the latter. This is how the phenomenon of homonymy arises, which is when a single term signifies a number of different meanings. Take for example the word that denotes the eye we see with, a spring of water, the hollow of the knee, an overweight gold coin, and the kind of rain that continues for days. The examples could be multiplied. This feature—which leads to confusion and ambiguity and to errors and misjudgments in what people do and think—was not the product of voluntary choice but of natural necessity, as we have explained. 1.6

Then those who practice the craft of rhetoric, the craft of poetry and rhymed prose, and the arts of eloquence more broadly look askance at the use of the same word over and over again, because they need to produce popular persuasion in different contexts—for example, in making peace between tribes; in rousing people to, or making them desist from, war; or in any other situation in which it is necessary to dilate on a topic and to reiterate a single idea to an audience so that it sinks into their minds and stamps itself indelibly on their understanding. This is especially true of poets, who are furthermore in a constant need of words that may serve in the place of other words bearing the same meaning, in order to get the meter right and arrange the structure of their speech more felicitously. It thus becomes necessary that several terms signify a single meaning. This phenomenon, which pertains to polyonyms, seems to conflict with the primary purpose behind the institution of speech. Yet, as you can see, it arises in response to a need. Had orators, poets, and 1.7

those composing in rhymed prose and meters not needed it, it would have been completely pointless. We have confined our explanation to these two categories because they are connected with the present question, and we refer anyone interested in learning more about the other categories to their extensive, in-depth examination in books on logic.

1.8 So much for our prefatory remarks. We can now address the question proper. Our response is as follows: There are heteronyms—words that vary with the meaning. These were the primary purpose behind the institution of language. There are homonyms—single words that each bear different meanings. Then there are polyonyms—different words that bear the same meaning. We have shown that these last two categories arose from necessity. Sometimes different words bear kindred meanings though they differ in their specifics, and sometimes they denote different qualities yet pertain to a single thing. This is why orators and poets use them as if they were polyonyms, on account of the affinity and close association between them, even though they are actually heteronyms. A good example is the profusion of terms used to designate the notion of "catastrophe"; they represent distinct qualifications, but as they refer to a single thing, they are deployed as if they had the same meaning. Something similar holds for the different terms for "wine," "sword," and the like. If you take a close and thorough look, you will see that these things have different meanings. But as they are qualifications attributed to a single subject, they are treated as though they were terms that signified the same meaning. This happens when people allow themselves a certain license in their speech, when they need some latitude, to avoid constraints and be less stringent with the facts. Had I not been assured of your refined intelligence, your critical acumen, and your nimble mind, I would not have alluded to the meaning of these matters but would have gone to the trouble of explaining the distinction between the meanings of the words "wine," "drink," "liquor," "alcohol," "inebriant," and other terms belonging to the same class; between the meanings of the words "sword," "saber," "blade," and the rest of the appellations and qualifiers belonging to the same class; and between the different terms and qualifiers used to signify "catastrophe." But I took the view that this would be gratuitous labor, prattling verbiage that would bring you no benefit.

Therefore, we need to probe different words whose meanings converge or are closely related, whenever we come across them. If we notice a point of distinction between their meanings, then we attribute these words to the imperatives of language and to the exigencies of the wisdom behind the institution of speech, classing them with the heteronyms that vary with the meaning. This is the clearest way and soundest method for dissolving questions and doubts. If, on the other hand, we do not succeed in uncovering a semantic distinction and probing does not bring one to light, then we attribute this to the other principle, and put it down to the category we clarified and explained, namely, the need that arises in poetry and rhetoric for using many words that signify a single meaning. I have taken it upon myself to discuss the specific terms that were used to illustrate the questions in the epistle, so as to provide a stepping-stone for dealing with similar cases—a closer look will reveal that there is a superabundance of these. God alone grants success. 1.9

The distinction between "haste" and "swiftness"

The distinction between "haste" and "swiftness" is as follows: 1.10
"Haste" is mostly applied to a sequence of physical movements and is mostly used in a disapproving sense. When you say to someone "you were hasty with me" or "he was hasty with him," it is understood that this is an expression of disapproval. This is not the case when you say "he was swift." Also, we only use "haste" to frame commands in addressing people who work in lowly occupations, and we only use it with our inferiors. By contrast, "swiftness" is a term of approval, and is mostly applied to nonphysical movements. For example, you use it to say that a person catches on swiftly and is

swift to learn, that he was swift to command and swift to reply. God is described as «swift at reckoning».[4] You use it to describe a horse as swifter than the wind and swifter than lightning. A glance is said to be swift, justice is swift, the heavens are swift-moving. "Hasty" could not be used in their place, nor could it be deployed in any of these contexts. The difference is clear, but people use the two terms interchangeably due to loose usage and the proximity between their meanings.

The distinction between "delight" and "gladness"

1.11 When people say "he was delighted," or "glad," or "exuberant," or "merry," the distinction between "delight" and "gladness" on the one hand, and between "exuberance" and "merriness" on the other, is plain. This is because "exuberant" and "merry" are only used pejoratively, in disapproval, while "delight" and "gladness" are not terms of disapproval. The distinction is too obvious and clear to require the further comment. "Delight" and "gladness" are terms similar in meaning. "Delight" is only used when this state has been induced in a person by someone else. "Gladness," by contrast, is a state that arises without the agency of another. The inflection of the respective verbs provides evidence for the soundness of this point. For the passive is always used: "I was delighted" and "he was delighted," and thus indicates an action produced by someone else, even if that person is not named. By contrast, when you say "I was glad" and "he was glad," the terms do not require the presence of another agent.

The distinction between "to be distant" and "to go far away"

1.12 There is also a distinction between the expressions "he was distant" and "he went far away." There are a variety of ways in which something can be distant, even if the term "distant" encompasses them all. When one proceeds by way of length, width, or depth, the dimensions differ, even if the general category is the same. As the dimensions differ and each is distinct from the other, so the words used to signify them necessarily differ. Although the term "distance" is used to refer to each dimension, as if it were the general category, it more narrowly applies to when one proceeds by way of length. The term "far away," by contrast, more narrowly applies to when one proceeds by way of depth. Its origin is connected with wells and other things that resemble them in depth. Then loose usage, combined with the fact that depth is also a kind of distance, led to it being used as a description of length.

The distinction between "to jest" and "to joke"

There is a distinction between the expressions "he jested" and 1.13
"he joked," because speaking in jest is the opposite of speaking in earnest, and is regarded with disapproval, whereas joking is not regarded with disapproval. The Prophet used to joke, and he would speak nothing but the truth; but he never spoke in jest. When people describe someone as a joker with a good sense of humor, they mean this in a positive sense. By contrast, if someone jests, he attracts blame and disapproval.

The distinction between "to block" and "to thwart"

In the expressions "he blocked" and "he thwarted," "blocking" pos- 1.14
sesses semantic priority, because it is, as it were, the cause of the thwarting. To thwart someone is to turn away from him, and this action comes after one has blocked, so the latter term, being close in meaning, is used in place of the former, though their meanings do not coincide.

I have refrained from commenting on the other terms you men- 1.15
tioned right after these ones, as it takes no more than a moment's reflection to uncover the distinctions between them. The term "to give" derives from the verb "to receive," which acquires a transitive meaning through the addition of a prefix; the same happens with "to rise" and "to make someone rise." "To hand over" (*nāwala*),

by contrast, follows a specific verbal paradigm, just as "to strive" (*ḥāwala*) does. These things are too evident to need further discussion.[5]

The distinction between "to sit down" and "to take a seat"

1.16 In the expressions "he sat down" and "he took a seat," the form of the act is the same, but the term "to sit down" is used when one sits after having been reclining or lying down, whereas the term "to take a seat" is used when one sits after one had risen to one's feet or had been standing up. People thus like to differentiate between the two formal acts, each of which is preceded by a different set of circumstances. The fact that people distinguish between these two words on the basis of the circumstances that precede them is demonstrated by the fact that one says "he was reclining and sat up straight," and not "he took a seat straight." In making this point, I do not mean to say that this rule necessarily holds true of every pair of words that signify a given meaning, and you should not take it as an ironclad principle that applies inexorably to all cases. If the difference between the meaning of two terms is not clear, the discussion we prefaced this question with provides ample latitude and scope for you to take the view that the terms converge, which is one of the categories of words that we enumerated.

The distinction between "aim" and "intention"

1.17 Toward the close of your question, you asked: What is the distinction between "meaning," "intention," and "aim"? There are indeed clear distinctions between these terms. Meaning is something that subsists in itself as an independent thing, which may then happen to become the object of an intention. Something can be a meaning without forming anybody's intention. The word "aim" originally referred to the target of an arrow. But insofar as it forms one's object and the end of one's movements and intentions, it resembles the aim of an arrow, so this word is used here by way of analogy.

The distinction between "silence" and "muteness"

You wrote at the conclusion of your question: "Why is it that the difference between 'to speak' and 'to be silent' can easily be made plain, whereas the difference between 'to be silent' and 'to be mute' is so elusive?" What a singular request; what a strange question! For how can the difference between two contraries that lie at the extremes and outermost boundaries of a spectrum and are divided by an enormous distance not be clearer than that between two similar things which are divided by a negligible distance and a sliver of space that only reveals itself to the inquirer after keen reflection and deep meditation? Yet the distinction between "to be silent" and "to be mute" is in any case not all that elusive. The expression "to be silent" can only be applied to subjects capable of speech and possessed of language. In the case of the expression "to be mute," by contrast, the capacity for speech is not a necessary precondition. For there is the expression "He brought things that cry out and things that are mute," meaning he brought a variety of assets that included both animate and inanimate things. The only assets to which the term "mute" is applied are those that are not living and that lack the ability to speak or utter a sound, such as gold and silver and the like. Other assets such as cattle and animals, on the other hand, are not described as mute. Assets described as mute are not described as silent, because "silence" refers back to prior speech or sound. True, one might say of a garment that has been worn out: "the garment fell silent." But that is by way of analogy. It is as though people noticed that a new garment rustles and makes other sounds, and so compared it to something that speaks; then they likened it to something that had fallen silent, when it had been worn out and ceased to produce these sounds. But that is merely a turn of fine language and a fancy metaphor. 1.18

On why people commend the keeping of secrets yet still disclose them—an ethical question

2.1 Why is it that people always exhort each other to keep secrets—going to great lengths to take oaths to keep them safe, decrying their divulgence as indecent, and adjuring each other to silence—yet then, despite all these precautions, they let secrets become public knowledge? How is it that secrets get out into the open and escape the protective veils wrapped around them, so that they are scattered abroad in social gatherings and immortalized in the pages of books, poured out for all to hear and recounted from one generation to the next? Why do people divulge them despite the care they take to have them concealed—indeed, despite the fear we feel about spreading them, the regrets we experience over uttering them, and the forfeited benefits, dreaded consequences, and wrecked relations their revelation entails?

Miskawayh's response

2.2 As philosophical inquiries have shown, the human soul has two powers, one a power to give and the other a power to receive. Through the power to receive, it establishes different kinds of knowledge and longs to learn new facts. This is the power that makes young people delight to hear fables early in their lives and to learn truths once they mature. This power involves passivity and a longing for the perfection that properly belongs to the soul. Through the power to give, on the other hand, the soul spreads its information among others and shares the knowledge it has acquired. This power does not involve passivity but is active in kind. Both powers belong to the soul essentially, not accidentally. Through one of his powers, thus, every human being has a keen desire to act—that is, telling people what one knows—and through another of his powers, to be passively affected—that is, asking people about what they know. Given this, it is impossible that the passive aspect be mobilized without the active aspect also being mobilized, or that the active aspect be mobilized without the passive aspect also being mobilized; because both of them belong essentially to the soul.

The reason why people divulge secrets is now plain. For as the 2.3 soul is a single entity, which both longs to ask for knowledge through one power and craves to impart knowledge through another, no secret is immune to disclosure. That is part of the wonderful providence with which God governs the world, as it explains how factual reports come to be passed down from ancient times and how the histories of different nations come to be preserved, why earlier generations take an interest in recording such facts and why later generations exhibit a keen desire to transmit and absorb them. This is why it has become a byword among philosophers and why they have put their view trenchantly and categorically in stating, "No secret can be concealed forever; sooner or later it will come out." It is also why ordinary people ask, "What can be concealed?" To which they reply, "That which will never be."

So it behooves someone who has a secret to entrust it only to 2.4 the kinds of people who have mastery over themselves and who know how to rein in the capricious movements and appetites of their soul, who in fact battle their soul and are accustomed to win this battle and to bring their soul to heel. This is something human beings achieve through the power of reason, the highest gift they have received from God, the greatest bounty He has bestowed on them, and the basis of the distinction he has granted them over other animals. Were it not for this noble substance, with its rule and oversight over the soul, human beings would be in the same condition as all those nonrational animals in whom the powers of the soul operate freely and unchecked, without restraint or supervision. By contrast, human beings wage mighty battles against their soul through this precious substance. What I mean by this is that human beings are battling their soul through the power of their reason. For they need reason to restrain their soul, to bring it under control, and to stand in the way of their base appetites, so that they only partake of these appetites to the degree that reason allows and determines, prescribes and permits. People who do not wage this battle unremittingly throughout their lives have no title to be deemed human; they are as wanton as animals that roam at will without the oversight of reason. When human beings abandon their high estate for that of lower beings, they forfeit their souls and consign them to the most injurious station, even as they deny God's bounty, refusing His most exalted gift, and reveal how averse they are to drawing near to their Creator. Philosophers have probed this topic at length, giving instructions to people about this inner battle in their ethical works; so let those who wish to learn about such matters turn to those sources.

2.5 The passions that affect the soul and the actions it carries out depending on their power are many. These are the appetites that people experience. No human being is ever free of them, but some have more and some less, so the degree to which rational beings must battle against them differs. The ignorant are those who abandon themselves to them and do not engage them in battle. Divulging a secret is one such appetite, which has to do with sharing information and with giving. If this is the relation in which the keeping of secrets stands to the struggle against the soul—so that an essential characteristic of the soul makes it ardently desire to reveal them, and the soul is only restrained and prevented by reason—it is fitting that this should be difficult and arduous, as is the case with other appetites that one must struggle against. One of these two powers may sometimes be stronger in some people and weaker in others. For there are people who love to speak and people who love to listen; there are people who are tightfisted with their knowledge and people who share it liberally; there are people who are keen to learn and acquire knowledge, and people who are slack to do so. Similarly, there are people who have a strong urge to disclose secrets, and others who are more steadfast and self-possessed.

We used to have a friend who kept company with a ruler and enjoyed high office, and who used to say to his companion, "If you happen to have a secret you would like to keep quiet and would hate to see trumpeted abroad, then please do not share it with me or hold me to the onerous demand of keeping it. It will jab and pierce my heart like an awl or a spearhead." I also heard him say, "I once discovered a secret kept by the vizier, and he gave me money and favors in exchange for my silence, putting them instantly at my disposal. I determined to keep my pledge, and I talked it through with myself and braced myself for the task. That night it was as if I had been bitten by a snake, and when I got up the next morning I burned with fever. I could find no other way of alleviating my distress than to go to an empty part of the house where a rickety old closet stood, and, after sending everyone away, to say to the closet: 'O closet, this is how things happened . . .' By God, this made me experience the relief a person feels when a heavy burden has been lifted off him. It was as if I had emptied a small container into a larger one. However, the sense of being weighed down soon returned to press on my chest, but luckily I found relief when the secret was disclosed by someone else." 2.6

Someone else expressed in verse what this person expressed in prose: 2.7

I do not keep secrets but divulge them,
nor do I let secrets stew in my heart—
Only the dim-witted spend their nights
tossed by secrets from side to side

(Or as another version has it: "Only the dupes . . .")

And then there is the saying about the king with ears like a donkey's. In order to emphasize the importance of keeping secrets, its author suggested that if even the trees and the soil cannot be trusted but will betray secrets, how can animals succeed? As the folk say: "Even the walls have ears."

Now, one poet said:

Brothers in honesty, I impart not the secret of one to the other,
though I possess them all—
My brothers may be scattered through the lands,
but their secret is entrusted to a rock that men cannot
cleave.[6]

Someone else remarked:

I keep secrets that make heads roll.[7]

Such talk is unsound and the claim does not stand firm. So pay close attention and be careful not to be deceived by it.

On why certain names are more pleasing than others—a composite question about the secrets of nature and the letters of the language

3.1 My question is: Why is it that one name falls more lightly on the ears than another, so that the very sound of it provokes people to delight? I have known people enamored of the poet al-Buḥturī who are transported by his words and zealously champion his verse to say: How fine al-Buḥturī's love poems to ʿAlwah are, how right he was to have chosen the name ʿAlwah. Yet they do not have the same experience with the names Salmā, Hind, Fartanā, or Daʿd. This is a phenomenon one encounters with names and cognomens, fine qualities and ornaments, outer forms and inner frames, ethical traits and natural builds, places and epochs, schools of thought and doctrines, practices and customs. If you investigate this topic, then join it to an investigation of that class of things that on the contrary weigh heavily upon one's soul, ears, and natural bent. For if there is a reason why one case is acceptable, then there must also be a reason why another case is objectionable; if there is a cause that makes one case agreeable, there must also be a cause that makes another case disagreeable.

Miskawayh's response

3.2 Names are composed of letters. There are twenty-eight letters, and each name can be composed of two, three, four, or five letters. The best way to respond to this question is to discuss the individual letters that form the basic units of names first, and then to discuss the names composed from them. That way one can clarify in turn why someone takes pleasure in hearing individual letters, then in their combination and composition, and finally in the positioning of one word next to another so as to form a public oration, a poetic verse, or some other category of speech. One may liken this to necklaces and pendants made up of beads that vary in size, color, type of stone, and setting. We know that the necklace made up of beads involves three aspects. One pertains to the individual beads, and to the choice of varieties of beads and types of stone. The second pertains to their arrangement, through which one bead placed next to another produces a different response in, and has a further type of purchase on, the soul. The third pertains to the proper positioning of each necklace, be it on the neck, the head, the forearm, or the chest. If this analogy is sound, the original letters are like beads, which vary naturally in ways that cannot be influenced by human effort and can bear no trace of human craftsmanship and no suggestion of skill and dexterity. It is thus in the other two forms of arrangement and composition that craftsmanship has an effect and in which the skill, keen vision, and refinement of human beings can be expressed.

3.3 Let me explain. Each of these twenty-eight letters originates from a different physical location, ranging from the deepest part of the lung to the front-most part of the mouth. This has been classified and clarified by the scholars of language and by the grammarian al-Khalīl and others, even though they disagree over the points of issue and positions of different letters. This is not the place to enter into the details of this topic, as it will only deflect us from our aim and purpose. Pressing on, then: Sound is produced through a particular set of organs; that is, the lungs and the windpipe, which is where the air is struck; for sound is a form of impaction in the air. The only way in which air can enter a person is through the lungs and the windpipe, which is accessed through the mouth; and the only way in which air can leave is through the same route. The impaction that constitutes sound thus only occurs in this area. Some sounds are closer to the lungs and farther from the lips, while others are closer to the lips and farther from the lungs, with many gradations in between. From the moment it exits the lung to the moment it reaches the lips, the breath—which is the air—has to cross a distance that extends between the deepest part of the throat and the tip of the mouth. Human beings have the capacity to break up the air through different types of impaction along the length of this distance. Sometimes they pierce this air in the back of the throat, sometimes in the front, or sometimes inside the oral cavity, up to a total of twenty-eighty locations.

3.4 One may liken this to a reed pipe pierced with a row of holes; when a person blows into it and his breath passes out of the instrument at a particular point determined by the successive movements of one's fingers, the sounds one hears vary depending on how near or how far that point is. The sound of the impaction that occurs at the last hole is not the same as the sound of the impaction that occurs at the first hole. Similarly, the remaining impactions between these two holes strike the ears differently, and do not resemble one another. Thus, one calls one sound "harsh" and another "sweet," one "sonorous" and another "gentle." Each of these sounds leaves an impression on the soul, has an effect on it and an affinity to it. Given the type of inquiry we are pursuing, our questioner has no title to demand that we discuss why the soul is more receptive to some sounds than to others. That type of investigation and inquiry pertains to the craft of music and its foundations and to the knowledge of the measurements of notes that differ according to their proportional relations—namely, the relation of equal, weak, half, and the like.[8] The soul is more receptive to some of these proportional relations than to others, such that one of the ancients said, "The soul is composed from a harmonic number."[9]

Since the windpipe is like the shaft of a reed pipe, and the way the letters are broken up in it resembles the way the sound pierces through different points of the reed pipe, and since the soul responds with varying degrees of receptivity to the sounds of the reed pipe, the same thing applies to the letters, so that there is no aspect or ground to distinguish between the one and the other. It has thus been made clear that the individual letters themselves affect the soul in different ways, and some affect it more strongly than others. If they have this quality taken as individuals and as simples, then the receptivity of the soul will also differ when they are in a composed state, except that their composition and combination involves a degree of craft, as illustrated by our analogy with the arrangement of beads and the arrangement of sounds in music. For what the musician does is to combine these sounds according to proportional relations that are agreeable to the soul. The person who combines letters must therefore also combine them and create an agreeable blend made up of two, three, or more letters, if he wishes them to be received well by the soul. 3.5

Thus far, we have explained why these letters differ, taken individually and in combination. On the basis of this account, it follows that certain names will be more beautiful than others, more pleasing to the ear and more easily received by the soul, while others will be less likely to achieve this. So as to bear out the analogy we coined with the beads and the necklaces and the placing of each necklace where befits it, there is a third consideration, one that concerns the arrangement of words next to one another and the positioning of them where they belong. This is where the craft of oratory, rhetoric, and poetry makes an appearance. For if one selects the letters that are combined to form names in such a way as to exclude everything odious and disagreeable, arranges them 3.6

in the places where they belong, and deploys them by placing one word next to another in a way that accords with the meaning, is not awkwardly situated, and is not repellent to the ear, then he has achieved as much as he can by way of craftsmanship, be it poetry, a public oration, or some other form of speech. Whenever a defect infiltrates one of these three levels, the craftsmanship becomes defective, and the soul recoils from the speech that has been arranged on that basis. We have given a synoptic account and sufficient explanation of the present topic, God willing.

3.7 As for what you requested at the end of your question—that I join this investigation to an investigation of those things that weigh heavily on one's soul, ears, and natural bent—I have obviously done that in the course of my discussion. For to elucidate the reason for one of two contraries is to elucidate the reason for the other. The odious sounds to which the soul is not receptive are many, and people do not care for them enough to combine them. They are instead encountered fortuitously as individual units, the way one hears the creaking of a door, the sound of copper being stripped by a coppersmith, and the like. The soul undergoes a change at such sounds and shudders all over, and sometimes the very hair on one's body stands on end and one experiences a sense of vertigo to the point where one feels uncomfortable. But this is well known and obvious.

On why people preach renunciation but do not practice it; on reasons, causes, time, and place—a question relating to voluntary choice

4.1 Why is it that people of all languages and creeds and all other customary beliefs and religious traditions counsel each other to adopt an attitude of renunciation toward worldly goods, of frugality and contentment with what is to hand at a given time and situation, even as people avidly seek them out and try to obtain them with extreme covetousness and greed, foraying over land and sea for the sake of some minor profit and paltry gain, to the point that one can hardly find a single person on the face of this earth who is not thinking back wistfully to those worldly things he has lost, doting rapturously on those he possesses, or yearning anxiously for those he may possess in future, and to the point where if you were to scrutinize people you would find none but are stricken into grief or perplexity or stupor by them? Those with the noblest intelligence are the very ones who are the most fatuous, those most vigorous in commending renunciation of worldly goods are the most grasping, and those who most strongly claim to hate them are most highly afflicted by their love. Give me the reason and the cause. Speaking of reasons and causes, what is a reason and a cause? What is the connection between the two, if such a connection exists? Can one substitute for the other? And if it can, can it do so at every place and time, or only at one place but not another, and one time but not another? Speaking of place and time, what is time and what is place? What kind of enmeshment does the one have with the other, and what is the bearing between them? Is a moment the same thing as time? Is perpetuity the same thing as a period? If so, how can two things be one and the same thing? And if two things be a single thing, can a single thing be two things?

Good God! This is a topic to make your mouth dry, press your 4.2
cheek to the ground, to plunge the soul into a state of ferment, to make the glutton choke on his next bite, to reveal the emptiness of claims to knowledge, and to make one confess the limits of one's adequacy and power. It is a topic that proves the unity of Him who encompasses these mysteries and truths, leads you to worship the One who knows these occult and subtle things, prohibits scorn and mutual derision, and commands mutual respect and fairness. It shows that knowledge is a boundless sea, for what eludes people exceeds what is attained, what remains unknown is many times what is known, what is presumed to be true is greater than what is

known with certainty to be so, what is obscure is much more than what is apparent, and what is imagined goes far beyond what is rigorously ascertained. God says, «They comprehend not anything of His knowledge save such as He wills».[10] Had the knowledge referred to in this verse remained subject to negation, nothing whatsoever would have been known, and had the exceptive clause not provided clarification, nothing whatsoever would have been left. But through the word "not," God negated what is required by His divinity, and through the word "save," He left what tends to the enjoyment and welfare of His servants.

4.3 Your question continued with denunciations and reproaches of human deficiency that I will leave to one side, without loss.

Miskawayh's response

4.4 This is a question imbricated with several difficult questions, yet you have subsumed them all under a single heading, and those questions you added at the tail end look like they ought rather to have been headlines. In putting your question, you succumbed to a fit of vanity and conceit, and like a proud stallion you roamed about, lustily swishing your tail back and forth, running sidelong across fields, swaggering in your pride and pressing ahead with your extravagance until I feared you would trip yourself up in the swell of your volubility. Shouldn't you leave this to the person tasked with discussing your question, and spare your respondent this malady? Show some mercy, Abū Ḥayyān, and God will show you mercy; let go of our throat and allow us to breathe. Leave us to our own shortcomings—for we know only too well that they are immense—and to our own struggle with doubt, for it is great. Do not censure us for being ignorant of things we know, and for not understanding what we have attained, thereby driving us to make pretensions and preventing us from seeking what we lack. You are behaving sinfully and treating us wrongfully. I pray to God not to hold your offence against you, or call you to account, and punish you for it. For unless He pardons and forgives, you are in danger of this: «He is worthy to be feared, worthy to grant forgiveness».[11]

4.5 The answer to the first question is as follows. Human beings are a composite of soul and body, and the designation "human" refers to these two elements taken together. The noblest of these two parts is the soul, which is the source of every excellence and in itself the means whereby human beings discern which beliefs are right and wrong, which actions are good and evil, which character traits are admirable and repugnant, and which statements are true and false. The other part—the body with all its particularities and appurtenances—is the more base and vile of the two. This is because it is composed of different internecine natural elements and it is always found in a state of becoming, never enduring for longer than the twinkle of an eye. It is in flux, perpetually changing, and that is why its world has been called a sophistic world.[12] These matters have been rigorously examined and explained in their proper places, and we refer to them only insofar as answering the present question requires. If, then, human beings are composed of these two parts and form a mixture of these two powers and their highest part is the one we mentioned—namely, the soul, which does not have its existence in the realm of becoming and is not composed of internecine conflicting parts, but is rather a simple substance in comparison to the body and a self-sufficient divine power—it follows that it is better for human beings to preoccupy themselves with this part rather than the other. For this endures, whereas that perishes; this is a single substance, while that is many conflicting substances; this exists eternally, while that only exists in a state of becoming with no stability.

4.6 A survey of the excellences of the soul and the deficiencies of the body would take us far from our present purpose. Having established and acknowledged these principles, it will be enough for answering this question to say that the person who perceives the excellences attaching to his soul and the defects attaching to his body must seek to augment these excellences so that he may raise himself to the ranks of divine beings and must reduce his concern for things which impede that possibility.[13] Insofar as preoccupation with the senses and with the particularities of the body impedes the virtues and modes of knowledge that are distinctive to human beings, all religions have deemed it reprehensible to abandon oneself to them and devote one's concern and attention to them, commanding that one take as much nourishment as is indispensable for one's material existence, and that one devote the rest of one's time to the pursuit of those virtues in which happiness lies.

4.7 This point emerges plainly and with the utmost clarity when one considers the difference that separates human beings from other animals. For the superiority of the former over the latter is grounded in the particularity of the soul, not the particularities of the body. Even though human beings are superior to them, as we know, the bodily particularities with which animals are endowed are more complete and extensive—and by bodily particularities I refer to strength, force, the ability to eat, drink, copulate, and the like. So the perfection and excellence of human beings comes from this special distinction that they possess to the exclusion of other beings. Anyone with a greater share of it has a greater claim to be called "human," and is worthier of being described as excellent. Thus, one says, "He is a man of great humanity," and this constitutes one of the highest forms of praise. Whoever wishes to acquaint himself with these fundamental principles, increase his understanding, and attain the highest conviction may look them up where he would expect to find them.

4.8 The answer to the question why, despite their awareness of this excellence, people ardently seek out and covet worldly goods, foraying over land and sea for the sake of paltry pleasures, is as follows. As human beings, the part of us which consists in our natural body is stronger than the other part. We experience a constant contest between these two forces, a common feature of things composed of different forces. In such cases, the strongest force will always have the more visible effect. This is why we are drawn to this part despite our knowledge of the excellence of the other. Even if we know that things are as we have represented, and are convinced beyond a shadow of a doubt, we are locked in a perpetual battle, in which one part gains the upper hand on occasion, while at other times we incline toward the other part, depending on the care we take.

Let me illustrate this with an analogy taken from everyday 4.9
experience. Someone who is ill, convalescing, and whose humoral mixture is out of balance, knows for certain that by following a diet and restraining his appetites he can recover his health and natural equilibrium. Despite this, he indulges many of his appetites, because their allure is too powerful and they get the better of his rational judgment and his physician's counsels. When the pain returns upon his gratification of his desires, he experiences a sense of remorse that makes him think he will never do this again. Yet it is not long before another appetite—or even the very same one—flares up in him. Even as he keeps admonishing himself, constantly reminding himself of the pain he will incur and of the desirability of health, admonitions and reminders are of no use, on account of what we have already mentioned: the powerful allure of present appetite. So, once again, he gratifies his appetite. This goes on without respite for as long as his illness lasts. The same thing occurs during times of health, when one satisfies appetites that one knows will disturb the balance of the humoral mixture and leave one vulnerable to illness. Deficient restraint and the powerful allure of nature lead one to defy one's sound judgment and to behave like a beast. If this analogy strikes you as sound, and if you find it compelling, you will have gained an insight into what was said above and you will have understood it clearly. You will now make allowances for those who would have you renounce worldly pleasures yet then turn to them themselves, and for those who advise you to abandon them yet then partake of them themselves, and indeed do so to excess.

The distinction between reasons and causes

4.10 Let's address the question regarding reasons and causes and their difference. A reason is that which motivates an act and for the sake of which an agent acts. A cause, in contrast, is that which acts itself. That is why reasons pertain more particularly to accidental things, whereas causes pertain more particularly to things having to do with the substance. The philosophers have used the term "cause" to refer to the Blessed Creator, to the intellect, the soul, and nature. They have thus spoken of the "first cause" and of second, third, and fourth causes, and they have likewise spoken of "proximate" versus "remote" causes in describing things that you will find fully expounded in their books. Yet this question, in one respect, resolves back into the very first question we answered, because these terms may be classed with heteronyms through one type of consideration, and with polyonyms through another. There's no need to go over it again as we have already discussed this topic at length.

4.11 Much has been said about time and place. It was a topic of discussion for the ancients, and it has been the subject of debate among the dialectical theologians of Islam. It is too obvious to "make your mouth run dry and press your cheek to the ground," all the more since the Philosopher treated it decisively, dismantling the different views taken on it, debunking the old doctrines, and specifying in the *Physics* his own view and the view of his teacher Plato. Whenever that philosopher has discussed a topic, there is no need to look further because he has covered the topic completely. His discussion has been commented upon by eminent members of his circle, has been translated into Arabic, and is available to read. Here I will mention the gist of the doctrines as the question appended to your first question requires, and I will leave detailed arguments aside, since they can be found in writing. It is preferable that I indicate the relevant sources and that these be read directly than that I should copy them out here. Time is a duration measured through the motion of the celestial sphere.[14] Place is the surface that encompasses both what is contained and what contains.[15]

The distinction between time, perpetuity, period, and moment

Regarding the difference between moment, time, perpetuity, and period, a moment is a definite amount of time that is distinguished from the larger totality of time as a particular. Similarly, a period is a duration that is longer, more extensive, and farther-reaching than a moment. Both terms appear in conjunctions that distinguish and separate them from the totality of time, which forms their encompassing whole, so that one speaks of "the moment that," or "the period when," relating them to a particular situation, person, or the like. If one wishes to be deliberately vague instead of conveying something clearly, one says: "such-and-such happened or will happen at a certain period or moment." One's listener then infers that one has preferred not to specify the moment or period, even though these are necessarily specific and determinate. Perpetuity, on the other hand, has absolutely nothing to do with time, period, or moment. It more specially concerns those things that do not exist in time and are not measured through the motion of the celestial sphere, because they belong to a higher order than that of natural things. I would put it as follows: The relation of time to natural things is like the relation of perpetuity to nonnatural things—and that is to say, to what is above nature. 4.12

These remarks are sufficient to provide your question with an indicative response. If you wish to learn more about it, you should consult the sources we have pointed out to you—the discussions of the Philosopher and his commentators—where it is examined in depth. God bless you, anyone who attains a sure knowledge of these matters through study will be enlivened by them to the wisdom of the One who created them and brought them into being, and they act as firm causes and powerful motives that lead one to acknowledge the unity of God. It is only on account of the bounty of God and the good He chooses to diffuse among us through such means that we can come to know and comprehend these matters: They belong to the part of God's knowledge that He willed us to comprehend. Our knowledge of time, place, the moment, and the present instant is of a 4.13

piece with everything else that God has enabled us to know. Behind such matters, however, lie occult and subtle mysteries inaccessible to human reason that no one has ever aspired to grasp. It is right and proper to acknowledge the weakness and impotence of human beings in such matters, as well as the things Abū Ḥayyān mentioned and the humbling limitations of human nature he decried. That is when we must sit on the ground and bow our heads in shame at our lowliness and abjectness, in view of our need for the Creator of the world and the Originator of all things.

4.14 By contrast, God is to be thanked for the matters we have discussed, for in order to discuss them we must speak of God's bounty and wonder at His wisdom, taking them as proofs of His generosity and power and of the good He diffuses in His creation, asking Him to increase our share of them, and ardently pursuing similar forms of knowledge through inquiry and examination. We must always hope that the One who confers them on us and puts them within our reach will diffuse more of the like, for they are things that have been assigned and made available to human beings and that it is their mission and task to attain. I will go further and say that human beings, who are perfected through reason, are duty bound not to cease striving and seeking to perfect themselves through learning. For as long as they live they must struggle tirelessly and unflaggingly to increase the knowledge that gives them membership of the victorious party of God and His close allies, those who triumph to the end, are granted safety, and «shall have no fear on them and shall not sorrow».[16] Those people, by contrast, who devote their lives to the acquisition of gold and silver and who expend all their effort on ephemeral and transient bodily pleasures and carnal appetites have distanced themselves from God as members of the party of Satan, laying themselves open to many sorrows, perpetual fear, and evident loss. Their relationship to the object of their desire is always one of two states: either wistfulness and pining for missed opportunities, or grief and desolation over lost possessions. For the things they seek have no stability, an infinite number of particulars, and no real existence, it being their nature to be in a state of becoming, change, and flux. We pray to the one God—the object of our heartfelt desires, to Whom we stretch out our souls, and before Whom our thoughts and hopes prostrate themselves—to diffuse among us the good we seek from Him, which we yearn for not as a means to something else but for its own sake, and to illuminate our minds so that we may perceive the reality of His oneness and the wonders of His creations, leading us to the highest happiness for which we were created by the shortest path and the best-guided way, the straight path of God. For He has a title to that, authority over it, and the power to carry it out.

On why people seek worldly goods through knowledge but do not seek knowledge through worldly goods—a question relating to voluntary choice

Why is it that people seek worldly goods through knowledge even though knowledge forbids that? Why do they not seek knowledge through worldly goods even though knowledge commands that? A brash and fractious fellow with questionable common sense might object, "We know people who have given up seeking worldly goods through knowledge and people who have sought knowledge through worldly goods." But let it be clear that this is not the point of the question. Should the person who makes such an objection get his thoughts in order, he would see what the question really aims at, and he would not compare unexpected events with widespread phenomena, nor would he contradict a rarity on the basis of a commonplace. 5.1

Response

Human beings are inescapably required to seek out worldly goods, for reasons we have already mentioned. They have a natural existence 5.2

through one of their two parts, and this part needs to be properly sustained in its material substance, because it is in flux and in a constant state of dissolution, and the elements that dissolve need to be replaced. Knowledge does not prohibit the acquisition of this basic amount; rather, it prohibits exceeding the strict measure of one's need. There are several reasons why such excess is reprehensible. First, it puts the body into a state of disharmony, when our object is to preserve its balance. Second, it prevents us from realizing that which is more distinctive of us as human beings—I mean the second part, that which constitutes our excellence. So, the use of knowledge to seek such amount of worldly goods as is strictly needed in order to preserve the health of the body is appropriate and in conformity with what reason dictates and knowledge commands. Seeking more than that is immoderate and exceeds the proper bounds. Seeking worldly goods in a balanced way is the most difficult achievement. You must have recourse to wise and knowledgeable people, and read books of ethics, to know what constitutes right balance and so adhere to it, and what constitutes excess and so steer clear of it.

5.3 Having provided this general perspective and indicated the sources that can be consulted, however, we need to add a basic further exposition and explanation. People vary according to the part of themselves they pay attention to. Some pay attention to the natural part, others to the intellect, and yet others to both. Consequently, people's aims vary, and their actions depend on the part they pay attention to. It is clear that it is misguided to only pay attention to one part to the exclusion of the other, because human beings are composed of both. It is right to pay attention to both if each is given a share of attention and a quota of effort in proportion to its merits and the loftiness or baseness of its rank.

5.4 Those who regard things according to the natural part plunge into the domain of nature, dedicating themselves to it with every ounce of their power and making it the locus of their ultimate end. They make the intellect an instrument for obtaining the effects and satisfying the needs of nature, thereby subjugating their highest part to the lowest one, as a king might be put in the service of his slave. However, those who regard things according to the intellectual part neglect the part that belongs to them by nature. They regard things from a divine perspective and aspire—composite human beings though they are—to partake exclusively of the excellence of the intellect, unblemished by the deficiencies of nature. This forces them to neglect the body, even though it is conjoined to them and necessity bids them to pursue the benefits that sustain it, or to remove the impediments created by its multiple needs. They thus wrong themselves and their fellow human beings. They wrong themselves because they disregard the part through which they are sustained, trying to secure their welfare through the sweat of another's brow, thereby wronging them by failing to help them in return. For justice demands that you help the person whose help you enlist, and that you labor in the service of those who offer you the fruits of their labor. It is through such help that polities are realized and the livelihood of human beings—who are political by nature—is put into good order. These are the people who call themselves "ascetics," and they are made up of a number of different classes. There is a group among the philosophers, and several factions among the exponents of different religious beliefs, creeds, and sectarian views. There is also a group in our own religion of Islam who call themselves Sufis, some of whom have declared that it is forbidden even to earn a living.

Having established the misguidedness of those who focus on 5.5
the one part to the exclusion of the other, we may now outline the correct approach, which is to pay regard to both parts and to give each part—nature and intellect—its proper due. We therefore say as follows. Human beings are composed from these two powers, as we have mentioned, and can only subsist through them. Therefore, their efforts must be directed both toward what is natural and toward what is intellectual. In terms of natural effort, the objective of human beings must be to preserve the health of their bodies and to maintain the mixture of their natural elements in a balanced state,

so that the acts that issue from them are complete and not deficient. This is achieved by seeking out, in a balanced way, food and drink, sleep and wakefulness, and motion and rest—to say nothing of the other adjuncts such as clothing, shelter to protect against cold and heat, and the things the body requires. They must entertain no other end, such as pleasure and exceeding the strict measure of need, out of a desire for ostentation and at the bidding of greed, cupidity, or any of those other maladies that make us falsely believe that this is what humans must aspire to. Their intellectual effort must also be directed at the preservation of the health of the soul, since it comprises a number of different powers and is susceptible to maladies when some of these powers surpass the others. The preservation of the balanced state constitutes its therapy, and the increase of knowledge constitutes its power and its means of attaining everlasting life and eternal happiness.

5.6 A detailed discussion of each of these excellences would require a great deal of space, but this amount suffices by way of brief exposition. So let people strive after that which secures the welfare of both parts, maintaining a balanced approach, without overshooting or undershooting the mark. For it is then that they will have attained a perfect and excellent state. Only fools who are to be ignored or dolts who should not be heeded will reproach them. God alone grants success.

On why people long for the past—a natural question

6.1 Why do people long for the earlier part of their lives, so that they cry like she-camels after their young and weep as if the world could not contain them, dwelling on images of things past? This is what one poet expressed when he exclaimed:

Though the cruelty of a time makes me weep
I weep even more to see its passing

Or as another said:

Many a day that brought me to tears
made me tear up anew when the next day dawned

And as another said:

I pine for the morrow, and when it comes
I weep over the day that has just gone

This feeling is present even when the past was full of poverty and need, distress and affliction. The reason for this must lie in some mysterious trait of the soul that human beings are unaware of. They can only uncover it if they inquire long and hard; free themselves from their deficiencies; throw themselves heart and soul into the pursuit of understanding, harvesting wisdom night and day without cessation; and if they have greater respect for fine words than for comely maidens and greater love for burnished ideas than for heaped gold. The measure of their dedication will determine the honor they reap, and the graces they enjoy in this world and the next.

Miskawayh's response

Two kinds of people long for lost youth and childhood: those who have lost the carnal appetites and pleasures at their most full-blooded and keenest in youth, and those who have suffered a decline in their hearing and sight or in any of the other bodily functions at the height of their power and in their prime, during childhood or their early years. The first aspect most often arouses the sense of longing, because those in the middle of their lives, who have reached the full vigor of maturity, do not long for their childhood, and old men do not lack any of the psychological features, capacity for judgment, and intellectual acuity they used to possess during 6.2

their youth—unless, to be sure, they have grown decrepit and senile, but in that case they are not said to have a sense of longing of any kind (this is simply not ascribed to them), and their views are not taken into consideration.

6.3 There is a third reason that makes people long for their childhood—this is when one's hopes for a continued existence run highest. It is as if people expect to have a long life ahead of them, and when part of their life passes, it dawns on them that this has been taken out of their appointed span and predetermined length of existence. They then long to go back to the beginning, out of a craving to live forever that cannot be satisfied through the perishable body. But it is the first aspect that poets have given voice to at length, addressing it blatantly in their poems. In the view of the philosophers, longing for the carnal appetites is like longing for servitude after manumission, or like longing to fall into the clutches of vicious beasts after one has escaped from their claws. For the powers of nature run riot in the young when appetite and anger seize them and overwhelm their reason, so that they take no counsel from their understanding and reason manifests itself but feebly. As we explained in our previous answers, the excellence and dignity of human beings is vested in their divine part, even though the other part is necessary. Thus, it is clear that the best age of all is the age at which the powers of nature grow weak, allowing reason to bring them under its power and rein them in so that they are led meekly and submissively, recalcitrant or restive no longer. At his most honorable age, the virtuous, upright man will not long for the most debased age. The surest proof of our position is that temperate, self-disciplined youths who have the power to subdue their appetites are pleased with their course of conduct, even if it entails great struggle, and are judged to be virtuous by all people of sound reason. When they grow old, they do not long for their youth, because self-discipline and the subdual of physical appetites now come to them so easily and with little strain.

6.4 Yet those who follow a philosophical path and adhere to religious Law are not beset by such impulses—I mean wild cravings to take pleasure, grief over pleasures missed, and regret over pleasures given up or inadequately indulged. They know that these are base passions that call forth vile actions, and that the philosophers have made their defects clear and devoted entire books to discrediting them, just as they know that the prophets have issued prohibitions and warnings against them, and that the books sent down by God give expression and provide testimony to all this. Could the virtuous man long for deficiency, the learned man for ignorance, and the healthy man for illness? These, rather, are impulses that beset ignorant people whose aim is to immerse themselves in nature and the senses, and to obtain their meretricious pleasures, not to seek health or attain happiness, nor to perfect human excellence. Such people are of no account, and their words and deeds should not be listened to.

On why men of knowledge tend to be conceited—an ethical question

Why are men of knowledge habitually given to conceit, even though true knowledge demands the opposite qualities of humility, gentleness, disregard of self, and a self-deprecating recognition of one's weakness? 7.1

Miskawayh's response

Men of knowledge truly worthy of the name do not succumb to the affliction of conceit. How could they, when they know its cause, and are aware that it is a malady caused by self-deception? For conceit occurs when a person judges that he possesses merit that he does not in fact possess. His judgment is false, but he persists until he comes to believe it. He is then like someone who sees a man fighting courageously in war against redoubtable fighters, bravely fending off enemies and killing opponents, while he keeps himself aloof from 7.2

the battle. He lies to himself and claims the other man's courage for himself, until eventually he comes to believe it. This fault is one of the most extraordinary deceptions the soul perpetrates, because in this case the act of lying is composite. One person might lie to another and get the other to believe him in order to mislead him. But it is indeed the essence of conceit and a cause for amazement that one should mislead *oneself* through lies and then believe oneself. Its composite character makes this kind of lie fouler and more repugnant than the simple lie we are familiar with. If men of virtue and knowledge are not given to the simple lie because they know it to be repugnant—especially since they have no need for it—they will be even less susceptible to the composite fault. This is why I said men of knowledge cannot be conceited. So this question is disqualified and ruled inadmissible. The kind of conceit that affects people who think they are knowledgeable falls entirely outside our concern.

On why people are sometimes ashamed and sometimes proud of wrongdoing; on the meaning of shame

8.1 Why are people sometimes ashamed of doing wrong, while at other times they boast of it? What *is* shame, to begin with? Defining it may bring us nearer to the goal and make it easier to attain the truth. What is the hidden meaning of the Prophet's saying, "Shame is one of the branches of belief"? Certain scholars have questioned how it is possible that shame, which is an effect of nature, should be a branch of belief. For belief is a mode of action. This is clear from how one speaks of a person as "believing" using an active verbal form, whereas one speaks of a person as "being ashamed" using a reflexive verbal form marking it out as a passive response, that is, a form of submission. Is shame praiseworthy in all circumstances, or does it depend on certain parameters? Is it only acceptable in certain conditions?

Miskawayh's response

Shame—which you wished us to begin with—consists in fact in a contraction of the soul through fear that a wrongful act proceed from it. It is an ethical trait that is becoming in young people, for it shows that they perceive what is wrong and are anxious not to perpetrate it, unwilling that it issue from them. Consequently, this effect comes over them. A sense of repulsion at wrongful actions is a sign of the nobility of the soul's substance and raises great hopes for its betterment. The author of the *Book on Estate Management*[17] said: "Shame is the soundest physiognomic feature and truest sign for those who would know whether a boy will distinguish himself, succeed in life, and respond well to the education of his character." This is due to the cause and nature of shame as we have just explained. Old men, on the other hand, should not be susceptible to this effect, because they ought not to be worried about acting wrongfully, on account of their knowledge, experience, and awareness of what is right and wrong, and since their souls should have been disciplined and secured against the possibility of doing wrong. For this reason they should not be susceptible to shame. The Philosopher made this clear in the *Ethics*.[18] 8.2

So, we have discussed what shame is, that it is a passive effect, and that it is a good thing for young people in particular to have it. We have also stated why it is good for them. The question why one boasts of doing wrong is not essentially related to this one. For this phenomenon is caused by ignorance of what is wrong, and it only affects ignorant people. So, when people realize that a given act is wrong, obviously they apologize and boast no more. Boasting occurs when there is no awareness of what makes an act wrong. In such a situation, the boast is the consequence of falsely discerning in an act something that makes it good—the boast is actually a boast about the good that is read into the act or falsely represented as having. Once it is realized for certain that the act is wrong, or it is no longer falsely represented as having the feature that makes it good, then the boasting stops and shame is felt. 8.3

8.4 The Prophet's saying, "Shame is one of the branches of belief," is fine, sound, and truthful. How could it not be one of its branches, when belief is giving credence to God, and giving credence to Him is to give credence to His attributes and acts, characterized by such extreme goodness that none of the things we judge to be good can match them or attain their level? They are the cause of the goodness of every good, and they diffuse goodness to everything, since they are its origin and point of beginning. Things acquire their goodness, beauty, and splendor from them and through them. The same principle applies to all the commands and laws that God has given, and to the requirements of reason, His first messenger and oldest deputy among all of His creatures. Whoever knows what is good necessarily knows its contrary, and whoever knows its contrary looks upon it with wariness and fear. He is thus exposed to the experience of shame that we outlined and described in summary fashion. Your beloved Abū 'Uthmān al-Jāḥiẓ[19] has said: "Shame is a garment that envelops you, a veil that screens you against evil. It is the brother of virtue, the ally of the faith, a companion in rectitude, a protective chaperone, and a vigilant eye—it fends off corruption and prohibits immorality and defilement." I quote his words because I know how enthusiastic you are about him, and how eagerly you welcome any argument he proposes.

On why people claim to have knowledge they lack—a natural question

9.1 Why do some people claim to have knowledge when they know that they do not have this knowledge? What is it that drives them to press that claim, makes them fight to defend something they know is untrue, and leads them to grasp at foolish and abrasive words?

Miskawayh's response

The reason for this is self-love and awareness of where excellence is to be found. Self-love means that people claim to possess what they don't. For knowledge and learning render the soul good, and are the means whereby it realizes and attains happiness. Without this, or without most of it, the soul becomes prey to repugnant qualities and to different types of unhappiness, all in proportion to what it lacks. Love tends naturally to conceal bad qualities, to display any good qualities that are present, and falsely to claim their presence if absent. Since we know this is how love behaves, and since our own soul is necessarily an object of love, we experience the effects that love usually involves. So there is nothing remarkable in people falsely claiming to possess the kinds of knowledge that constitute the excellences and good qualities of the soul, even if they possess none of them.[20] 9.2

On why it pleases people when others ascribe good qualities to them—a natural question

Why do people rejoice when others ascribe to them good qualities they actually possess? And why are they pleased when others describe them as having fine qualities they do not possess? 10.1

Response

The answer to this question is the same as the previous answer. For the good that properly belongs to the soul consists in sound knowledge and the actions that issue from it in accordance with that knowledge. So if the excellence or goodness of someone's soul is acknowledged by others, we necessarily rejoice for what we love, because its fineness and goodness have received recognition. We 10.2

rejoice when others describe us as having fine qualities we do not possess, for the reason discussed in the previous question.

On why it is bad to praise people in their presence and good to praise them in their absence—a question relating to voluntary choice

11.1 Why is it bad to praise people in their presence, so that it is universally dismissed as specious? And why is it good to praise them in their absence, so that it is ardently wished for? Is it because praising people in their presence suggests the intention to flatter and deceive, whereas praising them in their absence suggests a sincere intention to honor, or is there some other reason?

Miskawayh's response

11.2 Praising a person in his presence usually involves giving testimony to his virtues and leads to the person being deceived by this testimony, so that, carried away, he abandons much of his effort to acquire the virtues. In this case, the praise is aimed at winning the person's affection by displaying affection and love for him. Hence, it constitutes a kind of crafty and scheming behavior, and is censured and disapproved of. Praise given in a person's absence, in contrast, is proper because its intention is usually to truthfully acknowledge the virtues of someone else. In the process, attention is called to where virtue lies, and both the object of one's praise and the audience are galvanized to acquire ever more virtue and make it their constant practice, and they are incited to supply its means and causes. Sometimes the intention may be different; I mean, when the aim of the person praising someone in his absence is to deceive the object of his praise, hoping to gain his favor and derive personal advantages, if the praise reaches him and he is taken in by the pretense. This case then resembles the first in its craftiness, and it too is reprehensible. Sometimes the intention behind eulogizing another person to his face is to speak truthfully, not to flatter. In that case it is appropriate, except insofar as one supposes that the object of one's praise may be carried away by it and become remiss in his moral efforts.

It is thus clear that the value of praise depends on the intention 11.3
and aims of the person performing the eulogy, on his honesty or dishonesty, and on whether the praise is expected to benefit or harm its object. Yet our assessment is based on prevailing assumption and dominant practice. Since the account we have given is what usually holds true, it is generally wrong to praise a person in his presence and proper to praise him in his absence, even if it is possible that things may be reversed, so that it may be proper to praise a person in his presence and wrong to praise him in his absence.

On why people want to know what others say about them in their absence—a natural question

Why do people want to know what others say about them when 12.1
they leave their company, so much so that they even long to find out what will be said at their funeral oration, keen to learn the particulars of the event and the speech? And why don't they apply themselves to do the kinds of praiseworthy deeds they would like to be known for, despite the fact that their love of this is so deeply ingrained that they could never shake it off, even if they tried to defy and trick their own nature?

Miskawayh's response

As set forth in some of our earlier responses, the soul has two 12.2
powers, one of which is the power that makes human beings long to possess knowledge securely. Since the knowledge in question

extends generally over all types of things, it is all the more fitting that it should extend to our own soul, which is the object of human love and passionate attachment. Humans thus long for knowledge through their original nature and through a power that is essential to the soul, and this longing increases, becoming more powerful and intense because it specifically pertains to the knowledge of things to do with their beloved soul. They only fail to apply themselves to do the kinds of deeds they would like to be known for if some other impulse gets in the way, such as a competing immediate appetite with a stronger hold over them and greater attraction to them. See our earlier example of the sick person who knows that he needs his health and how to stay healthy and who nevertheless prefers to satisfy an immediate, inferior appetite, even if this means forfeiting the state of health that is his long-term preference. Were it not for these inferior appetites that get in the way of preferred forms of happiness, the excellent person could not be distinguished from the deficient one and the temperate person would not be praised, the glutton blamed. We would then derive no profit from instruction and moral admonition, and there would be no merit in toil and exertion over things that naturally involve hardship and strain. This is a sufficiently clear response to the question.

On why people disapprove of young people who act as if they were older—a question relating to voluntary choice

13.1 Why do people consider it idiotic when young men act like old men, comporting themselves gravely and stiffly, showing a predilection for seriousness and a horror of banter, shunning obscene language, fixing their eyes ahead when they walk and hunching over when they sit down, meticulously enunciating their words and staring at things with a squint?[21]

Miskawayh's response

When young men act like old men, they are signaling that their nature is not driven toward physical appetites, whose power and nature are at their fullest and sharpest extent during youth, when they are still developing. These appetites continue to increase to their maximal extent, and then they begin to decrease, following the pattern of all the powers of nature. So we know that a young man is lying when he claims the status of an old man in whom this power has declined, and we deem his lie and his inappropriate and unnecessary dissembling repugnant. A bald and absolutely unnecessary lie attracts greater opprobrium and provides evidence of the base substance of one's soul. Should the young man in question happen to be honest—that is, should that nature be deficient in him and his appetites blunt—he is absolved of the charge of lying, because there is evidence of a deficiency in his natural elements. The reason he is treated with indulgence is on account of the deficiency of some of his natural elements relative to the natural constitution of human beings; so, if he is honest, he will not be blamed or reproached. If, however, this person is honestly capable of controlling himself despite his young age, his inflamed appetites, and the inclination of his natural powers toward the pursuit of pleasure, it will not be long before his name is on everyone's lips and his renown spreads, and he will emerge as an infallible religious leader, a prophet sent from God, or an elect saint. People of discrimination have no trouble distinguishing the conduct of an honest person from the conduct of a liar, and the actions of a dissimulator from the actions of one acting true to his nature. Yet this honest young man is very much the exception: He is only encountered over many generations and across the eons. What we have discussed constitutes the general rule, and that is why people are quicker to judge on that basis. 13.2

Let us take your next question: "Furthermore, why do people consider it foolish when old men act like juveniles, flouncing about theatrically, attending amusement parties, seeking out singing, and showing a preference for wantonness and a penchant for licentious 13.3

behavior? And what constitutes wantonness and licentiousness in this connection?" The answer is similar to the first, in that it is simply its reverse. For when an old man claims that the powers of his nature are enhanced in his old age, one of two things holds true. Either he is lying and deserves our condemnation—especially since his lying involves laying claim to evils and deficiencies that he ought to have disavowed, even if he did possess them. Or he is telling the truth and deserves censure, insofar as he has failed to conquer the power that has dominated him during the long time he has been given to do so, to come to an awareness of the virtues and to train his soul and complete its edification. His situation is worse than that of the young man we discussed above, and is therefore more abhorrent and more repugnant in the eyes of those endowed with reason. Licentiousness is when one rushes to do the biddings of the appetitive soul without taking counsel from reason and without due regard for opinion. Wantonness, in contrast, is so termed because it derives from the notion of one's throwing off he bridle with which one's reason controls one's actions. The term for "reason" (*ʿaql*) has a similar bearing, as it derives from the rope used to hobble a camel (*ʿiqāl*). The same thing applies to another term for reason, "hindrance" (*ḥijr*).[22]

On why mean people tend to be mild-tempered and generous people volatile—an ethical question

14.1 Why is a mild temper characteristic of mean people and a volatile temper characteristic of generous people? Can a mild temper coexist with generosity and a volatile temper coexist with meanness? What holds true of these two as a general rule? For it is not the same for something to possess a feature stably and for something to acquire a feature through change.

Miskawayh's response

14.2 It seems to me that by "mean" you mean "avaricious," though they are not the same thing. I have based my discussion on this understanding, as it is supported by the rest of your remarks. I do agree that this is indeed generally the case, even though the situation is often reversed and you can meet a generous person with a mild temper or an avaricious person with a volatile one. But it is more appropriate for a generous person to have a volatile temper, for an avaricious person is someone who denies others the things they are entitled to under the right conditions, at the right time, and in the right manner. The avaricious person who denies other people their entitlements in these respects is unjust. If he perceives this defect in himself he must necessarily be forbearing toward people who complain, that is, who criticize. Obviously, criticism directed against an avaricious person must remind him of the injustice he has committed, and of his failure to fulfill his obligations as he ought to have. If the avaricious person immediately recognizes the truth of the criticism, he must necessarily be mild toward his critic, because his critic's words conform with the truth, and the soul naturally submits itself to and finds repose in the truth. Thus, for these reasons, it is in greater accord with the natural order that the avaricious person should be mild-tempered. Sometimes the opposite situation may arise, namely, that the avaricious person be ignorant of the obligations he must fulfill under the conditions we enumerated. Then he will not recognize when someone is speaking truthfully about him or when he is being unjust and when just, so as to be able to recognize that his acts are wrong. He is then afflicted with two defects: One of them is his withholding from others their entitlements, the other his ignorance of their entitlements. An ignorant person like this may then be vulnerable to volatility and impetuousness and may fail to be mild, for the reasons we have set out.

14.3 On the other hand, your question "Why is a volatile temper characteristic of generous people?" is disallowed, because the generous person is not characterized by a volatile temper. To be generous is to spend the right amount, at the right time, in the right manner, and the person who possesses this virtue cannot be volatile. For the volatile person cannot make these distinctions, so he exceeds the measure of the generous person, and then he is called prodigal and extravagant and does not deserve the laudable qualification of generosity. Yet it is a well-known feature of the Arabic language and Arab custom that they treat prodigality and extravagance as equivalent to generosity, so that in the Arab view the more prodigal and extravagant a person is, the more he deserves to be called generous. As a result, the Arabs failed to grasp where excellence lies and what deserves to be praised, and the volatility associated with wasteful and prodigal persons came to be deemed praiseworthy based on their custom. Yet this is not laudable for it does not allow for deliberation, and it leads a person to put things precipitately where they do not belong. This is the kind of person philosophers call prodigal. It has been shown in books of ethics that the generosity that constitutes a virtue is a mean between two blameworthy extremes, one of which involves deficiency while the other involves excess. Avarice is on one side of generosity, the blameworthy side that involves deficiency; prodigality is on the other side, that which is just short of excess. These matters are explained exhaustively in books of ethics, which anyone who wishes for greater detail should read.

On why people need to acquire knowledge but not ignorance—a question relating to nature and voluntary choice

15.1 Why do people need to acquire knowledge, whereas they do not need to acquire ignorance? Is it because ignorance forms their original state? And what is the cause of that? The sound argument is provided through addressing the cause.

Miskawayh's response

Philosophical inquiries have shown that knowledge consists in the soul's perception of the forms of existents as they really are. When one of the ancients described the soul as a place of forms, Plato expressed his approval of this view and declared that its exponent had hit the mark. For when the soul longs for the knowledge that constitutes its proper end, it transfers into itself the form of the object known, such that the form it obtains corresponds exactly to the form of the object from which it has been transferred. This then constitutes pure knowledge. If the form transferred into the soul does not correspond exactly to the object from which it has been transferred, it does not constitute knowledge. The greater the number of forms the soul accumulates, the greater its capacity to secure additional forms. In this respect, the soul is opposed to the body. For when a particular form obtains in the body, it becomes incapable of receiving another, unless the first form is effaced or unless the first and the supervening second forms are combined, producing a blend of the two forms, in which case neither of them is fully present. Things are otherwise with the soul. 15.2

The human soul is material and longs for the perfection that is assigned to it, attained by acquiring the form of all existents, by which I mean universals rather than particulars. It has the capacity to achieve that: the addition of the form of existents to it does not involve the displacement of some forms by others. Rather, in contrast to bodies, whenever the soul secures one form in itself it is capable of securing another, keeping all of them clear and separate from one another ad infinitum. Given all this, human beings need to acquire knowledge, that is, to secure the forms of existents and bring them into their possession. Ignorance refers to the absence of these forms and objects of knowledge. As we procure these forms, we need to exert ourselves and endure hardship and strain until we have acquired them. Their absence, by contrast, requires no exertion or arduous undertaking; these things are absent from the soul. The tangible analogy is a tablet that contains no writing; in order 15.3

to write on it and to trace out the forms of the letters one must exert oneself, whereas leaving it as it is involves no exertion. Unless, indeed, one follows the doctrine that the soul essentially contains the forms of things but has forgotten them, so that knowledge is a matter of recollecting and of eliminating the defect of forgetfulness from the soul.[23] In this case, the response to the question on the basis of this doctrine is clear, for the elimination of a defect inevitably involves strain, whereas leaving the defect untouched does not. Yet this doctrine is not to be commended, for reasons that it would be gratuitous to address in this context because it has nothing to do with the question proper, even though the discussion led us to it. But we can refer to the sources where it can be found discussed, namely, the books about the soul. These sources can be consulted directly. It has thus been made plain that knowledge consists in the soul's acquiring the form of the object known. The term "acquiring the form" (*taṣawwur*) derives from the term "form" (*ṣūrah*) and conforms to the morphological pattern *tafaʿʿul*. Ignorance consists in the absence of a form, so how could a word of the *tafaʿʿul* pattern derived from the word for "form" be used to refer to the absence of a form? That is impossible.[24]

On why people who provoke admiration also feel wonder at themselves; on the nature of wonder; on describing and knowing God—a natural question

16.1 Why is it that people who provoke admiration in others participate in the wonder of their admirers? Take the poet who composes an exquisite verse and provokes his listener to wonder with his marvelous rhetorical figures. Why does the poet experience wonder, when he is the object of wonder? We encounter this phenomenon in poetry and in prose, in oral responsa and written compendia, in mathematical calculations and skilled crafts. Speaking of wonder, what *is* wonder? And what does it reveal? People have said different kinds of things about it. A philosopher was asked, "What is the most wondrous thing of all?" He replied, "The sky and the stars." Another answered, "Fire," another, "The tongue, which speaks," and yet another, "Reason, which grasps." Another replied, "The sun," Aristotle said, "That whose cause is unknown,"[25] another said, "In fact, the most wondrous thing is ignorance of a thing's ground." So, if we followed this lead, everything should be worthy of wonder. On the basis of what the Philosopher said, everything whose cause is unknown should be worthy of wonder, be it worthless or precious. Another philosopher replied that "the most wondrous thing is human livelihood, for its foundation is deep; for all its dignity, reason is perplexed by it, and, for all their efforts, intelligent men reel before it." Another reply was, "Nothing is worthy of wonder!"—and many affirmed the truth of his words. What is all this divergence and disparity, when truth harbors no discord and falsehood no concord? Speaking of truth and falsehood, what is truth and what is falsehood? One may also range this under the present rubric. One of the ancients said, "The most wondrous thing is that men of many endowments should be thwarted while men of limited abilities should succeed in their designs." A Sufi whom I met, debated with, and learned from said, "The most wondrous thing cannot be denied for all its distance, yet cannot be espied for all its closeness, and that is the One True God."

Speaking of God, what is it one knows regarding the Divine 16.2
Being indicated through a variety of designations and locutions? Is it something that attaches to belief? Is it the unqualified sense of a conventional expression? Is it an allusion to a certain attribute, without any knowledge of the subject to which it applies? Or can knowledge not be spoken of in this connection at all? If He is qualified by a qualification, then the qualifier has limited Him through the qualification. If He is not qualified, then He becomes fair game for ignorance and invites comparison with nonexistent

things. If negation is impossible, affirmation becomes necessary. If affirmation and negation depend on the person doing the affirming and negating, then God will have preceded every affirmation and negation. And if He preceded all these expressions and intentions, then what is the role of the knower, and what is there for the person who believes in God's oneness to achieve? Alas! Alas! Great has been the clamor, much has been the error, and all views have run to excess. God has eluded the understanding of those who would understand and the imagination of those who would indulge their imaginations. People are left with knowledge no one agrees about and ignorance all partake in, with commands that aggrieve and prohibitions that vex, biting needs and crushing proofs, well-wrought words and high-flown locutions, immediate pleasures we long for and future goods we must toil for, external appearances that hang together and inner realities that are rent apart. To God we direct our complaint about the triumphs of capricious desire and the assaults of misfortune; for He is compassionate and loving.

Miskawayh's response

16.3 The author, succumbing to the same affliction as he did in an earlier question, appended to this question a number of questions that are grander, farther-reaching, and more abstruse than the main question itself. The only excuse I could find for him was to conclude that this is an ailment, a malady that overcomes him, and that it has nothing to do with an overweening pen, an impudent tongue that gets carried away, or an exuberant sense of mastery, just as it is not the type of thing that transports diviners in the act of divination, or that comes over Sufis cultivating rapturous states. On my reckoning it can only be a form of possession or insanity or impulse sent by Satan, against whom we must seek God's protection. For he filled his prose with rhyming cadences that repel the ears and offend the eyes and the mind. Had he not complained to God at the end about the assaults of misfortune, thereby acknowledging a defect and thus deserving mercy, we would have had our hands full treating his malady instead of penning replies to his questions.

I hope God will restore you to health! From the perspective of the senses and those who judge by them, the effects and acts of the soul are all marvelous. This is why most people wonder at, and feel perplexed by, the soul itself, coming up with all sorts of speculations about it. Despite their artful pursuit of such speculations, they invariably follow their usual practice in the domain of the senses and their way of conceiving sensible things, and make it out to be a body. Then their wonder increases when they discover that the acts and effects of the soul resemble none of the acts and effects of the body. Yet the wonder they feel at its effects would have been less had they grasped the nature of the soul. For it is not a body; and had they realized that it is not a body, there would be nothing marvelous about it having non-bodily effects. The poet who produces exquisite work and the thinker who reflects on some recondite question of mathematics or some other discipline engage in a reflective act of the soul and an intellectual mode of being, effecting a nonspatial movement of the soul in order to obtain a non-bodily result. They then discover that the desired result is produced by this movement of their soul performed with assiduity and dedication. Thereupon, they are themselves filled with wonder, first by this movement, which, they discover, proceeds from them necessarily and is not spatial as in the case of the body when it moves another body. They are then filled with wonder when the desired result follows upon this movement. In this response, they and their audience are equally liable to wonder, for they share the same ignorance regarding the soul and its effects and actions, so both groups have good reason to be amazed. In contrast, the person acquainted with the soul and its substance, knowing full well that it is not a body and that its effects and actions cannot be bodily, is not affected by this response in his soul, and the same applies to his audience, if they share in what he knows. 16.4

16.5 Wonder, included by my interlocutor in his presentation of his first question, is a form of perplexity that affects someone when he is ignorant of the cause of something. The less one knows about the causes of existing things, the greater the number of things one is ignorant of, and the stronger the wonder they excite. Conversely, if one knows more about the causes of existing things, there are fewer things one is ignorant of, and the wonder they excite is less. This is why some people said that everything is a source of wonder, while others said that one should wonder at nothing. The first group admits general ignorance and professes to be ignorant of the causes of things, while the second group claims for itself an august status, for they profess to know the causes of things.

16.6 God keep you! In your list of the different views about wonder you asked why all the divergence and disparity when truth harbors no discord and falsehood no concord? Wonder is not something that has a specific nature, nor does it exist externally; rather, it consists, as we said, in the perplexity of the soul when a given cause is not known. ʿAmr might know what Zayd does not know, so it is hardly surprising that they should diverge in the wonder they experience. For each of them wonders at something whose cause he does not know, and what is unknown to the one is the very thing that is known to the other. The issue would have been inscrutable and remarkable had it been a thing that existed externally and had excellent people worthy of having their opinions heard and their dissent noted been found to disagree over it, with some saying, "This is true," others, "This is false." Such a thing did indeed happen in the case of the question under discussion and in the case of time, place, eternity, and other related questions. Some people said that they are substances without bodies, while others said that they are accidents, and yet others said that they are neither bodies, nor substances, nor accidents. Each party came up with powerful arguments for its view. Yet all of these views were threshed out in the time of the Philosopher, when they were set firmly in place, their obscurities were dispelled, and what was sound was distinguished from what was infirm. It is not our task to dilate on these questions, quoting and discussing all these views. If you would like to learn about them, look them up in their proper places and assign them separate questions so that we can allocate time and reflection to each and every one, God willing.

You raised a query at the conclusion of this question—"What is it that people know regarding the Divine Being indicated through the word 'God' using a variety of designations and locutions?"[26] None of this is conceded— nobody claims to know any of this or that it attaches to it as you say, nor are these qualifications conceded in His regard. This topic is impossible to discuss in depth, as it forms the end of all philosophical endeavor and the objective of inquiry as a whole. It is not possible to discuss it without first acquiring all of the propaedeutic knowledge preparatory for it—that is, mathematics and physics, and after that, the aspects of metaphysics that relate to the knowledge of the soul and the intellect. Having learned about all these noble substances, one can come to know that they are affected by need, deficiency, and multiplicity, and that they require an original cause, an eternal creator that resembles them neither in His essence nor His attributes. This type of ignorance will be nobler than all the knowledge that preceded it, and it is indeed characterized by the difficulty and opacity you ascribe to it. 16.7

Were there another route to knowledge of this subject, it would have been followed by the ancients and people dedicated to the dissemination and propagation of wisdom. For they found only one route to this goal, though they neither set their sights low nor begrudged the effort. So they followed it, doing their utmost to smooth out its difficulties, pointing out the way for others, and guiding them to it. The ultimate happiness of human beings is vested in it, so let those who yearn for it muster the fortitude to follow the road that leads to it, be it difficult or easy, long or short. For this is the way of people who yearn for something: They follow the path calculated to secure the object of their desire whatever it may be, without regard for how rugged or how long it may be. Let 16.8

those who have not been granted the fortitude to follow this path be content with the license to use the terms and attributes applied to Him customarily by the true revelation; let them put their trust and credence in the philosophers and the prophets and those who follow their lead, for these are the only roads to follow. Assistance and success rest with God.

On why it is unseemly to eulogize long-time friends and acquaintances—a question relating to voluntary choice

17.1 Why is it inappropriate to seek the other's favor and unseemly to give praise when intimacy deepens and grows firmly entrenched, when closeness ingrains itself and acquaintance lengthens? It is on account of this that people have said, "Longtime brothers dispense no praise." This is something widely attested and well known.

Miskawayh's response

17.2 Praise, in someone's presence or absence, is giving the object praised his due for his fine qualities, acknowledging his possession of them, and informing him that the eulogizer is not just aware of them but grants and concedes them to him. The purpose is to win his favor and gain intimacy, to establish affection and good relations, to create a bond of amity, and to consolidate their mutual familiarity. If these things arise in the soul of both parties and the person praised realizes that the person praising him has treated him fairly, as is his due, acknowledging his excellence, and not cheating him of his rightful property, and if the two parties are established in the relationship of affection and love that is engendered though fairness and the fruit of justice, and if this state endures for a long time, there is no need to go to the trouble to make a second display of praise, because the original purpose has lapsed, and the original efforts have borne fruit. Such trouble would be pointless and foolish, to say nothing of how it implies that there are lingering doubts over the original praise, so that additional eulogies and repeated attestations are required because the original declaration was false, and little more than a shaky conjecture. This would involve a weakening of the very bond of affection that the question posited as being tight, secure, and robust.

On why blind people are often endowed with unusual powers—a natural question

Why is it that blind people make up for their lack of vision in other ways? For example, we find blind people who have sonorous diction, an agreeable voice, extensive knowledge, a good memory, great sexual prowess, an appetite for enjoyment, and a carefree nature. 18.1

Miskawayh's response

The soul has five avenues of perception through which it draws different kinds of knowledge into itself. One might liken these to windows and doors that give it access to things outside, or to messengers who bring the soul reports from five different quarters, its power being divided across these five routes. Or again, one might liken them to a spring of water that divides into five rivers flowing in five different directions, or to a tree with five branches, among which its strength is divided. One knows that if the course of one of the rivers becomes blocked, the water from the spring will be channeled into one of the other rivers or divided among them in equal or varying amounts, and the quota of water that would ordinarily flow down the blocked river will not be drained away, diminished, or lost. Similarly, if one of the branches of the tree is lopped off, the nourishment it was receiving from the base and roots of the tree is channeled into the remaining four branches, 18.2

visible on their shafts, leaves, and shoots, and on the flowers, seeds, and fruit they produce. Farmers and vineyard cultivators know this only too well, for they prune away the branches and shoots that absorb a great deal of nourishment from the roots so that it can be channeled to the other parts of the tree and produce fruit they can enjoy. They do the same with trees that do not produce fruit when they want their trunks to grow straight and thick, and to make them grow faster, as with trees like evergreen cypresses, junipers, and plane trees, whose wood is used for cutting, hewing, and carving. They consider which branch is the most promising for straight growth without any kinks, and they retain the one that has the greatest need of the root that nourishes it, removing the rest. With the nourishment directed exclusively to it, that branch will develop in the shortest time.

18.3 If this is evident from the behavior of nature, the same applies to blind people. When one of the powers of their soul that was devoted to the upkeep of one of their senses is cut off from its course, the soul channels it in one direction or in many. A surplus then becomes visible in the mind and the intelligence, in reflection, in memory, or in some other power of the soul. You can also see this plainly in other animals. There are animals that are impaired in one of their senses or, through their original nature and constitution, are entirely without a given sense, and their remaining senses are far keener than in other animals. The mole is an example: It lacks the organ of vision, but its sense of hearing is exceptionally keen. Bees are another example: Their sight is weak, but they are far more skilled with their sense of smell than animals that can see. If you consider what happens to them in houses with glass windowpanes, you will soon realize how weak the sense of sight is among bees, ants, locusts, hornets, and the animals that cannot blink, not having eyelids, their eyes covered with a hard stony integument that protects them from damage. For they think the glass is an aperture that leads to the open air and, in order to get out, they crash against it until eventually they drop dead. The reliability of their sense of smell is clear from the way they can direct themselves toward odorous objects from a great distance.

The cause of the sexual prowess or carefree temper blind people enjoy is once again the fact that the soul has lost one of the organs whose upkeep got in the way of these things; so when it directs its thought to something else, its effect on it becomes stronger. People care about many things that can be visually perceived—such as the various sorts of clothing, furniture, or amusements, and in general all that can be apprehended by the sense of sight—and the soul is under a powerful drive to acquire them. So, when it loses the sense of sight, it is cut off from most of the things that human beings care and think about, devising stratagems for obtaining them when they desire them and grieving for them when they lose them. As a result, the cares of blind people decrease. 18.4

On why people say that nothing good comes from partnership— a question relating to nature and voluntary choice

Why do people say, "Nothing good comes from partnership?" In our experience this is manifestly true. For we have never known of a kingdom to be firmly established, an affair to be accomplished, or a contract to be validly executed on the basis of partnership. Thus it is that God declared, «Were there gods in earth and heaven other than God, they would surely go to ruin»,[27] the highest testimony to God's unity and the nonexistence of any other gods. 19.1

Miskawayh's response

Partnership attracts this characterization because if you are self-sufficient and have the power to satisfy your own needs you do not ask for anyone else's help. So, if your power to do so falls short and you need someone else's help, the admission of deficiency leads you 19.2

to enlist another person to help you achieve what you want. Since powerlessness is deemed blameworthy, and deficiency is regarded with disapproval, partnership—the result of powerlessness and deficiency—is also deemed blameworthy and regarded with disapproval, as it reveals the deficiency and powerlessness of both partners. Yet among human beings, partnership is not deemed blameworthy in all situations. Rather, it attracts blame only in the case of things that can be achieved independently and single-handedly by others. An example is writing, or any other craft with several components that could be combined in a single person in such a way that the entire craft could be practiced single-handedly and independently. If someone is deficient in it and needs assistance, his deficiency and powerlessness become plain, and his craft defective. To take another example, a single person has the strength to carry a weight of twenty kilos on his own without any need of assistance; so if help is needed to carry it, his deficiency, powerlessness, and weakness are revealed. Moreover, things undertaken in partnership are affected by deficiencies and imperfections as a result of the different powers, diverging designs, and conflicting aims that enter into it; deficiencies that do not affect things undertaken single-handedly by a person acting on the basis of a single power, with a single design, and a single aim. For the latter can be conducted in an orderly and harmonious manner, and has a patent advantage over the first.

19.3 Partnership, on the other hand, is unavoidable with regard to things that a single person is not strong enough to do independently and unaided, such as carrying millstones, towing large ships, or other technical undertakings that are accomplished by large groups of people, through partnership and cooperation. Yet even if partnership is unavoidable in these cases because human power is limited, and even if those who pursue it attract no blame but are exempt on account of clearly extenuating factors, had it been possible for these things to be lifted through a single power and achieved through a single agency, we know that this activity would have been better ordered, less exposed to disturbance and disruption, and more likely to promote the good and to bring profit. Taken absolutely, thus, partnership reveals the powerlessness of the two partners and further introduces defects and disruption into tasks undertaken in partnership as compared with those accomplished separately, even though some cases are excusable and others not.

Human political rule is ordered well when a single agency and a single command are in place. Even if a group of people participate in it, they act on the basis of a single view and serve as instruments for the ruler, so that multiplicity is thereby unified and good order manifest. Hence, it is undoubtedly best that it should be in the hands of a single person and be exercised single-handedly, analogously to what was stated above. If the group of people cooperating in it disagree with each other and do not act on the basis of a single view, it becomes subject to the same defects, weaknesses, and imperfections that appear in other enterprises as a result of differences in people's designs and the presence of multiplicity, which serves to corrupt the unified order. How generalized and openly deleterious its disruption is will then depend on the wealth and advantage involved and on how serious its stature and august its position is. God clarified all of that most economically in the tersest words possible, with the plainest notions and clearest proofs available, when He said, «Were there gods in earth and heaven other than God, they would surely go to ruin». May He be glorified and may His praise be extolled. There is no god other than He. 19.4

On why people use intermediaries despite the problems with partnership—a question relating to voluntary choice

Why do people have recourse to intermediaries despite what they say about partners and the harm wrought by partnership, 20.1

as reported in the previous question? Thus, the vast majority of things both in the religious Law and the political domain are never achieved and put into order without an intermediary to weave and stitch, rend and mend, spruce and touch up.

Miskawayh's response

20.2 The exigencies of human life require people to act in partnership in the situations referred to in the previous question. Yet every human being, out of love of self and a desire for self-benefit, is keen to enjoy such benefits to the exclusion of his fellows. This produces the kind of corruption and mutual injustice I mentioned previously. Consequently, neither partner trusts the other, because each, with a stake in the matter, and out of desire for the benefit that will accrue to him, is vulnerable to blind desire and under its sway. As a result, they need an intermediary whose relationship to the matter is free from the defects of their relationship, so that, his judgment balanced and his opinion sound, he may give each his proper share without acting unjustly and without following the biddings of blind desire. The fact that partnership is blameworthy does not mean that human beings can do without it; for human weakness compels them to it, as we illustrated by reference to heavy weights or activities with many components. If people fail to work in partnership and to help one another, they forfeit them. Such forfeit is a forfeit of great benefits, so it is better to form partnerships, their defects notwithstanding, than to avoid them completely.

20.3 Most human affairs can only be accomplished through mutual help and partnership, because human beings are unable to act in isolation, are imperfect, and manifestly are created and originated beings. The more people there are acting in partnership in a given affair, the more discordant their views, the more uncertain the influence of blind desires, and the more pressing the necessity of intermediaries. Political governance is one of the cases in which blind desires proliferate and in which partnership and cooperative action are needed—thus a person who can judge honestly, unencumbered by blind desire and partisanship, is required. The intermediary, if he is actually free of this, will be better equipped to form fair judgments and correct views. If not, he must ensure that he has a smaller stake than the contending parties, or has greater self-control and discipline, being more effective at keeping blind desires in check. This will ensure he does not succumb to or follow the impulses of blind desire. Concord will be achieved, and justice—which produces unity and eliminates multiplicity—will be done.

On why people speak gladly about the needs of those they concern themselves with yet keep quiet about their own needs—a question relating to natural and ethical matters

Why do people speak so volubly about the needs of those they concern themselves with, yet are so reticent about their own needs despite their concern for themselves? What is the secret behind this? 21.1

Miskawayh's response

The basis on which human beings have been constructed, the principle on which they have been created, is that they are kings.[28] So, every human being is entitled to be a king in view of the auxiliary powers placed at his disposal, and everybody should be able to achieve this equally unless there is a defect or deficiency in his constitution. Everyone must have a sense of pride that prevents him from feeling abased, since everyone has to ask for help at different times, even though everyone's material basis is the same, and since one person is as likely to need others as they are likely to need him. This is why the civic state is necessary, why communities and cooperation arise, and why it is good for people to enter into exchange with one another, with one person giving his fellow what 21.2

he needs if he has it available, so that he may then receive its equivalent from him in turn. So it's tantamount to committing an injustice, if the person who solicits help does not compensate or enter into exchange with others, and if he does not offer anything in return or promise its equivalent. At the very least, he has demoted himself from the rank he was assigned to when created, so he becomes reticent and feels contempt for himself. But he does not experience this reaction when, by contrast, he talks about what another person needs. It is as though he has attributed this deficiency entirely to the person he is talking about, so his tongue loosens and he does not feel abased.

On why some people become famous after they die—a question relating to natural and ethical matters

22.1 What is the reason for the renown that comes to some people after their death, so that they spend their lives in obscurity and shoot to fame when they are dead, as for example Maʿrūf al-Karkhī did?

Miskawayh's response

22.2 This is predominantly due to the envy that besets most people, particularly when the person envied is close in status to the envier, or on a par with him, for example, in terms of lineage, political power, and geographical origin. For if people are similar in these external aspects and hold them in common, and then one of them comes into exclusive possession of a given excellence, the rest will vie with him over it and envy him for it. Eventually this leads them to repudiate him. That is why it has been said, "The last to recognize a scholar's merit are his own neighbors." Physical proximity and frequent association unite them and place them on the same footing, so they are prey to what I have said if one of them has exclusive possession of a given excellence. There may of course be other reasons for their failure to recognize his merit, but the cause I have described is the most frequent. On the contrary, it is easier for distant strangers to concede his merit and feel less envy, as there is nothing that unites them. People begin to acknowledge excellence and to concede what they had denied during someone's lifetime, when the object of their envy dies and his relationship to them is terminated.

On why men of virtue and reason feel envious toward their equals even though they know envy is blameworthy—an ethical question

How is one to understand the envy that besets men of virtue and reason toward those who are their peers in terms of merit, even though they know that envy is vile and has a bad name and that both latter-day thinkers and thinkers of yore have converged on censuring it? If there is no way for a person to divest himself of this reaction because it takes him in its grip, then what are the grounds for censuring it so vehemently? And if it is not something that grips him but rather something voluntary he generates in himself and roils his spirits by producing, how can one understand his choice? Can people who answer to this description be classed among the compos mentis or come close to the status of rational men? Aristotle was asked, "Why do envious people dwell longest in sorrow?" He replied, "Because they feel sorrow at normal things, and a separate sorrow at the good that comes to others."[29] 23.1

Miskawayh's response

Envy is a repugnant illness of the soul and a blameworthy trait. 23.2
People have mistakenly applied the term "envy" to things that do

not belong to the same class. This was precisely the mistake of my interlocutor, when he asked, "How is one to understand the envy that besets men of virtue?" For the man of virtue is not given to envy. Our discussion of envy will reveal its essential nature and thus its repugnant quality, putting it in its proper place and ensuring it is not confused with other things. We respond, then, as follows. Envy is a form of sorrow that comes over a person when a good thing comes to someone entitled to it. This foul passion is then followed by other foul acts, such as the wish that this good be withdrawn from the person who is entitled to it. This wish is then followed by many kinds of destructive exertions that result in numerous evils. So anyone who experiences envy in the sense that we have defined is evil, and an evil person cannot be excellent.

23.3 The term "envy" has mistakenly been applied when someone experiences this kind of sorrow for reasons that are not blameworthy. For example, a virtuous person may feel sorrow at the good that comes to the person who is not entitled to it, because he wishes things to happen as they ought, and because an evil person will put to evil purposes a good thing placed at his disposal, if it lends itself to such a purpose, or will derive no benefit from it whatsoever. Or, again, a virtuous person may feel sorrow on his own account when he does not receive the good that another person receives, if he is entitled to its like. The reason I do not apply the term "envy" to this reaction, however, is because his sorrow is not provoked by the good that the other has received, but because he has been deprived of its like. There is nothing wrong with someone wanting to have what another has; on the contrary, anyone who sees another enjoying something good should also desire to possess that good for himself—and this sorrow is not followed by the wish for the good to be withdrawn from the person entitled to it. The Arabs distinguished between these two types of person by using the term "envy" for the one and "admiration" for the other. The way we ourselves educate our children is by pointing out to them well-bred people and commending their virtues to them. Children with a good nature aspire to emulate the people of virtue, following in their footsteps, working as hard as they can to attain what they have attained. This method is beneficial for most young people. Children with a bad nature, in contrast, feel sorrow at the refinement and merit attained by others, and do not follow their lead. Rather, they try as hard as they can to deprive the other of it or to prevent him from possessing it; they deny his possession of it or reproach him for it. In that case they are envious and wicked.

My response to your remark "If there is no way for a person to divest himself of this reaction because it takes him in its grip," until the end of that segment, is as follows. Passions—I mean those not directed toward the attainment of perfection—are blameworthy, for they are material in nature. That is why it would be better for human beings not to be subjected to passions at all, if that were possible. Yet, as that is unachievable, they are obliged to eliminate all the passions they have the power to eliminate, in order to attain a state of completion and perfection, something they do by acquiring congenial character traits and manners. This happens to them first through the directive influence of their parents, then through the directive influence of the ruling power, and then through the directive influence of the laws and the principles of conduct promulgated for that purpose. For people derive outward forms and conditions from these things, and then they become entrenched as acquired possessions and stable states, which are the things that are called "virtues" and "good breeding." 23.4

On why we fear death but sometimes welcome it—a question relating to natural and ethical matters

Why do we fear death, and why is death sometimes welcomed? 24.1
Even if the first is the more frequent, the second is both starker and

more noticeable. Which should be held in the highest regard, fear or welcoming? There is much good to be harvested from a discussion of the topic.

Miskawayh's response

24.2 The fear of death comes in many varieties, as does the welcome given to it; some are praiseworthy, others blameworthy—for some lives are excellent and desirable, while others are bad and odious. Therefore death, their contrary, should vary accordingly. Thus, the death that is set against an admirable life will be loathsome, while the death that is opposed to a loathsome life will be admirable. These categories need exposition, in order to explain why one fears or welcomes death and to determine which of the two is superior. Some lives are burdened with great evils, terrible travails, and immense pains, as when a man is taken captive with his wife and children by a wicked people, and he sees his wife and children experience terrible sufferings, and his mind and body are subjected to intolerable torments, or when he suffers from an incurable illness, or when he is forced to perpetrate some evil against friends and parents. Nobody would choose to go on living under such loathsome conditions, because death is an excellent choice when faced with these tribulations and such an implacable enemy. This consideration leads us to conclude that when life is loathsome, death—its contrary—is desirable. So this kind of death should be welcomed; the reason for this is obvious.

24.3 The same applies if the situation is reversed. For there are admirable lives and well-regulated modes of living in which the body is healthy, the humoral mixture is balanced, and basic needs are met in honorable ways, and this enables us to strive for ultimate happiness and to realize the form through which human beings are perfected, while enjoying the help of excellent companions, the satisfaction of having fine children, and the pride that comes from good kinsfolk and an upright family. All of this is admirable, worth having, and excellent. The death that is set against it will therefore be loathsome, because it interrupts the perfection of happiness and the consummation of virtue, and deprives one of the good one stood to enjoy. So such a death must be feared; the reason for this is obvious.

This is one way of considering matters, one angle of examination. 24.4
Another approach is to say that the persistence of life is in itself preferable because it represents continued existence, and existence is a noble and precious thing, whereas its contrary, nonexistence, is a mean and base thing. What is noble must be desired, just as what is base must be avoided. If life must come to an end, nonetheless it leads to eternal life and to endless existence. Death then ceases to be odious, except in the way one might find odious a bitter medicine that brings health. Painful treatment and unpleasant medicine are to be preferred if they bring lasting health and continued well-being. Even if they are not preferable intrinsically, they are so extrinsically. Thus, discerning people who understand that the next world is superior and that the life to come is better than their present life welcome death as they would welcome unpleasant medicine and painful treatment, in order thereby to attain a permanent good, even if this choice is made on extrinsic rather than intrinsic grounds. Perhaps they may only suppose this to be the case, but they should still welcome death according to the strength of their supposition and the extent of their convictions. This is also the case with medicine when one entertains a strong supposition that the person prescribing it is knowledgeable. Without this belief and strong supposition, however, death is feared, because it is a kind of nonexistence, and nonexistence is something one recoils from. This is a valid explanation and clear cause.

Here is yet another reason why death is either welcomed or 24.5
feared. People who, through strong supposition, have gained firm insight regarding the life to follow in the hereafter, yet who have not equipped themselves for it or made the sort of preliminary preparations that they believe would lead to their happiness, will not welcome death but will hate and fear it. Conversely, those who suppose that they have made adequate preparations will welcome

it with open arms. This is evident among adherents of the various heretical groups and competing religions, the way the Hindus rush to commit themselves to the flames and carry out various kinds of bodily mutilation and slaughter, or the way the Kharijites pursued death with alacrity and gave up their lives in their famous battles. It is said that if a Kharijite were transfixed by a spear, he would spur on his horse to slide along the shaft of the spear, coming up against the one who had struck him, and then recite, «I have hastened, Lord, only that I may please Thee».[30] This is why the caliphal army attached lugs to the sockets of their spearheads, as a barrier to prevent a speared opponent from sliding along the shaft as far as the soldier who had impaled him. The adherents of heretical groups who endure different forms of torment, mutilation, and slaughter are too many to count. Still, we have described why death is feared and why it is welcomed and on what occasion and under what conditions each response is appropriate.

On why thin people tend to be noble and fat people ignoble—a natural question

25.1 Why are thin people more likely to be noble? And why are fat people more likely to be ignoble?

Miskawayh's response

25.2 This question seems to concern what usually holds true for the most part. Since innate heat is the cause of life and the cause of the excellences that are contingent on life—I mean intelligence, agility, courage, and the like—bodies with a greater share of it are superior. The correct way to view this is as follows: Bodies that are balanced with respect to thinness and fatness, tallness or shortness, and the other qualities are the most excellent. As your question is narrowly focused on thinness and fatness, we will also focus our reply with the following account. When heat combats the humors and succeeds in dissipating the excess moistures it contains and negating its contrary, the coldness that prevails over it, this results in agility and alertness and in bold and intrepid activity. Then come the concomitant excellences and, the first among them, the intensification of the heat that resides in the heart. The moistures, if they prevail, drown it out, impeding it and preventing it from exercising its effects. Ignobleness, and its concomitants, such as laziness, mental torpor, cowardice, and all its attendant defects, ensue.

Though fatness and thinness represent deviations from a balanced 25.3
state, thinness deviates by an excess of heat, which is the cause of excellences, and is thus more amenable than the opposite extreme—namely, fatness. Fatness is a deviation from a balanced state that tends toward coldness and the absence of heat, which counteracts and defeats these excellences. Books of ethics have demonstrated that the extremes of the excellences are all blameworthy, but, although they are similarly distant from the mean, some are closer to being praiseworthy than others. Thus, the state of balance that is lauded as generosity and liberality has two extremes: avarice and prodigality. Both, representing deviations from a balanced state, are blameworthy, but one, prodigality, is more similar to generosity than the other. For, taken too far, one of these extremes results in the nullification and negation of the thing praised, while the other results in an excessive increase of it. I declare that, in terms of a lack of balance, the two are on a par, but one is more similar to the state of balance than the other. This is a point that cannot be gainsaid or denied.

On why short people tend to be crafty and tall people foolish—a natural question

Why do short people tend to be crafty, while tall people tend to be 26.1
foolish?

Miskawayh's response

26.2 These also represent extremes relative to excellence, because a balance between tallness and shortness is what is laudable. But the tallness that results from an imperfection in one's natural constitution is closer to being blameworthy on account of the distance that separates the main organs from each other, particularly the heart and the brain, the two organs that have the clearest governing role. For these two must be separated by only a moderate distance so that the heat that is in the heart can modify the coldness of the brain, retain the brain's balance, and preserve the psychic spirit that is distilled in the ventricles of the brain, and also so that the coldness of the brain can modify the heat of the heart and help it retain its balance. This balance is disrupted and disordered, the overall structure is ruined, ensuing actions are impaired, and the excellences decrease, if one of the two organs is positioned too far from the other. In contrast, the physical proximity of the two organs does not produce the same kind of imperfection that their distance does.

On why some people overstate and others understate their age—an ethical question

27.1 Why is it that when people are asked about their age, some understate, while others overstate their age?

Miskawayh's response

27.2 Both types—I mean the one who understates and the one who overstates his age—share the same aim, even if what they say differs. And sometimes a person may say different things at different points in time or in different circumstances at the same point in time. This reflects a defect of character—it is to use mendacity to suggest that one possesses an excellence one does not in fact possess. The reason for this is self-love; because people want others to believe they possess greater merit than they do, and want others to excuse them for any deficiencies they happen to have. If an excellence or a deficiency manifests itself in the young, then they understate their age so as to let others know that they have acquired the excellence in a short space of time and that they could only have achieved this with great solicitude, staunch dedication, and nobility of soul, and by renouncing the appetites that get the better of their peers and refraining from the levity that prevails among people of their age. The shorter the amount of time involved, the greater their affinity to excellence and the greater the wonder they excite. By contrast, others may excuse the behavior of those who suffer from a deficiency as guilelessness and inexperience, in the anticipation that they will straighten themselves out, and the hope that they will mend their ways and turn from their errors.

Human beings have the capacity to cultivate the excellences and 27.3
increase their knowledge as long as they live, and they always derive pleasure from possessing a higher degree of merit than people of their age are expected to attain, or from being admired for acquiring in a short space of time the expertise that normally requires a long time. Persons who have reached middle age or who have lived long enough to have amassed extensive experience—people who have witnessed the ebb and flow of entire epochs, who have consorted with men of note, and who have been active in fields of learning—arouse profound respect in people's minds, provoke reverence in their hearts, and are treated with deference in social gatherings. Their counsel is sought out at difficult times, their opinions consulted. This status is much desired, so someone who is of an age at which he can plausibly make this claim or to assimilate himself to those who occupy these ranks exaggerates his age so that this status may be conceded to him and he can be considered to possess it. In mendaciously understating or overstating their age, both types, as well as the type who says different things at different times or in different circumstances, seek to present a false view of their merit

and claim status they do not possess. This is patently wicked, so the perpetrator is wicked. The best people do not succumb to this kind of viciousness, because they do not sully themselves with lies or make false boasts.

On why people end up loving particular months or days and why they form different conceptions of different days—a natural question

28.1 Why do people come to love a particular month and a particular day? How is it that people form a conception of Friday different from their conception of Thursday? Al-Rūdakī, who was congenitally blind—that is, he was born blind—was once asked: What do colors look like to you? He answered: Like camels.

Miskawayh's response

28.2 The reason people come to love one particular month is because of some happy incident they happened to have experienced during that time, as when they realized something they hoped for, obtained something they desired, anticipated the arrival of something they yearned for at a particular time, or experienced joy after grief or rest after toil. This experience may have persisted and been repeated over a period of their life at particular times, and so they warmed to that time, growing fond of it and coming to love it on account of what happened during it. This is why Muslim children come to love and develop a lifelong fondness for Fridays and to hate Saturdays. Because Friday is the day when they are required to rest and allowed to play, and it is followed by Saturday, which is a day when they must toil and stop the games they enjoy. Jewish children, by contrast, experience that in relation to Saturday and the next day, and Christian children in relation to Sunday and the next day. The same applies to feast days, on which people have been given permission to rest and dress up in their finery. The Prophet described them as "days on which one may eat and drink and dally with one's womenfolk." These days vary from religion to religion: Each group loves their own feast days, when they are permitted to dress up, enjoy themselves, and rest. By contrast, people for whom all circumstances are alike—people who are under no religious law and whose lives and circumstances are not governed by a particular order, such as the East Africans, the remote Turks, and the like—do not have this experience, and do not come to love any one particular day or month or specific time.

The explanation of why people develop a conception of Friday 28.3
different from their conception of Thursday is as follows. The form of time that is most manifest, most general, and most familiar is that produced by a single revolution of the outermost celestial sphere, that is, the celestial sphere that causes all of the other spheres to revolve and that, through its motion, causes them to move in a direction other than the one to which their own motions tend, namely, from east to west, departing from a given point and returning to it in the course of twenty-four hours. This form of time is most manifest to people on account of the appearance of morning and evening, which go from light to dark, caused by the sun's appearance above the earth for part of this period and its disappearance beneath the earth for another part. The repetition of these revolutions constitutes the days and nights. Each revolution contains human actions, motions, new births, and transactions that are not to be found during another revolution. These actions are subject to rulings and ordinances that apply over specific time frames and involve temporal limits stipulated within a given time frame. These need to be referred to different instances of the revolutions of the outermost celestial sphere that produce day and night, so that people's transactions may be properly executed, their ordinances may be soundly applied, and the temporal limits assigned to their actions and transactions may acquire a specific reference.

28.4 There is another form of time, one produced by a revolution specific to the sun as it traces its course. In this case, the sun departs from a given point and returns to that same point through a motion of its own, without the first mover's imparting motion to it. Unlike the former, this revolution occurs in the direction of west to east. A single revolution produced by the motion specific to the sun takes approximately 365 days and a quarter of a day to complete. This is also a form of time, but it is related to the motion of the sun, and is called a "year."

28.5 Then there is a further form of time that people are also familiar with and have come to know well; and though it is not as manifest as that of the sun, it follows close on it. It is constituted by, and arises from, a single revolution of the moon produced by a motion specific to it and not owed to the motion of the first mover. A single revolution produced by the moon's specific motion—also from west to east—takes twenty-eight days to complete, and is called a "month."

28.6 These three forms of time can be seen; they are manifest and plain because they are connected with the sun and the moon—the most luminous and conspicuous stars, and the largest in appearance. With familiarity, people have thus come to work on their basis, and so there has arisen a conception of each revolution that reflects the activities people allocate to it, the lives and births that unfold and occur within it, and the relation that people's motions bear to it in terms of their starting and end points. If we consider these revolutions in isolation from human motions and actions, and do not refer any other motion or action to them, there is nothing whatsoever to distinguish between them except the distinction that arises through iteration, which necessarily involves numbers—one being first, second, third, and so on, as far as numbers can reach. But if we consider them according to their different circumstances, refer different actions and effects to them, and give them a numerical sequence, there arise different conceptions that reflect the different things that take place in them and are referred to them.

In the case of the congenitally blind person you mentioned in your question, those who lack a particular sense do not form concepts regarding any of the corresponding sensible objects, because concepts regarding sensible objects are only formed in the soul after the objects have been perceived by the senses. For these are among the powers of the soul that derive information from the senses, and they only raise this to the power of the imagination after receiving it from the senses. The form of the sensible object then becomes fixed within the power of the imagination, even if the form of the senses is eliminated and disappears. But when someone lacks a particular sense to begin with, how is it possible for the sensible object to be raised to the power of the imagination? It stands to reason that someone blind from birth should be unable to imagine colors or form any relevant concepts. Similarly, if someone lacks the sense of smell or hearing from birth, he cannot imagine any corresponding sensible object for the reasons we have outlined. A learned practitioner of philosophy once told me he had asked a man blind from birth how he conceived of whiteness, and he replied, "It is sweet." It is as if, having failed to discover the form of whiteness in his imagination, he resorted to another sense whose objects were available to him, and so designated the one through the other and took them to be identical. 28.7

On the meaning and origin of injustice

What did the poet mean when he said: 29.1

> Injustice is ingrained in human nature, so if you find anyone
> abstaining from wrong, he does so for a special reason? [31]

What is the definition of injustice to begin with? For the dialectical theologians ply these topics with wild abandon without giving them their due, as if they were driven by anger and rivalry.

I heard someone say during his tenure as vizier: "I delight in injustice." What is it and how does it originate—injustice, I mean? Is it a product of human action, or is it an effect of nature?

Miskawayh's response

29.2 Injustice is the departure from justice. Since it is necessary to understand the meaning of justice in order to understand the meaning of injustice, we have devoted a separate discussion to the former, which you will find succinctly presented and expounded.[32] The meaning of the term "injustice" is similar to that of the term "inequity," which is the verbal noun of the verb "to be inequitable." "Inequity," however, is used in connection with following directions and other things, and refers to the act of deviating or straying from the course. "Injustice" represents the more proper antithesis of the kind of justice that concerns transactions between people. The term "justice" derives from "moderation," which means distributing with an equal measure, and this equal measure derives from the equality established among many things. The establishment of equality is what brings multiplicity into existence and preserves it in an ordered condition. Love spreads among people, their aims harmonize, their polities prosper, the transactions between them are successfully achieved, and their customs are sustained through justice and the establishment of equality.

29.3 A full exposition of these points, an investigation of the nature of justice, with an enumeration of its subdivisions and distinctive features, would have required a lengthy discussion that I fear would have struck you as excessive and would have violated the condition of brevity you stipulated at the opening of this epistle. This is why I have devoted a separate treatise to the topic, which you will find appended to this question, in the hope that, with God's help, it will meet your need. Had we come across a thorough discussion by a well-known philosopher or a separate work with detailed exposition, we would have indicated it as is our practice and we would have referred to it, for this is how we proceed. But we are only aware of one treatise by Galen, extracted from Plato's remarks, and it does not provide an adequate treatment of the topic, as it is merely an exhortation to justice and an elucidation of its merit, arguing that one should choose and love it for its own sake.[33] Once you have understood the nature of justice from that treatise, you will understand what deviates from it and does not pursue its course. When the arrow hits the mark, it only hits a single point, whereas there are an infinite number of ways to miss the mark and deviate from it. Similarly, justice is like a single point between things, dividing them right in the middle. It is thus possible to deviate from it in an infinite number of ways. How stark the wrongdoing is and how opprobrious the injustice will depend on how near or far it lies from the mark.

The poet's remark that "injustice is ingrained in human nature" 29.4
is an idea expressed in poetic form that cannot sustain a higher degree of critical scrutiny than befits the poetic craft. Were we to try correcting poetic notions using philosophical judgments and standards of logic as our touchstone, few sound views would survive, and the dignity of poetry would be trampled underfoot—not to mention that we would be doing it a greater injustice than the poet did to human beings when he claimed that injustice is ingrained in their nature. It is true that were we to set about constructing arguments for it and ferreting out finer interpretations, we would come up with some doctrine or other and hit upon some approach, but these responses would be built on reading truth into the fallacies, doctrines, and customs of poets in their craft.

To continue: Injustice, in the sense we have expounded, is similar 29.5
to other acts in that if it issues from a disposition of the soul without thought or reflection, it is called a character trait, and its bearer is unjust. This holds good for other acts ascribed to traits of character, for they issue from dispositions and stable states without reflection. If, in contrast, the act emerges after thought and reflection, it does not arise from a character trait, be it blameworthy or praiseworthy.

And if it does not arise from a character trait, how can it arise from nature? When agents repeatedly perform a certain act with reflection, that constant reflection produces a disposition from which acts subsequently issue without reflection; that disposition is called a character trait. If the thing that issues from this disposition is a type of work that has a durable form and leaves a durable effect, it is called a craft, and one derives a name from the work that refers to the stable state from which it issues—for example, "carpenter," "blacksmith," "goldsmith," "scribe." So if these works issue from their agents without reflection, these names are applied and these attributes are ascribed. Yet, nobody would call a person who might go to the effort of applying the tools of the carpenter, blacksmith, scribe, and goldsmith, and produce some simple action through reflection and thought, and thus by way of simulation and toilsome effort, a carpenter or a scribe. This is why a person who turns out a verse or two is not called a poet, and one who sews a thread or two is not called a tailor. All crafts conform to this principle, and the same thing applies to these works, as you can see, as well as to the acts that leave no durable effects. So too with character traits and the acts that issue from them; for character traits are dispositions of the soul from which the corresponding acts issue without reflection or thought.

29.6 You mentioned the vizier you heard saying "I delight in injustice." When blameworthy choices produce dispositions and stable states, they become evils and their bearers are called evil. In meriting the designation "evil" and in departing from the mean that constitutes the excellences of the soul, injustice does not possess a distinction not shared by similar traits. Evils and defects such as gluttony, avarice, or cowardice enter the soul, when the mean fails to be realized. What is peculiar to injustice is that it relates to transactions between people, and that it involves abandoning all concern for excuse and equality. In his *Ethics*, Aristotle has provided a clear exposition of this just relation and equality in transactions. He explains that a transaction involves a proportional relation between the seller and the buyer, and between the object sold and the object bought, and that the proportional relation of the first to the second is like the proportional relation of the third to the fourth in cases of reciprocal giving and exchange. This is also explained and set out clearly in other books by him.[34]

The well-known saying, "All will be well so long as there are disparities between people—should they become equal they would be brought to ruin," does not refer to disparities in the justice that is realized equally among them for the purposes of coexistence. Rather, it refers to the kinds of things through which civic association and communal life are achieved; disparity on the level of individuals makes for order on the level of the whole. It has been said that human beings are political by nature. Political association would collapse and communal life would come to naught if all people became equal in their ability to satisfy their own needs. As has been shown above, people perform different types of work and each performs his own separate work, so this generates the order of the whole and makes political association possible. One might compare this to writing, which is made possible as a totality by the different forms and shapes of letters and the different ways of positioning them relative to each other. These differences are what give writing its proper form as a totality. Were all letters equal and alike, writing would come to naught. 29.7

On the significance of a popular saying, and the meaning of certain words—a question about admonitions and about language

Why is it that people say to someone wearing clothes that are all new: 30.1
"Take along something unlike what you're wearing, to preserve you from harm"? Isn't likeness desirable in every situation? And speaking of likeness, what is the meaning of the terms "likeness,"

"accord," "resemblance," "similarity," "equivalence," and "affinity"? With a clear account of these terms, the truth regarding the terms "opposition," "divergence," "conflict," and "contrariety" will also become clear.

Miskawayh's response

30.2 The purpose of this popular practice is to ward off the evil eye. People believe that if something is perfect in every respect it quickly attracts the evil eye, whereas a lack or a visible defect will divert the evil eye and prevent it from causing harm. But you should not have mixed up these questions like this, for I see a difficult and lofty question side by side with another question, whose paltriness and simplicity bear no relation to the first. It is not for the respondent to propose questions and to frame doubts, so I have been forced to discuss all of them according to their rank. I do not say this to deny the evil eye and its effects, nor to pour scorn on the principles on which common people base their behavior. But the question took its point of departure from a popular practice, albeit one that has a distant foundation and can be traced back to a cause, and is based on certain facts.

30.3 Turning to the question about the terms "likeness" (*mushākalah*) and "accord," the term "like" (*shakl*) means "something similar" (*mithl*), and "likeness" derives from it, adopting the morphological pattern *mufāʿalah*. According to the scholars of the Arabic language, there is no difference between this term and the term "similarity" (*mumāthalah*). My view is that "similar" is broader than "like," because every like thing is similar, but not everything similar is like. The term "accordance" (*muwāfaqah*) derives from "accord" (*waqf*), as will be discussed in the next question, where we will explain it as part of our account of the terms "luck" and "fortune." "Resemblance" (*muḍāraʿah*) means alikeness, and it is produced using the morphological pattern *mufāʿalah* from the term meaning "something resembling" (*ḍirʿ*), which is its root and the source of its derivation. The terms "equivalence" and "affinity" have already been treated thoroughly in the question about justice. Their meanings are closely related, for one half of a donkey pack (*ʿidl*) is similar in weight to its counterpart on the other side; and the term "equivalence" (*muʿādalah*) derives from this term, on the morphological pattern *mufāʿalah*. At the end of the question, you said that once these terms were clear to you then the other terms would also be clear, so I have refrained from discussing them.

On why relatives and kinfolk are prone to outbreaks of extreme hostility—a question of ethics

Why does animosity run so high among relatives and kinsmen that it defies remedy—so virulent is the envy and so extreme the spite—to the point where goods are destroyed and blood is shed, where people abandon their homes and are brought to ruin? Are the evils one fears from neighbors in the same class as this animosity or not? 31.1

Miskawayh's response

Our earlier discussion about the definition of envy, the cognate notions that confuse people, and the different designations used make it unnecessary to cover the same ground in this answer. For we mentioned earlier that if a certain feature is shared by two people or a group of people, if they are united by a certain bond, with respect to which they are equal, even as they are equal with respect to their humanity, and if one person among them then happens to possess a good that the others do not have, he arouses the envy or desire for emulation of his peers. Relatives are a group of people who share a single line of descent and who do not consider anyone in the group to have a distinction over anyone else, so if one of them possesses a feature the others do not have, others vie against him. Moreover, ordinarily a common line of descent involves offering 31.2

aid and assistance and sharing in the same conditions; every party expects this from the other as a matter of course, so it is harder to tolerate and more difficult to resolve when this expectation is violated—it is akin to the disavowal of a debt or the denial of a right. If this is claimed, it excites aggravation; if it excites aggravation, it is rebuffed; if rebuffed, everyone swells with anger, and anger sows rancor and incites to evil deeds.

31.3 Add to this the strong interest relatives take and the probing inquiries they make into each other's affairs, which is simply not possible with more distant parties. So people set about demanding their rights and claiming their dues even without any to speak of; the grounds of anger are stirred, and anger makes them think more than the facts themselves allow. Everyone makes demands and expects the kinds of things that the others demand and expect, until the number and variety of demands bring matters to a point where they are beyond remedy and hope. The bond between neighbors is also a strong one, because it is a commonality that incites probing inquiries into other people's affairs and sows envy and all the other conditions mentioned in connection with relatives. But among the latter, unlike among neighbors, we can expect affection and mercy to operate. The evils that flare up among neighbors are unalloyed and the envy is pure, with no admixture of good and no reason for forbearance.

On why people become angry when others impute evil to them—a natural question

32.1 Why do people get angry when an evil that is actually to be found in them is ascribed to them? And why do they get angry when an evil that is not to be found in them is ascribed to them? Yet in the first instance, telling the truth is desirable and praiseworthy, and in the second lying is blameworthy and odious.

Miskawayh's response

The reason is self-love, which has already been explained. If a person is reminded of an evil that is to be found in him, he shudders to think of it, and if he thinks about it, he shudders at the thought of being confronted with it or vilified for it. For he knows how repugnant evil is, and he wants his beloved soul to be fault-free and far from every offense and reproach. So if an evil is imputed, he is first seized by distress and then by a desire to take revenge on the person who caused him this distress. Anger consists in the movement of the soul toward revenge, and this movement excites the blood of the heart and brings it to a boil. That is why anger is defined as the boiling of the blood out of a desire for revenge. The anger a person feels about an evil ascribed to him but not in fact found in him is as it should be, for he has been targeted with an unjust action intended to cause him distress. The benefit of anger, the reason it exists in human beings, is that it helps them to avenge themselves against unjust people or fend them off and prevent them from doing harm. So, if a person knows that someone has targeted him with an unjust action, he feels a desire to take revenge on him, his soul moves in that direction, and anger arises. Thus, the reason why anger is inflamed in both cases—when the truth is told, and when lies are told—has been clarified, as has the nature of anger. 32.2

On why a person who is being talked about suddenly appears out of nowhere; on the nature of coincidences—a psychological question

Why does a person who is the subject of conversation unexpectedly 33.1
appear at the very moment he is being mentioned? This is widely known to happen, even if it is not an everyday, familiar event—had it been, it would not strike people as astonishing and would not seem so momentous, but would be a commonplace. The same type

of thing happens when we turn around and see someone we had not been expecting to see. It is similar when we glimpse someone we think looks like someone we know, yet a closer look reveals it isn't that person, and then moments later we run into the person he looked like. Is all of this a matter of coincidence? If it is, what *is* coincidence? Does "coincidence" (*ittifāq*) consist in "concord" (*wifāq*)? And what is concord? Clarifying the latter notion will clarify the former and provide insight into it, or render it more accessible.

Miskawayh's response

33.2 The soul knows by its essence and apprehends things timelessly, because it is above nature, and time is contingent on natural motion; it is, as it were, an indication of the extensiveness (*imtidād*) of the latter, which is why the term for "extent" (*muddah*) was derived from it. For the latter is of the morphological form *fuʿlah* and the former of the form *iftiʿāl*, the root of both being the substantive term for "extension" (*madd*). Since the soul is above nature and its actions are above motion—that is to say, independent of time—the way it regards things is not the product of past, present, or future—rather, for it everything is on the same plane. Unhindered by matter and material objects or by the barriers put up by the senses and sensible objects, it apprehends things, and things appear to it timelessly. This feature of the soul may be more pronounced in some humoral mixtures, even to the point of divinatory powers and the ability to foretell events. The events foretold sometimes lie in the near, sometimes in the distant, future; the more distant the time and the longer the interval, the more marvelous, the stranger people find it. The time draws nearer and nearer to the present and the distance grows shorter and shorter, until the events foretold are separated from the present by only a small margin of time. This is what happens to the person who speaks of someone who then appears at the very moment he is mentioned. It's not the act of mentioning him that causes him to appear; rather the reverse: the proximity of his appearance apprises the soul and enables it to foretell it. The same thing applies to the case of turning around and seeing someone; the proximity of the person you turn around to see moves the soul and makes it direct the bodily apparatus to turn around. A deeper examination of this topic would not comport with our stipulation that we eschew lengthy exposition. Otherwise, there are marvelous things of this sort we could have brought up. This amount suffices for the purpose and provides an adequate account of the object of your inquiry.

We have promised to speak in a subsequent question to your question about coincidence, whether it consists in concord, and what accord is. I can assure you, however, that "coincidence" does indeed consist in "concord"; morphologically "coincidence" derives from it, and they have a single, shared root, as is indicated by the etymology.[35] We will give an adequate account of this when discussing "luck" and "fortune," God willing. 33.3

On the meaning of certain ordinary and technical terms—a question comprising some twenty questions, natural and linguistic, and including a discussion of luck and coincidence

What are the features that distinguish between the basic meanings denoted by different expressions used widely by people of reason and religion? These are terms that carry specific import, with obscure roots and crystal-clear meanings. What then is meant by the terms "power," "control," "ability," "capacity," "courage," "bravery," "valor," "succor," "granting a favorable outcome," "grace," "general good," "being enabled," "desertion," "assistance," "command," "sovereignty," "possession," "provision," "reign," "fortune," and "lot"? I have not mentioned "luck," because the word does not belong to the Arabic language.[36] Its meaning has been confused 34.1

with some of these terms, as has the term "lucky." All the terms "fortunate," "hapless," "endowed with a good lot," "possessing a good lot," and "possessing good fortune" carry particular meanings and serve particular ends, but it is difficult to expound them and arduous to inquire into them.

Miskawayh's response

34.2 Notwithstanding the diverse character of these questions, I found some notions to be more closely related and some less, so I have grouped the similar notions together and have not bound myself to the original arrangement. "Power" is an equivocal term used to refer to potentiality as against actuality. This is a specialized term only used by philosophers and not known to the generality of people. It refers to something that may possibly be manifested and enter actual existence. Thus one says a puppy has sight *in potentia*, or a person is a writer *in potentia*, even if this is not presently the case. It is also applied to the different elements the soul possesses, such as the powers of vision, perception, thought, discernment, anger, and the like. It is also used to refer to the quality that characterizes iron and similar objects, namely, firmness and insusceptibility to being bent or broken. It is also used to refer to the physical strength and hardiness that animals possess, and I believe this is what you had in mind in asking the question, because you mentioned this term alongside the terms "capacity" and "control." I have hit upon a definition that encompasses most of these significations and is relevant to your question: "Power" is a state of the entity that possesses it which manifests itself when confronted with its specific object. To clarify this definition as it pertains to animals: It consists in a balance between moisture and dryness in the nerves. For excess moisture in the nerves makes them flaccid when they are worked, and the one working them is then called weak. Excess dryness, in contrast, makes them snap and break or creates the risk of that, and makes them hurt when they are worked, and the one working them is also weak. The term "power" is only ever used relatively and in accordance with the standards relevant to its particular subject. One might thus speak of "a strong man" and a "weak camel," just as one might speak of a "strong ant" and a "weak elephant."

"Capacity" consists in the adequacy of a power to the demand placed on it; it is used in connection with animals and their strength more specifically, and in connection with corporeal burdens. It might also be used in connection with burdens of the soul by way of comparison and metaphor. One thus says, "So-and-so is capable of lifting forty kilos," meaning his power is adequate to this weight when placed on him. One also says, "So-and-so is not capable of speaking," "is not capable of rational speculation," or "is not capable of bearing sorrow and joy." When used in connection with inanimate beings, it is by way of extremely figurative speech. "Control" is the ability to manifest this power when one wills; this is why it pertains exclusively to animals and is not used in connection with anything else whatsoever on account of the definition we have given. "Ability" (*istiṭāʿah*) derives from the word for obedience (*ṭāʿah*), adopting the morphological form that indicates a request for obedience, according to the rules of derivation and the evidence of language. The basic meaning of this expression is metaphorical, based on the idea that we can only demand obedience from something when we have a claim to expect it on account of our control over it. The gist of this is that if you say "I was able to do such and such a thing" or "I am able to do this," you mean "If I demand obedience from it, it will offer it to me." The notion of ability goes back to that of control, even though the latter is essentially prior to the former; in this respect there is a distinction between the two. For the soul demands obedience from something on account of its control over it, and decrees that it must respond affirmatively to it. These elements are implicit in the word "ability," and this is proved by the derivation of the term. So dwell on this, and you will find it clear, God willing. 34.3

"Courage" is the employment of the power of anger in the right measure, at the right time, for the right object, and in the right 34.4

circumstance. It constitutes a character trait from which this action issues in accordance with reason, and is a mean state between two blameworthy extremes, one going too far in the direction of excess and the other going too far in the direction of deficiency. Excess occurs when this power is employed more than is right with respect to all the various conditions; this is called "rashness." Deficiency occurs when it is employed less than is right with respect to all the various conditions; this is called "cowardice." "Courage" is a term of praise, like generosity, temperance, and the like. The first manifestation of its effect relates to the person, and this is when it subdues his appetites and he only employs them as determined by reason, in accordance with all the various conditions. It also manifests its effect on others, when one person subjects another to injustice and wrongdoing, and he repulses him, in accordance with the aforementioned conditions, without excess or deficiency. "Bravery" is similar to "courage"; it is a term of praise that expresses the same meaning. But from a linguistic perspective, it comes from the notion of "elevation." The man who is called "indomitable" is, as it were, elevated above wrongdoing, rising above the level of those who are abased and despised, like a highland, which is the contrary of a lowland.

34.5 Though "valor" is similar to "courage," it specifically concerns actions relating to others, and is not used of a person's conquest of his appetites. Moreover, it is an adjunct of horsemanship; one thus speaks of a "valiant horseman." The notion of "valor" (*buṭūlah*) is appropriately grounded in that of "destruction" (*buṭlān*), for horsemen who possess this quality are constantly exposed to that fate, particularly given the fact that Arabs do not distinguish between the courage that is praiseworthy and the excess that is blameworthy, but rather consider the excess to constitute courage. What we call "courage" constitutes cowardice by their standards, as with liberality and generosity, for their approach to these is the same. I will add that sometimes courage leads to the destruction of life, and death is then good, excellent, and praiseworthy, having occurred in accordance with courage, that is to say, according to what reason determines, in the right manner, and on the basis of the other conditions. For should anyone fall short, I mean with respect to courage, he would be blameworthy and cowardly, as we have explained and clarified, and as emerged from our earlier exposition of the good death and the bad life.

"Succor" is the support of one power through an extraneous 34.6
power of the same category. "Desertion" is the failure to provide this support despite having the means to do so. "Succor," when it proceeds from human agents, can be either beneficial or harmful, on account of their ignorance of the consequences of things. But "succor" is a term of praise, for according to common usage it is the intention and aim one has at the time of acting, not its consequences, that is the focus. Succor from God, in contrast, is ever beneficial, never harmful, because of His knowledge of the consequences of things, and because He only does what is good and beneficial, being too exalted to do evil and beyond its reach—august is His mention, sanctified His name, too lofty for what the miscreants say! So, if we have clarified what succor consists in and what form it takes when effected by human beings and when effected by God, we have also clarified "desertion," its contrary, and there is no need to elaborate on it. "Grace" and "the general good" form the preserve of dialectical theologians, even though people generally are also familiar with them and aware of their meaning. You—God keep you—have steeped yourself in their notions and discussions, so you do not need me to take the trouble to clarify to you anything that pertains to them. May God increase your knowledge and grant you enjoyment of His blessings.

"Enabling" (*tamkīn*) derives from "possibility" (*imkān*), which is 34.7
the possibility that what is contained by something as a potentiality emerge into actuality. Its nature lies between the necessary and the impossible. The nature of the necessary can be envisaged as an extreme, and at the opposite extreme—I mean the point farthest from it—lies the nature of the impossible, while the nature of

the possible lies in between. This is why the possible has a wide compass, which neither the necessary nor the impossible have, for between the two extremes there extends a space that can be divided at many points, whereas the extremes do not occupy any space. Within the space that extends between these two extremes—the necessary and the possible—turn your attention to the point that lies exactly in the middle—this is what is most entitled and best fitted to be identified as the nature of the possible. Whenever the middle point approaches one of the extremes, it is the possible subject to a condition and qualification; and thus, people speak of a possible close to the necessary and a possible far from it. Similarly, they speak of a possible close to the impossible and one far from it. In contrast, if it lies in the middle, it is possible absolutely, and in that case there is no overriding reason for it to be associated with the necessary rather than with the impossible, nor is there an overriding reason for it to emerge from potentiality to actuality instead of remaining in its current state of potentiality.

34.8 "Enabling" is the noun of the verb "to enable." The principal parts of the verb are thus "to enable/enabling," as in "to honor/honoring" and "to speak/speaking." "Possibility" is the noun of the verb "to make possible." The principal parts of the verb are thus "to make possible/possibility," as in "to show honor/honoring." The term "that which is possible" adopts the same morphological pattern as "that which honors." The noun from which the verb theoretically derives is not used in the Arabic lexicon, nor does it come from it. For the thing has no verb connected with it other than the verb expressed with the transitive prefix. So if you say that a certain thing is possible, it is as though you were saying that this thing which exists *in potentia*—for which there is no ordinary noun in use, but which exists virtually, and its virtual meaning is "that which is possible"—has given itself to you, and has put you in the position to make it actual through your voluntary choice. "Possibility" is the noun from the expression "something gave power over itself." "Enabling" is an action performed on someone by something else whereby it puts him in the position to make that thing actual through voluntary choice. It is the verbal noun of "to enable," and the geminate verb form appears at this kind of lexical juncture to signify iteration and intensity of action, the way one says "he hit" and "he thrashed," "he was firm" and "he demanded emphatically." The term "enabling" can also carry another sense, namely, as a verbal noun deriving from the term "place," the way we say, "I established the stone in its position," when we give it the amount of space it requires so that it sticks firmly to the spot. In the same sense, we speak of a horseman as being "firmly fixed" in the saddle, and of a person as being "firmly established" in his seat. Talk of a person "establishing himself" with an emir falls in the same class by way of comparative and figurative use. As you can see, there is a vast difference between this meaning and the first.[37]

"Provision" consists in a living being's attainment of what it needs 34.9
as a living being. There are things that lead to the attainment of these needs, substituting for them and serving in their place—I am referring to the bases of human exchanges—and they are assigned the same status and are also called "provisions" insofar as they conduce to them. But the foundation is the former. God said: «There they shall have their provision at dawn and evening».[38] There are many causes through which these needs are obtained, some proximate, some remote, some natural and some nonnatural, and among the nonnatural, some that depend on chance and some that do not. Consequently, people have fallen into several kinds of error. One error is their attempt to reduce many causes to a single cause, and another is their search for proximity in remote causes. When that proved elusive, and they failed to uncover it where they sought it, they were plunged into perplexity, and the wonder they felt at the matter was proportionate to their ignorance of the cause.

"Mastery" comes from the expression "a certain thing passed 34.10
in turns among people" and "they passed it in turns among themselves," when they give it to each other alternately. God said: «so that it be not a thing taken in turns among the rich of you»,[39] that

is to say, so that everyone takes it in turns and it does not become the sole preserve of one set of people to the exclusion of another. It is a term that pertains to mundane objects of desire, particularly the achievement of domination. Its causes are also numerous, some remote and some proximate, some natural and some nonnatural. Among the nonnatural, some depend on volition and some on chance. Each of these divisions admits of further subdivisions, involving causes that are remote, proximate, or mixed, and entering into different types of compounds. So when the multitude fails to discern the cause, they are struck by the same sense of perplexity and wonder that they experience with provision.

34.11 The terms "granting a favorable outcome," (*tawfīq*), "coincidence," (*ittifāq*), "accord," (*muwāfaqah*), and "concord" (*wifāq*), have been mentioned above discretely and in a number of different questions, and we promised to treat them in this section, along with the terms "luck" and "fortune," for they are all similar and closely connected. The first four terms listed are close in meaning and derive from the term "agreement" (*wafq*). They belong to the class of relational terms, for they are only used to speak of the relation between two or more things. We say that a certain thing is in agreement with another, meaning that it conforms to it, corresponds with it, and is congruent with it. This is applied to any pair of things that exhibit congruence, whether bodies, character traits, or other things. As the saying has it, "Shann accorded with Ṭabaqah," that is, fell in with him and embraced him.[40] So the term "to accord" (*wāfaqa*) derives from "accordance" (*wafq*) and adopts the verbal morphological pattern used in Arabic when there are two entities at issue. Each of these entities is said to accord with the other, and is said to be accordant with it, as when we say that a person "contended with," and is "contending with" another. The term "coincidence" derives from "accordance," on the morphological pattern used when the subject itself is affected by the action, the way we say that a person or thing "drew near," "held fast," or "became disturbed." So these terms derive from the term "accordance."[41] On this pattern, it is only used when the subject has the characteristic mentioned.

It is said to be a matter of coincidence when a relation of congruence unites two or more things through an unknown voluntary cause, and these things are in accord with someone's volition; there must be an element of volition and some intention and choice involved. If volition is not involved and it has arisen through an unknown natural cause, but brings a person some benefit, it is a matter of "luck" for him. Since some things are brought about through natural causes, some through voluntary causes, and some through compounds—through both natural and voluntary causes—and since each of these may bring about something desirable or undesirable, even though its causes can vary from one person to another and from one purpose to another, contrasting names are used to refer to them in order to indicate the different kinds of causes involved. "Luck" is applied to those things with an unknown natural cause, remote or proximate, that happen to benefit a person independently of any volition or intention on his part. "Coincidence" is applied to those things with an unknown voluntary cause, remote or proximate, that happen to benefit a person and accord with a purpose or volition of his. Qualifiers that derive from these two terms are only applied to a person after something has happened to him repeatedly. That is, he is only called "lucky" if it has often been the case that natural acts occurred through unknown causes and brought about desirable and attractive ends. Similarly, a person is called "well-favored" if it has often been the case that voluntary acts occurred through unknown causes and brought about fine and desirable ends. 34.12

I will clarify these concepts using two examples, so as to set them out fully, in the open. I notice you asked to be exempted from having to understand the meaning of "luck" because you have found it does not belong to Arabic. It is as though you have forbidden yourself a truth unless it were clothed in Arabic words, so that if Arabic had not existed, you would have no desire to learn. But—may God grace 34.13

you with His support—we never abandon the search for meanings, regardless of the language in which they happen to be found and the expression they happen to receive. To continue, then. The following is an example of luck: If a stone should happen to fall from an elevated place and strike a man on some part of his body, bursting open his veins and making blood flow; if the man had previously been in need of bloodletting, then the falling of the stone that burst open the vein and made blood flow would act as a cause of health and help preserve him from illness. This would constitute good luck. The man would be considered lucky if many such things happened to him. Should the flow of blood not be beneficial and the man have no prior need to have it let, but if, on the contrary, the falling of the stone caused immediate pain and the flow of blood made his power sag and made him succumb to an unanticipated illness, this would constitute bad luck. An example of coincidence is if a person should leave his house driven by a particular volition and intention—relating to the pursuit of some necessary business—and on his way he should meet a friend whom he had been wishing to meet, or an adversary he had been looking for and failing to find. That would constitute a good coincidence, and if many such things happened, the man would be considered well-favored. Should the encounter be with an enemy he was fleeing or an adversary he was trying to elude, then this would be considered a bad coincidence, and if he repeatedly experienced this kind of thing he would be considered ill-favored.

34.14 Now the causes of voluntary movements are thoughts that arise and states that occur within the soul but are not produced by volition, for if they came about through volition, this would necessitate the existence of an infinite number of volitions, and that is inconceivable. These thoughts and states that constitute effects and acts must be attributed to an agent, yet we have said that human beings are not their agent, and thus they must necessarily constitute the act of some other being. They are to be attributed to God if they lead to benefits and good things. This is the "granting of a favorable outcome," which derives from the term "accordance."[42] God sometimes grants a favorable outcome without being asked, and sometimes after having been asked and supplicated—though all people perpetually request these things from God. So when these states and thoughts occur within the soul and it has recourse to movements that, in conjunction with other movements, bring about a single choiceworthy thing for someone in accordance with an excellent end of his, it constitutes the granting of a favorable outcome and the man is considered well-favored.

"Fortune" would appear to be an inclusive term that ranges over 34.15
both meanings, for a person is considered fortunate if he is granted a favorable outcome and has luck, and is also considered fortunate if he only enjoys one of these two things. "Lot" refers to one's share and portion. As everyone has a portion of happiness and a quota of good allotted to him from the celestial sphere depending on when he is born, everything of the kind that comes to him is attributed to his lot. "Hapless" means "held back," and derives from the term which means "holding back." This is why the term "door holder" is applied to a doorman.[43] The good that comes to other people is, as it were, "held back" from the person described as "hapless." The terms "possessing a good lot" (*ḥaẓẓī*) and "possessing good fortune" (*jaddī*) are qualifiers that refer back to the terms "fortune" (*jadd*) and "lot" (*ḥaẓẓ*), the way we describe a member of the tribe of Tamīm as a "Tamīmī" and a member of Bakr as a "Bakrī."

"Assistance" refers specifically to the type of succor that leads to 34.16
domination and conquest. We have already discussed what "succor" means. "Command" is an equivocal term, and its inflection follows the inflection of the term "master, patron" or "servant, client"—that is to say, it has one meaning taken from the superior party and another taken from the inferior party.[44] But the fundamental meaning in both cases is a state entailing a privileged relationship and entitlements, which incites the superior party to show compassion and solicitude and the inferior party to offer honest counsel and obedience. If this term is taken in accordance with the religious Law

and as a religious term, then it should be defined on the basis of the meaning indicated, even though the original sense is what we have mentioned.

34.17 “Possession” means to have exclusive effective authority over something. This may be established by nature, by the religious Law, and by convention. An example of possession established by nature is the ownership a person has over his limbs, his natural organs, and his movements, which he disposes in accordance with his will. An example of possession established through the religious Law is slave ownership that results from taking captive those who contravene the fundaments of the religious Law. An example of possession established by convention is the negotiations between those engaged in transactions. “Sovereignty” is identical with possession but with a more general reach and a more manifest element of control; it also involves coercion. The implementation of power in its case follows general interest based on solicitude. True sovereignty, that which deserves the name and necessarily attracts it in accordance with its meaning, is if it operates in accordance with the religious Law—upholding its ordinances, carrying out its rulings, compelling people to obey it, whether it agrees or conflicts with their wishes, be it by exciting their desires or their fears, and considering all of them without caprice or bias. If it does not operate in accordance with the religious Law and its abovementioned provisions, it constitutes an act of usurpation and the man exercising it is a usurper. He must not be called a “king,” nor should his craft be called “kingship,” and the power he implements is not in accordance with sovereignty. The meaning of “king” and the difference between a true king and a usurper have emerged plainly from this discussion. A fuller explanation of that point would exceed the space allowed here, but a brief reference suffices.

On the meaning of certain prepositional expressions concerning God

What do people mean when they say, "This is from God," "This is through God," "This is for God," "This is on God," "This is by God's arrangement," "This is through God's arrangement," "This is through God's will," and "This is through God's knowledge"? There is also a long report at the end of this question citing a highly lauded, distinguished teacher and mentioning some of his responses. 35.1

Miskawayh's response

35.2 It is impossible to answer for people in general and for the meanings they attach to these prepositions, given the plethora of meanings they attach to them and the variety of their views and approaches. It is unfair to charge us with this task; merely cataloguing people's views would be a lengthy venture, let alone answering for them and explaining their statements. What I can offer, taken in general, is to acquaint you with what I take to be the correct stance on these questions and with my own approach to them, and I will strive to set it out for you with the utmost brevity and succinctness, as stipulated in your prefatory epistle. I respond, then, as follows. All notions of this kind that are predicated of God and all acts, names, and attributes that are ascribed to Him are applied figuratively and by way of expansive usage—none of the literal meanings we ordinarily understand by these terms corresponds to anything that obtains in that domain. To begin with, according to the grammarians, the preposition "from" in these questions is used in ordinary language to denote the beginning of an aim, the preposition "for" to denote the end of an aim, and the preposition "through" to denote the means used. The other prepositions likewise bear meanings clearly expounded by the grammarians. I do not apply any of these literal meanings to God in anything but a figurative sense, for I do not say that His action has a beginning or an end or that He uses anything as a means, so that the preposition "through" might be predicated of Him without qualification and one might say, "This is through God's arrangement"; for there is no arrangement in His domain, nor does He have a need for this act or for any other act.

35.3 This is also my position regarding all other acts ascribed to Him, and it is likewise my position regarding the names and attributes predicated of Him, and that the Lawgiver has given us dispensation to use. My use of these names conforms to received report in acquiescence to command. Otherwise, who would dare apply, say, the qualifications "Merciful" or "Compassionate" literally to the Creator, who is exalted above the experience of passions? For mercy consists in a passion of the soul that causes praiseworthy acts to issue among us, whereas none of these elements and realities obtain in His domain. Yet, as human beings have limited abilities and powers and cannot be held to obligations they cannot meet and lack the power to discharge, they predicate of God the noblest of the names that carry praise and dignity among them, such as "Hearing," "Knowing," "Compeller," and "Almighty." It is my conviction that the religious Law specifically granted us permission to apply these names and attributes. Had we been left to our own judgments, we would not have ventured to use any of them through license or cause. So we examine closely any of these names, acts, or prepositions we hear ascribed to God. We permit their use when it is permitted by the religious Law, and we then reflect on what the speaker intended. If this involves goodness, wisdom, and justice, we let his view stand; we reject it if it does not, and is unworthy of being attributed to Him; we declare it spurious and its speaker a liar, and assert that our One Creator is above these false qualifications.

35.4 I then found you—may God grace you with His support—reporting under this question the responses of a distinguished teacher whom you showered with praise, whose statements you have confidence in, and whose responses you find satisfying, so I thought it best to also satisfy myself with them for your sake. For at the end of this question you wrote as follows, verbatim: The report in this section of the views of this teacher on a miscellany of topics, combining uncommon insights with choice words and agreeable compositions, has gone on at some length. If only everything that preceded could be succeeded by something similar—that would be a balm and a salve for the spirit. But the limits of time make it hard to realize what is imperative and mandated, let alone anything further, and above all I need to see this epistle to its completion.

On the nature of the sense of familiarity we feel toward particular places and people

What is one to make of the sense of familiarity a person experiences toward a place where he often sits, or an individual with whom he has been intimate for a long time? It is the same when a man acquires a familiarity with a specific bathhouse or indeed a specific room in a bathhouse, or with a specific mosque or indeed a specific column in a mosque. I heard a Sufi say: For forty years a quartan fever clung to me. When it left me I pined for it. The only sense I could make of my pining was the familiarity that had been kneaded into my very being, ingrained into my natural constitution, and branded upon my spirit. 36.1

Miskawayh's response

Familiarity consists in the recurrent exposure of the soul or nature to a single form. The soul is recurrently exposed to the forms of things either through the senses or through the intellect. It stores the forms that reach it through the senses in something akin to a storeroom—I'm referring to the location of memory—and at that point the forms are like strangers. The strangeness dissipates and intimacy ensues when a single thing and a single form recur several times and the form and its receptacle then become as one; and if the 36.2

soul looks once more into the storeroom, following our analogy, it finds the form fixed there and recognizes it, having grown intimate with it. This is what familiarity consists in. Every sensible object produces such familiarity through sight and the other organs.

36.3 The soul composes syllogisms from what it takes from the intellect, and derives forms from these, which are also strangers. After recurrent exposure, they become imprinted on it, and it grows intimate with them, though in this context one does not speak of "familiarity" but of "knowledge" and of a "stable state." That is why the different branches of learning demand a great amount of study. For at first this produces what is called a condition, which is like a drawn mark, and subsequently, through recurrent exposure, this becomes an acquired possession and stable state, and the union that we have mentioned arises. Nature, for its part, always follows the lead of the soul and imitates it—being like a shadow to the soul generated by it—so it follows the same course in natural things. That is why, when human beings accustom their nature to something, a form akin to nature is produced. Hence the saying "Habit is a second nature." An examination of the things that can grow habitual and become natural reveals that they are plentiful and clear—and in fact plainer and starker than the familiarity that is in the soul. This is the case, for example, when a person accustoms himself to phlebotomy or to urinating, defecating, and so on, at particular times; the same goes for digestion when eating and drinking and the other acts attributed to nature.

On why epilepsy is so hard to treat—a medical question

37.1 Why is epilepsy particularly recalcitrant to treatment compared with other illnesses? Physicians seem to despair of curing it. It is allegedly harder to treat among those of an advanced age whose bodies have begun to wear out, and easier to cure and more tractable among children, whose bodies are pliant, whose substance is moist, and who are quick to change.

Miskawayh's response

Epilepsy is a convulsion that affects the nerves, and the nerves begin from the brain, whence they spread throughout the entire body. The reason for the convulsion is a thick vapor that arises from viscous phlegm, and a thick gastric juice that blocks the passageways of the spirit found in the interior ventricles of the brain. Since the vapor dissipates quickly despite its thickness, awareness is quickly regained as it dissipates. Sometimes this blockage arises from the brain itself, sometimes it involves the contribution of the stomach through a thick vapor that ascends to the former from the latter, and, most commonly, sometimes it involves the contribution of another bodily part. Shortly before a fit occurs, if it arises from a bodily part other than the stomach, the afflicted person feels as if something were coming out of that part and being driven upward. The physician then binds that area and wraps strong dressings around it so as to prevent the vapor from ascending to the brain. 37.2

Children have weak and moist brains, and so they are quick to yield to vapors. During the developmental stage, their heat is suffused by an abundance of moistures, and vapor is simply an abundance of moisture that heat does not have the power to dissipate and commute. That is why vapors proliferate inside their heads, resulting in the blockages we have mentioned. Skillful physicians do not treat children using medications for epilepsy, but rather leave them be and minister to the area through dietary improvement. For if nature is fortified, the excess moistures in the whole body are dried out, and heat is kindled, then epilepsy automatically vanishes, because its cause—namely, the abundance of vapor—has vanished, and because the substance of the brain becomes firm and is little disposed to suffer impairments caused by its moisture and weakness. The physician's sole objective is, instead, 37.3

through specially prepared food, to improve the milk of the woman breastfeeding the child.

37.4 The opposite applies to people of an advanced age. For the weakness of all their bodily organs stems from their decline and from the weakness of their powers and bodily parts; an increase in their power is not to be expected. Rather, every day that passes diminishes and weakens them further. Thus, if their brain is exposed to thick vapor arising from the brain itself or from another bodily part, vapor begins to collect in it, and it grows more vulnerable to the vapor with every fit. At the same time, heat—which causes the dissipation of vapors—is too weak to dissipate them. That is why one despairs of effecting a cure. When matter is channeled to an area of the body and returns repeatedly, the passageways through which it flows widen to accommodate it, and nature constrains it through the kind of habit we mentioned in the previous question. The organ grows weaker, the matter flows with greater facility, the vapor increases on account of the foreign moisture arising in the bodies of those who are disposed to its formation and to its commutation into phlegm in their stomach, and the heat grows less capable of exercising a dissipating effect. As a result, it becomes almost impossible to cure.

On why people are so enamored of ascetic individuals

38.1 Why do people love those who are abstemious in their enjoyments, so that they prepare delicious food for them at great cost, carry it to them on their heads in jars, and place it at their feet? The more strenuously the ascetic man demurs, the more importunate they become. When he dies, they make his grave a place of worship, saying that he was "one who fasted much and partook little." By contrast, when confronted with people who gourmandize and eat to excess, they abhor and repudiate them, finding their presence loathsome and decrying the immoderation of their behavior. And why is it that people refuse to visit the tombs of kings and caliphs, but constantly visit the graves of the meek and wretched, and of those who went about in coarse and shabby garments?

Miskawayh's response

Human beings have an affinity to plants through their growing soul, an affinity to beasts through the soul that moves by voluntary choice, and an affinity to the angels through their rational soul. This last forms the basis of their eminence and dignity. The taking of nourishment is a distinguishing property of plants, though it also extends to animals on account of their power of growth. The rational soul, by contrast, has no need for food or drink. As angels are nobler than human beings on account of their essential lack of need for nourishment and the permanence of their substance, human beings who have a greater affinity to them through their soul are nobler than human beings who have a greater affinity to plants or beasts. Human beings regard plants and beasts with disdain and use them as they see fit, whereas they exalt and glorify the angels; thus, everything with an affinity to the former must necessarily be regarded with contempt and disdain, and everything with an affinity to the latter must be exalted and honored. This is too obvious to require extensive discussion or be worth the trouble of a response, but we did not wish to abandon the question entirely, so we commented on it to this extent. 38.2

On why some people squander their money despite the harmful consequences this entails while others are miserly even though this gives them a bad name

39.1 Why do some people eagerly squander their money despite knowing the dire consequences this begets, while others eagerly pinch every penny despite knowing the bad repute this attracts? And what is the difference between the notions of "provision" and "possession"? An established philosopher once heard me bemoaning my circumstances and said, "My dear fellow, you have little in the way of 'possession' but much in the way of 'provision.' There are many who have much 'possession' but little 'provision,' so praise the mighty and glorious God!"

Miskawayh's response

39.2 We have discussed in previous questions why people choose to do things that have dire consequences despite knowing this fact. We compared this to a sick person who knows that consuming harmful food will destroy his health—when the food is needed for the sake of health in the first place—and who chooses to consume the food as the result of an immediate appetite because he has a bad disposition and inadequate self-control, and capitulates to his beastly soul in defiance of his rational soul. So there is no need to go over the same ground again. Similarly, we have clarified the nature of "provision" and the distinction between it and "possession," so if you read the preceding discussion, it may serve as a response to this question.

On why some people keep their affairs private while others broadcast them for all to hear—a question of ethics

Why are some people eager to conceal what happens to them, suppressing any mention of what they do, and are averse to anyone becoming privy to their affairs, while others openly reveal their circumstances and pursue this with alacrity, letting people in on everything, be it great or small? What is the meaning of the Prophet's saying, "Make reticence your helper in your affairs, for those who enjoy blessings provoke the envy of others"? 40.1

Miskawayh's response

This question was also answered above when we said that the soul has two powers; it longs to take through one, and to give through the other. The soul is as susceptible to stinginess and liberality with respect to information as it is with respect to material possessions: Sometimes it is lavish, at other times niggardly. A person may be stingy with his knowledge yet liberal with his material possessions, and sometimes the reverse is the case. This was addressed exhaustively when we discussed the topic of secrets earlier. 40.2

On why self-praise is unseemly—a question about volition

Why is it considered unseemly for someone to praise himself, but proper for another to praise him? What does the person praised love about being lauded by the one who praises him? And what is the reason for that? 41.1

Miskawayh's response

41.2 To praise someone is to declare their outstanding nature and testify to their virtues. Since human beings love themselves, they see their good qualities but are blind to their bad qualities—they even see in themselves good qualities they do not possess. It is therefore considered repugnant for them to testify to things that cannot be accepted or seen in them. By contrast, the testimony of other people, who are at a remove and unencumbered by the defect of passionate love, is deemed admissible and their praise worthy of attention. Sometimes they may love the praised person with the love of a parent, brother, or friend, standing in a relation to him close to the relation in which he stands to himself; then they are vulnerable to the same defect or to something not far removed from it. In that case it is considered repugnant for them to eulogize, and such statements are unacceptable, though they are not as repugnant as in the first case—that is, the case of the self-praiser—since no one loves another person as much as he loves himself. What the person praised finds in the person praising him is the sweetness of having justice done to him, of receiving his due, and of hearing kind words regarding a beloved object congruent with one's will.

On why people disparage avarice even though they're avaricious; on the origin of avarice and generosity—a volitional, ethical, and linguistic question

42.1 Why do people disparage avarice despite the fact that avarice dominates them? Why do people praise generosity though it is rarely to be found in them? Are generosity and avarice natural or acquired? And is there any distinction between the terms "avaricious," "mean," "miserly," "ungiving," "vile," "petty," "stingy," "tightfisted," and "skinflint"?

Miskawayh's response

People disparage avarice because avarice consists in denying others the things they are entitled to on the conditions we mentioned earlier. Reason deems it to be repugnant in itself; its dominance does not prevent them from deeming it repugnant. It is a blameworthy character trait and an odious malady of the soul; just as there is nothing to prevent them from disparaging the maladies of the body even when present, there is nothing to prevent them from disparaging the maladies of the soul when dominant. Yet, unless people are honest with themselves and have cognizance of their merits and demerits, they largely disparage the avarice that afflicts the soul without acknowledging its presence in themselves. I heard a group of friends disparaging themselves for a number of moral defects, lamenting their great struggle to remedy them and ardent striving to remove them, bemoaning how bad habits had spoiled many of their character traits. Generosity is praised because generosity is in itself something good and beloved. Its definition has already been discussed; it is to the soul what health is to the body, so people value it and praise it, whether it is present in them or not. 42.2

You ask, "Are generosity and avarice natural or acquired?" Character traits as a whole are not natural. If they were, we would not be able to heal them, seek their improvement, or nourish hopes of altering them and eliminating them when bad. They would instead be like the heat and light emitted by fire or like the heaviness and downward inclination of the earth, and nobody seeks to heal these natural phenomena or alter or eliminate them. Yet, though generosity and avarice are not natural, we say that, through bad or good habit, they approximate nature in terms of the difficulty of treating them and eliminating their form from the soul. We only call them "character traits" when they have become a disposition of the soul from which a single act invariably issues without reflection. Before that, they are not called character traits, nor does one say that a given person is avaricious or generous unless that is his standing practice. A specific humoral mixture may predispose children and 42.3

young people to acquire a particular character trait, but they can be disciplined and habituated to the performance of fine actions so that they become a form and disposition of their soul whence that type of praiseworthy act always issues. That is analogous to how they might be predisposed to succumb to a particular illness but can be treated with food and medicine until the predisposition is reversed, their humoral mixture being modified until it becomes healthy and no longer inclined to succumb to that illness.

42.4 Regarding your question of whether there are any distinctions among the different terms you listed, I assure you there are indeed distinctions to be found. We previously distinguished between "avaricious" and "mean,"[45] with "meanness" being more inclusive than "avarice"—every mean person is avaricious, but not every avaricious person is mean. Meanness does not pertain exclusively to possessions and external effects but also concerns one's pedigree and the quality of one's ambition, whereas avarice pertains exclusively to giving and taking. The etymology of "stingy" and "ungiving" reveals their meaning.[46] "Tightfisted" and "skinflint" are terms that are used metaphorically and are taken from inanimate objects.[47] "Vile" and "petty" are terms that are used in a strongly pejorative sense, and each stronger than the rest, while "vile" is stronger than "small-minded" and "petty." As the popular adage has it: "So-and-so pinches pennies at the marriage feast." Aristotle refers to the very same adage, which proves to me that, with respect to this adage, his language agrees with ours, or alternatively that one people received it from the other. Such a person goes beyond avarice, which involves denying others what they are entitled to under specific conditions, and is so wretched as to treat his own self worse than an avaricious person treats others.

On why people blame treachery and praise fidelity even though treachery predominates among them—a volitional and ethical question

Speaking of disparagement of avarice and praise of generosity, what makes people unite in disapproving of treachery as despicable and approving of fidelity as admirable, even though treachery prevails and fidelity is rarely to be found? Are these qualities accidents that inhere in the original substance of things, or are they the product of conventional agreement? 43.1

Miskawayh's response

People approve of fidelity because it is known to be admirable through reason. People are political by nature, and thus are compelled to agree contractually among themselves to render certain matters binding, so that they may provide the conditions for accomplishing other ends through mutual help. These matters may pertain to religion, conduct, friendly relations, transactions, and sovereignty and domination—in a word, to everything requiring civic association and accomplished through acts of mutual assistance. They thus supply conditions that establish a set of terms among people which they always observe in accomplishing a given matter. If one group stands by and adheres to them, their ends are accomplished, whereas if they abandon them and break faith with each other, their ends are frustrated, and they fall short of accomplishment. Whether fidelity is admirable and treachery repugnant depends on the matter you propose to accomplish. If it is noble, dignified, and beneficial on a large scale, it is considered despicable to commit treachery and admirable to keep faith, and vice versa. 43.2

On the origin of the customs of different nations

44.1 What is the origin of the different customs found among the nations we see scattered across the world? The word for "custom" derives from the verb "to return" and the verb "to accustom oneself to."[48] So how did people establish their customs at first and then make them their continual practice? What was the stimulus that caused every group of people to adopt a different kind of attire, style of adornment, mode of expression, and way of movement whose limits they do not transgress and whose domains they do not overstep?

Miskawayh's response

44.2 To be sure, "custom" does indeed derive from the verb "to return." I cannot offer a response to the question about the origin of customs, about how people arrived at their first instances, what those instances were, and who was the first to reach them and to establish them for every group of people as regards their attire—I would not want it should someone offer to provide it for me, nor would I consider it real knowledge. There would be no advantage to be gained from it.

On why people don't grow young again after they've grown old—a natural question

45.1 Why is it that once human beings grow old and senile, they do not, following the way they developed, become middle-aged again, then inexperienced youths, then young striplings, and then children? What does this arrangement reveal; what does this order point to?

Miskawayh's response

Old age and middle age do not constitute the terminus of human development or the end of natural movement—that is, the movement of growth—such that you might propose (God grace you with His support) that an old man could follow its tracks back to where his movement took its departure from. Rather, you must know that the end of development and movement is when youth reaches its height; after that it pauses—this is middle age—and after that it declines—this is old age. For as long as the innate heat present in bodies composed of the four natures increases in power, it makes the body in which it is present develop by drawing into it suitable moistures that replace those that dissipate and serve as nourishment for the body. An amount of what is drawn in by the excess of power is left over, exceeding the amount of nourishment needed to compensate for that which dissipates. It adds this to the expanse of the body and uses it to extend the volume of its physical parts. It comes to a halt and ceases to add anything to the volume of the physical parts, when the power has reached its limits. At that point, its end is to nourish and so preserve the parts and extent of the body—that is, by drawing in an amount of moistures that distribute themselves through the body to compensate for those that dissipate, without any excess that might be channeled into increase and extension. Then the heat comes to a halt in middle age and grows a little weaker and begins to diminish; the body starts to diminish too and human beings experience a decline in that first movement. One's nourishment increasingly falls short of the amount needed, so that the moisture it replaces is not equal to the moisture that dissipates. Things continue this way until we become decrepit and reach the point of decomposition, the reverse of the composition from which we began. This is what constitutes natural, proper death. 45.2

Every constrained movement follows this course; initially it increases, then reaches an extremity, then comes to a halt, and then it starts to decline. The humoral mixture of human beings and of every being composed from the mutually opposing natures is 45.3

produced through a force that unites and constrains these elements, combining them harmoniously despite their mutual opposition and conflict; so their movement is constrained. Constrained movements tend to exhibit the pattern I have mentioned, unless the force that constrains them regularly applies to them one constraining act after another. What necessarily applies to the movement of development is thus what necessarily applies to every movement of its species. An old man cannot become middle-aged again, then young, then a child, because this is not the order followed by the movement, nor is old age the end of the movement, being, rather, the extremity of weakness and the counterpart of childhood. The middle period of human life, between childhood and old age, is the end, and then the decline and movement of old men follows the same course as in the beginning.

On the benefit people derive from likening some things to others—a question of voluntary choice

46.1 What do people gain from likening one thing to another, so that this element comes to their mind and they eagerly revisit it in verse and prose? And why is it that the likeness begets revulsion and stands in the way of acclaim if it fails to emerge, and the element is not skillfully chosen?

Miskawayh's response

46.2 What people gain is the joy they feel at the veracity of their imagination and at their ability to isolate forms from different kinds of matter, thereby unifying the form after it has been multiplied by matter. For to liken a peach to a chickpea is to isolate the shape that is found in their respective material bases and to regard the two as a single thing, despite the material difference between them in terms of how large or small, or how moist or dry, each one is, or in terms of color, taste, and other accidents. Grasping this, abstracting forms from matter, and reducing some forms to others, are characteristic acts of the soul, and the joy experienced is a joy of the soul. That is why we show such eagerness for them, just as we show eagerness for natural attainments. Indeed, though, the acts of the soul are nobler and more excellent.

On why some dreams are true and others false

Why are some dreams true while others are false? Why aren't all dreams true, or all false? What does their oscillation between these two poles reveal? Perhaps there is a secret to this that yields to examination. 47.1

Miskawayh's response

Philosophical inquiries have demonstrated that the soul is above time and that its acts are in no way bound by or in need of time, for time is contingent on motion, and motion is proper to nature. Given this, all things are present to the soul regardless of whether they belong to the past or the future, and it sees them from a single perspective. Sleep consists in the soul's suspension of some of its organs with the purpose of giving them rest—and by "organs," I mean the senses. When it suspends these senses, it retains other acts that belong to it essentially and properly, including the movement called deliberation and a revolving of the soul. This movement, essential to the soul, can take one of two forms. It is either divine, which is the gaze it directs toward its highest horizon, or natural, which is the gaze it directs toward its lowest horizon.[49] 47.2

When awake, the soul can see with the eyes a given object clearly at one time and dimly at another, depending on how keen or fatigued the visual power is, how far or near the object of sight 47.3

is, and how substantial or slender the objects that lie between them are. Under these conditions, the way objects are seen varies. A person may thus look at an animal under the influence of one of these contingent factors and think it is an inanimate object; he may think that a human being is a wild animal; or he may think that ʿAmr is Zayd. With the removal of those impediments and hindrances, he perceives the things fully. It is similar when the soul is asleep, that is to say, when it is not using the organ of sense perception. For it sees that aspect of an object that emerges from the first impression—I mean the high-level genus that encompasses the objects it ranges over—and then the object becomes progressively clearer to it, one form at a time, until it sees it plainly and distinctly. If it only happens to see the impression of an object, what it sees requires explanation and interpretation, but the dream does not require clarification if it sees the object clearly and distinctly, and the very thing it sees when asleep is what it will see when awake.

47.4 This part it possesses through the swift, noble gaze connected to its higher horizon, and it is the source of prognostications and veracious visions that form part of prophecy. The part that it possesses through the inferior gaze connected to its lower horizon involves it reviewing the store of sensible forms derived through the senses from objects of vision and hearing. These forms lie dispersed in no particular order and contain no indications of the future. Sometimes it may combine these forms haphazardly, the way an absent-minded or idle person without a specific purpose might behave, as for example when he fiddles with his fingers and with things at hand that are of no particular use for him. These dreams do not admit interpretation, and are merely the «muddled» dreams you have heard people speak of.[50]

On the nature of dreams

What are dreams? For they are an august topic, and one of the parts of prophecy. What is it that sees what is seen, and what is it that renders what is seen seeable? Is it the soul, is it nature, or is it the human being? I recoil from loftier inquiries about the soul and investigations of its nature and of what earlier and later thinkers have said about it. And if that defies one's ability and stands outside the pale of one's power, what should one say about inquiries into the intellect? For its horizon is even higher, its realm even nobler, its effects even subtler, its demonstrative force even more wide-ranging; its scales have an even firmer hold, its radiance imposes itself even more imperiously, and its benefits are even more evident. 48.1

Miskawayh's response

The soul sees objects of sight when absent as it does when present. 48.2
This is a result of the forms being realized in the common sense, something that human beings recognize from experience with a sense of necessity they cannot deny. How else would we acquire an image of Baghdad or Khurasan or the countries we saw once, of our houses and the friends we had there, or of everything we remember since childhood, were it not for the fact that these forms are realized in the common sense? This is particularly so given that it has been established beyond doubt that vision and all other forms of sense perception are passive effects produced by sensible objects and changes wrought by those objects, and these changes do not endure after the disappearance of the sensible imagined object. So, were it not for this comprehensive common sense where the forms of sensible objects endure without disappearing, whenever we saw or heard something that disappeared from our sight or our hearing, its form would disappear for us completely, so that we would not know its form unless we chanced to see or hear it a second time. Moreover,

we would not know that it was the same as the first were we to see it a second or third time. The same applies to the things we hear.

48.3 If we did not fix the forms of sensible objects one after the other in this power—I mean the comprehensive common sense—we would not be able to get anything whatsoever out of reading or out of seeing dance movements or movements that end at successive moments in time. For vision undergoes a change through the reading of each successive letter and through each successive movement, but the first state of change does not endure, for if it endured, the second would not be realized. But this is not what happens, for we continue to perceive these forms once gone as though they were right before our eyes and the soul could see them. The seeing called "memory" during wakefulness is called "dreaming" during sleep. Yet there is a further state that goes beyond the state of wakefulness, for with the suspension of the senses, the powers of the soul dispose themselves for seeing, and see the things that lie in the future, whether clearly or dimly, as a faint impression.

48.4 The etymological derivation of these terms shows you—you who are a master of language, may God grace you with his support—that they share the same meaning. For the terms "seeing" (*ru'yah*), "deliberation" (*rawiyyah*), and "dream" or "vision" (*ru'yā*) share the same root consonants despite the difference in their vocalization. Similarly, the verbs "he saw" (*ra'ā*), "he formed an opinion" (*irta'ā*), and "he deliberated," (*rawwā*) speak to the pattern of etymologically related words. You are familiar with these principles, as you have been well schooled in them. The same applies to the terms "to catch sight of" and "to have insight, as in to be discerning," "sight," and "insight."[51] The term "to look" (*naẓara*) is used to convey both meanings without any alteration: The act performed through the senses is referred to as "looking," as is the act of "seeing" performed through the intellect; both are designated by *naẓar*, with no change in the vowels or shift in the consonants.

48.5 So we have clarified what dreams are, what it is that does the seeing, and what it is that is seen. Dreams consist in the soul's perception during sleep of the forms of things in abstraction from their matter. The soul does the seeing, with the organ we have described. The abstracted form is what is seen. The previous question noted that some dreams may be true while others are false, that some may foretell the future while others may be idle or «muddled», though we did so with the utmost conciseness. For an analytical explanation of these topics would require us to compose several books in order to establish the general principles and provide a summary account of the subsidiary details. But the contrary has been stipulated, and your quick mind and receptiveness to mere allusions demand such a premise and promise—may God prolong your blessings!

On why friendship arises between apparently dissimilar individuals—a volitional and ethical question

Why does reciprocal affection arise between two individuals who do not resemble each other in external appearance, are dissimilar in physical build, and do not dwell in physical proximity, so, say, one hails from the city of Farghānah, the other from Tāhart, one is tall and well-built, the other short and unattractively diminutive, one is lean and meager, the other sturdy and tough, one is hirsute and covered in thick hair, the other smooth and with very little hair, one is more tongue-tied than Bāqil, the other more eloquent than Saḥbān Wā'il,[52] one is more generous than a rain cloud after a lightning storm, the other more avaricious than a dog nursing a fleshless bone it toiled to secure, so that the divergence and discordance between the two provoke the spectator and inquirer to wonder? 49.1

Speaking of divergence and discordance, what are they, and what are amity and concord? Indeed, you notice these individuals continually involved in relations of give and take, honesty and 49.2

fidelity, agreement and loyalty, contraction and growth, while sharing no common faith, joint opinion, uniting condition, or comparable nature. Such reciprocal affection does not obtain exclusively between males, but between males and females, and also between females. If we expand our remit, we can see a number of different permutations. The relationship may extend over time, or may be curtailed, with some lasting forever, while others endure for no longer than a month, maybe even less than a month. Perhaps most remarkable is when it creates enmity and rancor, envy and hatred, as if this very reciprocal affection were reciprocal antipathy, and heinous and uncommon atrocities are generated, including the destruction of wealth, be it ancestral or recently acquired, and the premature end of lives. Sometimes the enmity spreads to the children, as if it formed part of their inheritance—sometimes it grows even fiercer than it was among the parents. This is a difficult subject that gives free rein to wonder, and the causes are obscure. In this day and age, one seldom meets a mind keen to inquire into its mysteries and fervent about investigating its ambiguities. Yet what a relief it would be if those with no interest in such nuggets of wisdom left off incriminating with their calumnies those of us who try to unearth them!

Miskawayh's response

49.3 The causes of the friendships that arise between people divide into two high-level categories, namely, essential causes and accidental causes. Each of these subdivides into further categories, and the categories that pertain to amicable relations also apply to the causes of hostile relations. By understanding one of the two opposite terms one can understand the other, as the categories of the one mirror the categories of the other. The essential cause of relations of affection is powerful and stable and, if it extends over time, does not change and endures so long as the individuals do. It is an affinity between two substances stemming either from the specific constitutive elements of their mixture or from the soul and nature.

An affinity that stems from the elemental mixture might be found between two human beings or between two beasts. For a likeness in mixture unites and attracts like beings to each other without the operation of any intention, reflection, or choice, a phenomenon one encounters among many types of beasts, birds, and insects. Similarly, one encounters relations of hostility and antipathy between mixtures that lie far apart from one another without the operation of any intention, reflection, or choice. If you reflect on this, you will find that there are more cases than can be counted.

If we go up a level, from mixtures to simple elements, we encounter 49.4
the same phenomenon—I mean likeness and love, and antipathy and hostility. We are all familiar with the antipathy and animosity between water and fire, and with the way each element flees the other and strives to keep its distance from it, and also with the way each inclines to its own kind, seeking out its like to join itself to. If a harmoniously related mixture with a congruent composition is added, the cause becomes manifest and grows stronger, as it does in the case of magnets and iron and between the two vinegar stones—I mean the one attracted to, and the one repelled by, vinegar. The instances of this principle are so obvious among animals that they do not require detailed enumeration, making our response longer. If the agreement between two bodies by virtue of their substance and specific mixture necessitates affection, it is all the more fitting that agreement between two souls should also necessitate it, if there is affinity and likeness between them.

There are many accidental causes of affection, and some are 49.5
stronger than others. One such cause is habit and familiarity. The second is benefit, or the supposition of benefit. The third is pleasure, the fourth hope, the fifth crafts and practical ends, the sixth doctrinal affiliations and opinions, and the seventh partisanship. The length of time one of these relations lasts is determined by how long the cause abides. Examples of relations of affection based on benefit are the relations between subordinates or servants and their masters, between business partners and

merchants, and between those pursuing profit and those pursuing financial gain. Examples that are based on pleasure are the relations between men and women—though this also involves the affection based on benefit and the affection based on hope, hence its strength and tenacity—and the relations between lovers, between those who eat or drink or travel in each other's company, and the like. Examples of relations of affection based on expectation and hope abound, and perhaps the affection of parents toward their children contains an element of that. For when hope disappears and despair takes hold, parents withdraw from children, affection disappears, and hatred develops. The affection experienced by children is based on benefit, and additionally comes to be based in familiarity. I am certainly not saying that the causes I mentioned as being at work in the affection of parents are exhaustive, for there are other, natural, causes in operation; but there is a large share of this element involved. There are many obvious examples of relations based on crafts and practical purposes—so evident as not to require separate treatment. Examples of relations based on religious creeds and partisan loyalties are equally plain and evident.

49.6 These categories range themselves under the beastly, irascible, and rational powers of the soul. Those that derive from an affinity and likeness between the growing and beastly souls yield the causes of affection for pleasure or benefit. Those that result from a likeness in the irascible soul yield the causes of affection for victory, such as hunting parties, military expeditions, and the other partisan activities in which the irascible power is in operation. The ones that derive from an affinity and likeness in the rational soul yield affection for religion and doctrinal views. These may be found in compound or in isolation. The relation of affection is stronger when they enter into compounds and the causes multiply. The relation of affection is weaker when they appear in isolation, and the length of its duration also depends on this. The isolated accidental causes that derive from the rational soul are the strongest, followed by those that derive from the irascible soul. You can study and clarify the particulars on your own, so that my response does not violate the condition of synoptic presentation. When their causes disappear, so do these relations—none of them endures indefinitely apart from those based on what is substantial and essential, whether in the soul or in nature.

On the Definition and Nature of Knowledge

What is knowledge? What is its definition, and what is its nature? I have seen its proponents seizing upon different views of the topic. One group said: It consists in being cognizant of something the way it is. Others said: It consists in believing something to be the way it is. Yet others said: It consists in affirming something to be way it is. Exponents of the first view were then challenged: If knowledge is defined as being cognizant of something the way it is, cognizance would have to be defined as knowing something the way it is, and cognizance stands as much in need of definition as knowledge does. This answer is careless and misleading. 50.1

Exponents of the second view were challenged: If knowledge is defined as believing something to be the way it is, it is clear that either a thing's being the way it is existed prior to belief and only afterward became an object of belief, or the belief existed prior to the thing's being the way it is. For the way it is is what one is seeking to determine and for the sake of which standards are posited and reflection is required. The authors of the second opinion responded to this objection, adding to their original definition: Knowledge consists in believing something to be the way it is, combined with a repose of the soul and mental satisfaction. It was then objected: The word "belief" (*iʿtiqād*) is a morphological derivative from the term "to make a bond, to fix, to contract" (*ʿaqd*). We say someone "made a bond," that a person "believed," and that the speech in question is a "binding contract." The consonant *t* in *iʿtaqada* is a contingent element reflecting a particular purpose and is not one 50.2

of the root consonants of the word. Thus, the word indicates an act that is related to the binder who has a binding contract, and to the believer who has a belief. Yet the question was not about an act but rather about knowledge, which subsists in itself and is unconnected to the knowing subject. Can you not see that it is connected to him? Suppose you define it in terms of a person's believing a given thing so long as it is connected to him. What then was its reality prior to that point, when it had not yet been connected to him? This is the response of the Muʿtazilites, who are in the habit of making grandiloquent pronouncements, rolling their tongues at length over their words, submitting postulates and making distinct utterances, zealously and passionately defending their side. Those who offered this objection were told in turn: If knowledge consisted in believing something to be the way it is, then since God is knowing, God would believe things to be the way they are. To this they answered: God has no knowledge, for He is knowing through His essence, just as He is powerful through His essence and living through His essence. The objection was then made: The original objection did not concern this side issue, so don't dodge the arrow. If knowledge is defined as believing something to be the way it is, then the knowing subject must be defined as one who believes something to be the way it is. The question of whether this subject has knowledge or not can then be eschewed, and is moot on both views.

50.3 Exponents of the third view received this objection: "Affirmation" is an expression that signifies nothing more than the relation of an act to an agent. Affirmation is the act, and the affirmer is the agent. Yet notions like knowledge, ignorance, astuteness, intelligence, understanding, and discernment do not belong to the class of pure acts, even though they resemble them in the same way that verbs like "to be long," "to die," "to come into being," "to grow old," "to flare up," or "to abate" resemble them. The same consideration is directed against exponents of the fourth view,[53] I mean with regard to their claim that knowledge consists in discerning something to be the way it is. You must know that when defining something, the aim is to attain its essence stripped of accretions and free from extraneous elements, using terms exclusively assigned to it and expressions specially crafted to fit it. As long as the being of the thing is securely fixed in the soul and stands erect before reason, logic must necessarily arrive at its true nature or discern its most exclusive characteristics.

Miskawayh's response

I repudiate every one of these responses and their objections; for the people whose views were reported are unacquainted with the craft of definition, a difficult craft requiring wide knowledge of logic as well as extensive experience. These people think that definition is simply the substitution of one word for another, yet sometimes the word to be defined is clearer than the definition they posit for it. This is invariably how they proceed, except when they draw on the early thinkers and accurately transmit their views, as in the definition of bodies, accidents, and the like. The definitions they have proposed, however, are closer to drivel. Definitions, I say, are based on the proximate genus of the definiendum and the essential differences that constitute it and distinguish it from other things. When a genus and constitutive difference are not found for a given thing, it is only described. Description is based on concomitant properties that bear the greatest resemblance to essential differences. That is why we do not define "knowledge" as the perception of the forms of existents qua existents. Since forms are of two kinds—those that subsist in matter and material substance, and those that are abstracted and free from matter—the perception of the soul is also of two kinds. One is produced through the senses—this is its perception of that which subsists in matter. The other is not produced through the senses, but rather through the spiritual inner eye discussed in some of the earlier questions. Knowledge, as designated through the term *ʿilm*, specifically refers to the perception of the forms that do not subsist in matter. Another concept of knowledge, that designated through the term *maʿrifah*, refers to the perception of the forms that 50.4

are possessed of matter. But as a result of loose linguistic usage, the two terms are employed interchangeably.

50.5 I notice that you formulated objections against responses you judged to be inadequate that you might think also apply to this response, so I felt the need to address them. I therefore say the following. It is in the nature of a definition that it can change places with the term being defined; for the term defined and the definition signify one and the same thing, the only difference between them being that the term signifies in a general manner, whereas the definition signifies in a particularized manner. For instance, "body" might be defined by saying "it is that which is long, wide, and deep" or "it is that which has three dimensions," and this could then be reversed by saying "that which is long, wide, and deep is a body" or "that which has three dimensions is a body." This applies to all other sound definitions. That is why one can say "knowledge is the perception of the forms of existents," and one can also say "the perception of the forms of existents is knowledge," the only difference between the two being that "knowledge" signifies in a general manner, whereas its definition signifies in a particularized manner, as was earlier stated clearly.

50.6 So now it is clear that knowledge consists in perception and in the acquisition of forms. It is clear that these involve being passively affected, for forms are either abstracted and intellectual or material and sensory. When the soul perceives them, it transfers them into itself, so that these forms are imprinted in it, and when this occurs, it acquires their form. This holds true for both sensible and intelligible things. Now that this is clear, it will further be clear that it falls in the class of relational things, for perception is an effect produced in that which is passively affected by that which acts, and so is the acquisition of forms. Things of a relational kind cannot exist in isolation, nor can one "attain their essence stripped of every accretion" as you demanded from your opponent. For they have no being that is "securely fixed within the soul and stands erect before reason" except insofar as they are relational. Thus, the object of knowledge is essentially prior to the knowledge, just as the object of sense perception is essentially prior to the sense perception. The difference between essential priority and accidental and temporal priority has been clarified elsewhere. If the two are temporally simultaneous, and then the soul extracts their forms and establishes them securely within itself. . . .[54]

As for the entailment you forced on your opponent regarding 50.7
God—may He be exalted far above the attributes of created beings—you will know from earlier questions that we do not qualify God as "knowing" in the literal sense that attaches to the qualification "knowing" among us humans, and in no respect do we apply any of His attributes with the meanings they have when applied to other beings. Rather, we follow the religious Law and acquiesce in its commands, and we predicate of Him the most beloved epithets and describe Him using the greatest attributes that we as human beings are familiar with. For we have no means of accessing anything beyond what we know among ourselves, and no way of knowing what He merits in Himself. The sole thing we know about Him in reality is the pure fact that He is. Furthermore, everything that can be indicated through reason or through the senses has been created by Him. This being the case, if we find the religious Law sanctioning the use of names and attributes deemed praiseworthy and exalted among human beings, we accede to the command of the Law and apply them without referring them to the literal meanings known through language and the definitions acquired through it. This is a topic that I briefly touched on earlier, and I apprised you of the type of difficulty it involves. God is the one who grants success and assistance, and strength comes through Him alone.

On why people make apparently false statements when expressing admiration

51.1 Why is it that when a person sees a pretty picture or hears a melodious tune, he says, "By God, I've never seen or heard anything like that before," even though he has in fact heard better, and seen prettier, things?

Miskawayh's response

51.2 From the perspective of jurisprudence or linguistic necessity, this is neither perjury nor error. For no single thing resembles another absolutely, and we only say that "*this* is like *that*" in a qualified manner. It might be like it in terms of its substance, quantity, or quality, or one of the other categories. Or again, it might resemble it in two or more of these respects; but resemblance in all respects is impossible. This is why it is correct for a person to say, "By God, I've never see anything like it." From another perspective—and this is a natural perspective—you know that the senses are in a state of flux that derives from the flux of their objects. When the senses fix on a form and it then passes away and another appears, the new form occupies the senses, fixing itself in the place of the first. So what is present to the senses is only what has produced an effect on them, not what has passed away. The first form has been realized in the memory, and in another power; but the two may often not occur together, or the memory may not present itself, so what the person says will be based on the present moment and the presence or absence of memory.

On why people take pleasure in contemplating beautiful forms

Why does one take pleasure in beautiful forms? What is the evident rapture, the lingering look, the passion that seizes the heart, the ardor that enthralls the soul, the thoughts that drive out sleep, the images that swim before a person's eyes? Do all these things belong to the effects of nature, to the happenings of the soul, to the incitements of reason, or to the apportionments of the spirit? Or are they rather bereft of causes, and matters of mere senseless talk? Can phenomena that possess such dominance and conditions that exercise such an effect possibly exist by way of idle sport? 52.1

Miskawayh's response

The reason one takes pleasure in the form of human beings is due to a perfection in the bodily members and a harmonious relation between the parts of the body that are received with satisfaction in the soul. My response addresses what interests you in asking this question, oriented toward the human form that arouses passion, to the exclusion of other forms. So I say as follows. Nature imitates the acts and effects of the soul, imparting forms to matter and material objects according to their receptivity and the degree of their susceptibility. In doing so, it mimics the action of the soul on it—that is, on nature; yet the soul, for its part, is simple.[55] So nature receives complete noble forms from the soul, but when it seeks to engrave those forms on matter, material objects fail to receive them completely and fully on account of their poor susceptibility, and because they lack the power to grasp and secure the complete forms imparted to them. This failure on the part of matter can be sometimes great and sometimes small, and how well it responds to what the soul introduces into it will depend on its power to receive the forms. Thus, matter that agrees with a form receives the engraving completely 52.2

and correctly and in a way that resembles what nature has received from the soul. Matter that does not agree with it behaves in the opposite manner.

52.3 An example is the way nature produces flat noses, blue eyes, and reddish hair from matter when human beings are being shaped in the womb, in accordance with the receptivity of the matter at its disposal. This is not because it aims at deficient forms, for it always aims at what is most excellent. But moist matter will only consent to receive what is congruent with it. For black eyes and high-ridged noses are forms that require matter to have a proper balance between pliant moistness and firm dryness, and cannot be manifested by moist matter, just as a seal cannot be produced from molten wax. Sometimes the matter throws up impediments from the direction of quantity rather than quality, so that the physical constitution is not configured in the best manner. This is the case with the hair of the head and with eyelashes and eyebrows, for if there is a deficient amount of matter or the qualities are imbalanced, these are not engraved as they ought to be. Nature thus produces from it what is possible and achievable, and the ensuing form is not welcomed in the soul, for it does not correspond to the perfection the soul contains. Let's continue to use a clay seal as a basis for reflection: If the quantity of clay falls short of the amount needed for the stamp, or if it is dry, moist, or rough, the form of the stamp becomes deficient and it does not receive the engraving completely and perfectly.

52.4 The case of agreeable matter is the opposite, for it receives completely what nature imparts to it, and is engraved in a way that is sound and harmonious and that resembles what is in the soul. So the soul rejoices when it sees it, because it agrees with what the soul contains and corresponds with what it imparted to nature. Crafts imitate nature; so when a craftsman fashions a statue out of agreeable matter, and the latter receives the natural form completely and accurately, the craftsman is overjoyed and feels a sense of pride and self-satisfaction on account of the veracity of his work, and of his having actualized his potentiality in a way that agrees with what is in his soul and with what nature contains. Something similar applies to the relationship between nature and the soul, for in imitating nature, crafts stand in the same relation to nature as nature stands to the soul in imitating it. Moreover, it is characteristic of the soul that when it sees a beautiful form whose members are harmoniously related in terms of shape, measurement, color, and other features—a form that it receives with satisfaction and that agrees with what it imparted to nature—it longs to be united with it. It thus extracts it from matter, fixes it securely within itself, and becomes identified with it, as it does in the case of intelligible things. This is an act that belongs to it through its essence, and that it is driven toward, longs for, and is perfected by; yet it is ennobled through intelligible things, not through sensible things. When the soul does that and conceives a longing for natural things and natural bodies, nature seeks to bring about a union between bodies like the one the soul seeks in relation to abstract forms. Yet it has no means of achieving this, because bodies cannot join themselves to other bodies by way of union, only by way of external contact; hence, it experiences a longing for the external contact which represents the type of bodily union that lies within its power to achieve. This is a gross delusion and grave error on the part of the soul, for it demotes itself from a nobler state to a baser one, assuming a natural form for which it itself served as the source and original model, and thus failing to attain the intelligible noble forms that cause it to be elevated to the highest rank and the greatest happiness.

I have mentioned that which is universal and essential, and which 52.5
proceeds in a natural manner encompassed by craft and precisely determined by rules. The particular and accidental pleasure one might take—I mean, when a certain individual takes pleasure in something on the basis of a certain humoral mixture—is also due to a certain affinity, but it has the status of something individual, and individual things are infinite in number, and so cannot be encompassed by any craft or ordered by any rules. What one needs

to know is that every humoral mixture far from the balanced state has relations of affinity with things specific to it, while it conflicts with the humoral mixture that lies at the other extreme of the balanced state, so that what one person finds pleasant the other finds repugnant, and vice versa. The same applies to things determined by customs and different modes of perception. One sees this in the different kinds of food and drink that people take pleasure in. For humoral mixtures that lie far from the balanced state have an affinity for strange flavors and take delight in uncommon and extraordinary things. A broader survey of the phenomena will reveal to you all manner of extraordinary and uncommon things relating to smells, sounds, and the other senses.

On why people are more adept at counseling others than at managing their own affairs

53.1 Why is that when men of discrimination, ability, and intelligence are approached for counsel, they come out with wondrous subtleties, splitting hairs in half and outrunning the very clouds in the sky, yet when they turn to their own affairs and are called to be their own supporters and ponder the pursuit of their own advantages, they become like a mirage on a plain and express bland views, incurring shame from those who mentioned them as bywords for cunning and subtlety, and advertised the soundness of their judgment? What befalls and afflicts them? What alters them and causes their diminution? What distinguishes them with such a characteristic and brings them to such a result?

Miskawayh's response

53.2 The reason is twofold. One is the love human beings have for themselves and their fear of having error imputed to them or of committing mistakes, which induces a sense of bewilderment and confusion. The other is their susceptibility to blind desire. Blind desire is the enemy of reason, and error is always the adjunct of blind desire. When blind desire strikes, reason departs, and when reason departs, no good remains. Human beings are ever captive to blind desire, and blind desire makes them see wrong as right and error as sound judgment. Men of excellence and distinction are aware of this about themselves, and do not feel secure against the possibility that their judgment regarding their own affairs might be the result of how blind desire, rather than reason, makes them see things; so their thinking falters and their judgment regarding their own affairs becomes impaired. When offering their judgment on other people's affairs, by contrast, they are free from both conditions, so they judge things based on reason rather than blind desire, and are not led astray by self-love or fear of error. Hence, the judgment they deliver on other people's affairs is sound and as straight as an arrow. Sometimes they are subject to blind desire with regard to others' affairs, and then are affected by the same error that affects them in their own case. This demonstrates the soundness of our account concerning why they get matters right in other people's affairs and fall into error in their own. The judgments of rational people regarding their own affairs can be sound, and their errors can be minimized, if they place themselves on guard and steer clear of blind desire, except that people have been naturally formed to love themselves and in subtler contexts to confuse blind desire for sound judgment. In such cases, the mistakes they commit are excusable and they can be spared from their consequences.

On why the sight of open wounds provokes horror and fascination

Why is it that people recoil in horror from an open wound, 54.1
shrinking from looking at it and from drawing near it, repulsing

all images of it from their mind, and trying to distract themselves from it with other things, yet the more violently they shrink from it, the more violent their fascination with it becomes? And what about the following? For this is another subcategory within the earlier category of wonder. To continue the question: The person who treats the wound comes into contact with it through his eyes as he looks at it, through his hands as he treats it, and through his tongue as he speaks of it. Do you think the reason he can do so is the fact that this is customary and habitual for him, having had long experience with looking at, and coming into contact with, wounds? Or is it because he needs to earn a living, meet his needs, look after his dependents, and defray expenses? If it is because of custom and habit, how did matters stand with him at the beginning of this custom and habit? If it is because of his profession, how did he manage to resist his natural inclinations and discipline himself in such a way? Is it possible for someone to grow habituated to something that is neither in his nature nor his habit, and, with perseverance, to become like a person born in that condition who has experienced it his whole life?

Miskawayh's response

54.2 Philosophical inquiries have established that the soul is one in reality, and that multiplicity is only introduced into it through the multiplicity of individuals. This being so, when a person sees another suffering from something unnatural, such as a wound, an imperfection in his physical build, or a deficiency in his form, he responds as he would in his own case, as though he were looking at his own soul and body. For the soul in the one case is the same as the soul in the other, so such a response is only proper. His fascination with it and its perpetual presence in his memory are due to the fact that when the soul receives a form, it extracts it from its matter and fixes it securely within itself, binding it through the power of memory. The soul does not resemble a mirror, which, confronted by an object, receives its form as long as that object stands before it, and loses the form when the object disappears; nor does it receive forms the way the eye does. For these bodies are natural, and they receive the form of physical objects accidentally. Souls, by contrast, receive forms in a nobler and loftier modality, and they retain those forms securely fixed even when their bearers are no longer in front of the eyes.

There has already been some discussion of this point in these questions, and at that juncture we provided an account of how the soul rapidly receives the form of an object through the power of imagination and how this form endures afterward in the power of memory, so that it sees it when asleep and when awake. For we can summon at will the forms of our fathers and grandfathers and the cities we have lived in as though they were standing right before us, even if they are absent or no longer exist. An explanation of the reason for this and a more detailed account of the topic can be found in the appropriate sources. The person who treats the wound you asked about, who has grown habituated to it through custom, can do so due to the recurrence of the form and because the act has become like a fixed trait for him. As we clarified earlier, when the soul is recurrently exposed to particular forms, these forms produce something stable in it that is akin to an inherent characteristic. And we noted that if this were not so, we would not be able to educate the young or to inculcate fine habits into children during the early stages of their development. For the soul acquires a familiarity with acts that are performed consecutively and without cease, regardless of whether they are good or bad. When a person continues to perform them, they become a stable state and an acquired possession, and it becomes hard to eliminate them. 54.3

On why people love the present world; on whether the religious Law can conflict with nature

55.1 What causes love for the present world? We know that God says, «No indeed; but you love the hasty world».[56] And the poet says,

> The soul is rapt in the love of the present world.[57]

This has fomented strife, fermented change, plunged reason into confusion, and created the need for prophets and political governance and for restraints and admonitions. If love for the present world is given with our natural disposition, ingrained in the material of our being, and beaten into our mold, how is it possible to banish and remove it? How can divinely imposed obligations conflict with the demands of nature? Doesn't the religious Law reinforce nature? Doesn't religion serve as a foundation for political governance? Doesn't reason rule in favor of religious devotion? Isn't the next world comparable to this one? What view should one take before this abyss? How can one cogently reproach someone who loves what was rendered lovable to him and what was made the exclusive object of his ardor in the same way that he was created male or female, tall or short, blind or sighted, boorish or gallant? If blame is disarmed for one of these sets, it will be disarmed for both, and if it clings to one, it will cling to both. This is an inquiry that leads to questions about compulsion and free choice, two subjects requiring well-defined inquiry and renewed consideration, for the facts leave the mind divided and prevent one from satisfying one's desires and attaining one's ends in inquiry.

Miskawayh's response

55.2 The "present world" refers to the senses and to the pleasures of eating, drinking, voiding, and resting that form their adjuncts. It is the beastly soul to which these sensible things specifically pertain. You should understand that this soul is with us from the beginning of our development and from when we are born, so we acquire a powerful attachment to it through the long, continuous passage of time. That is why its power is so manifest, why it dominates so strongly, and why it exercises such a controlling force. It is only at a later stage that we look to the soul that discriminates through the power of reason. Its effects make themselves progressively manifest, and it gains in strength when one reaches middle age and attains one's full vigor and physical maturity. In order for that to happen, we need to mobilize ourselves in resistance to that other soul, denting its force and attenuating its power through intense effort and sustained perseverance, depending on the power it has, the mastery it enjoys over us, and the attachment we feel toward it. We also need to strengthen the rational soul by acceding to its rule, by giving it authority over us, and by implementing its resolutions. This is why we find it difficult to accept the rule of the latter and easy to accept the rule of the former soul.

Our response to your question "How can divinely imposed obli- 55.3
gations conflict with the demands of nature?" is as follows. It is in the nature of the beastly soul to submit to the rational soul, and to be restrained by the latter's commands. Were this not in its innate disposition and its natural grain—that is, being receptive to instruction and issuing its specific acts in accordance with what reason commands—this would, I swear, be an imposition of obligations that conflict with nature. Yet nobody desires to eradicate this power completely. Rather, we demand that it agree to order its acts on the basis of what reason prescribes; and, as we have said, it is naturally disposed to accept this kind of instruction. The cases mentioned by way of analogy—tallness and shortness, and so on—do not conform to the same principle, for instruction plays no role in these things, and what is involved is rather an effect that matter receives from its giver depending on its substrate, and it is not possible to oppose this in any way or through any cause. To elaborate, the moisture

contained by matter is extended and drawn upward through heat, this being the direction in which heat moves. The tallness thus produced depends on the matter, the amount of moisture acted upon, and the heat acting upon it, and the way it is in fact manifested cannot be otherwise. The distinction between the two types of things you proposed to fuse is now clear, and the reason for the love of the present world and the value of the discipline God provides to people through religion and different forms of instruction is revealed, in a succinct and clear answer to the question.

On why people take their own lives

56.1 I wonder: What causes a person to take his own life when failures crowd him, when poverty besieges him, when circumstances defy his power and capacity, when his demands and desires meet with closed doors, when passionate love oppresses him and shows itself recalcitrant to cure? What does he hope to achieve through this course of action? What is his aim in pursuing what he proposes? What looms before him and consumes his good judgment, rendering him oblivious to a spirit he knows intimately, a soul he loves passionately, and a life he holds dear? What is it about nonexistence that filters into his imagination and snatches him from the grip of experience and delivers him to the cruel shifts of fate?

Miskawayh's response

56.2 Human beings are a composite of three powers of the soul, and stand in the midst of these powers, as it were, pulled now by one, now by another. The direction in which their acts incline depends on the relative strength of a given power. Thus, sometimes it is the irascible power that dominates them, and if they are imbued by it and their acts incline toward it, their powers appear as though they were exhausted by anger, with the other powers receding from view, as if they did not possess them. Similarly, if the appetitive power rages, the effects of the other powers recede from view. Human beings are at their optimal and most judicious state when they are dominated by the rational power, for it is this that exercises rational discrimination and disposes all the other powers so that their acts emerge in accordance with its dictates and prescriptions. Human beings then occupy the eminent rank that God has prepared and willed for them. If this is so, we should not think it strange that some of those powers should be stirred up when human beings encounter some difficulty or when a door closes in the face of something they desire, so that an act issues from them that is neither entailed by reflection nor mandated by discrimination, as a result of the fact that the effect of the rational power recedes from view and the other powers gain the upper hand.

You can witness this firsthand in the different states that visit you. 56.3
For at various times you find your soul experiencing certain states, which it chooses and pursues, refusing counsel and right-minded command. Later, when you emerge from the fit that had come over you in that state, you are amazed at the acts that issued from you. You rebuke yourself for them, as if it were someone else who had chosen and pursued them. Things continue this way until the moment arrives when once again that first power stirs up in you, and you are not prevented from succumbing to the same thing by your previous experience of yourself and the admonitions you gave yourself. This is because we are composed of different powers of the soul. It is only after strenuous treatment, extensive reform, and long practice that human beings can isolate a single power and perform the acts of all the others on the basis of the one that is most excellent and noble. For persistence in a habit and implementation of a resolve over a long, uninterrupted period of time produces a trait of character, and this exercises the controlling force and becomes dominant. That is why we command the young to comport themselves well, and why we hold them to the principles of conduct instituted by revealed laws and commanded by wisdom.

56.4 Your question does not require, and the present space does not permit, a more in-depth exposition of this point and an account of its causes. Should someone doubt what we have said and suppose that human beings, composites of these three powers that they are, ought to abide in a single state composed from those powers, as is the case with all other entities that form blends and composites of natural dispositions, they should realize that their analogy is unsound. For the powers of the soul in human beings have their own essential movements that increase and decrease, and also external conditions that stir them up. The same does not apply to the powers of natural entities. Ponder the matter, and you will find that things stand as our synopsis has indicated and outlined.

On a Philosophical Puzzle Relating to the Act of Suicide

57.1 I asked one of our teachers in Baghdad about a man who had been walking along the bridge when suddenly a number of armed officers surrounded him and set about hauling him to prison. Seeing a razor blade gleaming in a fancy shop, he seized it in the twinkling of an eye and slit his throat with it; he was soon lying in a pool of his own blood, having breathed his last and left the land of the living. I ask: Who killed this man? If we reply that he killed himself, then is the one who did the killing the same as the one who was killed, or is the one who did the killing different from the one who was killed? If the one is different from the other, then how did they come to be conjoined in view of this disjunction? If the two are the same, how did they come to be disjoined in view of this conjunction? I have appended this question to the previous topic because it tends in the same direction and treads in its footsteps.

Miskawayh's response

This question seems to be premised on the notion that human beings are a single thing that involves no multiplicity, and from this perspective the aporia gains in force. Yet this misgiving disappears once it is clear that human beings possess and are composed of many powers, that they incline sometimes toward one power and sometimes toward another, and that their acts also depend on the power toward which they incline and by which they are dominated, as we showed in the previous question. 57.2

I respond to his question "How did they come to be conjoined in view of this disjunction?" as follows. The reason for this is that the Creator knew that this being composed of a soul and a body requires things for its sustenance, such as food and the like, that its life can only be sustained through matter that it can only attain through movement and striving, and that there are many things that hinder and prevent access to it. He consequently gave it a power to use to attain its needs and repulse whatever opposes its needs, so that it might survive. It is in the nature of this power to be stirred up and roused more than it ought on certain occasions, and less than it ought on others. These two conditions involve defects: Rashness is the concomitant of the first, cowardice of the second. Through their power of discrimination and reason, human beings are capable of using this power in the right manner and of training it so that it is only roused and stirred up at the right time, in the right measure, and for the right objects. When they achieve this rank, they are courageous and praiseworthy, and they are as God willed them to be in creating them. 57.3

The question still harbors a possible point of doubt, for someone might ask: If the person who kills himself performs that action in accordance with the irascible power, then he is courageous, and the courageous person is laudable. Yet we know that the person who does this to himself is blameworthy. So how do things stand with regard to him, and where is praiseworthy courage to be located? To this I respond: Be assured, this act is indeed among the effects 57.4

of the irascible power, but it is an expression of its defective state and of how it falls short of what is right, not an expression of how it goes beyond it or of the balanced state we have termed "courage." For the person who feels fear about something that happens to him, such as poverty or some adversity, and who does not face up to it and greet it with firm resolve and full strength of mind, is a coward and a weakling. This cowardice leads him to say, "I shall relieve myself from the burden of enduring this hardship that has come upon me." This is the cringing attitude and weakness that is termed "cowardice." We have mentioned that the irascible power may sometimes be slack and fall short of what is right. It then involves a defect and a failing; this is not called "courage," nor is the person commended or praised.

On moral change and acting out of character

58.1 How does it come about that at a certain moment in time the hardened hypocrite turns sincere, the person steeped in doubt conceives certainty, the one slumbering awakens, and the one given to perfidy becomes well-intentioned? How does it likewise come about that the person who has always been sincere turns hypocritical and the one who has made a habit of integrity provides grounds for suspicion? Along the same lines, how is it that the person who has kept faith for sixty years commits betrayal, and the one who has been a veteran of betrayal for sixty years abstains from it? What is the meaning of these disparate happenings and singular phenomena? We similarly find that the liar sometimes tells the truth though it serves no objective and the truth teller lies for no definite reason, and it doesn't generally turn out to be the case that the former tells the truth for the sake of attaining a benefit and the latter tells a lie for the sake of repelling harm.

Miskawayh's response

This question is closely related to the previous two, and the response it invites is closely related to the response given to those questions. For hypocrisy, good will, and the other things he mentioned in his question are effects of the rational soul. It is evident that this soul also has its state of illness and its state of health. When it is in a balanced state with respect to its other powers, it is healthy, and when it departs from this balanced state, it is ill. If it departs from a balanced state at one time, it is not impossible that it should return to it at another. Just as truthfulness, good will, sound reflection, and the proper disposition of actions according to the circumstances represent its health and balanced state, their contraries represent its illness and departure from a balanced state. Yet we certainly do not concede that it tells the truth at one time and lies at another for no reason, or for the sake of repelling some harm. On the contrary, it always supposes that its action is right on account of something it sees in it. This supposition may be misguided and mistaken. Yet it is inconceivable that the soul should perform that action without being motivated by some desire and without aiming at what it mistakenly sees in it. 58.2

On the meaning of a certain saying concerning God's beneficence

What did the scholar mean when he said, "God extended His benefits to all people, but He did not extend the surplus of His beneficence to all?" How could one expound the meaning of this statement? By what means could one determine its truth? Is there something that promotes the welfare of people that God omitted and did not liberally dispense ab initio without express solicitation? How could this be, when He initiated the bestowal of benefits before there was merit and desert, and when He created people 59.1

without a need for their existence? Supposing one said, "Without being avaricious, He afflicted people with need and then withheld what they needed." One ought to object: One should not thus deny His munificence with regard to manifest matters because uncertainty adheres to matters of speculation; it is possible that the hidden realm of things He has withheld includes things that may happen but that are unknown, and permeated by His providential disposition they might unfold in accordance with His wisdom in a manner that cannot be denied or gainsaid.

Miskawayh's response

59.2 The statement "God extended His benefits to all people, but He did not extend the surplus of His beneficence to all" is a remark made in the rhetorical style, and its meaning is correct if one disregards the labored feel imparted to it by its author. A statement uttered by Christ makes this point plainer. For it is reported, in a translation from his language to ours, that he said, "Do not worry and do not ask, What shall we eat, what shall we drink, and what shall we wear? For God has granted these things to all people in the measure of their need, but they desire surplus. And know that not everyone who prays to God will see the face of God, but only those who have fully attained His satisfaction through righteousness."[58] These are Christ's words as translated and reported.

59.3 Let us interpret these remarks—that is, let us clarify the first remarks whose meaning you inquired about: The clear and manifest benefits given to all people consist of the gift of life and the removal of the impediments that block access to the things necessary for its preservation. For its preservation depends on innate heat, and the preservation of innate heat depends on aeration—which expels the smoke generated by the heat and the greasy moisture from the locus the heat adheres to—and on the replacement of the dry air in that smoke with air that is moist, salubrious, and agreeable to the matter of that heat. This is achieved through an instrument for blowing air that resembles blacksmiths' bellows, namely, the lung and the respiratory organ in all beings that have a heart and a locus for this heat, and what is akin to the lung in other animals that have no heart and no need to aerate the heat blazing in the greasy moist matter. Furthermore, the removal of impediments applies to the very air that constitutes the matter of that heat, and then to the moisture, without which, given the heat's consumption of it, the quantity of it found in the body would be depleted—I am referring to water.

These are the elements necessary for life, the lack of which, even 59.4
for the blink of an eye, would lead to the destruction of life. The removal of impediments with respect to them is clear, abundant, and manifest, and extends to all animals. The subordinate elements necessary for the longevity and well-being of living creatures—such as the existence of arteries and other blood vessels, of organs for obtaining nourishment, of powers for attracting, transforming, changing, retaining, and repelling, and of powers with a presiding role and others subservient to them (the presiding powers always govern and put the subservient ones to service, while the subservient ones constantly offer their obedience and service)—has all been expounded clearly in the craft of medicine and is so evident that there is no need to broach the topic again. Finally, there is the choice that living beings have between one type of aliment and another, which goes beyond what is necessary for their preservation. For they have also been granted, in accordance with their need, a power that enables them to make choices and to secure what they need. The entirety of this has been extended to all people, and none of it has been withheld from them.

The "surplus of beneficence" consists in proximity to the 59.5
Creator, and this can only be achieved through striving, desire, and application. God has also pointed the way to this, and it is left to human beings to direct themselves toward it. For the surplus of beneficence is not held back from them; indeed, the door lies open, and the barrier has been lifted. But people set up barriers for themselves, and hold back from application and desire and from pursuing the method and pathway pointed out to them

and recommended to their desire. This they do by preoccupying themselves with the superfluities of their subsistence, which they have no need for as living beings, and by inclining toward the pleasures of the senses, which hinder them from attaining their object, their end, and their ultimate happiness. For the present context, this suffices as a response to the question you have posed. God alone grants success.

On why noble-minded people love cleanliness

60.1 What is the secret behind the fact that noble-minded people prefer cleanliness, love ritual purity, and pursue neatness? But if that is so, what good is there in the Prophet's statement, "Shabbiness is a part of faith"? A certain ascetic said, "Frugality is a part of nobility, and opulence a part of prodigality." I heard a Sufi say, "When the heart of a Sufi grows pure, it stands against coarseness inured." Taken as it stands, this remark requires some qualification, but the Sufi stayed silent after pronouncing it. I heard a philosopher say, "When the heart is purified, evil is nullified." While this makes for an elegant turn of phrase, the reason for it is elusive, and its proof straggles behind.

Miskawayh's response

60.2 First, we must discuss the cause of cleanliness and filthiness so as to clarify the meaning of each notion, and then examine the repulsion human beings feel toward filth and the attraction they feel toward purity. I therefore say the following. If the four elements do not enter into heterogeneous mixtures, human beings do not feel repelled by them and do not term them "filth." The sense of repulsion is aroused only by certain kinds of mixtures. We find upon examining the mixtures that when these four elements enter a specific kind of blend based on a certain harmonious relation, they achieve a balanced state and produce the human mixture. This mixture has a certain compass, and that which does not depart from it is a human being in form and mixture, whereas if it deviates from this mixture and departs from it, it is not a human being. Its departure and deviation must be oriented more toward one of the four elements than to the others. If it inclines in the direction of heat and the remaining elements stand close to the human mixture or remain in the same state, the extent of its departure in the direction of heat is examined. If the departure is very great, the mixture constitutes a lethal poison for human beings. If it falls below that level, the mixture's noxiousness for human beings depends on the degree of its departure from a balanced state as regards heat. This is not called filth. The same applies when it departs in the direction of dryness and coldness. For if these run to excess and oppose the balanced mixture to the point that they destroy it, they constitute poisons. If they do not destroy that mixture, they harm it and displace it from its form. No matter whether the thing that departs from the human mixture is a plant or an animal, it is affected by what we have mentioned.

This is how matters stand when single elements run to excess 60.3
while the others remain balanced. The departure of two of them from the balanced state also admits of different varieties and occurs in different ways. Yet when moisture in particular increases to excess, or when heat increases to excess, this mixture produces a state that is called "putridity"; this when heat is unable to dissipate the moisture, so that it conflicts with the balanced mixture from this respect. As a result, human beings find it repugnant and feel a sense of aversion toward it, be it encountered in an animal or an inanimate object. This sense of repulsion and repugnance comes in different varieties, depending on the way in which the corresponding mixture departs from the balanced state. I will give you an example. Since the mixture of human beings is close to the mixture of horses and there is an affinity between them, they feel positively disposed

toward each other on this account. Yet human beings feel repelled by this mixture and find it repugnant if it grows distant and results in dirt, worms, dung beetles, and flies. For these kinds of animals are made of putridities resulting from the increase of moisture and the decrease of heat, as we have described, and are distant from the mixture of human beings.

60.4 The same applies to the superfluities of the body. Once nature has seized upon nourishment, extracted what is suitable, sifted it out, gathered it in its receptacles, and gradually assimilated it into the body; and once it has rejected whatever is unsuitable, sifting it out in the same manner, and gathering it in other receptacles—namely, the organs of excretion—the part sifted out and stripped of all suitable elements comes to be at the farthest remove from similarity, and is affected by a dominance of moisture and a decrease of heat that causes it to become putrid. As a result, human beings find it repulsive and repugnant, and wish to be relieved of it. This is true for all superfluities filtered out of the body. It is unsuitable because it has all been rejected and sifted out by nature—and whatever is unsuitable arouses repugnance. This is called "filth," yet so long as it remains within the body and has not extruded from it, it is tolerated by necessity. Once it extrudes, we feel disgusted by it and find it repugnant and loathsome. These are what are called "filth" and "squalor" by nature. There are other things that human beings find repulsive through habit and also become comfortable with through habit, but they have nothing to do with the topic we are considering in this question.

60.5 The Prophet's statement, "Shabbiness is a part of faith," has nothing at all to do with the type of thing we were just discussing. A person with a shabby appearance hates filth and loves cleanliness, and does not disagree with you concerning any of the aspects of purity you value. If he does disagree with you, it has nothing to do with his shabby appearance, but is rather in the way someone without a shabby appearance might disagree with you. The same applies to the state of austerity that was the subject of the remarks by the Sufi you reported. These notions represent different topics from those we were considering, and their discussion is connected to the notions of temperance, contentment, and moderation, virtues examined in depth elsewhere. The statement, "When the heart of a Sufi grows pure, it stands against coarseness inured," and the statement, "When the heart is purified, evil is nullified" refer to the different grades of certainty and the different ranks the soul may attain with respect to knowledge. Upon my life, when someone has attained a certain rank with respect to proximity to His Creator, evil has been nullified in him and he has been inured against coarseness. An analytical account and exposition of these topics would run to great length—our discussion has brought out what is sufficient and adequate to the purpose.

On the merits of singing versus playing musical instruments

What is better, singing or playing musical instruments? And who is better and nobler, the one who sings or the one who plays a musical instrument? 61.1

Miskawayh's response

Music is a form of knowledge that may be conjoined to practice, and its practitioner is called a "musician." As knowledge, it is one of the four mathematical sciences that the student of philosophy must receive a degree of instruction in. As practice, it does not number among these sciences, but consists in the production of well-proportioned notes and rhythmic patterns calculated to move the soul using an appropriate instrument. That instrument may either be part of the body or extraneous to the body. If it is part of the body, it consists in natural organs that were designed as a means for carrying out different tasks and are ordinarily put to other uses. 61.2

If it is extraneous to nature, it consists in artificial instruments that were designed as a means for carrying out the production of notes and rhythmic patterns. When natural instruments are put to uses other than those for which they were designed, it is in their nature to suffer disturbance and be displaced from their shapes, undergoing mutation and change. It is wrong and deserves censure if the person who puts them to that use seeks to obtain vile and defective things. If he seeks in doing so to make the effects of knowledge manifest to the senses, so that they clearly discern the proportional relations composed in the soul, and to make manifest the wisdom involved, this is admirable and deserves approval, even if it involves a departure from what is customary and familiar in the view of some people.

61.3 But the objective people have in practicing music today is to arouse vicious appetites and to help the beastly soul prevail over the rational, discriminating soul, so that it may partake of its pleasures without being ordered and licensed by reason. If one pursues that by means of natural instruments, one inevitably incorporates appropriate words, which are used to combine the specific notes with the specific rhythmic pattern. If, in addition, these words are cast in erotic verse deploying the deceitful and distorting artifices of poetry, their power to move the soul becomes composite and multifaceted, and one's impulses gain force and grow strong enough to do away with temperance and arouse lust and covetousness; because poetry alone has these effects. These are causes of evil in the world, and any cause of evil is itself evil. This is why it is abhorred by reason, forbidden by the religious Law, and prevented by political power.

61.4 If the instrument is extraneous to the body, the best kind is that which makes the least use of bodily members and allows the human shape and stature to remain in its proper form without suffering disturbance; it is simultaneously more amenable to displaying the science of composition, more capable of distinguishing notes, and more successful at articulating the true nature of those notes that are similar, but not related by harmony as determined by the science of music.[59] We know of no better instrument for this than the one designated as the "lute," for its four strings are mounted in correspondence with the four natural elements, and its fastened frets have proportional relations that are suited to the task of distinguishing notes.[60] There is no note in the world that it cannot be used to reproduce and play. We have only heard reports about the Greek organ, and have only seen pictures of it.[61] What al-Kindī and others have said about it has not helped it emerge from potentiality to actuality. Even if the instrument were to be constructed, it would require a degree of skill on the part of its operator that would be impossible, or very difficult, to find. When the lute first emerged into actuality, it required a skillful person to play it, and knowledge alone was not enough to play it without practice and skill. The same would hold true were this instrument to emerge into actuality. That is why we refrain from declaring it superior, but categorically affirm that the lute is superior.

On why some people master different subjects more easily than others

62.1 Why do some people master different forms of knowledge with facility, with the submissive cooperation of their desires and the ready acquiescence of their nature, while others cannot get to grips with a given subject, even though they wear out their minds, pass sleepless nights, frequent intellectual gatherings, and spend a long time studying with others? The first person may live in penury, whereas the second may enjoy ample means. Some have said it is a matter of different gifts, others that it is a matter of different lots in life, others still that it is a matter of different natures, dispositions that make one incline to some things, souls that make one decline others. According to others, it is a matter of supernal influences, sublunar receptions, and celestial conjunctions, whereas someone else said: God knows best what He has created and what He has done, and all we can do is undertake inquiry and take instruction. If they lead us to clarity, that is a blessing that neither human beings nor jinn can give sufficient thanks for. If they conduce to obscurity, that is a situation that human beings can accept without shame.

Miskawayh's response

62.2 Even though the soul is noble and lofty in its essence, the acts that issue from it depend on the instruments at its disposal. Thus, if a carpenter's axe is missing and he uses the borer or saw instead, his act—which requires an axe to be accomplished—cannot issue in a perfect way, and he cannot fully realize the forms of the material he is hewing—not because of any remissness on his part, but because he lacks the necessary instrument. So it is with the soul when it is galvanized to seek some understanding and roused to pursue some knowledge and fails to find the instruments it requires. When this happens, it is in the same position as the carpenter in our example. For some forms of knowledge require a powerful imagination, and the imagination depends on a certain balance in the mixture of the anterior ventricle of the brain. Other forms of knowledge require sound thought, and sound thought is achieved through a certain balance in the mixture of the medial ventricle of the brain. Yet other forms of knowledge require an excellent and sound memory, and excellent memory arises through a certain balance in the posterior ventricle of the brain. Some of these mixtures require a certain degree of moisture for their specific balance, while others require a certain degree of dryness, and the same applies to the remaining two qualities.

62.3 As these ventricles are contiguous, each communicates its quality to the other. Thus, the moisture of one provides moisture to the other on account of their contiguity, even if the latter does not require moisture for its specific balance. That is why it is rare to find a person who combines the three excellences together—namely, an accurate imagination, sound thought, and an excellent memory. If one of these dominates, the ease with which a person takes to the form of knowledge corresponding to that mixture will depend on what he was endowed with and what capacity he was given. A person who lacks balance in all of them will lack the ability to benefit from any and all forms of knowledge. Sometimes the excellences may be realized in a sound mixture, but their bearer neglects his soul, the way a carpenter might have the instrument he needs but fail to use it out of laziness and a preference for comfort and ease, and because he is distracted by amusements and idle activities. This is the kind of person who deserves blame for squandering his lot—he loses his soul. God said about him: «Surely the losers are they who lose themselves».[62] The person who uses the instrument available to him to the extent of his ability and who realizes its excellence according to his capacity, by contrast, is exempt from blame. That does not depend on ampleness of means or poverty, but rather on the presence of the relevant instrument and a propitious mixture and, beyond that, on a person's level of application.

Therefore, those who say that this is a matter of different gifts, 62.4
lots, natures, supernal influences, or the like speak truthfully, and none of their views you have quoted are false. Each points to a sound aspect and a manifest ground, even though all of the aspects and grounds are to be traced back to a single ungrounded Ground, a first Cause that is the cause of every other, an Originator of all, and a Creator of everything. We ask Him to supply us with His grace, beseech Him to place us beyond reproach, ask Him to make us thankful, and commit our affairs to Him. He is our sufficiency and our master, and in Him our trust reposes—an excellent master is He and an excellent ally!

On the nature of physiognomy

63.1 What is physiognomy, and what does one seek to obtain through it? Is it sound, or is it sound at some times and not others, or for one individual and not another?

Miskawayh's response

63.2 Physiognomy is a craft that seeks to unearth people's character traits and the acts that flow from character traits by means of the elemental mixtures, natural appearances, and attendant movements. It is a sound craft grounded in strong principles and firm premises, and its possessor and practitioner must school himself in three principles in order to master it and rule on its basis; if he does so, he will not err, nor will he be deceived. The three principles are: the four natures; the elemental mixtures and the things that attend and entail them; and the appearances, outward forms, and movements that attend character traits. We will explain these points following our usual approach of keeping the exposition short and merely alluding to the subtler points, and beyond that indicating the sources where they can be found properly discussed.

63.3 You ask, "What does one seek to obtain through it?" What one seeks to obtain through this craft is an advance cognizance of people's character traits so that one may enter into relations with them with the benefit of such insight. Physiognomy may be practiced on horses, dogs, and all other animals that human beings derive benefit from. It may also be practiced on inanimate things, as in the physiognomic study of swords, clouds, and other objects. But it is the physiognomic study of human beings in particular that has attracted the most thoroughgoing attention, on account of the multiple benefits it brings, as we will explain, God willing.

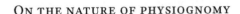

63.4 To your question "Is it always sound, or only at one time and not another, and for one individual and not another?" I respond that it is sound always, at all times, and for all people, but with the proviso mentioned—namely, that one has mastered the principles of which we promised to give a general overview, referring to its proper sources for a detailed exposition. The reason we have said it is always and perpetually sound is that its components and indicants remain stable and do not undergo alteration. They are not like the external forms in the celestial sphere that suffer mutation and change. Rather, the external form, appearances, and elemental mixture of human beings and the movements they necessarily perform as a result of these aspects remain stable and endure as long as they live. Thus, the person who uses these indicants as the basis for his judgment also finds them in a uniform state when he examines them.

We return to our enumeration of the three principles to say: 63.5
The use of the natures themselves as indicants takes the following form. When the heat that is located in the human heart—which is the cause of life—exceeds a balanced state, it naturally leads to an increase in respiration on account of the heart's need for aeration through the lung, to an expansion of the cavity in which it is located through increased movement, and to its accumulating a quantity of smoke that surpasses the right balance and that is proportionate to its increase and to the amount of greasy moisture contiguous to it. The effect of the conditions I have enumerated is that the person whose heart-based heat has these characteristics possesses a heavy way of breathing, a broad chest, a sonorous voice, and thick hair around the chest and shoulders—unless a preventative factor arises, as happens in the case of the person whose skin is affected by dry mange or the pores of whose skin are blocked or narrow. Whoever encounters these characteristics and judges that they are entailed by a predominance of heat judges correctly, but he must not hasten to pronounce any other diagnosis before he has inquired into the other two principles, that he may rest in full confidence. For heat is attended by anger, courage, and speed of movement, but this is contingent on certain conditions. Thus, the brain has a role to play

in the acts of human beings, and it modifies the heat of the heart, given that it is cold and moist; therefore it must be examined. If the person who possesses this mixture has a small head relative to his chest, then one may pronounce the diagnosis we have outlined. If the investigator adds to this the other indicants furnished by the remaining two principles, there can be no doubt as to the soundness of his diagnosis and the accuracy of his reasoning.

63.6 As for the use of mixture, the second principle, as an indicant, we know that every mixture has a physical structure suited to it and an external form congruent with it, and this physical structure has a particular character trait of the soul as its concomitant. For nature always produces a specific physical structure from every mixture. That is why only a donkey is produced by nature from the sperm of a donkey, a date tree from a date pit, and wheat from a wheat grain. Similarly, the physical constitution of a lion is always and only produced from the mixture peculiar to lions, and the physical constitution of a hare from the mixture specific to hares. We know that that physical structure is always attended by a specific character trait by natural necessity. The mixture of a lion's heart is hot, so it is attended by boldness, and its heart is disposed to blaze, so it is quick to feel anger. Since its mixture agrees with its physical structure, nature equipped it with an apparatus for breaking the neck of its prey and ripping it with its teeth, removed its impediment as regards the bodily parts it employs in conformity with this mixture, and supplied it with its strength and physical force. The mixture of hares is opposed to this mixture, so hares are languid, cowardly, and weak, and have little vigor, and thus nature equipped them with the apparatus of flight. Hence, they are light and good at running, and no acts of courage or daring issue from them. Every lion is courageous and daring, while every hare is cowardly and skittish, so that people would laugh if someone were to recount how a hare daringly advanced on a predator and the predator took to flight. So, if the physiognomist finds that a person's features and physical structure bear a resemblance to one of these two animals and judges that he possesses a closely related mixture and its ensuing character, he will not be far from the truth, particularly if he includes the other two principles in his consideration.

The reasoning that applies to the two examples we have mentioned can be extended to every mixture specific to a given animal. That is to say, every mixture is attended by a particular character trait, such as slyness and deceitfulness in foxes, malice and duplicity in wolves, fawning and geniality in cats, and thieving and burying in magpies. It is only in human beings that natural character does not manifest itself fully as it does among these animals, because human beings can discriminate and reflect, and can conceal their blameworthy character traits by assuming their contraries, by simulating praiseworthy actions, and by manifesting that which is not in their nature or in their inborn constitution. In that case, one will need to uncover their natural character using one of two things as the basis of one's judgment: either long acquaintance and inspection of their affairs, or the basis we are presently considering, enlisting the craft of physiognomy against the natural character traits they conceal. If a person's mixture and physical structure have an affinity to the makeup of a hare, we judge that he possesses a hare's character, and if they have an affinity to a lion, we judge that he possesses a lion's character, along with all its other indicants. 63.7

The use of appearances, external forms, and movements—the final principle—as an indicant amounts to the following. Every state of the soul, such as anger, satisfaction, joy, and sadness, among others, involves appearances, movements, and external forms that always attend that state, and that manifest themselves most strongly in the eyes and the face. Physiognomists place special reliance on the eyes, asserting that they are the gateway to the heart. They use their external form, color, and many other aspects—too many to enumerate in the present context—to unearth the majority of a person's character traits and dispositions; and they successfully form accurate assessments, particularly if they include the other two principles in their consideration. For the way the eyes of a joyful 63.8

person and the eyes of a sad person appear and move, for example, is manifest. If, thus, we encounter a person whose eyes appear and move in a way that corresponds to one of these two states by physical constitution and by nature, we judge that he possesses this natural disposition. Similarly, if a person's eyebrows knit, his forehead becomes wrinkled, and a frown appears on his face when he is at rest, we judge that he possesses this natural disposition, and that he has a bad character.

63.9 These, then, are the three principles on which physiognomists rely, and they are strong and natural, as you can see. Polemon has written a book on the subject, and they say that he was the first of the authors whose works have come down to us and about whom we have information to arrive at this knowledge. He was then followed by others who composed books on the topic that enjoy wide repute. So a larger share of this knowledge may be acquired from its proper sources. There is also another type of indicant that can be used as a basis for judgment, which may not be natural but is closely linked to it, namely, habit. For we have already mentioned the saying, "Habit is a second nature." We know that a person who has grown up in a particular city and a particular nation and has spent a long time in the company of a particular faction becomes like them and adopts their ways, as happens with people who spend time in the company of soldiers, amusement seekers, or any other class of people. It is even supposed that a person who spends a long time in the company of beasts acquires something of their character traits—something you can observe clearly among camel drivers and shepherds, who live in the open country and rarely mingle with people, and how those who deal with women and children sink to the level of their character traits and grow to be like them.

63.10 This provides a general overview of physiognomy. It is imperative that you guard against forming a judgment on the basis of a single indicant, and that you strive after all the indicants provided by the three principles. In this way, you will be like those trustworthy witnesses whose veracity raises no doubts in your mind, your judgment will be accurate, and your physiognomic insight sound, depending on the experience you have acquired in the craft once you have familiarized yourself with its principles. How much profit there is in this knowledge, and how promptly it is delivered! Throughout my many peregrinations across the world, I see many varieties of people, mingle with nations of different kinds, and witness extraordinary traits of character. When I make use of physiognomy, it brings great profit and immediate benefit.

However, physiognomy may err when confronted with the phi- 63.11
losopher who has achieved the fullness of wisdom. The reason for this is that he may have had a corrupt mixture and a natural character of a piece with it, yet he may have reformed and refined it through prolonged exertion, and he may have given himself a pledge to preserve upright conduct and cleave to agreeable traits, as is reported about Polemon, who was the first person to arrive at this knowledge. For he was brought to Hippocrates while the latter's identity was masked, so he met him in person without knowing who he was. He contemplated him and pronounced the judgment: "Adulterer." Hippocrates's students leapt to their feet to attack him. But Hippocrates forbade them, saying, "The man has spoken the truth on the basis of his craft, but I forcibly restrain my soul from manifesting its natural disposition."[63]

On why people covet things denied to them

What is the secret behind the saying "Men covet what they have 64.1
been denied?" Why are things that way? How is it that people are quick to lose interest in what they have been given, while their passion redoubles to seek what has been withheld? Should we not rather feel covetous toward what is available and indifferent toward what has been denied? Is this why we feel no desire for cheap things, but feel desire for expensive ones? And is this why we do not feel as

keen to see the emir when he rides forth as we are to see the caliph when he appears in public?

Miskawayh's response

64.2 The soul is self-sufficient and self-content, with no need for anything external. Its need and want for things external arise on account of its conjunction with matter; for with regard to wanting and needing, matter is the opposite of soul. Human beings are composed from both, so they long to gather many kinds of learning and material possessions. They collect learning and knowledge in a thing that resembles a storeroom, which they can consult whenever they wish and from which they can extract whatever they will. I am referring to the power of memory, where we deposit the things derived from external sources—that is, from scholars and books—or generated through internal thought and reflection. Human beings entertain the same desire for material possessions and sensible objects that they do for the things already mentioned. That is why they are led astray by them and mistakenly multiply them to excess, until philosophy brings them to an awareness of the kinds of knowledge and sensible objects they ought to acquire, and then they make it their aim to pursue both things in moderation, without exceeding that limit.

64.3 The reason they covet what has been denied is that they seek the things they do not have and are unavailable in their storeroom, and they take steps to acquire and attain them depending on the inclination they have toward either the intelligible or the sensible. Upon attaining them, they feel pacified, knowing that they have stored them away and will find them waiting for them whenever they go back to them (if they are the type of things whose essence it is to endure). Then they turn their longing in another direction. This continues until they realize that particulars are infinite in number, that one cannot hope to attain what is infinite in number, and that there is nothing to be gained from yearning for it and no point in seeking it, whether it regards matters of knowledge or sensible objects. Among objects of knowledge, one rather ought to pursue those species and entities that are permanent, everlasting, and always in a single state; this is accomplished by referring the infinite number of individuals to the unity with which the soul can unite itself. Among sensible objects that can be acquired, one ought to pursue those that are necessary for the body and that serve to sustain it, without multiplying them to excess; for it is impossible to encompass them in their entirety given that they are infinite in number.

Thus, everything that outstrips need and the measure of suffi- 64.4
ciency gives rise to sorrows, anxieties, illnesses, and all kinds of woes. People often go astray on this head, because of the human aspiration to do away with the basis of privation—for privation means need, and self-sufficiency means independence, that is, having no needs whatsoever. That is why one says that God is self-sufficient, because He has no needs whatsoever. But when people have numerous possessions, the number of their needs grows with the number of their possessions, and the forms of their privation increase in proportion to the impulse to acquire more. The laws of the prophets and the ethical teachings of the philosophers have made that plain. The reason we feel no desire for things that are cheap and widely available is that we know we will find them whenever we try to obtain them. Expensive things, by contrast, are only available at certain times and are obtained now by one person and now by another; everyone wishes to be that person in order to attain what others have failed to, in line with what we have explained about human beings.

On why people inquire into what will happen in the future

Why do human beings inquire into future outcomes? Why are they 65.1
affected by them, and what influence do they wield over them?

What good do they garner if they take this to great lengths, and what evil do they fear if they incline to indifference? What did the ancients mean when they said, "He who watches himself is met with adversity; he who abandons himself is preserved from it"?[64]

Miskawayh's response

65.2 There are two reasons why human beings inquire into future outcomes: first, the eagerness they feel about things that are to be, and their longing to know what is to be before it has occurred, for reasons that were discussed in the first question; second, in order to prepare for them if they are the sort of thing for which preparation avails. This is why human beings long for omens and augurs when they lack other forms of proof such as the configurations of the celestial sphere and the movements of the stars, and why they sometimes have recourse to diviners and put credence in many false speculations.

65.3 Taken at face value, the statement of the ancients, "He who watches himself is met with adversity; he who abandons himself is preserved from it," seems to conflict with the first proposition. For this saying refers to how someone who watches himself tries to protect himself against things that must unavoidably befall him. He tries to escape from what is predetermined—I mean, from the necessary entailments of the destinies mediated by the movements of the celestial sphere—and his attempt becomes the cause of its happening to him. The poet was referring to this when he said:

> If you guard yourself against fate and try to flee,
> you will only run toward it.[65]

By contrast, the person who gives himself to it and is content with it is preserved from what is not predetermined and, even if he does not try to preserve himself from it, it does not befall him, as the poet said about those who have the opposite quality:

Guarding against things that will not be,
and fearing things that cannot deliver them from fate.[66]

To this topic pertains an explanation of the things from which one should try to preserve oneself and the things one should not—by which I mean, things in which thought and reflection avail, and ones in which they do not. If a topic arises that demands it, I will examine it closely, God willing.

On the influence of companions on a person's character and on the benefits of companionship

How is a person affected in his good and evil qualities by his companion? Why is it that an evil person is swifter to exert influence on a good person than a good person on an evil one? What benefit does the soul derive from companionship? 66.1

Miskawayh's response

What we gain from a companion is the possibility of following his example and imitating him. Two natural objects that are physically contiguous must inevitably influence one another. The same applies to the soul, for nature imitates the soul, being like a shadow to it. In nature, stronger elements tend to transmute weaker elements into themselves and assimilate them to their being, as we notice with things that are hot and cold and those that are moist and dry. Illnesses arise in the body on account of the influence exercised by one contiguous object on another, and it is through this means that they are treated by medications. The soul in us is material, so evil comes naturally to it, whereas good comes to it through effort and learning. We human beings thus need to toil at the good in order to acquire it and bring it into our possession. It is not enough for us to 66.2

realize its form, but we must grow familiar with and habituated to it, and spend a long time reproducing the condition it has generated in us, before it can pass from being a transient condition to being a stable state and an ingrained trait.

66.3 By contrast, we do not need to toil at evil to acquire it. All we need to do is let our soul follow its bent and leave it to its nature; for it is lacking in good, and lack of good constitutes evil. As has been established by philosophical inquiries, evil is not something that has a subsisting essence, but rather consists in the privation of good. That is why it has been said that matter is the origin and wellspring of evil insofar as it lacks all forms. Simple primary evil consists in privation and then enters into compounds. What causes it to enter into compounds are the privations associated with matter.

66.4 A full exposition of these points would take too long, but what you can retain for the purpose of answering your question is that the soul imitates and follows the example of the soul it keeps company with, and that evil comes to it more swiftly than good for the reasons we have mentioned—namely, that the soul that is in us is material. By this I mean that it receives forms from the intellect. Intelligibles become intelligibles for us once their forms are fixed within the soul. That is why Plato said that the soul is a place of forms. Aristotle admired this comparison of Plato's because it is a fine figure of speech and an eloquent way of indicating the idea he had in mind.[67] Therefore, on the basis of this principle, we ought to avoid associating with evil people, mingling with them, and cultivating their company, and we should listen to the words of the poet who said:[68]

> Ask not about a man, but consider his companion:
> we follow the example of those whose company we keep.

We must also warn young people and children against that as forcefully as possible; as was established, confirmed, and highlighted in the discussion of an earlier question.

On why people scorn certain forms of ostentatious demeanor and why individuals aren't simply allowed to do as they please

Why do people scorn those who keep the lower end of their garment long and drag it behind them; who wear their turbans very large, puff up their collars with cotton, and have their shirt openings very wide, swaggering about and belaboring their speech? What makes these people and their ilk repulsive? What renders them and their cognates unseemly? Why isn't everyone left to his opinion and choice, his desire and predilection? Surely there must be a secret reason that unites men of reason and discrimination, and men of excellence and distinction, in deeming these things repugnant? So, what is this secret and reason? 67.1

Miskawayh's response

It is affectation that renders these things objectionable. The only reason someone diverges from how people customarily dress and act, setting himself apart from them by behaving differently, and being prepared to shoulder the cost of his actions, is that he has a purpose that conflicts with their purposes and an aim that is different from their aims. If his goal is to acquire fame and call attention to himself, the only possibility is that he is seeking to create an impression ungrounded in reality and to demand a status he does not merit. For had he merited it, it would have been clear and manifest, and would have been acknowledged without any need for affectation or incurring such steep costs. He is thus in fact a lying counterfeiter, and his only reason for engaging in this is to deceive the good-natured and cozen the unwary—the characteristic behavior of impostors, whom we should guard against and keep our distance from. Additionally, our instinctive response to divergence is involved: Divergence causes alienation, excites repulsion, and 67.2

generates animosity. What people and men of merit seek, and what prophets also seek through the norms and laws they have imposed on them, is to establish the concord and harmony that generate relations of love and affection, so that all may share in the good and acquire the unified form that is the cause of every virtue, for the sake of which people come together in polities, as it enables them to live well, enjoy life, and attain the goods desired in the mundane world.

On what the soul seeks in this world and on the nature of human beings

68.1 What does the soul seek in this world? Does it have something it seeks and desires? If these elements attach to it, it can no longer be thought to occupy a lofty rank and possess a momentous standing, for this is the hallmark of need and the first ingredient of powerlessness. But for the fact that it would widen the scope to excess, I would have asked: What is the soul's relation to human beings? Does it subsist through them, or do they subsist through it? And if that is so, in what way is it so? A wider topic yet, a veritable ocean of discussion, is the subject of human beings. For man is a mystery to man. Then you adduced various quotations that contribute nothing to the question, so let us occupy ourselves with our response.

Miskawayh's response

68.2 Were it not that the term "seeking" suggests the wrong idea regarding the condition of the soul and how its effects are manifested in this world, I would have applied it and permitted you to apply it, as others have. But I have seen the physician al-Rāzī and others of his stripe become ensnared in a doctrine remote from the truth as a result of this and similar words that philosophers apply loosely—or rather on account of the contingent need for words, when the words are too narrow to encompass the subtle meanings to which they apply them. Yet I shall indicate the views you should follow on this topic. For when the elements enter into different kinds of mixtures through the celestial sphere's different kinds of movements, they generate the different kinds of forms and shapes that nature fashions, and through the medium of nature receive different kinds of effects from the soul. For the soul manifests its effects in every mixture according to its receptivity; it puts every natural instrument, according to its suitability, to every use it can possibly be put to, and brings it to the utmost state of excellence possible for it.

The soul performs that act for no other purpose than the mani- 68.3
festation of wisdom. For the wise agent manifests wisdom for no other purpose beyond wisdom, since the grandest acts are those that are not desired for the sake of something else, but rather for their own sake. Whenever an act is desired for the sake of another end and another objective, that objective has a higher status than the act. This comparative chain cannot extend ad infinitum, and thus the last end and the most excellent act will not be the one that is performed for the sake of some other thing, but rather the one that itself constitutes the ultimate end and purpose. That is why someone who practices philosophy must have no other aim in practicing philosophy than philosophy itself, and why someone who does something fine must have no other aim than the fine. That is, he must not be looking to obtain a benefit, secure an honorable reputation, attain preeminence, or anything else besides doing the fine itself, simply because it is fine. The Philosopher has indicated that the soul is perfected in this world by receiving the forms of intelligibles in order to become an actual intellect after having been a potential intellect. It becomes identified with the intellect when it intellects it, for it is in the nature of that which is intellected and that which is intellecting to form a single indistinguishable thing. One grasps this clearly after one has spent a long time studying the different parts of philosophy and has come to its final part.

68.4 On the topic of human beings whose breadth you lamented and on which you recounted faltering views that availed you nothing, what you need to take as your mainstay is that this term has been appointed to designate the entity composed of a rational soul and a natural body. For everything composed of two or more simple elements requires a singular name that expresses and conveys the notion of composition, as happens when the form joined to the matter of silver is called a "ring," and the form of a bed joined to the matter of wood assumes the name "bed." Something similar happens when two or more natural bodies are joined and compose another thing that is designated with a singular name. This is what happens in the case of vinegar when it is compounded with honey or sugar and is then called "oxymel"; likewise with the way one designates the different types of medicine or electuaries that blend many ingredients and the different types of composite foods and drinks; each is designated using a specific name. The same thing happens when matter passes from one form to another, as in the case of inspissated grapes called "juice" at one time, "wine" at another, and "vinegar" at yet another, depending on the transformation the form has undergone within a single substrate. Man is thus the rational soul when it uses the corporeal instruments called a "body" to perform actions in accordance with discrimination.

On the nature and attributes of God

69.1 Here—God grace you with His support—you quoted various exchanges between a questioner and a dialectical theologian, but did not direct yourself to any topic we should make the subject of inquiry. For the question pertains to the names and attributes of God, and we discussed that topic thoroughly earlier so there is no need to rehearse it again. So you should go back to the earlier discussion and look it up, and, God willing, you will find it adequate to the purpose.

On why people experience fear in the absence of an apparent cause

Why do people experience fear in the absence of anything fearful? Why do people thus frightened and affected feign hardiness to prevent others from discovering their base disposition, inadequate strength, and lowly anxiety, even as their limbs buckle, they cry out in commotion and are visibly changed, their heart pounds, and they exhibit the effects of what would be plain in the expression of their face, the look in their eyes, the words on their tongue, and their disturbed behavior, even if they tried to conceal it? 70.1

Miskawayh's response

The reason is the expectation of an untoward occurrence. The sense of fear is appropriate if its cause is sound and its ground is clear. If it is not, and fear results from misjudgment and impaired thinking, it indicates a malady or a humoral mixture with original impairment. Depending on the nature of the unwelcome event, fortitude is proper, endurance of the harm it causes is praiseworthy, and human beings exhibit the effects of courage or cowardice. Even the most steadfast and self-possessed, the most perspicacious and keen-minded are unavoidably disturbed when something untoward suddenly happens to them, particularly something terrible. Aristotle says, "He who does not feel anxious at sea when faced with a raging storm and confronted with terrors that exceed the limits of human power is a madman."[69] Many untoward occurrences follow this pattern and approximate to it. The anxiety a person experiences depends on the extent and measure of these occurrences. Even if 70.2

the expected or the untoward event is such that it is within human power to repel or alleviate it, yet one becomes overwhelmed by anxiety and loses self-control, failing to face it with composure; prone to excessive anxiety, he is cowardly, and from this perspective merits blame. The remedy is to train oneself by confronting and undergoing hardships, by enduring them patiently, and by bracing the soul prior to their occurrence, so that they do not catch one unawares and off guard. If courage is a virtue and its contrary a deficiency and defect, given what was said earlier regarding the passionate sense of attachment people feel toward themselves and the love they have for their own soul, is there anybody who does not wish to conceal his deficiency and display his virtue?

On why people fly into a rage when they can't open a lock

71.1 Why do people get angry and annoyed if, for example, they are trying to open a lock but it won't open, and then they fly into a rage and bite the lock and curse? This is a phenomenon that is widespread among people.[70]

Miskawayh's response

71.2 This phenomenon and its like are among the most repugnant things that affect people, and they deserve blame if they do not rectify it by means of a good and praiseworthy character. For anger makes the blood of the heart swell, out of a desire for revenge, and this revenge is blameworthy if it is not carried out in the right manner, against the right people, and in the right measure. How much more, then, if it takes the form you have described. I have provided a response to your question about the cause of anger. Rational and discriminating human beings must subdue it when roused on the wrong occasion and not accelerate its progress; they must not behave like beasts, adopting the habits of wild animals. For those who aid it through thought, and, through the power of reflection, inflame it so that it burns and blazes, will later struggle to remedy and subdue it. Human beings deserve blame for it if they leave it to the biddings of nature and do not make the effect of discrimination and the power of reason manifest in it. In his book on ethics, Galen mentioned this very case regarding the lock, and he expressed his amazement at the ignorance of people who act like this, or who kick donkeys and punch mules. Such kinds of actions indicate that the individual in question has only a very small quotient of humanity and is dominated by beastliness, which is to say that he has poor discrimination and makes little use of thought. This is not the only phenomenon to affect the common people and the rabble. When appetite, lust, or any of the other expressions of the irascible and beastly soul flare up in them and commence their natural movement, they fail to use the resources with which God endowed them, by which He distinguished them, and on account of which He rendered them human—I mean the effect of reason through good reflection and sound discrimination. It is to God that we turn for help; strength comes from Him alone.

On why people with small heads have light brains

Why do people with small heads have light brains? And why is it that not everyone with a large head has a weighty brain? 72.1

Miskawayh's response

The brain requires balance with respect to both quality and quantity, and realizing one does not render the other dispensable. If its substance is excellent in terms of its quality, but its quantity is deficient, it will necessarily be bad. If it is extensive in quantity, 72.2

it will not necessarily be bad, for it may be extensive and have an excellent substance, yet it must also have a good relation to the heat of the heart, so that the coldness and moisture of the one and the heat and dryness of the other, taken together, may produce the praiseworthy, desirable balance. When it departs from this balance, it is attended by a corresponding share and portion of badness. Yet there are a number of unequal ways of departing from balance, and it is better that it should be excellent, extensive, and in excess of the amount required than that it should be excellent and fall short of the amount required. If it combines bad quality and bad quantity, the individual will accordingly be an idiotic imbecile.

On certain beliefs concerning the relation between a person's facial hair and his character

73.1 Why do people believe that men with no hair on the sides of their face, and those who are short, are malicious and cunning, yet they do not believe that men with long beards and thick hair, a tall frame, and a handsome appearance have a good mind and sound judgment? Why do they deem a sparse beard felicitous?

Miskawayh's response

73.2 This question pertains to physiognomy. In all things, what is praiseworthy and commendable follows on a particular elemental mixture that constitutes the balanced state. By contrast, the two extremes that stand on either side of the balanced state—excess and deficiency—are blameworthy and repugnant. If an abundant, long, and large beard that grows all over the face is a sign of sound intentions and guilelessness, it necessarily follows that the light, sparse hair that represents the opposite extreme should be a sign of malice and cunning. Both of these are extremes that depart from the commendable balance. I reckon that poor choice also has a bearing on the matter. For a man who leaves his beard greatly untended is capable of trimming it down with a minimum of effort in order to arrive at the correct balance and praiseworthy appearance. Thus, leaving it in a blameworthy state even though it wears him out and he is always trying to fix it, or leaving it until it becomes unseemly and disheveled, is a sign of faulty choice and poor discrimination. The one who lacks a beard, by contrast, can do nothing about it, and is exempt from blame.

On why people racked by suffering find it easy to face death

Why do people tormented by suffering find it easy to face death even though they know that nonexistence means a lack of life and being, and that however acute the evil one suffers might be, it is conjoined to this cherished life? They also know, moreover, that existents are nobler than nonexistent things, and that nonexistent things have no dignity. So, what makes it easy for them to face nonexistence? What is it that comes over their heart? Does their choice come about through reason or a corrupt humoral mixture? 74.1

Miskawayh's response

This question makes a valid point, though it is expressed in a confused manner and contains premises that are not conceded, for when human beings die, they do not become nonexistent tout court. Certain of their contingent aspects are nullified, and certain of their qualities cease to exist, but their substances do not cease to exist. It is absolutely impossible for substance to cease to exist, in view of the fact that substance has no contrary and in view of other facts established within the fundamentals of philosophy that do not belong to the present context. Substance qua substance is not susceptible to nonexistence. When a person dies, his parts dissolve 74.2

into their original components, that is, the four elements, which they do by changing into them. The four substances themselves endure in perpetuity. It has been established that the substance of human beings that consists in the rational soul is even worthier of substantiality than the four elements; therefore, it also endures eternally.

74.3 Your question did not center on this issue, and there was a mistake in the use of unsound premises and the unguarded use of words, but it was necessary to call attention to the mistake before turning to address the point of the question. Life is only cherished if it is excellent, and by an excellent life I mean a life free from evils and adversities, in which the acts performed are complete and excellent, and in which a person is not afflicted by undesirable events such as extreme disgrace, grave injustice, or calamities affecting his family or children. For were a person to be given the choice between this bad life and an excellent death—that is, to be killed in battle while defending his womenfolk and resisting the humiliation and adversities we have described—both reason and the religious Law would mandate that he choose to die and be killed while doing battle against the people who inflict those things on him. A similar question came up earlier, and we provided an adequate reply thereto. That was the question you posed about "why we fear death but sometimes welcome it."[71] So please consult that, for it meets the purpose.

On why people denigrate things they fail to attain and are hostile to things of which they are ignorant

75.1 Why do people denigrate the things they fail to attain and disparage the things they do not possess? In the same vein, people are hostile to things they do not know, so that "People are hostile to the things they do not know" has become a venerable adage. Why this hostility? Why don't they love them and seek them out and try to comprehend them, so that the hostility may cease and so that honor may be established, beauty perfected, words of praise justly uttered, and statements of the truth veraciously made?

Miskawayh's response

This is one of the repugnant traits of character that afflict people. It is akin to envy and tends in the same direction. The person who coined the proverb "Man is an enemy of what he does not know" meant to express blame and reproach, as with the saying "People are a tree that sprouts injustice and envy." The reason for it is, first, the love of one's own soul, and second, an erroneous approach to the acquisition of the things that serve to embellish it. For when a person loves his soul, he loves its form, and knowledge is the form of the soul. One of the consequences of loving the form of our soul is that we hate whatever we do not have as our form. So, if we possess a certain type of knowledge, we love it, and we hate it if we do not possess it. We fail to understand that it is better for us to solicit what we do not know through active pursuit, even if it entails effort, in order that this become another beautiful form we possess. Perhaps what prevents us from doing so is our aversion to humbling ourselves before a teacher once we have attained eminence in a different subject and among a different set of people. 75.2

You ask: "Why don't they love them and seek them out and try to comprehend them?" This is what one ought to do, and what the author of the proverb sought to encourage by calling attention to the fault, so that it might be avoided by doing what is better. I heard a scholar saying that an illustrious and high-ranking judge set out to learn geometry at an advanced age. He said: I asked him, "What is it that drives you to this, even though it detracts from your status and sets fools' tongues wagging, and even though you will not attain a great share of it, given your age and given the fact that mastery of this knowledge requires a long time and a sharp mind that is only 75.3

found during youth and the early part of life?" He replied, "Watch your words! I realized I nursed a sense of hatred for this knowledge and a sense of hostility toward its possessors, and I desired to pursue it in order to love it and not to hate a form of knowledge or be hostile to its possessors." This is what it means to submit to the truth and swallow its bitterness, in keenness to taste the sweetness of its fruit and out of a desire to train the soul to endure what it finds repugnant when this redounds to its beauty and profit, compelling it to do those things that reform and refine it.

On why it is easier to make enemies than friends

76.1 Why is it that if a person wanted to, he could make multiple enemies in the space of a single hour, whereas if he tried to make a friend and establish cordial relations with a single companion he could only achieve this over a long period of time and with great effort, much trouble, and financial loss? The same holds true for every good we hope for and every matter we desire, in all domains. Don't you see that it is easier to rend than sew, simpler to destroy than build, less difficult to take life than to nurture and give it?

Miskawayh's response

76.2 Your question answers itself. It reminds me of a story I heard about al-Aṣmaʿī. I was told that a student read out the following verse to him:

> The canny man is suspicious of you,
> as if he has seen and heard things about you.

The student asked, "Abū Saʿīd, what does 'canny' mean?" He responded, "Someone who is suspicious of you, as if he has seen and heard things about you." I also say regarding this question: The reason people are able to make enemies quickly but can only make friends after a long time and at great cost is that the former involves rending, the latter mending; the former involves destroying, the latter building. Apply this to the rest of your question, and you have your answer.

On why atheists act morally

What drives unbelievers and materialists[72] to do what is good and choose what is fine, to return deposits given in trust, persist in kindness, take pity on the afflicted, help those who cry out, and assist those who seek refuge with them and place their grievances before them? They behave this way even though they anticipate no reward, expect no return, and fear no judgment in the next life. Would you say that what motivates these noble traits and praiseworthy characteristics is their desire to be thanked and spared repugnance, or their fear of the sword? Yet they may act this way at times when they cannot be supposed to be taking precautions or seeking to secure gratitude. This can only be for some secret reason that lies in the soul and some mystery that lies with reason. And do these things contain something that points to the unity of God? 77.1

Miskawayh's response

There are certain acts, aims, natural attributes, and dispositions that human beings possess qua human beings prior to the advent of the religious Law. Their judgment contains certain rudiments and their reason contains certain basic principles for which they do not require a religious Law. Rather, the Law comes in order to call attention to and confirm what they already possess, enlivening what is latent within them and present in their natural constitution, which God bound them to and inscribed within them from the beginning of creation. So everyone naturally endowed with 77.2

reason and a share of humanity possesses a drive to acquire excellent traits and a longing for good qualities that is simply grounded in the excellent traits and good qualities necessitated by reason and mandated by humanity. Sometimes, to be sure, it may be conjoined with a desire to be thanked, to acquire a good name, or to obtain other things. The desire for gratitude and its concomitants would not have been commended, were it not a fine thing and an excellent quality. If the Creator were not one, this condition would not be universal among people, and no one would have responded to those who urged it and exhorted him to it, had he found nothing within himself to attest to it and corroborate it. Upon my life, this is the clearest proof of God's unity.

On why some people willingly become the butt of other people's jokes

78.1 What comes over certain people so they become a laughingstock? People laugh at them, ridicule them, and slap them about, and they submit to such treatment with patience and contentment, though they have little or nothing to gain. How do they acquiesce to this unseemly state of affairs without demur? Sometimes the person in question may even belong to a family of great eminence and lofty standing. Similarly, someone else may adopt effeminate manners or become involved in singing or games—and so on, to the end of the story he recounted regarding a man who grew up following a blameworthy path, though hailing from a great family.

Miskawayh's response

78.2 As we mentioned earlier, in the question regarding physiognomy, every elemental mixture is attended by a specific character, and the acts of the soul issue in accordance with that nature and mixture. People are beasts in the guise of men when they abandon themselves to nature, yield to their blind desires, and fail to use the power they were endowed with in order to remedy this and discipline their soul. The character trait you mention in this question is one of the traits that attend an unbalanced mixture and that become unruly when people are left to the biddings of their nature, leading them to follow the foulest paths. It is imperative that those so afflicted strive to treat them, and that others strive for this on their behalf. Apropos this topic, we have already remarked that this is possible, and were it not possible, there would be no value in reforming and disciplining character, in praising people or blaming them for it, in restraining them from it and urging them to it, or in the exercise of governance by parents and rulers. Indeed, polities are founded on this basis. If someone fails to respond to treatment using such therapeutic means, it will be necessary to treat him through the imposition of punishments. The illnesses of the soul and the illnesses of the body are very similar to each other. A person must be treated through force and coercion when he fails to treat his bodily illness voluntarily and by his own preference. The same applies to the illness of the soul, until we reach a point when we despair of the person ever reforming; then he needs to be relieved of himself and others relieved of him, in order to purify the earth from his existence in accordance with the dictates of the religious Law and virtuous governance.

On why people love to occupy positions of eminence

Why do people love to occupy positions of eminence? Whence 79.1
was this trait instilled into them? What did nature intend to signify through it? Why do some people take their quest for eminence to extremes, taking spear thrusts and sword strokes in their chests, spending sleepless nights, bidding rest adieu, and crossing sprawling desert wastes? Is this trait of a piece with the rancor a person feels

about the way they are addressed when receiving or sending correspondence? And how does that relate to the preceding discussions? For people are extremely competitive over these points, severing relations with each other and taking things to the limit.

Miskawayh's response

79.2 It has been demonstrated that people have three powers: the rational, the beastly, and the irascible. Through the rational power they long for knowledge, fine conduct, and the excellent traits that lead them to wisdom; its effect manifests itself from the brain. Through the beastly power they are driven toward the appetites by which they obtain all bodily pleasures; its effect manifests itself from the liver. Through the irascible power they are driven to seek positions of eminence, long for all kinds of honor, experience zeal and pride, and solicit power and illustrious status; its effect manifests itself from the heart. The relative strength of each of these powers depends on the mixture of these organs, designated as the principal organs of the body. This mixture may depart from the balanced state, either toward increase and excess or decrease and deficiency. In that case, they need to adjust them and lead them back to the mean—that is, to the balance appointed for it—and not give themselves up to them by abandoning their efforts to rectify and discipline, for these powers flare up for the reasons we have mentioned. If left to their own devices and no effort is made to reform them and treat them by imposing restraints, and nature is followed instead, conditions deteriorate and they gain the upper hand, growing so unruly that we despair of treating and curing them. We control them and are able to discipline them in the first instance through the soul that presides over all of them, that is to say, the discriminating power of reason that is called "divine." It is this power that ought to be in command and to preside over the rest.

79.3 So it is natural for human beings to love eminence, but this love must be regulated in order to be appropriate and as it ought. If it runs to excess or to deficiency in someone as a result of a particular mixture or bad habit, he must rectify it through discipline, so that it may move in the right manner, under the right conditions, and at the right time. These powers and their effects have already been discussed at the relevant juncture, so we will confine ourselves to these remarks.

Furthermore, just as some people, as a result of the movement 79.4
of the power of the beastly soul within them and their failure to bridle it, take spear thrusts in their chest and confront terrors by land and sea in order to satisfy their appetites, so too other people confront these terrors when the power of the irascible soul goads them to attain honors and positions of eminence. Everything depends on reason, which presides over these powers, and on the effort a person makes to fortify this soul so that it may dominate and subjugate the other two powers, with the result that they proceed at its command, move in the directions it prescribes, and stop at the limits it sets. For this is the power that is called "divine," and it has the insight to treat and reform them, and the capacity and an exclusive title to preside over them fully. But as Plato said, the former is as pliant as gold, whereas the latter are as strong as iron, and human beings need to have the will and strive hard to subject them to it—for they will indeed be subjected and submit. God is our helper; He is sufficient for us, and an excellent guardian is He!

On why we honor people for the achievements of their ancestors but not those of their progeny

Why does one honor people who have a father or grandfather who 80.1
was highly regarded, with many glorious deeds and acts of courage and leadership to his name, whereas one does not honor people who have such a son? I mean, why is it that honor flows from ancestors to descendants and does not flow from descendants to ancestors?

Miskawayh's response

80.2 Fathers are the cause of their children's existence, and their disposition flows into them because the latter represent their causal effect and are constituted from their elemental mixture and their seed. For that reason, children are like parts or copies of their fathers, so it is not strange that the cause should manifest its effect in them or that they should be expected to incline toward the ancestral disposition. The opposite proposition—namely, that the effect should serve as grounds for the cause, reversing the process—is one not countenanced by reason and rejected by basic intuition. The merest reflection suffices to answer this question.

On why the progeny of illustrious people evince an elevated sense of entitlement and self-importance

81.1 And why is it that if someone's father is known for the attributes we have mentioned or for other attributes such as being devout and God-fearing, his children and his grandchildren must swagger about, dragging the hems of their garments along the ground, comporting themselves haughtily and holding people in contempt, thinking that they have been granted the power to rule and presuming that you are obliged to serve them and your salvation depends on them? What scourge, what bane is this, and what is its origin? Did such behavior exist in bygone times and among the peoples of earlier eras we know about?

Miskawayh's response

81.2 Our answer to the previous question indicates the answer to this. For the honor that attaches to a causal effect depends on the honor that attaches to its cause. So if that honor is due to religious devotion and its cause is divine, the descendants who issue from it feel a sense of pride in it that others do not, though within determinate limits and to a specific degree. To overdo this and to end up regarding themselves in the ways you report are of a piece with the other forms of excess we enumerated earlier. You ask, "Did anything of the kind exist in bygone times?" Upon my life, this has existed among every people and in every era. Noble descent is still for the most part passed on to children, and one expects to see it reflected in their dispositions, so that rulership remains within a single family for a long time, and people refuse to accept anyone else and will only submit to them. This is found among all peoples—Persians, Byzantines, Indians, and the other races. Similarly, children are reviled for their ignoble stock and corrupt origin, and are expected thus to incline; so they are disparaged and eschewed on its account. But your question includes a reference to religion, which, as you know, has a different status with respect to elevated rank and dignified standing, even if the capacity of prophethood itself does not, and is not expected to, flow into offspring. For the glory and honor that attend prophethood, the inclination that people naturally feel toward it, and the interest in serving as leaders and rulers taken by members of the family in which it appears depart from the customary order, particularly if there is an exclusive claim and the condition of excellence is met. Turning away from persons with such attributes will then constitute an injustice and a transgression. And that is all I have to say.

On whether it would be more consistent with the true order of things if all people were honored equally

Could true wisdom possibly lie in people's enjoying an equally high degree of honor instead of occupying disparate levels within it? If that is where true wisdom lies, then what actually obtains among people must be the result either of a compulsive force they cannot 82.1

elude or of ignorance that cannot be held against them. By "equality" I am not referring to people's equality in terms of estate and adequacy of means, or poverty and need; the propriety of this has been certified by wisdom, as it follows the natural bent of the world and accords with reason. I am referring, rather, to people's equality in pedigree, for this has led to widespread insolence, domineering manners, and contemptuous behavior. Wisdom rejects the imposition of anything that is evil or that leads to evil. That is why the Prophet said, "The lives of believers are valued alike; the least among them may make covenants in their name, and they will stand as a single man against other parties."[73]

Miskawayh's response

82.2 People command honor through their own account and through the effects of wisdom that manifest in them. How apt are the words of the Imam ʿAlī, peace be upon him: "A man's worth lies in his proficiency." Our earlier remark regarding the nobility that runs in one's pedigree was based on the fact that there is a strong hope that people with a prior connection to excellence will also manifest it themselves, particularly if its cause is near to them. How could people command an equally elevated degree of honor? For were they equal in this regard, this would constitute neither honor nor an elevated degree of it. What would they be elevated and honored above, if all stations were equal? But with regard to the humanity that extends to all of them alike, and with regard to the principles and conditions that attend humanity, people are equal; they differ with regard to other elements, in which some are more endowed than others.

On different forms of divination

83.1 What is the form of divination called "augury," and that called "taking omens," all about? Why are so many people obsessed by them? And why was one of them excluded from the religious Law while the other was licensed? Do they rest on a foundation that we use as our reference point and depend upon? Or are they sometimes based on what people suspect and perceive, and at other times on chance and compulsion? The statement on the topic transmitted from the Prophet is well known, but is not framed in such a way as to produce certainty, and its text does not provide substance for a considered opinion. He says, "Let there be no transmitting of illness and no augury."[74] But it was said on another occasion he was fond of good omens. Those who transmit reports about the Prophet have claimed that when he was staying in Medina at the house of Abū Ayyūb al-Anṣārī, Abū Ayyūb heard him calling two servants of his, saying, "O safety!" and "O prosperity!" They also report that he said to Abū Bakr, "May this house be safe for us and enjoy prosperity." How can this be, and how is it to be understood? Does it confirm that he approved of augury, or does it stop short of that? Next, you quoted what Ibn Ismāʿīl said in connection with al-Zaʿfarānī's story.[75] You also quoted Ibn al-Rūmī's words, "Omens are the tongue of time, and the sign of the accidents of fortune." And you said: How often something occurs unexpectedly, without a statement or prediction to precede it, so that when a prediction accompanies it, it is held to be the greatest wonder and the most remarkable thing.

Miskawayh's response

As we have already noted, human beings yearn to discover things that exist, things that will exist in the future, and things concealed from their view. They have a natural longing and desire to know about them, depending on their ability and according to their capacity. Occasionally they can attain knowledge of some of them through a suitable nature combined with sound judgment and accurate intuition, and they exercise divination with regard to certain matters such that they hardly ever get them wrong. They then are on the firmest footing in this domain and are practitioners of the 83.2

highest rank. Occasionally for some matters this is not possible, and, through the medium of astral indications and the movements of the heavenly bodies and their influence on the lower world, they judge rightly or wrongly depending on their ability to gather, and then to combine, indications. This craft contains a great number of general principles and subsidiary rules that stem from these principles. Errors are not due to any weakness in the principles of the craft, but rather to the weakness of the person inquiring into it, or to the fact that he wants more from this craft than it incorporates, so that he refers to it things that exceed its purview; and sometimes he may fail to grasp these grounds and other similar natural indicators.

83.3 It is not in the nature of the soul to perform an action without motive or grounds, pointlessly, as it were. Thus, if we are confronted with two possibilities, one of which does not preponderate over the other, we try to give our soul an argument for undertaking one course of action rather than the other. We then have recourse to weak grounds, and labor to find improbable causes that might enable one of the two equivalent views to acquire preponderance over the other within our soul, so that we can attain it and adopt it. It is the way of virtuous men to harbor good opinions, sound hopes, and fine intentions, and in such cases they tend to see things as good omens. Omens may be expressed through simple sounds with no trace of articulate language, but they are usually expressed through intelligible speech. They may be conveyed through pleasing images and agreeable shapes, but mostly they are conveyed through the physical features of human beings. The Prophet said, "If you send me a messenger, let him have a beautiful name and beautiful face."[76]

83.4 Those who engage in augury, by contrast, are the opposite of those who nourish fine intentions and good hopes, so their approach is repugnant; they generally tend to augur from things, and the sorts of indicators they use are simpler and more copious. Some they draw from people's moles, from horses' spots, and from different kinds of physical features. Others they draw from incongruous mixtures and repugnant creatures, such as owls, vermin, scorpions, rats, and the like. Yet others they draw from disagreeable sounds, such as the braying of donkeys, the grating of iron, and the like. Some they draw from names and nicknames, deriving words from them that share some or all of their letters; for example, deriving the term "raven" from the term for "estrangement," the term "ben tree" from the term for "separation," and the term "date pits" from "distance."[77] Some they draw from physical defects, such as when a person is missing his right eye or has a crippled foot, and others from movements and directions, as when a bird passes from left to right or from right to left, and when something is crooked or inclining. This is due to a weakness of the soul and the natural disposition, and to its succumbing to despair and despondency. These perceptions exacerbate its condition, and this is why they were forbidden. Of all the nations, the Arabs in particular were extremely keen on this method and clung to it very tenaciously. Yet their own poet put it well when he said:[78]

> Ziyād asked his augurs to inform him
> about it, but no one could.
> He stayed behind as if someone had offered him
> a piece of Luqmān ibn ʿĀd's wisdom.
> He learned that the only omen to be had from augury
> is the augur himself—he is destined for perdition.
> Indeed, things do coincide at times,
> but augury is rife with false predictions.

On why some people dislike being addressed as "old man" while others relish it

Why do some people hate it when others address them as "old man" out of respect and veneration even though they are not old, while others wish to be addressed that way even though they are in the 84.1

flush of youth? Indeed, we encounter such reactions among people who are actually old and who hate that mode of address, though in this case the reason for their dislike is evident. Our question, however, is about young men who hate being addressed as "old man" when it is meant as an honorific, and about young men who are not addressed as "old man" but affect that status, even though the loss of youth is painful and gray hair is a heinous sight.

Miskawayh's response

84.2 People differ in this regard as a result of the different ways in which they view themselves and the ways in which they perceive the aims of those addressing them. For a person may want to manifest his virtue at the beginning of his life, in his early years; so, if he is addressed as "old man," he may think he has been deprived of that virtue and has been assimilated to those who acquired that virtue over a long period of time and after extensive experience. It may also be hateful because there may be a particular motive for wanting to be young or there may be a penchant for amusements and blind desires, which are deemed reprehensible in old people. So, if a person is addressed as "old man," he views this appellation as a hindrance and restraint, and assumes that the individual uttering this form of address expects him to act the way he expects old people to act, and will not excuse him for venturing to do the things he has set his mind on. Sometimes a person may take into account the level of respect that has accrued to him, which only accrues to old people, whereas he is still young, and he may rejoice at the honor bestowed and the speed with which he has achieved the status of a seasoned and experienced man. So the pleasure or anger with which one responds to this qualification differs depending on the way one views matters.

On why people take comfort from knowing they are not alone in their misfortune

What causes people to take solace when others share the troubles they are experiencing? What causes them to feel anxious, oppressed, and disconsolate when misfortune singles them out and calamity is confined to them? What secret quality of the soul is expressed therein? Is it praiseworthy or reprehensible for people to respond that way? How should they treat this reaction if it carries them away, and to what should they impute it? Why do our troubles make us wish other people shared in them, and why do we find comfort in that? Our companions report a Persian saying that runs: "If your threshing floor has been burned, you want the threshing floor of others to burn." 85.1

Miskawayh's response

Anxiety, sorrow, and grief are among the contingent effects the soul is subject to, and they resemble other effects such as anger, appetite, jealousy, mercy, cruelty, and all the other ethical characteristics human beings are praised for adhering to in the right manner and in accordance with the other conditions we have enumerated many times, and blamed for adhering to in a way that conflicts with those conditions. The soul is refined through the acquisition of character traits so that these contingent effects affect it as they ought, under the right conditions, and at the right time. The sorrow that affects a person in the right manner is the one that arises in response to a calamity that befalls him on account of a wrong he committed or an action he was remiss in or made some voluntary contribution to, or an unhappy chance that singled him out among other people and whose cause he does not know. Even though this kind of sorrow is inferior to the first, it is not held against people. By contrast, no reasonable person feels sorrow over things whose occurrence is 85.2

necessary or inescapable. Nobody feels sorrow at the setting of the sun since it occurs necessarily, for example, even though it prevents the realization of many benefits, causes harm to everyone, and stops people from seeing and from pursuing their daily business. Similarly, no reasonable person feels sorrow when winter and cold set in or when the summer heat appears; instead, we gear up for it and make preparations.

85.3 Nobody feels sorrow over natural death, because it is necessary. It is only when it appears at an unexpected time or takes an unanticipated form that people are aggrieved by it. Thus, parents are aggrieved by the deaths of their children, because they had anticipated that they would die before them. By contrast, children are not greatly aggrieved by the death of their parents, for matters follow the course they had anticipated, though it might occur slightly earlier, for example, or when it ought. In the case of the traveler or seafarer who happens to be the only one of his companions to suffer some hardship relating to his property or body, his sorrow is due to suffering misfortune and bad luck. The cause of this type of event is unknown, and one excuses him most readily on that account. Those who wish others to suffer the same kinds of evil that have afflicted them have a wicked nature, especially if this brings them no profit and avails them nothing; in that case, it is right to reprimand and discipline them. The poet put it well when he said:

> The wounds of another do not heal my wounds;
> let them have their sufferings, and me my own.[79]

On the virtues of different nations, such as the Arabs, Byzantines, Persians, and Indians

86.1 What is the virtue that runs in the different nations, such as the Arabs, the Byzantines, the Persians, and the Indians? You then asserted that you omitted the Turks because Abū ʿUthmān al-Jāḥiẓ does not take them into consideration. You went on to make a number of related points that I have not quoted, because the question at hand is fully contained in what I have quoted.

Miskawayh's response

As this question addresses itself to the special characteristics of different peoples, and as wonder is aroused by the characteristics a given group possesses to the exclusion of others, I have made this the subject of my inquiry, and have not sought to rectify the terms of the question. This has been my approach with all the other questions, because their author follows a rhetorical style, and does not proceed the way the logicians do in investigating a question and applying their methods fully to it. So I respond as follows—God grants success. In our earlier discussion, we explained that the soul uses bodily instruments and that its acts issue in accordance with their mixtures, reporting Galen's view and indicating the location where that discussion can be traced. We illustrated this through the example of innate heat and other elements, explaining how, when they are present, the rational soul uses them such that they obtain in the right manner, for the right people, and at the right time. We also stated that virtue and praiseworthy character are realized through training and the correct determination and ordering of actions, and by persistence until it becomes an innate trait and stable state. If this principle has been retained, there could be nothing easier than to reply to this question. 86.2

In every nation a mixture prevails, even if on rare and unusual occasions certain mixtures may be found that conflict with it. This is due to the type of soil, air, and foodstuffs, and the mixture attendant upon those aspects, and to those influences of the celestial sphere and the stars that you find so odious. For that world is what influences this one on a general level, first by distinguishing the elements from each other, then by mixing them in different proportions, and then by imparting forms and shapes to them. Your demand to be 86.3

reprieved from the truth has no merit, and you have no means to grant yourself reprieve from it. So adhere to it, because it must be accepted. Were it not that your question concerns a different topic, I would have devoted my attention to this one; but this constitutes one of the principles on which it rests, so one must mention the principle in discussing its subsidiary. On this basis, when one of the noble mixtures is balanced—that is to say, in the noble organs: the heart, the liver, and the brain—and to this are added the virtuous traits of character we have mentioned, which means ordering the acts that issue in accordance with the relevant mixture, refining them, and adhering to them through repeated action and sustained habit—this leads to realizing the virtue that arises from them. Whether that is found in a nation or an individual, and whether it is due to noble character traits existing from the beginning or to gradual discipline once a felicitous mixture, a propitious aim, and a continued habit are in place, virtue is realized and does not disappear.

On why intelligent people are more susceptible to grief

87.1 Why do people with greater intelligence experience much grief whereas those who are more ignorant experience little grief? This phenomenon is encountered among different individuals and among different races, such as the blacks and the fair skinned. For black people are evidently merrier and more ignorant, whereas fair-skinned people are more intelligent and reflective, and more strongly given to worry. This is the case even though it is said that joy comes from the blood, and fair-skinned people have a greater amount of blood,[80] more balanced humoral mixtures, readier access to what brings joy and is conducive to merriment, and greater mastery over worldly things in every respect. This phenomenon is also observable among intimate companions, one of whom is naturally prone to worry, while the other is a natural jester.

Miskawayh's response

Grief arises from two different quarters: one is reflection, and the other is humoral mixture. Grief arises from reflection if a person expects some evil to happen. Grief arising from the humoral mixture occurs when the mixture of the blood deviates toward blackness or burning, roiling the spirit that is produced by the vapor of the blood in the passageways of the arteries. How clear the vapor is, how well it expands, and how swiftly it moves and courses in that cavity all depend on the clarity of the blood. Once the cause of grief is known, its counterpart, the cause of joy and happiness, is also known. People of intelligence often expect worldly evils to happen because of how their thought roves, whereas those who do not reflect much and do not expect any evil to happen have no reason to feel grief. The type of humoral mixture we mentioned has been firmly established by Galen, his disciples, and other physicians who came before or after him. The humoral mixture in question will be either adventitious or contingent, on the one hand, or natural and original to one's constitution, on the other. If it is contingent, it constitutes an illness, and must be treated through the means used to treat the various kinds of melancholy and the different sorts of atrabilious illnesses that are caused by the blood's degeneration through burning and by its deviation toward black bile. If it is originally present and part of one's constitution, then it cannot be treated, because it does not constitute an illness; one thus finds entire generations of people and nations whose humoral mixtures are like that. 87.2

As for what you have said regarding the blacks, East Africans in particular are characterized by joyfulness and animation; the reason for that is the balanced state of the blood of their heart. It is not the case, as you supposed, that their mixtures follow upon the blackness of their skin, for the blackness of their skin is caused by the sun's proximity to them and by its passing vertically above their 87.3

heads at the lowest point of its orbit, so that it burns their skin and hair, producing in it—their hair, that is—that frizzy quality which in fact signifies that their hair has been singed. As heat overwhelms their exterior, it draws the innate heat out of their interior toward itself; for heat inclines in the direction of heat. As a consequence, the innate heat in their heart does not become too great. If the innate heat in the heart is not strong, the blood found there is not exposed to burning, and instead it tends toward clarity and fineness. The blood of East Africans is always fine and pure, and that is why courage also is rarely found among them.

87.4 Most fair-skinned people, by contrast, live in the northern climes and in the cold countries, where the sun is distant and the innate heat grows strong in their heart. Because their exterior is encompassed by the cold, their skins remain white and their hair lank, and their heat returns to the inside of their bodies in order to escape from the cold in the air around them as a result of the sun's distance. That is why they are more courageous and why the heat of their heart is stronger; as a result, their blood tends toward turbidity, blackness, and imbalance. The balanced people, who dwell in the intermediate climes, far from both the north and the south, are those freest from these flaws, who have the soundest mixtures and are closest to a balanced state.

On why intrinsic merit and worldly fortune do not coincide

88.1 Speak to me about the queen of all questions whose answer is the prince of all answers; a question that forms the lump in one's throat and the mote in one's eye, the morsel one chokes on and the dead weight on one's back, the malady that wastes one's body and the pained sigh one heaves, such is the immensity of the affliction and suffering it visits upon people. The question: Why are excellent men left deprived, while deficient men attain success? This is the reason why Ibn al-Rāwandī threw off the bonds of the faith, why Abū Saʿīd al-Ḥaṣīrī professed himself a skeptic, why some people disbelieved in Islam and others cast doubt on divine wisdom. When Abū ʿĪsā al-Warrāq saw a eunuch coming out of the residence of the caliph with horses driven before him and a throng of people running around him, he lifted his eyes to the heavens and said, "I proclaim your unity in many languages and tongues, I summon people to believe in you through many arguments and proofs, I buttress your religion through every kind of testimony and evidence, and then I walk about like this, naked, hungry, and thirsty, while a black man like that luxuriates in silk and embroidery, surrounded by servants and attendants, with his retinue and entourage." Some say that this was Ibn al-Rāwandī. Whoever it might be, the account of this topic is clear, the chain of transmission reaches far back to bygone ages, and inquiry into this mystery is obligatory. For it is a gateway to securing a tranquil heart, a peaceful breast, and a sound mind, and to obtaining God's approval. Were it to turn out that the only thing one can do in this connection is to entrust things to God and patiently endure according to what the proofs dictate, that would suffice.

The astrologists say: The eighth mansion is in opposition to the 88.2
second mansion; it seems that it indicates hostility when a mansion is counter and in opposition to another. An established scholar reported that Ibn Mujāhid said: Excellence is to be counted as part of the sustenance granted by God, and deficiency is to be counted as part of the deprivation inflicted by God. An established scholar once told me: Be assured that the distribution of different lots in life is just, and that the Distributor acts fairly. He gave you erudition, excellence, eloquence, and discernment, and He gave your fellow wealth, high standing, sufficiency, and a life of comfort. So consider how the blessings were distributed between you, and then consider how the afflictions were also distributed between you. He granted you excellence, but afflicted you with poverty; He granted him plenty, but afflicted him with ignorance. Isn't justice to be

found in this reflection, and doesn't the truth lie with this thought? Upon my life, a view of this kind would not command assent from materialists, believers in metempsychosis, or dualists,[81] but in any case it replaces blindness with insight. Were we to devote separate responses to the questions of this epistle, it would sate the objector and slake the skeptic. God is our helper in carrying out what we have in mind and intend.

Miskawayh's response

88.3 This question is just as you have stated and described in terms of how difficult most people find it and how inscrutable the underlying rationale has appeared to different kinds of inquirers, to the point that discussions of the topic have come to resemble a drawn game of chess. The players contest it until fatigue and weariness overtake them and they let it end in a draw; they then return to it on successive occasions, but from the outside everything always looks the same. I was keen to devote a separate treatise to this topic when asked to do so by a close friend—a treatise incorporating a general and thorough discussion that would fit the purpose and meet the need. For with these kinds of questions, which make the rounds among people and are notorious for the doubt and perplexity they provoke, one should not content oneself with these kinds of answers, which you asked to be delivered with the utmost conciseness and in which I have incorporated only allusions to subtler points—particularly as I do not know of any extensive account of the issue by earlier thinkers, so that I might have adumbrated the main points and referred to that work for a more detailed exposition. Yet, having made it the object of my inquiry, it is impermissible that I should leave it without a discussion midway between the dilatory and the succinct. I shall expend my utmost effort to set it forth clearly and dispel the perplexity it has produced in people. I draw my hope of success from God; God is my sufficiency.

88.4 I thus respond as follows. It is an incontrovertible principle acknowledged by all right-minded people that every existent in the world, be it natural or artificial, has a proper end, perfection, and purpose for the sake of which and because of which it was brought into existence. That is to say, it was brought into existence in order to accomplish that purpose, even though it might be used to accomplish other things besides that ultimate purpose and ultimate perfection, and even though it might be good for things that have no relation to the purpose for which it was intended and willed. For example, a hammer is designed to be used by a craftsman for pounding and flattening physical objects in the directions required, yet at the same time it can serve to break things apart, thus being used for some of the functions for which an axe is used. Similarly, a pair of scissors is designed to be used by a tailor for cutting clothes, yet at the same time it can serve to sharpen reed pens, in place of a knife. The same applies to all other artificial implements.

Natural entities follow a similar pattern. Thus, teeth were designed 88.5
in different positions and with different forms because of their different perfections, that is to say, the different purposes they are used to accomplish and the different acts for the sake of which they exist. The front teeth are sharp and have the kind of shape that is good for cutting, as is the case with knives, whereas the rear teeth are broad and have the kind of shape that is good for crushing and grinding, as is the case with millstones. They can also be used to accomplish other acts. The same applies to the hands and the feet. For people may venture to put each of these to a use other than the one for which it was created and for the sake of which it was made, whether because they have a need for that or because they wish to provoke astonishment and admiration, the way some people walk on their hands or use their feet to knock people down or to write. Yet even though it is permissible for these acts to issue from these instruments and they are used to accomplish something other than what constitutes their perfection and what is proper to them, this will be marked by disorder and deficiency when compared with the instruments that are used to accomplish the works that are proper to them, that are required from them, and for the sake of which they

exist. If that holds true for all artificial implements and individual entities of a natural kind, the same applies to all species. For when we contemplate any given species, we find that each species is disposed to perfections and purposes that are proper to it. It is similar with the genera of these species. For rational and nonrational animals cannot have the same purpose and perfection. That is to say, it is in no wise and by no means possible that human beings, who were distinguished through this form, created according to this pattern, endowed with discrimination and reflection, and rendered preeminent through reason—the most glorious gift given to them and the most excellent feature specifically granted to them—should not have a purpose proper to them and a perfection for the sake of which they were created and because of which they exist.

88.6 If this principle has been set in place and secured assent—and it could not be sounder or stronger, as you can see—we can now investigate these artificial implements and natural individuals from another direction. For we find that they converge in some aspects and diverge in others. Thus, a hammer has in common with a knife, a needle, and a saw the form of a tool made of iron, but it is then set apart through a form that is proper to it and distinguishes it from other tools. Human beings have in common with plants and beasts growth and nourishment, the pleasure taken in food and drink and all other bodily comforts, and the excretion of superfluous substances. What we wish to know is: Is each entity's exclusive possession of a purpose that is proper to it and a perfection that is assigned to it due to the aspects it has in common with, or to the aspects where it diverges from, other entities? We find that this is due to the form that is proper to it and that distinguishes it from other entities, and through which it is what it is. That is to say, it is the form of an axe, which constitutes it as an axe, that determines its specific property, perfection, and purpose; and the same applies to all other entities.

88.7 Next, we turn our attention to human beings, which share in the substrate of plants and animals, and we say as follows. Insofar as human beings are animals, they have in common with beasts the purpose and perfection of animality, that is, the pursuit of pleasures and appetites, the quest for physical comforts, and the drive to replace the parts of their body that dissolve. Yet, as animality is not the form that is proper to human beings and that distinguishes them from other beings, these things do not issue from them in the most complete manner. For we find that most animals outstrip human beings in all the features we enumerated and surpass human beings in their ability to locate them, devote themselves to them, and obtain greater amounts of them. As the form that is proper to human beings and distinguishes them from other beings consists in reason and its special attributes, discrimination and reflection, these are the features in which their humanity must be vested. So the person with a greater share of these attributes has a greater degree of humanity, just as, when a person has a greater share of the form proper to him as a result of the features we enumerated, his merit is in starker evidence in all its varieties.

Now let us return to the specifics of the question you raised, to 88.8
expound it on the basis of the principles set out above. I therefore say as follows: Upon my life, were it the end of human beings, the purpose on account of which they exist, and the perfection to which they were disposed, to accumulate as many possessions as possible and to enjoy food and drink and all other pleasures and comforts, it would be necessary that they exact them fully through their proper form, that they acquire them in great quantities, and that each person's portion of them be commensurate to his share of humanity, so that the most excellent human beings would be the ones who excel most with respect to possessions and their enjoyment. But, as the form proper to them is the one we have mentioned, we know that their aim and purpose is what issues from that form and is accomplished through it, such as to acquire true knowledge and learning, and to deliberate and reflect on them, so that through such means they may attain a rank loftier than that of the beasts and the other beings in the world of generation and corruption, reflecting

the superiority they have over them intrinsically and on the basis of their form. This is a rank that they can only attain with the reflection and voluntary choice that pertain to reason.

88.9 No one could possibly object to what we have stated by arguing that this reflection and choice must rather relate to pleasures, for we have shown at this juncture and many others that lowly animals possess the latter in greater abundance and larger quantities without reflection or reason. The dignity of reflection in fact emerges, and the benefit of reason stands out, when it is used in relation to the most excellent beings. The most excellent being is the one that has a permanent existence and does not cease to be or undergo change, and does not need or require anything external to it but is, rather, self-sufficient, diffusing its generosity over all beings and assigning them to their proper stations according to their rank and receptivity, and depending on their merit. Thus, the form of humanity is perfected by reflection, thought, and choice when they are used in relation to divine things, elevating one to noble stations that none can speak of or refer to save those who have reached them, who have grasped the object of reference, and who have come to know the blessings extended to human beings. If one then seeks to sink down in creation and return to the level of the beasts and of those that are ranked with them, who have lost themselves—as God said, «Surely the losers are they who lose themselves»[82]—upon my life, this is the manifest loss that one always asks God to preserve one from.

88.10 I have been impressed by the words of Imru' al-Qays, for all the crudeness of his Bedouin style, his foreign kingship and youth, and his pursuit of the poetic forms he cultivated and lost himself in, immersing himself in its notions:

> I see us hurrying toward an unknown fate,
> beguiled by food and drink.

What is this hurry we are in? What is this unknown fate? He is making a subtle point, revealing a fine intelligence and remarkable gifts. Don't you see that he says we are "beguiled by food and drink"? That is to say: What is willed and intended for us is something else, yet we are beguiled by them. So it has emerged clearly that, since those things the common people call "sustenance" do not constitute the end of human beings, the purpose for which they were created, or their intrinsic aim, they must not pursue them and marvel at those who happen to receive them, even if they long for them and desire them. For they do so not in their capacity as rational human beings but in their capacity as beastly animals. With regard to those necessities on which their life depends and which allow them to proceed toward their end, the impediments have been removed and nobody has been wronged. If you ponder these points, you will find them plain, God willing.

On the meaning of coincidence

What does "coincidence" mean? And the remarks that follow. 89.1

This question has already appeared, and it has received a thorough response that nonetheless fulfills the proviso of brevity.[83] After that appears a question about the meaning of "granting a favorable outcome," which has also come up before. So one may consult the answers provided to both questions earlier. 89.2

On the nature of compulsion and choice

The answer to this question lies in devoting a separate discussion to the question of compulsion and choice, to thus ask: What is compulsion, and what is choice? What is their relation to the world? How do they relate and fit together? That is, how do they diverge in their convergence? For you see them in the world attributed to those 90.1

who combine reason and sense perception, yet you also see them attributed to those who possess sense perception but not reason.

Miskawayh's response

90.2 There are many movements and acts that issue from human beings but that do not resemble one another. For there are certain acts that they manifest insofar as they are natural bodies, and through which they exhibit an affinity to inanimate objects. There are other acts that, besides being natural bodies, they manifest insofar as they grow, and through which they have an affinity to plants. There are other acts that they manifest insofar as they have a sensitive soul, and through which they have an affinity to beasts. Then there are other acts that they manifest insofar as they are rational and discerning, and through which they have an affinity to the angels. Each of the above acts and movements that issue from human beings has many varieties and is grounded in different motives and causes. It can also be considered from different aspects, and it is affected by a large number of impediments and different hindrances, some of them natural, some of them a matter of chance, some of them coercive. When a person considering this topic fails to distinguish these acts from each other and to consider them from every aspect, he is confused by these facets and cannot discern the right way to consider them. As a result, he is overwhelmed by perplexity and his uncertainties and doubts proliferate. On our part, we shall set out these movements clearly and discriminate between them, and then we shall discuss the basic nature of compulsion and choice. The issue will then become much simpler and accessible to understanding, and it will not seem abstruse, with God's will.

90.3 I therefore say as follows. Whatever the different varieties and discrete aspects an act admits, it requires four elements in order to be manifested. The first is the agent who manifests it. The second is the matter in which it is realized. The third is the purpose to which it is directed. The fourth is the form that exists in advance in the mind of the agent and that he seeks to produce in matter by acting; and sometimes the form may be the act itself. These four elements are necessary for an act to be realized and manifested. There may also be a need for an instrument, for time, and for a sound structure, but these are not necessary for every act. As your question concerns the type of human action that is connected to choice, we must also mention that. Furthermore, each of the above elements necessary for an act to be realized divides into two categories, proximate and remote. An example of a proximate agent is the wage laborer who wields the building tools when making a house. An example of a remote agent is the person who designs the house, who gives instructions to build it, and orders all of the required tools to be brought. An example of proximate matter is the bricks used for the walls and the wood used for the door. An example of remote matter is the primary elements. An example of proximate perfection is the inhabiting of a house. An example of remote perfection is the preservation of material goods and the deflection of the harmful effects of heat and cold and the like.

As for the varieties of acts we mentioned, they differ according 90.4
to the varieties of active powers present in human beings. For the appetitive power, the irascible power, and the rational power each have a specific act that issues only from it. Some of the causes and motives consist in longing and desire, and others consist in thought and reflection; and these may form compounds. Some of the impediments we mentioned are a matter of chance, others are coercive, and still others are natural. An example of those due to chance is when a person goes out to visit a friend and comes across an adversary who had not been looking to find him, and who impedes him from completing his action, or when a person gets up to do something and stumbles or falls into a well. An example of the coercive is when thieves tie a person's hands in order to prevent him from striking them, or when a person is shackled by the authorities to prevent him from running away and fleeing. Examples of natural impediments are semi-paralysis, apoplexy, and the like.

90.5 There is a further way of considering acts that needs to be called to mind. For we may sometimes consider an act not as it is in itself, but under the aspect of its relation to another person. For example, we may consider Zayd's action under the aspect of its constituting an act of obedience or disobedience toward another person, under the aspect of its being loved by ʿAmr and hated by Khālid, and from the perspective of its being harmful for Bakr and beneficial for ʿAbd Allāh. This way of considering things does not pertain to the act itself, but rather to its relation to another person.

90.6 Having considered acts, their different varieties and aspects, and the conditions required for them to be manifested and realized, we may now consider the nature of choice. So we say as follows. The term "choice" linguistically and morphologically derives from the term "good." When one says that a person chooses something, it is as though he does himself some good, that is, he does what is good for him, whether in fact or according to his opinion, even if it is not in fact good for him. So human action connects to it from this facet, and is what issues from a person as a result of thought and deliberation, in order that he should do what is good for him. We know that people do not think or deliberate about things that are necessary or impossible; they only think and deliberate about things that are possible. When we refer to what is "possible," we mean that which is not impossible, and the postulation of whose existence entails no absurdity.

90.7 This is the aspect of acts that is connected to choice and to which human action especially pertains, and it requires the conditions we have enumerated in order for an act to be fully realized. However, a person who considers this aspect is liable to lose his way and get tangled up in those other aspects that are not connected to human beings and do not have their origin in them. He might consider things based on one particular aspect of acts and fail to consider the other aspects, so that his judgment on human action would be based on that one aspect alone. That would be akin to a person's considering an act from the aspect of the matter that specifically pertains to it and is necessary for its realization, while abandoning the other aspects also necessary for its realization. One might illustrate this with the example of paper used by a writer. Should one consider the writer's action from this aspect—in circumstances when he is unable to get hold of paper, that is—one might suppose that he is incapable of writing from this aspect and that he is barred from acting on its account. Yet this aspect does not connect to him insofar as he is a writer and chooses to write. The same applies if he lacks a reed pen and a sound limb or any of those elements that are conditions for any human act to be realized. Someone who considers matters this way will then rush to the conclusion that the person is under compulsion and will deny his having a choice.

The same thing will happen if someone considers his action 90.8
insofar as he is endowed with choice. For if one considers this aspect and relinquishes the other aspects also necessary for his act to be realized, one will also rush to the conclusion that he is a capable agent and deny his being under compulsion. This is how it is with all things that are compounds formed out of simpler elements. For if a person considers that compound on the basis of only one of the parts that compose it and leaves out the other parts, he is assailed by numerous doubts concerning the parts he left out. Even though human action is designated by a single term, its realization is contingent on many things indispensable for its completion. So, when the person considering it only has regard for one of these elements and omits the others, he is assailed by doubts concerning the elements he has neglected.

The right approach is that taken by those who give separate 90.9
consideration to each of these elements and refer action to all of them, who assign every aspect a share in the act, and who do not consider human acts to be entirely a matter of choice or entirely a matter of compulsion. That is why it has been said: God's religion lies between excess and deficiency. For those who assert that all that is required for human action to be realized is that the agent possess the power to act through choice go too far and neglect the material

elements, coercive causes, and impediments we enumerated earlier. This leads them to affirm the position of delegation. Likewise, those who assert that, for their acts to be realized, it suffices that these impediments be removed and that the material elements be vouchsafed them fall short to the extent that they neglect the power to act through choice. This leads them to affirm the position of compulsion. If our explanation and concise account of the matter stands, the correct view has emerged, and it provides a response to your question about compulsion and choice.

90.10 It is plain knowledge that if a person is unable to act because of the absence of some of the elements necessary for his act to be manifested, accidental to it, coercive, or a matter of chance, this is referred to the relevant aspect. For example, if he fails to act because the matter or one of the other necessary four elements is lacking, he is judged to be powerless. If he fails to act because of a coercive or chance impediment, he is exempt from blame from that aspect and in accordance and proportion to it. By contrast, when a person possesses the power to act through choice; when those hindrances have been lifted from him and all relevant impediments removed from him; when, additionally, the action at stake is of a kind that, considered from a relational perspective, represents an act of obedience to a person one is obligated to obey, an act of assistance to a person one is obligated to assist, or some other type of obligatory relational act; then if this person fails to act, he is subject to reproach and not given exemption, for he has the capacity and ability to act. That is why he experiences regret and receives punishment or is rebuked and blamed by others. This aspect, which, among the various aspects of action, pertains to human beings in particular and is connected to the kind of thinking and deliberation that is termed "choice," constitutes the benefit and product of reason. But for this, there would be no profit in the existence of reason, and its existence would be pointless and senseless. We know for certain that reason is the most exalted entity and the noblest thing that God bestowed on human beings. We also know for certain that the lowliest entities are those whose existence brings no benefit and no profit and that have the status of pointless and senseless things. So, if we followed this proposition, the most glorious entity would be the lowliest. Yet that is an impossible contradiction. Thus, this proposition cannot be true, and its contrary is true.

On the Reason for the Wanderlust Experienced by Certain People

Why do some people experience a hankering after travel from when 91.1
they are children till they are fully grown men, from youth to old age, so much so that they disobey their parents and roam from one end of the world to the other, enduring the hardships of travel, the mortifications of living away from home, and the humiliations of being a nobody? After all, they know the words of the poet:

> The stranger is ill-regarded
> wherever his mounts set down.
> The stranger's reach is short,
> his tongue ever dull.
> People give aid to each other,
> but he has few to aid him.

Others grow up in their mothers' arms and on their wet nurses' shoulders, undisturbed by hankerings for other lands and unoppressed by a longing for anything, as though they were a stone ever fixed on its slope or a pebble immobile in the stream. Perhaps you will say: It is the positions of the astral bodies, the degree of the ascendant, and the configuration of the celestial sphere that imposed these conditions on them and wedded them to these characteristics. You will then be confronted with a more exacting question concerning the influence of these stars and their ability to dispose these causes despite their ostensible state of subjugation, and with the more pressing and vexing task of responding to it.

Miskawayh's response

91.2 The power of desiring sensible objects divides into as many categories as there are senses. Just as the sense of sight may be stronger in one humoral mixture and the sense of hearing stronger in another, so it is with the desiderative power that is present in that sense: It is this that longs for the sense to attain its perfection and to emerge from actuality into potentiality. This means that all senses are senses in potentia until they perceive their objects; once they perceive them they become senses in actuality. If matters stand as we have described, it is hardly surprising that this element should be stronger in some senses and weaker in others, so that some people long to hear things, others to see things; some long for the tastes of food and drink, others for smells and different scents, and yet others for things like clothes and such that can be worn. Sometimes a single person will long for two or three things or for all of them together.

91.3 Each sensible object has countless species, and each species includes an infinite number of individuals. Despite their volume, vast quantity, and tendency toward an infinite number, they do not constitute perfections for human beings insofar as they are human beings; their perfection, that is, the perfection that completes their humanity, lies in what they perceive through reason—which is to say, in the various types of knowledge. The noblest are those that conduce to the noblest objects of knowledge. Their close association with learning and proximity to understanding and discernment is the reason why sight and hearing are the noblest senses. One grasps the first principles of the various forms of learning by means of them, and progress toward the forms of knowledge proper to rationality is made from them. Since this is how things stand concerning the longing for what completes the existence of the senses and actualizes them, and since it is manifest and familiar that some people long for a certain species, enduring every hardship and trouble to fulfill their desire, then it is neither remarkable nor surprising that others should long for a different species and show a similar endurance.

Yet we find that some of these cases have been considered in the Arabic lexicon and assigned a name, whereas others have been neglected. So "greed" and "gluttony" are the words used when the power of desire in those who long for food and drink runs to such an excess that they experience the eagerness to obtain them that I described, one that entails all manner of strains and hardships. Yet there are no words for those who experience the same thing with respect to objects of smell or hearing. I believe that this is due to the prevalence of the former, the opprobrium that attaches to it, and the number of sins and wrongs it entails. It is now clear why some people long to leave their homes and roam the earth. For the desiderative power that specifically concerns sight loves to multiply and renew the objects of sight, and they think that individual objects of sight can be fully encompassed, so they endure many hardships in order to perceive that species. We may come across people of even greater endurance whose desiderative power drives them toward other kinds of sensible objects and the effort to multiply them. So ponder all of these together, review them afresh, and examine their particulars, and you will find that all conform to one and the same principle. 91.4

On why people desire knowledge, and on the benefits of knowledge

Why do people desire knowledge? What is the benefit of knowledge? 92.1
What is the danger of ignorance? What is the advantage of the kind of ignorance that all people share? And what is the secret behind the kind of knowledge people possess by nature? For to strive to uncover these principles and penetrate into these specifics is to

evoke a wealth of knowledge and sound judgment, even if the inquiry into them and their antecedents and consequents is arduous to the soul and onerous on the shoulder. But for the Creator's aid, who could cross these barren wastes and voiceless deserts? God protects the purehearted, supports the obedient, and helps those who cry out.

Miskawayh's response

92.2 In the course of discussing these questions we have already pointed to the response to this one, but, in order to dispel the present uncertainty and remove the present doubt even more fully, it is necessary to go over some of the discussion again. Knowledge represents the perfection of human beings qua human beings, for it is the form that renders them human beings and distinguishes them from other beings—that is, plants, inanimate objects, and beasts. The form that distinguishes them does not consist in their external lineaments, their shape, or their color. This is proved by the fact that when we say "So-and-so has a greater degree of humanity than so-and-so," we do not mean that the person in question has a more complete bodily form or is more perfect with regard to his physical lineaments, his color, or anything else besides his rational power, through which he distinguishes between good and evil things, right and wrong actions, and true and false beliefs. This is why human beings have been defined as rational mortal animals. So it is not their lineaments, their shape, and all their other ends and adjuncts, but their rationality that distinguishes them—that is to say, distinguishes them from other beings.

92.3 As this is the element of human beings that renders them human beings, the greater the degree of their humanity, the more excellent they are in their species. This also applies to every existent in the world: When its act issues in accordance with the form proper to it, its act is better, and the better its act, the more excellent and noble it is. For animals, we can take the goshawk and the horse as examples, and for tools, the reed pen and the axe. For when the act proper to its form issues perfectly from each, it is nobler in its species than those that fall short. Similarly with plants and inanimate objects. For every individual existent has a proper form from which its act issues and that renders it noble or base, depending on whether that act is complete or deficient. So is there anything that can yield greater benefit than that which perfects your existence, completes your species, and delivers your being, distinguishing you from inanimate objects, plants, and nonrational animals and bringing you close to the angels and God? Is there anything that can brook a danger more calamitous and vexatious, more injurious and disastrous, than that which pulls you lower down in creation, casts you back to the vilest level of your existence, and demotes you from your noble station to the base station of inferior entities?

I believe you take the view that knowledge ought necessarily to 92.4
yield benefits such as honor, power, or money, through which one might then obtain the objects of one's appetites and different kinds of pleasures. Upon my life, knowledge may produce that result, but contingently and not essentially. For the end of knowledge, to which it drives and through which human beings are perfected, does not consist in the ends of the senses or the perfection of the body, even though it might achieve these in many circumstances. Used for that type of purpose, it serves to perfect one's beastly and vegetative form, so that it is used for the vilest things when designed to be used for the noblest.

On why people and other animals respond so powerfully to certain kinds of sounds and musical effects

Why do beasts and birds listen so intently to a heartrending melody 93.1
and a resonant voice? What element of this so impinges on people of intelligence and learning that it can even cause them to pass

away? This occurrence is familiar and well-known to those with wide experience of the world.

Miskawayh's response

93.2 We already had much to say on the topic, in our response to the third question you posed in this book, about why human beings like some names and hate others, why they find some letters heavy and others light, and how the soul is affected by sounds that vary in sharpness, loudness, and other qualities. Here we will extend these points to the degree that your extension of the question requires. We respond as follows. Even though the soul is an active form insofar as it constitutes the perfection of a natural body, it is material and passive insofar as it receives the impressions and forms of things. That is why two kinds of causes pertain to it: those through which it acts, and those through which it is passively affected. The soul receives the proportional relations of the different impactions to one another, just as it receives the impactions themselves in single or compound forms. For both the individual sounds and their ensemble are not the same as their proportional relations to one another. Proportional relations are a form of relation, and the relational mode of consideration is not the same as the consideration of things themselves, just as the influence of the one is not the same as the influence of the other.

93.3 As these proportional relations are many and varied, what necessarily applies to them is what applies to all things characterized by multiplicity. That is to say, they have two extremes, one a state of excess and the other a state of deficiency, and they have a balanced state relative to these extremes. If the extremes are many, the balanced states are also many. The soul rejects deficiency and excess, and inclines to the balanced state. As it possesses powers whose manifestation depends on the various mixtures, those powers have different relationships to different proportional relations and different balanced states. The masters of music strove to represent these proportional relations and to study these balances by assigning to them representations from the category of quantity using numbers, even though the category of quality would seem more appropriate for some. For the craft is formed out of these two categories, that is, quantity and quality; but quantity—which consists in numbers—is easier to grasp, so they represented the aspects of quality by means of quantity, and then presented each of these summarily, as you will find expounded in their books.

We have outlined in a general way what the effects of the different sounds that reach the soul are, and which are enjoyable and which odious, so it will be clear that any excess in this regard and deviation toward one of the two sides must affect people accordingly. It has been shown at many junctures that the soul and the body are closely intertwined, and that the one often manifests its effect on the other, for the states of the soul alter the humoral mixture of the body, and the humoral mixture of the body also alters the states of the soul. So, if a certain effect grows so strong in the soul that the humoral mixture is impaired and departs from its balanced state, it ceases to receive the effect of the soul and death ensues, for death consists in nothing more than the soul's ceasing to use the bodily instruments. We know that if the blood of the heart, which possesses a particular balance, spreads through the body and becomes finer than it ought to be because of joy, or returns to concentrate in the heart more than it should because of grief, both situations result in death, or something just short of death, depending on the strength of the effect. It is very common for bodies to exercise a natural effect on bodies and for that effect to be conveyed to the soul, provoking a movement in the latter that becomes the cause of another effect in the body, which leaves it shaken and makes it depart from the balanced state. If you ponder this phenomenon in connection with the things that occasion anger or sadness in strong degrees, it will become plain to you. This suffices for this context; if you wish to explore the topic more fully, then turn to the books of music, for they will meet your need, God willing. 93.4

On why older people are more liable to hope; on the meaning of "hope" and related terms

94.1 Why is it that the grayer one's hair becomes, the brighter one's hopes grow? Abū ʿUthmān al-Nahdī said: I reached 130, and I abjured everything but hope, for that is keener than ever. What is the cause of this condition? And what hidden message does it contain? First, what is "hope"? Second, what is "wishing"? And third, what is "anticipation"? Do these phenomena promote worldly welfare? If they do, then why do people exhort each other to limit their hopes, to abandon their wishes, and to make God the sole object of their hope and anticipation? For He conceals sources of shame, takes pity on the shedding of tears, accepts repentance and forgives transgression, and all hope pinned elsewhere is vain, all anticipation ephemeral.

Miskawayh's response

94.2 This question took an act of the soul and connected it with an act of nature, of the sort that depends on the body and the bodily mixture, and then a comparison was struck between the two, though they are distinct and do not resemble each other. This is why it provoked a sense of astonishment, for hope, anticipation, and wishes are qualities proper to the rational power; gray hair, the deficiencies that affect the body, and the failure of the powers subject to the humoral mixture are natural features arising in instruments that tire through exercise and weaken with the passage of time. By contrast, the acts of the soul grow stronger and their effect intensifies through repetition and continuous performance; this is the opposite of what applies to the body. For example, intellectual reflection becomes stronger and keener the more it is exercised, achieving in a short time what it had previously taken a long time to achieve and swiftly apprehending things that had previously seemed obscure. Sensory vision tires and grows weaker when exercised, and its effect decreases until it disappears.

The distinction between the terms "hope," "anticipation," and "wishing" is obvious. For hope and anticipation attach to voluntary matters, and to things that bear this aspect. Wishing, by contrast, may attach to things that are not the subject of voluntary choice or deliberation; for there is nothing to prevent us from wishing for the impossible and for things that involve no discrimination. Hope pertains more narrowly to subjects that have voluntary choice, whereas anticipation seems to carry both meanings. A person may anticipate rain and fertility, whereas hope can only attach to a person endowed with the capacity to act and deliberate. Wishes, as you know, are diffuse and tend in every direction. A person may wish he could fly, become a star, or ascend to the heavens and view his life from there, but he cannot anticipate it or hope for it. Furthermore, we might anticipate rain, but we can only put our hope in the one who brings down the rain and creates the downpour. These are clear distinctions. 94.3

To your question "Why do people exhort each other to limit their hopes, to abandon their wishes, and to make God the sole object of their hope and anticipation?" my response is as follows. All objects of hope, anticipation, and wishing are limited in duration and finite in number. They are evanescent in themselves and bound to succumb to corruption, fade away, and perish; none of them abides in the same state for a single moment. So, were someone to gratify his desire for them by attaining them, they would soon evanesce and fade away in themselves, or the hope, anticipation, and wish attached to them would soon evanesce and fade away. By contrast, the things that relate to God are everlasting and neither come to an end nor fade away; rather, God diffuses them eternally and is everlastingly generous with them. There is no strength but through Him; He is our sufficiency, our helper, our supporter, and our guide to the straight path. 94.4

On why women are more jealous than men; on the nature and moral status of jealousy

95.1 Why are women more jealous over men than men are over women? The phenomenon is encountered in varying degrees, yet however that may be, there is a hidden force here that explains why its grip on one group is tighter and on the other is slacker. With some people, jealousy has led to the destruction of life, the loss of blessings, and the abandonment of their home. Then in the subsequent question you asked: What is jealousy in the first place? What is its basic reality? What is one to say about its principles and its specifics? What does its etymological derivation reveal? Is it commendable or is it blameworthy? Is the person who experiences it deserving of praise or censure? By bringing up these topics, you are more certain to arrive at instructive insights and reach the goal you desire, and by uncovering them you will also gain knowledge of other topics and pass on to topics beyond them.

Miskawayh's response

95.2 Jealousy is a natural ethical trait that is present among both human beings and beasts. It is praiseworthy if it conforms to the conditions that apply to all traits, that is, if it is put in its proper place and neither oversteps nor falls short of the requisite measure, after the pattern of all the ethical traits we mentioned earlier, such as anger and appetite. For these are natural ethical traits; the ones praised are those that do not depart from the balanced state and attain the place proper to them. The basic reality of jealousy consists in guarding one's womenfolk and the protection of their chastity for the sake of preserving progeny and lineage. So the person who deserves to be commended and not censured is the one whose jealousy is directed to that end, and who neither oversteps what is right by ruling on the basis of groundless accusations and by giving credence to false suppositions and, on their basis, hastening to mete out punishment, nor falls short of what is right by overlooking clear indications and by failing to be roused to rancor by things seen and heard if these are true. He is the one who, with his ethical trait balanced between these extremes, feels anger in the right manner and for the right reasons.

Those who are remiss or immoderate in jealousy are like those 95.3
who, in all ethical traits, overstep the balance, be it to excess or deficiency. We have shown clearly that excess and deficiency in every ethical trait expose the person to many kinds of evils and all manner of adversities and woes; and one's ruin is proportionate to the degree of excess or deficiency exhibited and to the conditions mentioned earlier in our discussion of ethics. There is no single pattern or principle for whether the female has a greater share of jealousy than the male, or the male a greater share than the female. Sometimes the male may exceed his female partner in his response, while sometimes the female may exceed her male partner, as happens with the power of anger and other ethical traits. Yet protective action is more appropriate for males, and this trait is more specific to them, as it involves the exercise of the power of anger and courage; this is more appropriate to males than to females, though females also have a share.

There is no harm in mentioning and highlighting a particular 95.4
aspect here, as many people err on this point. It is repugnant if the power of jealousy is excited and this is caused by appetite, by the desire for sole possession and for exclusive enjoyment of a condition shared by nobody else, and if this response concerns women who are not one's own and is not directed to the preservation of one's lineage and seed. It is a good and fine thing if it conforms to the conditions I have mentioned. The sudden onslaught of this power, however, is a repugnant defect. We find certain animals unaffected by jealousy, such as dogs, billy goats, and swine. The names of these animals serve as terms of abuse when used to describe human beings. We also find some that are prone to jealousy and protective

behavior, such as rams and other stud animals, and these names serve as terms of praise when human beings are likened to them. I know of no other reason why "male goat" serves as a term of abuse and "ram" as a term of praise apart from the manifestation of this particular trait in one and not the other. These are the facts concerning jealousy, its basic reality, and which expressions of it are to be praised and which blamed.

On why more people die young than die old

96.1 What is the reason there are more people who die young than die old? This is attested by the fact that we see fewer old people around us; otherwise there would be more of them, for they would pass from youth to middle age, and from middle age to old age. Death, prevalent among the young, depletes their ranks, and only a fraction pass from that stage to old age, so they are few and far between.

Miskawayh's response

96.2 Life is contingent on the humoral mixture peculiar to each person. This mixture is like a point within a circle; that is, it is a single thing and any departure from it toward the points that surround it, whether near or far, can extend ad infinitum. All people, and all animals generally, have a balance between heat, moisture, coldness, and dryness peculiar to them, and if they deviate from the balance to one of the extremes, they succumb to illness or death. Moreover, there are many things that displace them to the extremes, including, among other things, foods, drinks, and the air that reaches them through breathing. Many of their natural and nonnatural movements displace them from this balance, and many other unforeseeable impairments befall them from external sources. Given the plethora of innumerable causes that displace people from the balanced state, and given the paucity and sparsity of causes that keep them in that state, there is little to wonder at in the situation you described—but it would indeed be worthy of wonder if the opposite obtained.

But for the enormous care directed to the preservation of all animals and human beings in particular, and the consummate and extensive protection afforded to them, there would not be a great length of time between their existence and nonexistence. So let your thoughts dwell on all I have mentioned: on the impairments internal and external to the human body and their different movements, that is, the way the element of fire it incorporates inclines to an upward movement and the element of water it incorporates inclines to a downward movement; on the ardent desire to annihilate and transmute the other natural to each; on the struggle required to preserve the balance, so that the power of the one does not exceed that of the other, set against the existence of numerous appetites and inclinations toward things that are calculated to increase the one and decrease the other. You will then find that everything is preserved with enormous care to the greatest extent possible in such circumstances, until finally some natural element that cannot be withstood presents itself. 96.3

One might compare this to a lamp preserved through a wick and oil while different material elements come to it from the outside—large quantities of oil and strong flames that cause it to be extinguished, and strong winds that it cannot resist and in the face of which it cannot possibly be preserved. If it survives all this for a long period of time, it unavoidably succumbs to natural exhaustion. That is, across the passage of time the heat inevitably depletes what nourishes it, and exhaustion ensues accordingly. This is a sound comparison adequate to its target. If you examine the innate heat and its need for what preserves its powers without excess or deficiency, its complete consumption of the original moisture along with the different material elements that come to it from the outside, and its power or lack of power to exercise a transmuting effect, you will grasp the object of your inquiry and the basis of my comparison will become clear. 96.4

On why people seek likenesses

97.1 Why do people seek likenesses in all they hear, say, do, and ponder? What is the benefit of likenesses? How are they independent of their source, and where do they find their purchase? Likenesses and similitudes, the fact of being alike and the act of likening, are noble objects of concern, a subject for limpid words.

Miskawayh's response

97.2 Likenesses are struck for objects not perceived by the senses drawing on objects perceived by the senses, because of the familiarity and intimate relationship we have with the senses from the beginning of their development, and because they form the foundations of our knowledge, from which we progress to other kinds of knowledge. So if we inform a person about something he has never perceived or speak to him about something foreign to him, something he has never personally witnessed before, he asks for a model derived from the senses. Once furnished with this, he feels a sense of ease and familiarity because of his intimate acquaintance with the object of comparison. This phenomenon may also arise among sensible objects. Thus, were we to speak to someone about ostriches, giraffes, elephants, and crocodiles, he would ask for visual representations so that he could see them with his own eyes and subsume them under his sense of sight. He would not be content to use the sense of hearing for something that is to be grasped through the sense of sight, and he would finally refer the object to that specific sense.

97.3 The same applies to objects of imagination, for were a person tasked with imagining an animal the like of which he had never set eyes on, he would ask what it is like, and would demand that his informant represent it for him. Take the phoenix as an example; even though this animal does not exist, any attempt to imagine it must be based on a visual image composed out of animals that have actually been seen. It is all the more natural that the forms of intelligible things should be foreign and unfamiliar, for they are too subtle to become objects of sense perception and too remote to be provided with a sensible model except by way of approximation. The soul finds comfort in a likeness, even if it is not a true likeness, as it helps it alleviate the strangeness of the foreign. It becomes easier for it to contemplate their likes upon a more intimate acquaintance with intelligible things and an acquisition of the ability to contemplate them without a model through the eye of reason. Every good is attained through the grace of God.

On why we find it easier to represent extreme ugliness in our imagination than exquisite beauty

How it is that the imagination has the power to depict the most 98.1
repulsive images, the most odious forms, and the ugliest limnings in the human soul, yet it lacks the power to depict the most beauteous images, the finest forms, and the most pleasing limnings? Don't you see that when a person's imagination is exposed to the most repulsive things, he is filled with disgust, overcome by shuddering, gripped by aversion, and overtaken by revulsion? Indeed, if the imagination were capable of representing the highest beauty, a person would make that his occupation whenever he was on his own and free from care. So what is the meaning of this? And what is the reason for it? No wonder! For there are things about human beings and their relation to the soul, the intellect, and nature that carry us to the ends of wonder and plunge our hearts into perplexity. Glory be to Him who deposited these rarities into these vessels and made the attainment of these ends possible, who adorned their exterior and beautified their interior, who disposed them between security

and fear, between justice and wrongdoing, and withheld from them the knowledge of the "why" and the "how" in most of those matters.

Miskawayh's response

98.2 Beauty is a form contingent on a balanced humoral mixture and on the existence of sound relations between the different parts of the body as regards shape, color, and other external features. It is rarely the case that all components of this state are brought together in a sound manner. That is why nature itself is not capable of producing it in matter in a perfect way, for the operative causes do not provide assistance; that is, it does not often come about that the matter, the shapes, the form, and the humoral mixture are such that the last form is received in the soundest possible manner. If nature is incapable of generating the balanced state and the sound relation that results in complete beauty, is it a surprise that the imagination should be incapable of it? For the imagination depends on the senses, the senses depend on the humoral mixture, and the humoral mixture depends on an effect of nature. For example, what one desires from many strings set on many frets is that a pleasing note should issue therefrom; and that note is achieved through the whole of the instrument and its parts—the strings, the frets, and the different strokes applied to them. So the note, even though it is a single thing, is produced through the cooperation of all parts. If one part falters, the note that issues is repulsive, its relative distance from a sound that is pleasing being commensurate with the extent of the powerlessness of the causes and the inadequacy of some of them.

98.3 So it is with matter in its need for a particular mixture of elements and many other forms. All of these in combination prepare it to receive the forms of beauty, which consists in a particular balance and a particular sound relation between mixtures and bodily parts with regard to external aspect, shape, color, and other features that, taken jointly, constitute beauty. Even though beauty is a single thing and a single form, it resembles that single pleasing note which requires a large number of external features and an abundance of different forms in order for that pleasing balance to emerge. The imagination moves with facility when it is a matter of departing from the balanced state, whereas in order to attain and preserve that state, it must expend great effort and rely on many prerequisites that it must bring into balance. The same applies to every kind of balance; it is difficult to preserve and persist in, but it only takes the merest movement to depart from it. The difficulty of realizing it becomes even greater, should this balance require external elements to complete it and a variety of things to assist it.

On why sudden joy affects people so violently

99.1 Why does joy have such a violent effect when it assails one suddenly, so that it can even kill? A variety of stories about its effects have been recounted on good authority. When the mother of a certain man was notified that her son had assumed the office of governor, her vision blurred, she keeled over, and she went into convulsions until she died. Ibn al-Khalīl said to me: The bewilderment that comes over a person who discovers a hidden treasure is due to the extreme happiness and overpowering joy he experiences. This is the reason for his public behavior and his movements, and the reason why he finds it difficult to keep what is happening to him a secret and maintain it under control. Yet we hardly encounter this phenomenon when grief and sorrow descend upon us and overwhelm us. We rarely find that someone's gallbladder has ruptured, his physical constitution has become infirm, and his limbs have gone limp and sinews weakened because of a piece of news that vexed and oppressed him, or some evil that befell and overtook him. Though this does happen, it is rare. And when it has the same effect as joy, that is all the more astonishing and the secret behind it all the more remarkable.

Miskawayh's response

99.2 We have already answered this question in the course of discussing the earlier ones.[84] We said that the soul has an effect on the mixtural balance of the body, just as the humoral mixture has an effect on the soul, and we clarified all of that and provided examples. We know for a fact that joy causes the face to redden and that fear causes it to blanche—one causes the blood to expand over the exterior of the body, and the other to sink into the recesses of the body. The heat in the heart is responsible for this; at one time it expands and causes the blood to become fine, and at another time it contracts and causes it to thicken. Joy is attended by the former condition, grief by the latter. If it runs to excess in either direction, it results in a departure from the balanced state, and death or severe illness supervenes, depending on the extent of the departure from the balanced state.

On why we experience states of suffering more intensely than states of well-being

100.1 Why do people feel the pain that befalls them more acutely than they feel the state of well-being they are in? A single day's suffering leads to a dozen days' moaning, whereas going about cosseted in well-being makes no impression on them, and they only notice it when visited by some hurt or affected by some fear. This is why the poet said:

> Though the wheel of fate brings its miseries,
> the suffering teaches you the meaning of joy.[85]

This is corroborated by how we find the complaints of the afflicted outstripping the gratitude of the healthy; this must be because the former experience something the latter do not.

MISKAWAYH'S RESPONSE

This is because well-being is a state congruent with and in agreement with the natural state that results from the balanced mixture set for that body. Congruence and agreement are not things that can be sensed; things that supervene and do not involve agreement are what is sensed. Sensation was granted to animals to use as protection against injuries that befall them, and so that the pain produced in them by things that happen but that do not agree with them should cause them to remedy and redress these things before their mixture becomes impaired and they quickly succumb to destruction. The science of anatomy and discussions of the benefits of the parts of the body have explained why nerves were generated from the brain, dispersed throughout the whole body, and woven into those parts of the body that require sensation.[86] So wherever in the body there are nerves there is sensation, and those parts of the body that do not have them lack sensation; the only parts of the body that do not have them are those that have no need for sensation. 100.2

The noble parts of the body were provided with nerves in order for them to be able to sense things more acutely and to sense the injuries that come upon them more quickly. The purpose of this is to make us hasten to eliminate the pain we experience through treatment, and not neglect it through indolence or other factors. Were a person to be free from sensation and from pain and its locus, it would not be long before he succumbed to destruction through a multiplicity of injuries. Congruent states, by contrast, do not need to be sensed. This is how things stand with all of the five senses in their natural states; they do not sense the things that are congruent with them, but rather, sense the things that do not agree with them. 100.3

The sense of touch, shared across the entire body, perceives that which exceeds or falls short of the balance set for it. For example, the body has a particular balance with respect to heat, and it does not sense the temperature of the air that it encounters if it is congruent with it or agrees with it. By contrast, the body senses the air if it departs from the particular balance of the body, whether 100.4

in the direction of cold or heat, and rushes to remedy or rectify it. The same applies to cold, moisture, and dryness. Each of the other senses has a balanced state proper to it; it does not sense that which is congruent with it, but rather only senses that which opposes it and displaces it from its balanced state. Take the eye: It does not sense the air or any of the objects that lack color and a modality that would displace it from its balanced state. The same applies to hearing and to the other senses. This topic is discussed thoroughly in the appropriate sections of the books of philosophy, so let these be consulted.

On why seeing someone laughing causes others to laugh

101.1 We sometimes see a person laughing at some remarkable thing he sees or hears or thinks of, and then another person sees him and begins to laugh at his laughter without sharing in the object of his laughter. And sometimes the second person's laughter makes the first person laugh even harder. What is it that passes from the person who's laughing out of amazement to the second person laughing?

Miskawayh's response

101.2 One individual soul can have many kinds of effects on another individual soul, some rapid and others tardy. We have already said much about this. The rapid effects they have on one another include sleeping, yawning, and other forms of relaxation. It is a well-known fact that when a person grows drowsy or feigns drowsiness in the presence of a person who is wide awake and feels no tiredness, he causes the latter to grow drowsy and sends him off to sleep. The same applies to people who yawn and shirk work. Something similar may happen with someone who sets to work energetically, so that his energy passes over to another person, though the first person remains more energetic and this quality is more evident in him. The reason for this is that the soul is one in its essence, even though it is characterized by multiplicity through the multiplicity of individuals. So it is hardly surprising that certain rapid effects of the soul should be conveyed from some individuals to others without any time lag. This process does not require that anything should "pass" through any physical transfer and motion that unfolds in time. It is enough for the two souls to see each other, for the effect the one exercises on the other occurs without any lapse of time. On this subtle point, one should recall the effect on the observer of the object of observation; for though accomplished by means of the body, it requires no lapse of time whatsoever. Thus we cannot say that, when a person observes a fixed star, there is a lapse of time between the moment he opens his eyes and the moment he sees it.

On why human beings are so attached to the world despite the misfortunes and suffering they experience in it

Why are human beings so passionately attached to this world— 102.1
clinging to it, cherishing it, and laboring after it—despite the vicissitudes, accidents, calamities, and other woes they see it contains, and despite the extinction to which its inhabitants are exposed? Whence did human beings acquire this attribute?

Miskawayh's response

How could they not be passionately attached to the world when 102.2
they are natural beings and form part of it? For they originate in it, develop in it, and are born out of it. Don't you see how they begin as a drop of sperm and develop like plants, deriving their nourishment by means of roots connected to their mothers' wombs, and drawing their sustenance the way a tree does? God transfers them

from that location when they are completed and become «another creature»,[87] and He molds them into animals; then they take nourishment through the mouth and breathe, and reach the rank of nonrational animals. They remain thus until they receive the form of rationality for the first time and become human beings. Then they progress in their humanity until they reach the ultimate ranks they are intended to attain—and only a few isolated individuals across many eons arrive at the final rank that constitutes the ultimate end of humanity.

102.3 The vast majority of people occupy a station close to the beastly one, and their rationality and discrimination do not go beyond imparting a certain order with a rational structure to this beastly nature. For them to abandon this nature and reach the point you demanded is out of the question. This is only attained by philosophers who achieve the fullness of philosophical wisdom and exhaust all of its parts through both knowledge and action, or by prophets, who occupy that station by means of divine inspiration and guidance. Even so, they need the material substance of human existence, which they derive from this world, though they do so without passionate attachment and without clinging to it greatly or cherishing it. This topic is inexhaustible and wide-ranging, and people have discussed it at length. What I have indicated and stated suffices. I have no more to say.

On why people say the world would fall to ruin if it weren't for fools

103.1 Why was it said: But for fools, the world would fall to ruin? What worldly or religious benefit do the lives of fools bring? Is what was said true?

Miskawayh's response

It has been established that human beings are political by nature and that they do not live in isolation as the birds and wild beasts do. For the latter can satisfy their own needs, having been provided with plumage and with the ability to attain the things they need for their welfare and nourishment. Human beings, by contrast, are naked and powerless and lack the ability to attain the things they need for their welfare and nourishment without cooperating and forming communities; and this constitutes political association. Furthermore, political association can be characterized by a state designated as "flourishing," and by another state designated, relative to the first, as "ruin." This state of flourishing is realized when helpers abound and justice reigns through their power of political authority, which orders their affairs, preserves their stations, and relieves them from adversities. By an "abundance of helpers" I mean that people's physical powers and intentions should work together to effect a plethora of actions, some of which are necessary for life to be sustained, others of which are conducive to living in a good condition, and yet others are conducive to the embellishment of life. Flourishing is the conjunction of all these aspects. If political association lacks any one of these three, it is in a state of ruin. If it lacks two—specifically, both the good condition and embellishment of life—then it is in an advanced state of ruin. For it is only ascetics who content themselves with just the things that are absolutely necessary to sustain life, and they do not cause the world to flourish, nor are they to be counted among those who can do so. 103.2

The subsistence of the world, its complete flourishing, is accomplished through three things, which are like high-level genera that then subdivide into numerous species. The first consists in working and cultivating the land through planting and sowing, and tending to it with means that put it in good order and prepare it for the use desired of it. I refer here to using tools derived from mined materials such as stones and iron for tilling, grinding, and irrigating the land 103.3

with water that comes from springs, rivers, canals, waterwheels, and the like. The second consists in the implements of soldiers and the weapons they use to protect the people we have described from enemies, so that the people can live as a group and fulfill the purpose they have come together to achieve through cooperation. Additionally, soldiers have craftsmen and attendants who train horses for them, and who fashion shields that serve for protection, as well as other weapons that serve for repelling and driving off the enemy. The third consists in procuring and supplying, which is accomplished by transporting to another place things rare in one place, and to the land things that are found in the sea. These three elements constitute an adornment and beautification that further ameliorate the condition of the world, and there are people specifically devoted to each of the subdivisions of the three elements we have mentioned.

103.4 You must understand that to live is not the same as to live excellently or in a good condition; you will then understand that flourishing is connected to how excellent life is. We know for a fact that these things can only be achieved by incurring many risks, exposing oneself to fear, enduring hardships, and confronting terror. People would all become ascetics were they to content themselves with necessities, cast aside the superfluities of life, and act purely on the basis of what reason demands. And were that to happen, the good and beautiful order present in the world would disappear, and they would lead the abstemious lives led by people who dwell in sparsely populated, defenseless villages, or led by people who live in tents, yurts, or reed huts. This is the state of polities designated as ruin.

103.5 To your question "Are the people who cause the world to flourish to be called fools?" I respond: It is not permissible for everyone to call them that. For this derogatory appellation is more fittingly applied to the people we have described—those who dwell in villages and remote parts of the earth and who show themselves unequal to improving their living conditions—than to those who have used their intelligence, perspicacity, and acumen to develop this plethora of fine crafts that work to the advantage of people. That is only admissible for those who have acquainted themselves with, and distinguished between, all forms of knowledge and learning, assigning them to their proper stations, abstaining from those they abstain from out of experience and knowledge, and choosing those they choose based on reflection and secure conviction. The reason why philosophers have abstained from inquiring into the flourishing of the world is that it conduces to the flourishing of the body. They ascertained that the soul is superior to the body, and perceived that there is another world that belongs to it, with a beauty that befits it, and with its own crafts, forms of knowledge, and pathways. It is more taxing and arduous to venture on these paths than to venture on the hazards of the mundane world, and more demanding and toilsome to persist and persevere in these crafts and forms of knowledge through inquiry and action than to persevere and act in the mundane world. Therefore they chose contentment, and contented themselves with as much nourishment in the mundane world as is necessary. Yet it is they who created the foundations of the different crafts and trades for that other people, and who left them to that other people when they showed themselves unequal to any other tasks. Then the philosophers occupied themselves and their disciples with the loftier and more excellent matters.

On the anxiety experienced by people who have something to hide

What is the reason for the anxiety experienced by the person 104.1
who hides something shameful, harbors something dubious, and conceals some wicked deed? His face and behavior give him away such that people remark: The guilty person might as well declare, "Here I am, take me in." What is this phenomenon all about? How is it provoked? And through what means can it cease?

Miskawayh's response

104.2 This question only provokes perplexity in people who do not acknowledge the reality of the soul and the fact that all the voluntary movements of the body have their origin in it and are accomplished through it. I cannot see how anyone who knows that the soul governs the body of living beings, and particularly of human beings who are vested with voluntary choice and governed by the rational discriminating soul, could find any cause for perplexity. For when the soul is aware of something and it produces acts that are contrary to what befits that awareness, it experiences the kind of disturbance that nature experiences when its movement is to the right but it is moved to the left by a force inferior to or equal to its own force. Disturbance appears in the former, just as it appears in the latter.

On why we are more likely to heed a preacher who practices what he preaches

105.1 Why is it that when a preacher is honest, his words have an effect, his preaching achieves results, and it is easy to follow his example, to obey him and adhere to what he has said? And why is it that if the opposite holds true of him, his words have no influence, be they ever so pure, and his preaching does no good, be it ever so eloquent? Why does it matter if he dissociates himself from the truth of his words when the words are true, the evidence sound, and the proof incontestable? How can his action fortify his words while its contrary can enervate his evidence? Doesn't wisdom subsist in itself, and isn't it the guarantor of its own soundness? That is why it has been said: When sermons come from the heart they enter the heart, and when they come from the tongue they go no further than the ears.

Miskawayh's response

Preachers command people to do what they consider the most proper course of action. So, if they go against their own word, they give others the impression that they have lied and been deceitful, and that the reason why they exhort people against enjoying the mundane world is for it to be left to them and be available for their enjoyment. Observers who fall short of that rank and are unable to reach the same level of reflective examination form the notion that preachers derive their ability to preach from their heightened ability to fool people and to disguise falsehoods as truths, for if they believed the words they spoke, they would act on their basis. These are the kinds of things that occur to people's minds when they hear a preacher who does not behave as he preaches. It may be that the majority of preachers one sees do not in fact subscribe to what they publicly express, and their goal is rather to distract people's attention from what they possess, to gain a position of eminence by having people flock to them, or to satisfy some other worldly desire. So what impact can the words of such people have once the people they are preaching to have become cognizant of their designs and have discovered where they are tending? It is the opposite with those who do good works and strive for righteous behavior, whose heart is sincere, and whose deeds are in accord with their knowledge, their words, and their intentions. They become models whose example is emulated and whose words are trusted. They attract a great number of adherents, and many pursue the same reflective inquiry that they do and place credence in their judgment. 105.2

On why people regret their failure to honor and benefit from great men during their lifetime

Why do people feel great regret at their failure to honor and acclaim men of excellence and to acquire wisdom from them once they are 106.1

gone? Why did they shun them when they had the chance to consult them and the opportunity to devote time to them, when they had fewer cares, were more open in their views, and clearly had more power?

Miskawayh's response

106.2 This question has already been answered, and there is no point in repeating the discussion.[88]

On why Arabs and non-Arabs declare their pedigrees in times of war

107.1 Why do Arabs and non-Arabs declare their pedigrees during times of war and unrest? To declare one's pedigree is to state who one's fathers and forefathers are and to state one's relation to famous events and notable deeds of the past. What is it that rouses them and makes them bristle and advance, enter the fray and boldly venture forth, risking their lives as they storm ahead? At that moment they may hear some verse, remember some proverb, or see someone of inferior family, station, stock, and origin conducting himself in a way that is superior to the way they are conducting themselves, and a sense of pride seizes them and drags them by the bit to their death. What are these curiosities and these wonders pertaining to this ethical constitution that lie widely dispersed and deeply buried in this physical constitution? Glory be to the One through whose knowledge, command, and action this is accomplished. He is God, to whom all things submit themselves, whether freely or grudgingly, and to whom all things point, whether covertly or overtly.

Miskawayh's response

107.2 Anger exists as a potentiality in human beings until it is actualized by something that causes anger. The same principle applies to all powers of the soul. The things that actualize it are of two kinds: those that arise externally, and those that arise internally. Examples of things that arise externally include violations of honor, insults, and the like. Examples of things that arise internally include the remembrance of wrongs and grudges and all those states that tend to fuel this power. It is characteristic of the soul that, when it is at rest and a person seeks to elicit a powerful action from it, his bodily members do not comply with his desire. He is then forced to move and rouse the soul, and that movement of the soul determines the degree of powerfulness of that action. We perceive this clearly in people who are feeling happy: When they try to display anger or to behave in the way angry people do, their bodily members abandon them, and they exhibit signs of forced behavior. Sometimes they provoke others to laughter, and also laugh themselves, though they are in the most pressing need of the power of anger. In that situation, it is necessary for them to rouse their irascible power by remembering something that stirs up that power so their action can issue in the right manner.

This situation arises in times of war if the war does not specifically 107.3
concern the person fighting in it—I mean that the fighter might be participating in a war that does not specifically concern him with the aim of helping others or of obtaining some financial reward. Confronted by the sight of war, he fails to be seized by a sense of zeal and pride, and then needs to declare his pedigree, which involves remembering acts of courage performed by his forbears, in the hope that this will stoke his passions, rouse his courage, and elicit a powerful movement from his soul. If roused, this power becomes like a fire, which begins feebly and then grows stronger as it engages in actions and applies itself to them with dedication. Those acts become like the material fed into a fire, which kindles it until it flares up and blazes fiercely, and he becomes like someone in a state of intoxication, so diminished is his self-control and his capacity for discrimination. This is the state the fighter seeks to produce in himself.

On why people distinguish between different kinds of air, water, and earth, but not different kinds of fire

108.1 Why do people say, "This air is more agreeable than that," "This water is fresher than that," "The ground of such and such a region is firmer than that one," and "The soil of such and such a place is softer, more putrid, or more briny than the soil of that place," yet they do not then say in analogy: "The fire of such and such a region is superior, better, and purer, or emits stronger heat, burns more strongly, and has a fiercer flame," but instead they attribute these qualities to the differences between materials, saying for example that its power is plainer to see in dry timber and is faster to take hold in combed cotton?

Miskawayh's response

108.2 The four elements have in common the fact that each admits the power of the other in smaller or larger degrees, so that some are purer in their form and species than others; yet fire in particular is less receptive to the power of the others and more resistant to entering into mixtures. That is because the form of fire dominates over its matter. To explain the point: Earth is receptive to forming mixtures with water and air that displace it from its proper form, resulting in the mud, salt, and the various aspects that account for the differences between soils. Similarly, water receives from the earth contiguous to it and the air surrounding it many kinds of tastes and smells, purities and impurities, such that it undergoes an evident departure from its proper form. The same holds true of air, insofar as it accepts different effects from the earth and water, with some of it becoming thick and some moist, dry, and balanced. So the effects of these three elements on one another are manifested in such a way that they are plainly perceived by the senses, and the effects of some relative to others become deficient in a such a way that every person can judge that they have departed from their balanced state. Their departure from their balanced state causes evident harm to bodies.

With fire, by contrast, its proper form dominates over its matter, so that it is not receptive to forming mixtures that result in one of its effects—be it the effect of burning, which constitutes its act, or the effect of light, which constitutes its specific property—becoming deficient in a way that is plain to the senses. Fire may indeed also receive a certain effect through mixture and through contiguity with nearby objects, but it is extremely meager in comparison with the effects received by its counterparts. For example, the fire whose material consists in black naphtha and unmixed sulfur has a different color when compared with the fire whose material consists in clear oil and pure violet ointment; for the former is red, whereas the latter is white. But the act one wishes the fire to effect on this ensemble—that is, to burn and emit light—does not suffer deficiency. Suffering deficiency as a result of the specific materials characterizes it in all geographical regions alike and is not exclusive to one as opposed to another. If people obtain what they want from the action of fire, they content themselves with meeting their needs, and give no consideration to the materials specific to given countries, particularly since the materials are common among them. This is not how things stand with the counterparts of fire. 108.3

On why people feel happier when they unexpectedly obtain something they weren't seeking than when they obtain what they were seeking

Why do people experience a greater sense of happiness when they 109.1
come into some money or realize some good when they're not

expecting or anticipating it than they do when they attain what they were seeking and achieve what they were pursuing? Is it because in the one case they must seek something deferred, or is there some other reason?

Miskawayh's response

109.2 Every occurrence that concerns a person's soul and body and that reaches him in a gradual manner is felt without much acuteness and manifests a weak effect on him. When it reaches him suddenly and in one fell swoop, it is felt acutely. In the case of the body, this is exemplified by the fact that we take little notice of the illnesses that make us depart from the balanced state in a gradual manner, and sometimes we take no notice of them at all. By contrast, if they bring about this departure in a non-gradual manner, we experience a great amount of pain. This is how it is with consumption and similar illnesses; for they make us depart from the balanced state toward the farthermost extreme, right to death's door, but we do not feel the pain because it occurs gradually. Were this to happen differently, all at once, we would be exposed to an amount of pain that would be difficult to bear. The same thing applies to pleasures, for pleasure in fact consists in a person's return in one fell swoop to his balanced state. Pleasure and pain are similar conditions in that they appear all at once, in a non-gradual manner, and they are thus alike in the intensity with which they are felt. This question concerns an effect that sometimes comes to people in a gradual manner and sometimes in a non-gradual manner. The way a person responds to things he has not anticipated and has not arrived at gradually by pursuing them is similar to the way he responds to the examples we gave, which happen in one fell swoop; he thus feels them acutely, and their effect on him is strongly manifested.

On why fine edifices fall to ruin when left uninhabited

Why is it that fine buildings and imposing mansions quickly become dilapidated when uninhabited, but not when they are inhabited and frequented? You might suppose that this is because the inhabitants undertake repairs when necessary, restore them when they're dilapidated and fallen to ruin, and care for them by replastering them and sweeping them clean. Yet rest assured that this is not the reason. For you know that they have an impact on the dwelling by walking on it, by causing it to support their weight, by wearing down layers of plaster and daub, and by all those other movements that have a similar tendency and effect, even if they do not weaken it in view of the repairs and restorations they undertake. So the question about the cause of this persists, and you will hear it in the course of responding to my questions in this book.[89] 110.1

Miskawayh's response

Most types of damage to buildings are either due to decay caused by rain and water, when the drains are blocked by objects swept by the wind into the pipes and watercourses, for this causes the water to back up and flood the foundations of the walls from outside and inside the building; or result from defective cracks that appear in the exterior of fine buildings, exposing them to the air, rain, cold, and snow. Sometimes the damage may be caused when the wind blows reeds or chaff from the chopped straw of the bricks into the watercourse, for this diverts the water in the wrong direction and causes the entire building to become dilapidated. The damage done by vermin springing up at the foundations and by spiders on the ceilings, effectively wearing away at all of the building's features over time, is plain. Dilapidation of this type produces a very ugly effect that is repulsive to behold and renders a distinguished 110.2

building unseemly. Sometimes the inhabitants of a building might neglect a room, be it intentionally or unintentionally, so when it is opened up it cannot be entered because of the activity of animals that creep along the ground (rats, snakes, and insects that build nests by boring holes, such as woodworms and ants), the food they collect, spiderwebs, and dust covering the ornaments. This assumes that it has been spared from seepage, and from water that destroys the walls and the ceilings over which it flows, causing them to crumble from the clay the water sweeps down from the roof and breaking all of the timber, supports, and stays. If the building is occupied, the inhabitants prevent these great causes of dilapidation from taking effect. The decay produced by inhabitants is negligible in comparison with these things, so the building is more likely to flourish and less likely to become dilapidated.

On why men of sublime character beget knaves

111.1 Why do men of a noble, honorable, valiant nature beget ignoble, disreputable scoundrels? The former beget the latter with all the disparity between their souls' aims and traits and for all the propinquity between their origins and roots.

Miskawayh's response

111.2 Discipline and governance have a large hand in reforming the character traits of the soul, though they are contingent upon the humoral mixture of the body. Sometimes the humoral mixture of the son may be distant from the humoral mixture of the father, and this may be compounded by faulty discipline and bad governance, though even one of these is enough to produce corruption; so the two dispositions and comportments become different.

On why our longing for home grows more intense the nearer we come to it

Why is it that when a person is far from his homeland and birthplace—where his eye takes its delight, his head finds its rest, his soul tastes its joy, and his spirit derives its warmth—his sense of longing is less fierce, his sense of disquiet more abated, his feelings less inflamed, his soul filled with greater cheer, and his heart filled with greater delight, yet as he approaches his home and his eagerness to set foot there increases, his patience gives out and his equanimity deserts him? The poet thus said:[90] 112.1

> Longing burns fiercest on the day when the native returns

Is this a phenomenon that has a general or a particular application? What is its cause? Does it have a cause?

Miskawayh's response

This phenomenon is encountered and attested among natural things as well, for if you cast a stone from a height down to its resting position on the ground where it belongs, from the time it begins to move, the closer it gets to its resting position, the more vigorous the movement grows and the faster it becomes, and it attains its greatest velocity when close to the ground. The higher the point from which the stone is thrown, the starker and more manifest this phenomenon is. The same holds true of fire and the other elements when cast from a place that is not proper to them. The closer they get to their resting positions, the more intense their movement and inclination become. We do not ask "why" regarding such topics, for they form first principles of nature, and our only aim can be to become cognizant of them and to know that this is how they stand. The same applies to the soul, insofar as its inclination is weaker 112.2

when it is far from the place it is accustomed to; the closer the soul draws to that place, the more intense both its inclination and the movement called "longing" become.

112.3 The reason I have said that one does not inquire into these topics by asking "why" is that "why" is used in inquiry when one is searching for a cause or foundation. Yet these constitute foundations in themselves, and they have no other cause beyond the fact that this is how things stand in themselves. That is, they themselves constitute their own foundations, and they do not stand that way because of some other cause. For example, should a person inquire, "Why does the eye see by means of these specific ocular layers? And why does it see things according to the angle between itself and the object of vision—large if the object is large, and small if it is small?" or should he ask, "Why does the ear perceive things by means of an impaction of the air in this specific fashion?" it would not be necessary to respond, for with evident things that constitute first principles, the *that* is identical to the *why*.

On the Meaning of the Dictum That Judgement Sleeps While Passion Keeps Watch

113.1 Why was it said: Judgment sleeps while passion keeps watch—this is why passion defeats judgment? This is a remark ascribed to the sage of the Arabs, ʿĀmir ibn al-Ẓarib. Doesn't judgment belong to the party of the intellect and its supporters? So how could it be defeated given its lofty status and noble position? And what is the meaning of the remark made by another early thinker: "The intellect is the friend we disavow; passion the enemy to whom we bow"? What is the cause of such friendship joined to such disobedience? And what is the cause of such enmity joined to such subordination? Does this show the reality of things to be reversed and subverted? For what is manifested deviates from what is mandated and conforms to an order that is infirm.

Miskawayh's response

This point was framed for literary effect and in a rhetorical manner. In terms of content, the point is that passion is very strong in us, whereas judgment is weak; the reason is that we humans are natural beings and within us the element of nature dominates over the element of the intellect. For we live in the world of nature, and the intellect is foreign and has a weak effect upon us. That is why it fatigues us to inquire into intellectual matters, but it does not fatigue us as much to inquire into natural matters. The effect of the intellect on us is very limited, though it is noble in itself and occupies an exalted rank. And even though in comparison with the intellect nature is weak and occupies a lowly rank, it is strong in us because we live in its world, form part of it, are composed from its elements, and all of its powers are present within us. This is evident and needs no lengthy explanation. 113.2

On a remark concerning logic made by the dialectical theologian Abū Hāshim to the philosopher Abū Bishr Mattā

Abū Bishr Mattā, the commentator on logic, once attended a learned gathering and, as a reproach of logic, the dialectical theologian Abū Hāshim asked him:[91] Isn't "logic" simply a derivation from the term "speech"? So tell me: Was Abū Hāshim being fair? Did he hit upon the truth, or was he guilty of partisanship in saying something that he never should have, despite his status and extreme caution in how he expressed his doctrines? An exposition of this point would yield hidden caches of knowledge and illuminate the ways of wisdom. 114.1

Miskawayh's response

114.2 Abū Hāshim was right about the morphological pattern, but was wrong in expressing disdain and reproach—if that was indeed his aim. For the only reason why some form of knowledge could be reproached is if someone has made a mistake, not because of its name. The same point would have applied had Abū Bishr responded in kind by asking, "Isn't 'dialectical theologian' (*mutakallim*) simply derived morphologically from the term 'talking' (*kalām*)?" He could also have considered all other forms of knowledge and posed similar questions. "Doesn't 'legal knowledge' simply derive from the expression 'I understood something,' adopting the morphological pattern?" and "Doesn't 'grammar' simply derive from the expression 'I headed toward something,' that is, 'I directed myself toward it'"? It often happens that a name is applied to a particular form of knowledge that is not merited by its station, and that a name is applied to it that demeans its station; the former does not benefit the knowledge in question, nor does the latter harm it. I know some people who called themselves the "discerners" and called their forms of knowledge "true discernment," when this was a far cry from how things actually stood. Others called themselves "the deserving," "the people of truth," and suchlike, and in doing so made false claims. That is as much discussion as the topic deserves.

On why some Arabic words are feminine and others masculine

115.1 I once saw a man asking an established philosopher: The Arabs treat the noun "sun" as feminine noun and the noun "moon" as masculine. What is the cause of that? And what was their object in agreeing on this practice? For if it lacks a cause, it is akin to a convention established to serve no particular aim. This scholar offered no response, and so I have not named him, for to mention his name while revealing the limits of his abilities is to expose him and impugn his dignity, and he does not deserve that his many successes in reaching the truth should be denied on account of this minor failure. The questioner then said: The astronomers treat the sun as masculine and treat the moon as feminine, and this also constitutes an agreement among astronomers. Here, the philosopher responded, providing an account of their views. The reason he was unable to deal with the other question was not inadequate erudition, but he could not recall any response given on the topic by the authorities on the Arabic language. The issue at stake is hidden from view, not merely of those who have skimmed the surface of knowledge, but indeed of experienced navigators, who have sailed its open seas, braved its waves, and plumbed its depths. Alas, the waters of this knowledge run deep, and the ship that sails on it floats high. It is not every heart that can compass every thought, not every person that can utter every word, and not every agent that can bring forth every deed.

Miskawayh's response

The grammarians, on their part, do not assign causes to these 115.2
things, and they point out that the Arabs may treat something that is in reality masculine as a feminine noun and treat something that is in reality feminine as a masculine noun. An example is the fact that women's reproductive organs themselves, which are the ground for the feminineness of everything feminine, are treated as a masculine noun by the Arabs, and there are feminine terms used to refer to the reproductive organs of men. Examples abound of nouns like "eagle," "fire," and such, which really ought to be treated as masculine but are treated as feminine. Yet the question asked specifically about the sun, and I think the reason why the Arabs treat it as feminine is that they believed that the lofty stars were the daughters of God—may He be exalted far above such notions—and they worshipped whichever they deemed noblest. They referred to the sun in particular by the name of a goddess, for one of its names is "al-Lāt." So it is possible

that the reason they treat it as feminine is because of this name and because of their belief that it is one of God's daughters—indeed, the greatest one in their view.

On whether a human being could know everything

116.1 Is it possible for one human being to grasp all forms of knowledge, in all their varieties and paths and in all their different languages and locutions? If it is possible, is it also obligatory? If it is obligatory, is it encountered in reality? And if it is encountered, is it known? If it is possible, what is the ground of its possibility? And if it is impossible, what is the ground of its impossibility? A response to this question would shed light on the hidden recesses of the world.

Miskawayh's response

116.2 One of the ways in which philosophy has been defined is that it is the knowledge of all existents qua existents, but not according to the terms you set out in your question—that is, when you referred to "their varieties and paths and their different languages and locutions." For it is not possible for a single form of knowledge to encompass the entirety of these terms, since its particulars are infinite in number, and what is infinite in number cannot enter existence. But the objective with every form of knowledge is to arrive at its universals, which contain all of its particulars *in potentia*. In medicine, for example, it is enough to learn the principles and ordinances through which the type of illness and type of treatment can be determined; to seek to know all the particular elements of the different illnesses would be impossible. This is how the books by Galen and other physicians are written: They instruct a person in the principles and treatments of the different illnesses. Once a physician begins practicing the craft, he comes across innumerable particular elements relating to a single illness, and the illness continues to harbor particular elements that no one who comes after him could ever enumerate. If this is how things stand, the response to your question is subject to the qualification I have mentioned. There is no point in seeking to learn the different paths and locutions, for one's objective in pursuing the different kinds of knowledge is the knowledge itself, and whatever the path used to reach it and whatever the language used to express it, knowledge would meet the purpose.

To your question "Is this obligatory?" I respond: It is indeed 116.3
obligatory, because philosophical inquiry is obligatory inasmuch as it constitutes the perfection of humanity and the attainment of its ultimate degree. When an entity has a specific perfection, its end is to attain that perfection. People who fall short of attaining their perfection, even though they possess the means and the obstacles before it have been removed, are held to account.

Regarding your question "Is it encountered in reality?" it is 116.4
indeed so, because philosophy is encountered, and it is the craft of all crafts, and none of its parts have been ordered as it has been ordered itself. For it starts from the lowest level at which the learner begins and reaches the highest grade possible for him to reach. All of this involves principles and explanations that enjoy the utmost firmness, and they are known and available. There is nothing to prevent us from reaching them, nor are they begrudged to those who seek them, and they are a grace to those who learn them.

On why new incumbents are harsh toward the officials they replace

What is the meaning of the anger felt by the new incumbent of an 117.1
office toward the official he has replaced? This is how this question is articulated. For example, you are appointed governor of a particular

province, or judge in a particular city. You arrive in the province and find the former governor whom you are to replace. You treat him harshly, get angry, and scowl openly at him. Yet he has done nothing to anger you, nor has he ever done you any harm. You have never met, and there has been no exchange of any kind, good or bad, between you. The anger experienced by public floggers and executioners belongs to the same class.

Miskawayh's response

117.2 The new official intuits that the official he is replacing must hate and loathe him, and human beings are naturally disposed to loathe those who loathe them and to hate those who hate them. As a result, every newly appointed official experiences this reaction vis-à-vis the incumbent. Sometimes other elements may be added; for example, the official being replaced might have been deposed because of an act of great treachery or a great felony, such as rightly provoke anger. In addition to that, often the new appointee has been ordered to detain his predecessor, to take him to task for embezzlement of funds, and to liquidate his assets. These are things that provoke anger and enhance its material basis, particularly as the official being replaced will defend himself, deny every evil ascribed to him, and try to protect his assets to the best of his ability. So how could anger be excluded from this context? Doesn't this in fact constitute its true and proper occasion? The behavior of floggers and executioners admits a different kind of justification, for they are recompensed for practicing their trade, and if they fail to execute it properly they will be exposed to censure and derision, and the only way for them to execute their trade properly is by rousing themselves to anger. This is supplementary to the first reason I mentioned regarding the new official and the incumbent being replaced.

On why human beings are considered to be orphans after losing their father rather than their mother

Why is it that with human beings someone is deemed an orphan when he loses his father, whereas among other animals this is based on the loss of the mother? If you say: The reason is that among the latter the mother is the provider, the same holds true of human beings. There must be another secret behind this, and the matter must admit further consideration. 118.1

Miskawayh's response

Insofar as human beings are animals and via this aspect share kinship with the beasts, they need nourishment to sustain them and preserve their animal nature. Insofar as they are human beings and via this aspect share kinship with the celestial sphere, they need the things that enable them to attain this station through instruction and discipline, for discipline is to the soul what nourishment is to the body. The person who attends to the first condition is the mother, and the person who attends to the second is the father. As the second is their noblest condition and that through which they become what they are—human beings—it follows that their status as orphans must be based on the loss of their father. As the perfection of the animal nature of other animals consists in bodily nourishment, it follows that their orphanhood must be based on the loss of the mother. A person might lose his mother before he reaches the point of receiving instruction from the father and while in need of suckling. He is then called an orphan on account of the loss of his mother, and there is no objection to designating him as such. 118.2

On why chess is so hard to master

119.1 Al-Ma'mūn said: "I wonder at myself. I have the ends of the earth under my power, yet I cannot master a small square"—he was referring to chess. This is something commonly reported among people, so what is its cause? For his wonder was aroused by the obscurity of the cause.

Miskawayh's response

119.2 Without the addition of constant application and regular training, acquired knowledge and prior learning do not suffice in crafts, for otherwise a person cannot become skillful. The craftsman is the person who is skilled in his craft. Take the scribal craft as an example; if the person who knows its principles acquires knowledge but lacks practice, then, despite any prior knowledge and assiduous learning, he comes to a standstill, and none of the knowledge he has previously acquired regarding it avails him. The same applies to sewing or building, and in general to every professional craft, such as leading an army and military combat. Neither courage nor knowledge of its modalities suffices without the acquisition of training and practice; this is when it becomes a craft. Since chess is a craft that conforms to this pattern, neither deliberative power nor good imagination nor excellent judgment suffices without the addition of active engagement and practice. For every move that changes the shape of the game is met by an opponent's countermove, be it apt or inept. All this needs to be determined, and all potential patterns need to be represented in the imagination, move by move, in all their different configurations, and this can only be achieved through practice and training.

On why people dislike changing their name or patronymic, and why they have a sense of aversion toward certain names and titles

Why are people averse to changing their patronymic or their name? I once knew a man who, on account of a contingency that prompted him to do so, changed his patronymic, and he felt unhappy and ill at ease. His patronymic was "Abū Ḥafṣ" and he adopted the patronymic "Abū Jaʿfar." His reason for doing so was that he asked a Shiʿi for a favor and did not wish to be known as Abū Ḥafṣ.[92] Why is it that some people hate certain things because of their name rather than their intrinsic nature, or their title rather than their inner substance? What is the meaning of the revulsion the soul is quick to feel when confronted with particular sobriquets and titles? What is the meaning of the tranquility that comes over the soul when it encounters particular appellations? And yet the two are similar in appearance and close in imagination. 120.1

Miskawayh's response

Names bind themselves to meanings, and with the passage of time speakers of a language grow so used to them that the two come to be virtually identified. This is what led a group of scholars to the controversial assertion that the name is identical with the thing it names, and what led a group of eminent learned men to assert that names correspond to particular meanings by nature.[93] This seems to involve saying that only the letters that in fact combine to designate the meaning "standing" or "sitting," "star" or "earth," are fit to be used for referring to those meanings and no others, for those letters have come to belong to them by nature. This claim imposed upon the greatest philosophers the task of refutation and composing books on the topic. Therefore, it is little wonder that a person should grow so accustomed to his own name that he should think 120.2

that he himself has undergone a change if it is changed, and if he is addressed with another name, he should think that someone else has been addressed, and that, indeed, it should seem to him as though his very self has thereby been altered.

120.3 I heard an accomplished scholar consulting a doctor and expressing concern that his symptoms might mean that he had been stricken by melancholy. I asked him: What is it you find unusual in yourself? He replied: It seems to me as though my right side has become my left side, and my left side has become my right—I have no doubt about that. After questioning him extensively, I discovered that he had worn his ring on his right hand for a certain period of time in order to ingratiate himself with a powerful friend of his; when he left him, he happened to return his ring to his left hand, and he experienced this reaction as a result of custom and habit. If you consider this example, your question will become easy to answer, and you will grasp the similarity that joins habit and nature.

120.4 The answer to your question about the revulsion people experience toward something on account of its name, title, or sobriquet is closely related to the answer to this question. For names and titles also provoke revulsion on account of what they designate, because of prior habit. So, were a person to agree with another to reassign the name "coal" so that it designated camphor, whenever the word "coal" was mentioned, the image of something black would come to mind, and the fact that this had been reassigned to another object that is white and sweet-smelling would do nothing to prevent it. This is due to habit, unless of course the combination of the letters is repugnant and the letters themselves provoke distaste. The explanation of the latter phenomenon was discussed exhaustively in the earlier section of these questions.[94]

On the mannerisms of people whose mind is preoccupied, and on why people have so many different ways of behaving when they feel anxious or unhappy

Al-Tawḥīdi asked: Why do people who feel anxious or who are preoccupied with ruminating about some contretemps love to touch their beard, tap the ground with their finger, or fidget with pebbles? People may vary in that respect, so that we find one person who, when anxiety attacks and grief bites, loves to be among large crowds, around people, and in packed social gatherings, endeavoring thereby to raise his spirits and experience a cheering effect. Another person, by contrast, seeks refuge in solitude and is only to be found in deserted places, confined spaces, or dark roads. Yet another likes solitude but longs for leafy gardens, blooming meadows, and flowing rivers. Furthermore, things vary among these people, so that we find one person who, faced with the adversity that overshadows his thought, exhibits a purer nature, a quicker heart, and a greater presence of mind, reciting rare poems and composing magnificent epistles, acquiring large bodies of knowledge and turning the experience he confronts into sound counsel, whereas another person is stunned and stupefied, his judgment takes flight and his mind is plunged in confusion, so that he would fail to accept guidance were he to be given it, he would fail to comprehend any order, and he would fail to take heed of any prohibition. 121.1

Miskawayh's response

The only time the soul puts the limbs out of operation is during sleep, though this is not the right occasion to go into the reasons. Reason disapproves of inertia, and during wakefulness the bodily members must necessarily move, whether intentionally and voluntarily, in a skilled manner and for specific purposes, or by way of idle play and 121.2

diversion and in a state of inattentiveness and distraction. This is why the religious Law prohibits inattentiveness, why the principles of good breeding forbid laziness, and why citizens and their rulers have been commanded to avoid inactivity and to occupy themselves with different kinds of work. Because inactivity is repugnant and reason is averse to it, people in their leisure time busy themselves with games of chess and backgammon despite their foolishness and despite the fact that they consume part of one's life and fritter away time to no profit, for nobody wants to sit about without occupation and without moving unless it is an unavoidable necessity, for the reasons we mentioned above.

121.3 The limbs of the person lost in thought or feeling anxious do not become inactive, but through discipline a person must habituate himself to performing seemly movements, the way staffs were appointed for the use of kings, which is also deemed reprehensible and viewed as a kind of frivolousness, being considered to belong to the same category as infatuation with rings. Touching the beard and plucking the fibers off a new garment are considered symptoms of illness, for they are a disordered type of movement that does not conform to the standards of good breeding; in fact, they are an idle type of movement which indicates that the person soldiered on until, in one fell swoop, he lost his reason and his discrimination. A person possessed of discrimination and intelligence will not engage in this; he must be made conscious of what he is doing and must desist from it if it is his wont. The variations between different people—such as those who like to associate with people and those who like solitude, and all the other things you recounted and whose subdivisions you listed—are contingent on the humoral mixture. People affected by black bile and by melancholy thought like to be solitary and apart, and find it congenial, whereas people affected by sanguine thought like to associate with and be around people, and are sometimes fond of excursions and entertaining spectacles.

121.4 Let's take the points you made about those who turn out poetry, compose epistles, and busy themselves with different forms of knowledge—all of this depends on the habits of the people beset by thought and worry. If previously they had been the type of people who occupied themselves with them or devoted much thought to them, after the supervening incident, they resort to their former state and return to their habitual activity with a soul that has been roused and compelled to think, acquitting themselves with skill in their familiar activity. It is unavoidable that their thoughts be directed to the kind of thing that befell them—that is, that they compose poems and epistles relating to the matter that affected them, but with the assistance of thought—for example, by applying themselves to some other poetry and referring it back to the worries troubling and galvanizing them; then their words and their poetry come out keener and purer than before. People who are stunned and stupefied and whose mind is plunged into confusion, by contrast, are those who did not practice poetry or compose epistles before they were visited by the matter that preoccupies them, and who did not have a habit of resorting to thought and of using it to unearth hidden subtleties. So, when they are beset by an incident that requires them to think, they cannot find the means, and are struck by the kind of bewilderment and dazed condition you have described.

On different ways of approaching God's attributes

122.1 I saw someone pose the following question: Why is it that the only way the adherents of God's unity describe the Creator is by denying Him any attributes?[95] He was told: Explain your point and clarify your intention. He said: People follow two approaches in discussing the attributes of God. One faction says: He possesses no attributes—such as hearing, knowledge, sight, life, and power—yet even though these attributes are to be denied, He is qualified as hearing, seeing, living, powerful, and knowing. Another faction says: These are names that belong to a subject qualified by attributes that consist in knowledge, power, and life, and these must be applied and affirmed. Both factions agree on the view that God is qualified as "knowing" in a way unlike the way other beings are qualified as "knowing," qualified as "powerful" in a way unlike the way other beings are qualified as "powerful," qualified as "hearing" in a way unlike the way other beings are qualified as "hearing," and qualified as "speaking" in a way unlike the way other beings are qualified as "speaking." Furthermore, the faction that affirms God's attributes has resorted to the view that He has knowledge that is unlike the knowledge of other beings, and they have adopted a stance of negation with regard to all of it. Pending further clarification, it seems, on the face of it, that both factions affirm and deny, give and take. That is the end of the question. The response can be given in a few lines and, with the assistance of understanding, in brief, and by way of an expansive exposition if required in the relevant context, God willing.

Miskawayh's response

122.2 Your remark, "The response to it can be given in a few lines and . . . in brief . . ." is close to what I have said. For every attribute and every subject of attributes that one's imagination alights on and that one's tongue pronounces is given by God's generosity, originates with Him, and is a bounty He bestows on His creation; it is impermissible that God be qualified by means of things He has originated and created. That suffices as a brief response, but it is necessary to provide minimal clarification and exposition. We therefore say as follows. It has been demonstrated that the One, the First Creator, is prior in existence to all intelligible and sensible things and that He is first in reality, that is, there is nothing that precedes Him as a cause or ground or in any other way. A being that is not preceded by a cause exists eternally, and a being that exists eternally exists necessarily. A being that is such has always been, and a being that has always been has no cause, and is neither composite nor characterized by multiplicity. For were it composed or a composite, there would be something that preceded it—namely, its elements or parts. Yet we have said that He is first and has not been preceded by anything, so He cannot be composed or characterized by multiplicity. The attributes affirmed of Him by those who affirm them might either be eternal alongside Him or originated after Him. If they were eternal alongside Him and their existence were conjoined with His existence, there would be multiplicity, and if there were multiplicity, it would inevitably be a composite of parts. If the parts were prior, or if the unity—particularly the one from which the parts were composed—and the multiplicity were prior,[96] He would not have been first, yet we have said that He is first. Were His attributes posterior to Him, He would be free from them in the beginning of time and He would be truly characterized by unity, but what accrued to Him would have accrued to Him on account of a ground and a cause—may He be exalted and glorified far above what the purveyors of falsehoods claim—yet we have said that He has no ground or cause.

The reason for our application of generosity, power, and all other 122.3
attributes to Him is that when reason divides something into affirmation and negation, right and wrong, existence and nonexistence, it is necessary that each of the opposing extremes be considered and that the best of the two be ascribed to Him, insofar as it is unavoidable that we refer to Him using an attribute at all. For example, having learned about power and impotence, which form opposing extremes, we find that one of these is praiseworthy, while the other is blameworthy, so it is necessary that we ascribe to Him what is praiseworthy for us. We do the same with regard to generosity and its contrary, and knowledge and its reverse. Nevertheless, we must not proceed analogically on this basis unless we have been given license by a religious Law and granted permission by a divinely revealed book, so that we do not ascribe to Him figments of our own devising unsanctioned by norm or ordinance, and we should be on the strongest possible guard against doing such a thing. But

we have pledged to avoid going on at length in our answers to these questions, so let us confine ourselves to this modest amount. Those who wish to dwell on the topic at length and to expand on it may read about it in the relevant part of our book, which we have entitled *The Book of Triumph*, or in the books composed by others on this topic, God willing.[97]

On why we find it easier to remember what is correct than what is defective

123.1 Why are people more successful at remembering what is correct than what is erroneous? This is attested by the fact that if we were to task a simpleminded person with acquiring literary culture and developing the habit of correct speech, he would be more adequate to that task and bolder in pursuing it than a learned judge, a trustworthy witness, or a man of letters whom we tasked with acquiring the disposition of a commoner or emulating his erroneous and corrupt speech. That is why we find a hundred people who can recite to us Abū Tammām and al-Buḥturī, yet we cannot find three who can recite to us al-Ṭarmī and Abū l-ʿIbar.

Miskawayh's response

123.2 What is correct is a single thing and follows a course indicated by reason and demanded from everyone by our sound natural constitution. By contrast, deviations from the course, errors committed in it and against it, are infinite in number, hence their insusceptibility to precise determination. If a person deviates from it, he does so in a haphazard and contingent way, not on the basis of an indication provided by the understanding or a proof on the part of reason. The retention of something of this kind is extremely difficult, for retention consists in the recollection of a form bound by reason, and that form represents a demand of reason or a prescription on the part of one of the powers of reason. Human beings are assisted by their natural constitution in responding to this prescription, and they are also assisted by their natural constitution in recollecting it. Veering from it, by contrast, is like veering from the central point of a circle. For there are an infinite number of points of a circle that do not constitute the center but there is only a single point that is uniquely determined, which is the one equidistant from the entire circumference of the circle.

On why prosodists tend to produce flat poetry

Why do versifiers and prosodists produce bad poetry and their works lack luster and élan, whereas the reverse is true for naturally gifted poets? Isn't prosody founded on nature? Doesn't it constitute the measure of nature? Why then does it betray one's expectations? We have seen people possessed of taste and a natural gift for poetry committing mistakes by slipping from one meter to another, and we have not seen this happen to any versifiers or prosodists. So why are they, despite such excellence, more deficient than those they excel over? 124.1

Miskawayh's response

Naturally gifted poets who are not of pure Arab descent[98] stick to a single meter, and do not abandon it so long as their nature acquiesces to it. But we sometimes hear the early poets of pre-Islamic times using meters disagreeable to our nature and displeasing to our taste, which find them agreeable and well-measured and use them as regularly as they use others. An example is the line by al-Muraqqish: 124.2

> Traces of Bint ʿAjlān in al-Ṭaff not yet effaced,
> though a long time has passed.[99]

This is a poem included in al-Mufaḍḍal's *Anthology*—and there are others like it that I do not wish to prolong this response by citing—whose meter was agreeable to the nature of those people, yet it is repugnant to our own nature, and we regard it as rhythmically unacceptable. Similarly, they might sometimes employ variations[100] in the meters they approve of that the naturally gifted poets of our own time consider rhythmically unacceptable, though they are correct. The reason is that those people would redress things by voicing particular sounds at various points in the poem that would make the meter come out right. We have no knowledge of those sounds, so when we recite the poetry properly it is not pleasing to our nature. This is proved by the fact that when we do know these sounds in certain pieces of poetry, we find them pleasing and to our taste. An example is the line of the poet:[101]

> In the mountain pass with no cleft
> lies a slain hero whose blood will be avenged.

If this meter is recited in a segmented fashion using the sounds proper to it, it is to our taste, whereas if it is recited the way other poetry is recited, it is not to everyone's taste. This is how things stand with those metrical variations in poetry that the taste of the Arabs approves of but our own taste regards as rhythmically unacceptable. Were music not embedded in people's natures and were the measures of different sounds and their relationships to one another in rhythmic patterns not naturally ingrained in the soul, different souls would diverge about which specific open syllables they found agreeable; agreeable open syllables are the proportional relations musicians seek and on which they ground their judgment and principles.

124.3 Prosodists and versifiers track the open and closed syllables found in every verse, and study them in terms of their number and in comparison with the elements that are facing and parallel to them. If one element is lacking, whether an open or closed syllable, the reciter redresses this by voicing a certain sound so as to remedy the problem. Whenever that is not possible, his taste finds it awry and his nature does not go along with it. People's taste falls short in prosody because they are mistaken about some of the metrical variations permitted by prosody. The Arabs have a specific approach to this. People guided by taste but unaware of the sound through which that metrical variation is accomplished form the notion that it is permissible in every context, and accordingly fall into error. They also impugn their nature, so that they come to believe that poetry with metrical defects is of the same order as poetry that contains metrical variations, and that just as poetry that contains metrical variation is allowable, the former—which they think belongs to the same class—is also allowable. The basis of this error and the way people are led to commit it have been identified. For his part, the person who invented prosody understood meter and possessed taste and natural gifts, and he developed a craft based on his outstanding natural disposition that can also serve those who lack an outstanding natural disposition with regard to taste, allowing them to use the craft to make up for their deficiency. This also applies to the crafts of grammar, rhetoric, and other scientific crafts of the same class. However skilled practitioners of a craft may be, they are not in the same class as people of superlative, outstanding natural dispositions.

On the meaning of the dictum that the learned live longer than the ignorant

What did an ancient thinker mean when he said, "Even if they live shorter lives, the learned live longer than the ignorant"? What does this indicate, and what is the secret it harbors? For on the surface it implies a contradiction. 125.1

Miskawayh's response

125.2 Philosophical inquiries have established that life is of two kinds: the life of the body, which is the beastly life that all animals share with us, and the life of the soul, which is the human life realized through the attainment of various kinds of knowledge and learning. This is the life that excellent people strive to attain. So, ignorant people who live a bodily life must be viewed as not living at all, meaning that they are not human beings and do not live human lives. The learned must be said to be those who are really alive, whereas the others are dead.

On why it is harder to speak eloquently than to write eloquently

126.1 Why is eloquence with the tongue harder than eloquence with the pen? The tongue and the pen are only tools, and draw from a single source, so why is it that for every ten people who write excellently and express themselves eloquently, there are three who, when speaking, fail to acquit themselves well and express themselves eloquently? One of the indications of how rare eloquence with the tongue is is the greater esteem shown by people for those who are eloquent with the tongue than for those who are eloquent with the pen.

Miskawayh's response

126.2 The reason for this is that the eloquence achieved through the pen is achieved with reflection and thought, and with enough time for critical judgment, choices, erasing and adding things, and deliberation about replacing one word with another. If people extemporize when their words and meanings are incompletely formed they succumb to stammering, stuttering, and slurred speech—precisely the repugnant inarticulacy we seek to guard against. Eloquent people, for their part, are endowed with presence of mind, and words flow from their tongue so rapidly that they do not confine themselves just to expressing the ideas inside their mind but have some time left over to embellish their phrases, to arrange them by deploying the most agreeable ones in turn, to look for affinities, balance, and rhyme—in short, to achieve things that ordinarily require much time and prolonged thought.

On the significance of the fact that human beings are the only animals to stand upright

What is the significance of the fact that among all animals, human beings are the only ones that stand upright? Abū Zayd al-Balkhī the philosopher has pronounced some remarks on the topic that I will recount. 127.1

Miskawayh's response

If that excellent man you mention has pronounced some remarks on this topic, it is appropriate for us to ask you to exempt us from delivering any of our own. If you do not grant us this exemption, it is appropriate that we content ourselves with an allusive rather than an elaborate discussion of the point. We therefore reply: When the material substrate of heat is soft and well-disposed in terms of moisture and susceptibility to extension, heat causes the body to which it attaches to extend in its direction—that is, upward—in a straight manner. Things bend and incline toward the earth for two reasons: either because the heat is weak, or because the material substrate to which it attaches has limited susceptibility. One can perceive and contemplate that phenomenon in relation to trees, some of which grow branches that dangle toward the earth, while others extend upward in a straight manner, and yet others grow in a composite way, depending on the resistance of their matter, for the 127.2

movement of composite entities is also composite. Trees and plants that grow on the ground and do not stand erect do so because of the large number of earthly parts they contain and because the heat is too weak to make them extend upward. Trees that stand erect and sprout branches that spread right and left and incline toward the earth do so because the movements of the fire and the earth have formed a composite, producing a composite shape that combines standing erect and downward inclination. Trees that, like rods, extend upward, such as cypresses and the like, do so because the earthly parts and aqueous moisture they contain are soft, and the heat is strong, so there is nothing to hinder the straight movement that fire produces. If you ponder these examples with due attention, it will not be difficult for you to transfer the principle to animals, God willing.

On why certainty is less enduring than doubt

128.1 Why is it that when certainty obtains, it does not last long enough to take root, whereas when doubt assails, it drops anchor and stays put? This is demonstrated by the fact that when a person who is certain of something is given reasons to doubt it, his spirit is jolted and he is filled with unease, whereas when you take a person who harbors doubt by the hand, give him guidance, and offer wise insight, you only make him more recalcitrant, and all you get is insolence and repugnance.

Miskawayh's response

128.2 I believe that the person who posed this question about certainty was unaware of its real meaning, and fancied that the term "certainty" refers to some loose notion of learning or light conviction.

This is not how things stand; for certainty constitutes the highest possible rank that knowledge can reach, and doubt cannot possibly assail a person after certainty has been formed. For example, once someone has come to know that five times five makes twenty-five, doubt is not possible at any point in time. Similarly, once someone has come to know that the sum of the angles of a triangle is equal to the sum of two right angles, doubt is not possible. This is how it is with the kinds of knowledge that are established with certainty by means of demonstrative proofs and by means of the first principles through which demonstrative proofs are known. The kinds of belief that fall below certainty admit of many ranks, as explained in the *Book on Logic*,[102] and each rank is vulnerable to doubt depending on the degree of conviction it involves. Given this, the heart of the person who has attained certainty never succumbs to a doubt that "jolts" his spirit; he is tranquil and at ease and utterly immune to being moved by doubt.

You mentioned that if one offers guidance and wise insight to the doubter, this only makes him more recalcitrant. This happens for one of two reasons: either because the person offering guidance does not approach the doubter gently and does not introduce him to wise insight in a gradual way, instead burdening him with more than he can bear; or because the wise person might sometimes forbid things that nature inclines to through blind desire. Through our earlier exposition, you know that the forces of blind desire are dominant, and stronger than the forces of reason. The doubter thus becomes like a person pulled in different directions by two ropes, one weak, the other strong. He inevitably submits to the stronger one, until with the passage of time his resolve is strengthened and the strong part grows weak and the weak strong, in accordance with what the philosophers have indicated and the prophets have legislated. 128.3

On why we laugh harder when a person keeps a straight face

129.1 Why do people laugh harder at a ridiculous person who makes them laugh when he does not laugh himself than they do when he laughs? This phenomenon arises whenever someone amuses you but does not laugh.

Miskawayh's response

129.2 The person who provokes laughter typically goes after things distorted from their proper place in order to amaze his listener and make him laugh. By not laughing, he shows himself to be composed and indifferent to the cause that should naturally induce amazement and laughter; this conflicts with the state of the listener, so a second cause is joined to the first.

On the meaning of the scholars' proposition that a rare instance attracts no ruling

130.1 What is the meaning of the statement we hear from scholars of all persuasions: "The rare instance attracts no ruling"? We hear jurists, dialectical theologians, grammarians, and philosophers saying this. So what is its secret? What is the truth behind it, and what is its cause? Why is it that a rarity carries no ruling, and an anomaly admits no explanation?

Miskawayh's response

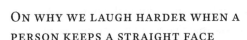

130.2 It is not the case, as you suppose, that scholars of all persuasions use this expression. It is used by those who belong to the kind whose knowledge derives from incidental observation and from widespread views, for according to some people these constitute first principles of the sciences they cultivate. By "first principles" I mean that they assign them the status of accepted foundations on a par with necessary foundations such as those provided by the senses and by reason. Having done so, they inevitably come across things that conflict with their assumptions, so they classify them as "rare" or "anomalous." For example, a person of this type happens to observe that it rains on a particular day of the year—on a Saturday in December,[103] say—and continues to do so for years. He therefore rules that this forms an ineluctable necessity; any event that contravenes this rule is declared anomalous and rare. The same applies to people who consider a particular day of the month blessed and another ill-starred, as the Persians do with the first day of the month, which they call "Hurmuz," and the last day of the month, which they call "Anīrān." Thus there persists the ruling that things follow this specific pattern, and any contravention of the pattern is said to be anomalous and rare.

The same applies to all of those who base their rulings on prin- 130.3
ciples that are not natural or necessary, for they are not as consistent as forms of knowledge established through demonstration, whose principles are based on necessary matters. We see this firsthand among the ordinary people who do not know the causes or grounds of things. For if one of them sees one thing take place upon the appearance of some other thing, he attributes the former to the latter without inquiring into whether or not it was its cause. Thus, if he sees some delightful circumstance the moment Zayd appears, he asserts that Zayd was its cause. If Zayd happens to appear at some other time and another delightful circumstance happens, his opinion is reinforced, and his sense of insight increases. If it happens a third time, he pronounces his ruling with categorical certainty. This applies to most things that concern this category of people. It is little wonder then that they claim it is an anomaly when the pattern is contravened. There are many instances of this phenomenon; the reason is that sometimes true causes may be involved, as when one

rules in wintertime that rain will fall on such and such a day because that is what happened in the previous year. Since it is winter, this may happen a great number of times, but the cause of the rain is not that specific day; there are other causes, even if rain happens to fall on that day.

130.4 If people who engage in philosophical inquiry follow others' examples or draw their premises from such sources, they will inevitably fall prey to the same thing others do. This is why it is imperative to assign things to their proper places. Things that rest on demonstrative proof do not undergo change, and one should not anticipate that anything will arise that opposes them or casts them in doubt. If they do not rest on demonstrative proof but involve a proof that is consistent and sound, one may place one's assurance and trust in them. The ones that do not rise above the level of weak convictions must not command assurance or trust; one should anticipate that something will arise to overturn them, and they are not immune to doubt or objection.

On the Possibility of Certain Kinds of Coincidences Obtaining

131.1 A certain dialectical theologian said: We know for certain that it is impossible that all the inhabitants of a particular quarter should, by coincidence, touch their beards at a particular hour, in a particular season, and in a particular situation. If this is possible, is it possible that all the people living in a town should happen by coincidence to do so? If this is possible, is it possible that everyone in the world should happen by coincidence to do so? And if it is not possible that this should happen by coincidence, what is the cause? The theologian mentioned certainty and necessity, then did not go beyond the first question. Upon my life, the fact stands but the question of the cause remains. The truth of the matter will be fully expounded in your book of responses, God willing.[104]

Miskawayh's response

The logicians have probed the notions of the necessary, the impossible, and the possible in depth, and Aristotle, the author of the books on logic, has provided a consummate discussion of the topic. The appropriate position to take in this context is the following: The "necessary" is that whose affirmation is always true and whose negation always false. The "impossible" is that whose affirmation is always false and whose negation always true. The "possible" is that whose affirmation is sometimes true and sometimes false, and whose negation is sometimes false and sometimes true. These things have different natures, and your question concerns the nature of the possible. If it were allowed that all people should do that at one particular moment, it would be assigned the nature of the necessary, and that is incoherent. Moreover, Aristotle has explained that individual propositions which concern what is possible and are in the future tense cannot both be true or both be false, and cannot distribute truth and falsehood.[105] An example is the proposition "Zayd will bathe tomorrow" and "Zayd will not bathe tomorrow." These propositions cannot both be true. Otherwise, the very same thing would both exist and not exist. Nor can they both be false; otherwise, the same thing would both exist and not exist. And we cannot say that they distribute truth and falsehood, as this would nullify possibility. This view is liable to provoke perplexity, so Aristotle nuanced his account further, with the following explanation. With regard to possible things, affirmation and negation are true indefinitely. With regard to necessary and impossible things, affirmation and negation are true definitely. That is to say, possible propositions distribute truth and falsehood by virtue of their nature qua possible. Necessary propositions distribute truth and falsehood on the basis that they are necessary. These remarks are clear and 131.2

plain to those with the slightest training in logic. Those who wish to probe them in depth may consult the proper sources, where they will find satisfaction.

On the role of analogical reasoning in the linguistic sciences

132.1 A scholar of grammar and lexicography was asked: Is analogical reasoning consistently maintained across all phenomena that relate to words? He replied: No. The questioner asked: Is analogical reasoning violated across all of them? He replied: No. He was then asked: What is the reason? He replied: I don't know, but one has recourse to analogical reasoning in one context and one avoids it in another. I posed this question to a philosopher and he offered an answer that, despite its difficulties, will be presented before you, God willing.

Miskawayh's response

132.2 The analogical reasoning of the grammarians is not grounded in necessary first principles, and this is why it is not consistently maintained. The reply given by this grammarian concerned the analogical reasoning that pertains to his craft, and that was what was required of him. By contrast, all the forms of reasoning used by philosophers are consistently maintained, especially the kind of syllogistic reasoning termed a "demonstration," and none are subject to violation. Some of my remarks to the previous query—regarding the claim that the rare instance attracts no ruling—could serve as a response to this, so you can refer back to it, God willing.

On whether God created the world for a cause

A person asked: Did God create the world for a cause or for no cause? If for a cause, what was that cause? If for no cause, what is the argument for that? This is a complex question with many ins and outs, and it is no easy task to discuss it. 133.1

Miskawayh's response

It is not possible to say that God created the world for a cause because of the point we made before—namely, that a cause naturally precedes its effect. If the cause is also caused, it must have a cause that precedes it. This would continue ad infinitum, and that which is infinite cannot exist. Thus, it is only possible to say one of two things: Either the cause has no cause, or the world has no cause other than the Creator's essence. If we said that the world has a cause other than the Creator's essence, that cause would have no cause and would have to exist from eternity, as it would exist necessarily. If that were the case, everything conceded regarding the Creator's essence would have to apply to it. And if that were the case, it would have to be first and to have always existed. This is something we predicated of the Creator based on demonstrative proofs that concluded in its predication. Yet it is impossible that there should be two entities to which this qualification applies, that is, that both of them should be first and have always existed. For these two entities must agree in one feature—one that renders both of them first and such that they have always existed—and must differ in another feature—one that renders each distinct from the other. The feature they have in common and the feature that distinguishes them must be a constitutive or divisive difference, so that they acquire a genus and a species, for this is the basic reality of "genus" and "species." The genus is naturally prior to the species. The species, which 133.2

requires a constitutive difference, is not first, for it is composed of an essence and a constitutive difference, and a composite entity is posterior to the element from which it was composed. These are mutually contradictory facts, and they make it inadmissible to claim that the two entities are both first and have always been. Even the lengthiest explanations of this issue come down to this core point, which is sufficient for people endowed with an excellent mind and developed intelligence.

On why a life of comfort makes people feel oppressed and leads them to behave wantonly

134.1 Why do people feel oppressed when surrounded by constant comforts and attendant blessings? This sense of oppression encourages exuberant and impetuous, wanton and unrestrained behavior, and gets them mixed up in evil, so that they end up in awful situations and get into ghastly scrapes. Then they grind their teeth in anger at their bad choices and in regret at abandoning sound judgment and at turning their back on those who offered them well-intentioned counsel, in addition to the pain caused by the malicious pleasure of the ill-intentioned. What is the secret reason for the impetuosity and the element that makes one act fitfully? This is why we have one of the exceptional sayings of the Arabs: "Repletion gave him impetus"; that is, a full belly made him unrestrained, abundance made him wanton, and luxury provoked him, agitated and swollen with lust, to willful arrogance. That is why one of our pious forefathers said, "Well-being is a secret possession that only inspired saints and prophets sent by God can endure." This is so even though everyone without exception loves well-being and inclines to comfort, and seeks protection against evil and its corollaries and consequences.

Miskawayh's response

Comfort must follow prior discomfort. Pleasure clearly constitutes a relief from pain. Since comfort follows discomfort, it is experienced as pleasant and delightful when we are delivered from the cause of discomfort. If comfort continues uninterrupted and the pain of discomfort departs, then comfort is not realized but is rather nullified, as is its meaning; and with its nullification comes the nullification of pleasure. As pleasure is nullified, people err in longing for pleasure, whose true reality they are ignorant of. That is to say, they long for pleasure, but are ignorant of the fact that it is simply relief from pain. So people essentially long for discomfort in order to experience subsequent comfort. Once a person grasps this and perceives it clearly, he stops longing for pleasure, and when he feels the pain of hunger he attends to its treatment through the remedy called satiation, without aiming at pleasure itself, instead seeing pleasure as a concomitant of his purpose rather than as his primary end. That is why people who are cognizant of this fact limit their desire for corporeal things, that is to say worldly things, those which are connected to the senses and are termed "pleasurable." Ignorant people, however, cannot avoid being affected by what we have described, so they perpetually succumb to it, and become embroiled in innumerable troubles, pains, and maladies. The outcome is remorse and regret. 134.2

On why some things are best when they're new and others are best when old

Why is it that some things achieve their consummate form when they are fresh and tender, and are only commended and judged to be good when in that state, whereas other things are only chosen and commended when aged and old, marked by the passage of time? Why don't people regard everything from a single perspective? 135.1

Why are things divided according to these two perspectives? Is there a secret behind this that can be revealed?

Miskawayh's response

135.2 The perfection of things varies; for some the form that constitutes their perfection is completed in a short period of time, while for others the form is completed over a long period of time. Therefore, the length of time people must wait for their perfection, and the preference they show toward them, vary accordingly. Every entity begins, reaches perfection, and then enters decline, until it is eventually annihilated and returns to the point from which it began, so its optimal state is when it has attained perfection. Its progression to that point and its decline are deficient states, though the former is better than the latter. As this rule applies consistently to things that form part of this world of ours—that is, the world of generation and corruption—it follows that people's judgments regarding the form of perfection that is good and commendable in each of these various things must also vary for the reasons we mentioned.

On why people who display great piety are prone to arrogance

136.1 Why is it that if a person fasts or prays beyond the stipulated amount common to all, he conceives a scorn for others, treats them peremptorily, and puffs himself up in social gatherings, swollen with pride and stung by some gadfly as though he were the recipient of divine afflatus, was assured of forgiveness, and had exclusive rights to Paradise? Yet he knows that action is susceptible to different kinds of impairment, through which the reward of the agent may be undone. This is why God said: «We shall advance upon what work they have done, and make it a scattered dust.»[106] The phenomenon that affects him must have a cause, which will be revealed in the response to the question. One of our companions used to laugh at an anecdote on this topic. He said: One day a Jew converted to Islam in the early morning, and before evening he had struck a muezzin, cursed a second, and unleashed his anger on yet a third. "What kind of behavior is this?" people asked him. "We religious devotees are a sharp-tempered lot!" he rejoined.

Miskawayh's response

Arrogance affects everyone who knows that he possesses a certain virtue but who also suffers a deficiency from another perspective, and who fears that that virtue might remain hidden or that nobody else might know he possesses it. For this is the meaning of arrogance; that is, the person affected tries to get another to concede and acknowledge that he possesses that virtue; if the other fails to acknowledge it, he succumbs to all manner of disturbed movements. That person spoke truly who said that the reason for the display of arrogance is some baseness discerned in the self. The way to avoid being affected by this phenomenon is for a person to seek to possess virtue for no other reason than that he should become virtuous in himself, and not in order that this should receive acknowledgment or honor for it. It is right and proper if it happens to be acknowledged, but if it is not, he should not seek this from others and should be unconcerned about the fact that others do not know about it, for we know that it is a defect to love and seek honor. Some people have been ruined by the love of honor, some have been affected by pomposity, and others have fled human society, and other such odious things. What the person endowed with reason should do is to seek to possess the virtues so as to acquire a disposition honorable and praiseworthy in itself, regardless of whether he is honored or not, and whether it is acknowledged or not. In this it resembles health, for health is desired for its own sake, and the reason a person is keen to possess it is simply in order to be healthy, not in order that he should be thought to be so, nor in order to be honored for it. Similarly, if it is given to one to achieve 136.2

the health of the soul by realizing the virtues, one must not demand honor for it or acknowledgment of one's achievement. Whenever this guiding principle is contravened, one falls prey to all sorts of ignorant behavior, among them arrogance and the condition described.

On why a warm manner is more pleasing than a cold benefaction

137.1 One of our companions reported that Hārūn al-Rashīd asked Isḥāq al-Mawṣilī, "How are your relations with al-Faḍl ibn Yaḥyā and Jaʿfar ibn Yaḥyā?"[107] He said, "Sire, I only gain an audience with Jaʿfar with difficulty, and when I reach him I kiss his hand, but he doesn't glance at me or grace me with a single word. Then I go home and I find his tokens of kindness and charity and his gifts and presents waiting for me, and I am at a loss what to make of him. No sooner is my hand on the door knocker than al-Faḍl has received me, and he treats me amiably and gives me special attention, asking about all of my affairs high and low and vivifying me with his cheerful mien, beaming countenance, joyful air, and gentle tone. This overwhelms me and makes me feel I could never thank him enough, and I am left nursing a sense of bashfulness toward him. This is how things stand." When he heard this, al-Rashīd said, "Abū Isḥāq, which of the two are you fonder of, and whose actions have the strongest effect on you?" "Al-Faḍl's," he replied. This is the end of the report.

137.2 My question is: Why did Isḥāq esteem al-Faḍl's action more highly than Jaʿfar's? What al-Faḍl expends is contingent: It does not endure and yields no profit, whereas what Jaʿfar expends is a substance that endures and is an object of pressing need on which desires are fastened and hopes pinned. The proof of this is that no one on the face of the earth sets out to obtain a man's cheerful mien or wanders the earth in search of a friendly face. Yet both land and sea are replete with people seeking wealth, begging, and servicing hopes at others' doorsteps.

Miskawayh's response

I believe the story has been reported the wrong way around. It was al-Faḍl who was described as being arrogant, and he was the one who showed honor by bestowing gifts, and it was Jaʿfar who was described as having a bright, cheerful manner. What is undisputed is that Isḥāq preferred the person with the beaming countenance, even if he rarely received tokens of generosity from him, to the person who was lavish and acted kindly, because of the pride and hauteur the latter conjoined to these acts. There are enormous variations between people with regard to the point you are asking about and find surprising. For there are those who love riches and material comfort, and there are those who love honor and high standing. Those who love riches might love high standing and honor, but only as a means for acquiring wealth. Those who love high standing and honor may love wealth and riches, but only as a means for acquiring high standing and honor. Each of these factions alleges that it is truly astute and that the other faction is ignorant and foolish. The truth of the matter is that each is driven toward something natural, but extravagance has led both to excess. For wealth must be sought in moderation and acquired in the proper way, and then spent under the appropriate circumstances. When a person falls short in any of these respects, he becomes greedy, is gripped by baseness, and falls into avarice and wrongdoing. A person must possess a form of excellence that makes him deserving of honor, and honor should not be sought out without a just claim or in the arrogant manner censured in one of the previous questions. Honor is nobler than wealth, and is attended by pleasure, if things are as we described and honor attends excellence. 137.3

137.4 In general, money is not desired for its own sake, but rather serves as an instrument for attaining a plethora of wishes and wants. The reason it is loved is because it is equivalent to all objects of desire, that is, because lovely objects may be obtained by its means. Taken on its own, and abstracted from this one characteristic, it is simply a stone with nothing to distinguish it from other objects. Honor, however, may be desired for its own sake if a person desires it on account of merit grounded in virtue, and this is due to the spiritual pleasure and psychological joy he derives, for even though it arises from the irascible soul and this soul is inferior to the rational one, it is superior to the beastly soul, which delights in bodily pleasures that it shares with plants and lowly animals.

137.5 You remark that one sees more people who love wealth than people who love honor—this is as it should be. For the people who resemble the beasts represent the majority, while only a small number distinguish themselves through the virtues. Just as those who distinguish themselves through the virtues of the rational soul are few in number, those who distinguish themselves through the virtues of the irascible soul are fewer than the multitude.

On why those closest to a king are less inclined to prattle about his person than those at the farthest remove from him

138.1 Why is it that the elite members of the king's circle, those who are his close intimates, do not speak about the king the way those who are distant from him—such as doormen, soldiers, and stablemen—do? For we find the latter displaying a lusty appetite for speaking about the king, taking their claims about him to an extreme and spinning yarns about him.

Miskawayh's response

138.2 There are two reasons for this. One is that those close to the king have refined manners and have been judged fit to serve him, and among the manners they have been held to is that they refrain from speaking about the king. For speaking about him involves demeaning him, violating his dignity, and impugning his venerability. By contrast, the latter class of people, because of their bad manners, fail to discern and pay heed to any of the things I mentioned, and, as is natural and befitting to commoners, they make groundless boasts and untrue claims, out of a belief that by doing so they may gain honor and standing among their peers. The other reason is the fear of punishment among members of the king's entourage, for the king metes out punishment for this offense and views this as a principle of good government, lest those who speak about him end up divulging a secret or making public words that should not be made public.

On Ibn Sālim al-Baṣrī's claim that God perceived the world while it was nonexistent

What was the confusion that Ibn Sālim al-Baṣrī[108] succumbed to when he voiced his unique position, claiming that from pre-eternity God looked at the world, viewed it, and perceived it, during the entire time it was nonexistent? For he and his supporters have created a widespread ruckus among the learned. If his claim is false, in what respect is it false? If it is true, in what respect is it true? 139.1

Miskawayh's response

The confusion the author of this position succumbed to is compound. For he considered the way in which living beings like us perceive things, and he found that there are two types of perception, one intellectual and the other sensory, with the sensory subdividing into the imaginary and the visual. In the visual sensory type, the visual object is perceived through an organ possessed of layers, moistures, and a hollowed nerve leading out from the 139.2

ventricle of the brain. It requires a transparent medium that lies between it and the visual object, as well as balanced, moderate light; moderate distance; and the absence of any intervening barrier or obstacle. We have said that the imagination is contingent on sense perception, so it is not possible to imagine something that cannot be perceived, or something the like of which cannot be perceived. Intellectual perception, by contrast, does not require any of the senses; rather, reason itself has an intrinsic power through which it perceives intelligible things. The discussion of the latter type of perception harbors a greater amount of subtlety and obscurity than the discussion of sensory perception.

139.3 The person addressing the point at issue mixed up these types of perception, and knowing that the Creator knows everything that is, he called this knowledge "perception" and assumed that it is of the same kind as our perception and our imaginary knowledge. So his confusion was a compound formed out of these false assumptions. It is an arduous task, and one that presupposes many kinds of knowledge, to investigate and distinguish these types of perception so as to determine what pertains to living beings possessed of reason and sense perception like ourselves and how such beings perceive existent things, and then to establish that the Creator transcends them all. For in our case, all of these—that is to say, all kinds of knowledge and learning—are forms of passive affection, as it is impossible for us to know anything of a sensible or intelligible kind without being passively affected. Yet God cannot be passively affected. Rather, He knows things in a higher and loftier manner than we do. What we have said provides sufficient clarification of the reason for the confusion this man suffered in assuming his particular position.

On why the poets love to dwell on the apparitions that come to them in their sleep

Tell me about the infatuation of poets with apparitions that visit them while they are sleeping, about their passion for evoking them, and their presence in erotic verse. We encounter this among all stripes of people, and it is a familiar phenomenon among those who, overcome by tender feeling, have become the plaything of ardent love, whose eyes have grown fond of the form and beauties of a particular individual, and whose heart has become attached to this person in desire and love. 140.1

Miskawayh's response

The term "apparition" refers to the form of the beloved when acquired within the imaginative power of the soul, so that this form stands before one's eyes and in front of one's fancy whenever one is alone. This is a condition that affects everyone who has a passion for a particular thing, for its form imprints itself on this power called the imagination, located in the anterior ventricle of the brain. If this power is repeatedly exposed to the form of the beloved, the latter engraves itself in it and remains there; so whenever a person goes to sleep or wakes up, that form invariably arises within it. It is especially in sleep that we find the person we long for, for in sleep we see images based on things contained in our soul. Thus, we might see in our sleep that we have gained access to the other in accordance with our desire. This results in dreams about sexual intercourse, and in the discharge of the substance that prompts our longing and drives us to be united with our beloved. The greater part of that effect passes away, and this subsequently leads to a complete recovery. 140.2

On why people are reluctant to advertise their merits

141.1 What makes people reluctant to call attention to themselves by advertising their merits, displaying their qualities, establishing their name, and publicizing their attributes? This simply results in obscurity, and obscurity is a form of nonexistence and has a familiar relationship to deficiency. For what is obscure is unknown, and the unknown is the contrary of the nonexistent;[109] and there is no debating the nonexistent and no disputing the existent. This question originated in the following circumstances. One of our masters showed us a book he had composed, and we discovered that he had not noted on the outside "Written or composed by so-and-so," nor had he even noted that he was the owner of the book. We asked him, "What is your reasoning?" He answered, "There are secret reasons that make it attractive to me." Then he brought out several books written during his youth and containing his name, and he said, "These are the relics of my days of deficiency."

Miskawayh's response

141.2 Merit calls attention to itself, and does not need people to call attention to it themselves. For the virtues that are truly virtues shine out like the sun, and cannot be hidden, even if their possessor wished it. Those that can be hidden are deemed virtues but are not. People employ reason to scrutinize the claims of anyone who sets about praising himself and making claims in order to draw attention to his virtue, so his imperfections become apparent and the points on which he is deceived about himself become manifest. If he happens to be speaking truthfully, and he indeed possesses the virtue in question, he reveals, by taking such pains to manifest it, that he is not confident in people's judgments and their powers of scrutiny; or he may be confident, but is boastful and proud.

People do not like any of these character traits because they are base. The great-spirited person, by contrast, belittles the virtues he possesses because he aspires to more; for however high the degree of merit a person acquires, it is nugatory compared with that which surpasses it. He is subject to the natural disposition of human beings and under its control, and the limitations vested in human nature prevent him from acquiring it fully and attaining its utmost degree, or he is distracted by deficiencies that hinder him from seeking the highest level of human virtue.

On the relative merits of verse as against prose

Someone posed a question about the ranks of verse and prose, their respective merits, the relation of one to the other, and the classes people occupy with regard to them. Most people place verse higher than prose, without offering a clear argument in support of their view; even so, they make that claim and avoid delving into the hidden aspects of the truth involved. A small minority place prose higher, and attempt to argue their case. 142.1

Miskawayh's response

Verse and prose are species that form subdivisions of speech; speech constitutes their genus. The correct mode of division is as follows: Speech divides into that which is arranged in verse and that which is not arranged in verse. That which is not arranged in verse divides into that which employs rhyme and that which does not employ rhyme. The process of division continues until the final species is reached. Let us illustrate this with an example familiar to you: Insofar as it is a genus, speech follows the same principle as the term "living being." For living beings divide into the rational and the nonrational, nonrational beings divide into those that can fly 142.2

and those that cannot fly, and one continues the process of division until one reaches the final species. Rational beings and beings that can fly have in common the fact that they are living beings, which is their genus, and rational beings and beings that can fly are then differentiated by virtue of rationality. Similarly, verse and prose have in common the fact that they are forms of speech, which is their genus, and verse is then differentiated from prose by virtue of meter, through which verse is constituted as verse. Since meter is an additional quality and a surplus form relative to prose, poetry excels over prose on account of its meter. Verse and prose have meanings in common, so it is not through this aspect that the one is distinguished from the other; rather, each of them may be sometimes true and sometimes false, sometimes sound and sometimes defective. The relation of verse to speech is like the relation of melody to verse. Just as melody imparts to verse a form that is additional to the one it had previously possessed, similarly, the quality of versified arrangement imparts to speech a form additional to the one it had previously possessed. Abū Tammām put the point eloquently when he said:

> They are jewels strewn about, but if you unite them in verse
> they become necklaces and strings of pearls.

On why people feel oppressed when things are prohibited to them

143.1 Why do human beings find interdiction oppressive? Similarly, when a command is issued, it seizes us by the throat and stifles our very breath. And yet we know that the order of the world requires commands and prohibitions, and this can only be achieved through someone who commands and prohibits, and through something that is commanded and prohibited. These are basic elements and principles, but their meaning is withheld from us here, and by gaining an overview human beings may be perfected and distinguish what is obscure from what is clearly distilled.

Miskawayh's response

The commands and prohibitions you refer to arise in connection with those appetites that wantonly drive human beings to evil actions, and concern the necessitation of actions that involve hardship but lead to our good. Human beings naturally incline to immediate gratification of their appetites without regard for consequence, and to a preference for ease and repose here and now over what will bring repose throughout the time to come. Thus they find it oppressive when their appetites are forbidden and when commanded to perform acts involving hardship. This is a condition that cleaves to human beings from childhood. For what they find most onerous is their parents' denial of their wishes and admonitions to do things that are difficult yet beneficial. When they grow to adulthood, the people they find most oppressive are their physicians and healers, those who dispense counsel to them in deliberative matters, and those who rule over them and impose upon them what benefits them and serves their welfare. This is the condition of most people, who are governed by their appetites and follow their blind desires. Yet one may also encounter among them people of outstanding natural disposition, sound judgment, and firm resolve, who only do what is finest and suppress their blind desires, enduring the toilsome burden of doing so on account of the excellent and meritorious outcome they anticipate. Such people are few and far between, indeed a rare exception; commands and prohibitions are not addressed to people such as these—they have no need of being galvanized by promises and threats, or warnings of painful retribution in the life to come. 143.2

On why preachers are affected by stage fright when addressing large audiences

144.1 Why are preachers overcome by inarticulacy, stuttering, and embarrassment when they stand in the pulpit among large numbers of people on days of assembly, even though they have memorized and mastered what they want to say and are confident of its excellent quality? What is it that they experience, one wonders, that makes their minds stray from the track, makes their tongues defy their orders, plunges their thoughts into confusion, and takes complete possession of them?

Miskawayh's response

144.2 When the soul applies thought in one particular direction, its application in other directions is hindered. This is why no one is able to think simultaneously about a question of geometry and a question of grammar or poetry. In fact, we are incapable of attending at the same time to a mundane and otherworldly matter. People who do so apportion a separate segment of time, however small, to each matter, but there is no way for the time occupied by the one and by the other to coincide exactly. This happens to us because we human beings are enmeshed with matter, and because the soul employs material substance and instruments. This is clear and plain and immediately evident to all. On days of congregation, our thoughts become absorbed by the things that absorb people's attention—the faults they might find or the deficiencies they might be mindful of—so we consume ourselves with fearful anticipations of the prospect and with the need to guard against it; and this impedes the acts proper to the occasion. This disorder within the soul is what brings its instruments into disorder, producing in them a variety of disjointed movements, such as stuttering and the like.

For when the user of an instrument is in disarray, his instrument inevitably follows suit.

On the anxiety that affects onlookers when they see preachers affected by stage fright

Why does someone who looks at and attends to someone else feel embarrassed and ashamed, particularly if there is a relation between them, if they are joined by a bond of kinship or are united by a common characteristic or shared doctrine? What is it that separates the one who is looking from the one who is being looked at? And what is it that connects the speaker to the listener and makes him shut his eyes and seal his ears as he faces him? This is something I have seen with my own eyes—indeed, something I have been driven to myself. This second question annexes itself to the first because wonder takes hold of us and curiosity stands firm until such time as the underlying cause and the prevailing facts have been brought to light. When the cause becomes evident, the ruling is established, and once the veil is cast aside, the ardor of those who try to peer through it abates. Praise be to God, who controls those well-guarded subtleties and secrets withheld from pure intellects and sharp minds. 145.1

Miskawayh's response

It is necessary to rehearse here in summary form our account of the causes of shame and embarrassment. Shame is a contraction that affects the soul as a result of a fear of doing wrong. Since this is what shame is, the soul of a person, when he is related to the speaker, is beset by a disturbance similar to the one that besets the speaker because he fears he will do something wrong or say something he will be criticized for, just as the speaker is afraid. We had 145.2

occasion to point out earlier that the soul is one, and multiplicity only enters it through the multiplicity of material substrates.[110] Otherwise, it would be impossible for anyone to convey what is in his soul to the soul of another and make himself understood. What has already been said about this topic suffices for the purpose, for what is required at this juncture is to bring out that what Zayd does badly also concerns ʿAmr from another perspective, even if ʿAmr is a stranger. How much more so when the two are united by some relation or a bond of kinship?

145.3 It is not necessary for something to separate the one looking from the one being looked at, for the acts and effects of the soul are not of this sensible, bodily order, especially given that both the speaker and the listener are experiencing one and the same thing—a fear of doing wrong, and an apprehensiveness about slipping up and making mistakes. For this is the state of mind, as we said, from which shame and embarrassment stem. When the listener is convinced that the speaker will perform badly and miss the mark, his fear and apprehension turn into certainty or into something not far removed from that, so the shame that affects him intensifies and he succumbs to the disordered kind of movements you spoke of. The same thing happens to the speaker if he lacks self-confidence or if he isn't used to standing up and speaking in such a context. His apprehension mounts and his shame increases, and with the increase of shame comes an increase of disorder, and it becomes impossible to speak as freely as the soul permits when its power is full, it is in a state of composure and equanimity, and its movements are calm.

On why we hate hearing the same thing twice

146.1 Why do we hate hearing the same thing twice? Why does the person who hears the same thing twice find it oppressive, even though the second time is no different from the first? If there is a difference between the two, then what is it?

Miskawayh's response

From uncommon reports and unfamiliar discourses the soul derives a nourishment similar to that which the body derives from its aliments. To offer to the soul for a second time information and knowledge it has already assimilated is like offering to the body for a second time food it has already eaten its fill of. Given the same food twice, the body finds it oppressive and turns away from it. It is likewise with the soul's relationship to knowledge. The analogies I have drawn here between bodies and non-bodily things have to be taken with discrimination, so as not to tarnish these exalted matters in ways that corrupt one's imagination and lead one's fancy down roads that comport ill with the intended meaning. I pray that the statements to which I have confined myself will suffice for those perusing the present questions; for I have been addressing my answers to a reader who already has a purchase on these subjects and so commands respect. Whoever is not at this level must school himself well in these subjects first, and only then, God willing, peruse these answers. 146.2

On whether the religious Law can conflict with human reason

Someone put the following question to me: Is it possible that the Law handed down by God should contain things that reason rejects—that it opposes, declares repugnant, and rules impermissible—such as the sacrifice of animals or the imposition of blood money on the clan of an offender? I earmarked this question for you and have fixed my hopes on seeing it answered by you, for you are a storehouse of arcane learning and recondite wisdom. Kindly answer it; otherwise, 147.1

I will convey to you the answer I gave to this question, and give you an account of what took place between me and this disputant; if you find it sound, you can tell me so, whereas if you find it weak, you can give me the benefit of your judicious counsel. For the shores of knowledge lie distant, its depths are unfathomed, and its waves tower and crash. But for God's great bounty toward creatures as infirm as us, we would be unable to inquire into anything or to reach any conclusion. Yet God is kind and gracious toward His servants, providing beneficence before it has been solicited, and good before it has been sought.

Miskawayh's response

147.2 It is not possible that the Law handed down by God should contain things that reason rejects and opposes—those who raise such doubts are ignorant of the provisions of reason and of what it rejects. For they always confound it with acquired customs, and they suppose that if people's natural disposition recoils from something, this amounts to an opposition on the part of reason. I have heard many people giving voice to these misgivings, and I have attended their verbal jousts and disputations, but they never go beyond what I have said. We must preface our response with a few remarks that help clarify the distinction between what is rejected by reason and what is rejected by the natural disposition and found repugnant by human beings as a result of acquired custom. So we respond as follows: When reason rejects something, its rejection holds forever; it can never change at any point in time, and its position can never be other than what it is. The same thing applies to everything reason judges to be good or bad. In general, all of the judgments of reason are valid forever. They have held necessarily from the beginning of time, and there can be no change in this status. This is something that is widely accepted as true and that cannot be gainsaid or doubted. Matters of natural disposition and custom, on the other hand, may change with shifting circumstances, causes, times, and customs. In talking about what is "natural," I am referring to the natural disposition of animals and human beings, not to primary nature in the absolute sense. For "nature" is an equivocal term; but we have clarified what we mean by "natural disposition."

If that is clear from examples and facts that muster general assent, then we can return to our question and say: The sacrifice of animals is not something reason rejects and denounces, but rather belongs to the second category, that is, to those things which some people's natural dispositions reject because of acquired custom. For were it one of the things that reason rejects, it would always be so, and reason would never approve of it, dictate it, or feel at ease with it. Yet we see people who reject the sacrifice of animals because it has not been part of their custom; and then, once they become accustomed to it, they find it easy and have no trouble performing it, and it becomes just like any other act they perform. And we observe how butchers and slaughterers—indeed, even those who have taken part in wars—find it easy to countenance things that others find hard. Similarly, when an animal is in agony because of an incurable illness, any rational person who takes pity on it and is loath to watch it suffer from something incurable would order that it be slaughtered so that it might find reprieve in a speedy death. So one must ask: Is reason, in ordering it to be slaughtered, now declaring good something it had formerly judged to be evil? Or has its eternally enduring act undergone a change due to a sudden contingency or newly arisen factor? Yet we acknowledge that it is not in the nature of reason for this to happen, and that is because it is an eternal substance, and its substance consists in its rulings. Thus, its rulings have eternal duration. 147.3

We do not suppose that the rulings of reason on questions of arithmetic or geometry or other types of natural proof have changed in the last ten thousand years, or will change over the next ten thousand years, or over shorter or longer spans. We are confident that they have always been and always will be the same. Those things, by contrast, which are disapproved of at one time and approved of at another, that are rejected on one occasion and accepted the next, 147.4

have their origins elsewhere than pure reason. Matters relating to political governance always involve such things. Likewise, bodily illnesses[111] and impermanent things on the whole are always exposed to change, and the relevant rulings change as they do. Indeed, it is impossible for them to adhere to a single state, for insofar as motion necessarily adheres to them, they are always passing from one state to another or passing into nothing. Motion itself consists in the change of moving things, for they are all changing. Similarly with time and what it attaches to; it changes as it changes. But the sense of repugnance people feel about slaughtering animals is due to the fact that they share in their animal nature. For when something bad happens to a beast, it crosses their mind that something similar will happen to them because they share animality with it. This thought produces in them the kind of revulsion that is produced in all animals whenever they envisage the occurrence of something bad. Yet once they grow familiar with this act, their sense of revulsion falls away, and slaughter and butchery come to seem no different to them than sharpening a pencil or carving wood. It is the same with those who take part in wars, and come to see them as normal even in the midst of fearsome carnage.

147.5 There is another case in this context that is even clearer than those I have mentioned. When a person is confronted with an abominable evil at the hands of enemies—as when one sees one's wife and children undergoing things one cannot bear to witness—reason deems it permissible for one to give up one's life and opt for a noble death instead of an ignominious life. The license granted herein by reason—the license to choose death, that is—extends to all cases in which it is ignoble for a person to continue living. Questions of this kind should therefore be addressed as follows: When reason judges any of these things to be good or bad, it does so on the basis of contextual factors and conditions. It neither rejects nor accepts a given act taken by itself and in isolation; that is, it does not pronounce a timelessly valid, primary ruling like those we know and are well acquainted with.

This is how matters stand with regard to things known as good and evil. Many ignorant people believe that everything falls into either of these categories. Yet this is not the case. For material prosperity and worldly power are neither good nor evil, and one must first consider the uses to which their owners put them. If they put their prosperity and wealth to good use, then their prosperity is good; if they use it for evil, it is evil. Similarly, anything that can serve two contrary ends should not be identified with one or the other; it is more appropriate to say that it can serve for both without distinction, like tools that can be put to a good or a bad use. For tools are not described as beneficial or harmful, nor can the notions of "benefit" or "harm" be applied to them until they have been put to use. Thus, one must say that things judged good or bad under particular circumstances and on the basis of particular customs are, from the viewpoint of reason, neither good nor bad absolutely, and one must first examine those who produce them and put them to service, as well as the time and circumstances in which they occur. For if an act is called "retaliation," it is good because it involves the preservation of human life, while if, on the basis of a different consideration, it is called "murder," it is bad because of the destruction of life it involves. 147.6

In this question, I deviated from the practice adopted throughout this book, of writing concisely and restricting myself to the key points. This is because of the sheer amount of verbiage I hear from ignorant Manichaeans and those who, duped into following their example, have gone over to their views, falling for the deceit through which they have gained access to the hearts of simple people and turned them away from the true laws. Yet were you to ask any of them about the distinction between taking "bad" and "good" in an absolute as against a restricted sense, they would only be able to give you a confused account. For all that, it is not impossible that any rational person among them who saw an animal covered in open ulcers, suffering from a colic recognized as untreatable, or lying with its limbs broken after falling into a ditch, tossing and turning in the 147.7

throes of a prolonged death—that such a person would give the signal for it to be killed, even if he did not take on the task himself. Other kinds of evils may afflict an animal that lives a long life, commensurate with those we mentioned, from which the only redemption, if one is judicious enough to discern it, lies in a speedy death. Yet such a person would not take on the task of killing it himself, and would ask another to do it, on account of custom and of the way his feelings are fixed. And were a rational person such as this to have the misfortune of being subjected to torture by a ruler who wished to bring about a slow death, in order to make him suffer woefully from the torture, he would be quick to rule that he should do that which he had previously rejected, and take a fast-acting poison or ask to be relieved of his life. Similarly, if his children and family were subjected to something he found abhorrent, he would prefer to die rather than to see it happen. So how else could something loathsome come to be readily chosen as desirable, and something deemed bad be deemed good from the perspective of reason, unless things are as we have described?

147.8 The answer to this question has thus emerged clearly, and it has been made plain that all those things that are bad at one time but not at another cannot be attributed to pure reason and to its timelessly valid primary judgments, and indeed that the terms "bad" or "good" cannot be predicated of them absolutely. Rather, they must be ascribed to natural dispositions and acquired customs, and one may then say: x is bad under such-and-such conditions, or good given such-and-such factors, in a restricted, not in an absolute, manner, and without attributing this to pure reason. People have discussed the reason why communities should be governed by the principle of levying blood money on the clan of an offender. The reasons why it is good are evident, particularly as the foregoing question has elucidated them and has clarified the right view to take on similar points of confusion.

On a remark made by Aḥmad ibn ʿAbd al-Wahhāb concerning the possibility of uttering something that is completely false versus something completely true

Aḥmad ibn ʿAbd al-Wahhāb said in response to Abū ʿUthmān al-Jāḥiẓ's work, *The Square and the Round*: Nobody can say something false that contains no truth of any kind, whereas one can say something true that contains no falsehood of any kind. 148.1

Miskawayh's response

If truth and falsehood pertain to that specific type of the divisions of speech designated "statements," and statements are what logicians call "declarative" utterances—that is, utterances that convey information—and if those divisions are as discussed by practitioners of that craft, statements can indeed be purely false just as they can be purely true. If Aḥmad ibn ʿAbd al-Wahhāb takes a view of truth and falsehood that is different from what these people are familiar with and have spoken about, then I know nothing of the matter and cannot speak about it. 148.2

On why excellent souls find repose in the truth and find falsehood repugnant

In this question you mentioned a question quoted by Abū Zayd al-Balkhī, the answer to which he also reported. Abū Zayd al-Balkhī the philosopher said: A philosopher was asked, Why do excellent souls find rest in the truth and find falsehood repugnant? He said: The reason for that is as follows . . . 149.1

Miskawayh's response

149.2 Excellent souls find rest in statements that are acceptable, either as a result of a powerful conviction or necessarily as entailed by a demonstrative proof. Anything that does not fall into this class inevitably meets with rejection and refusal in the soul. I believe that the person who posed this question meant to ask the unqualified question: How does the soul find rest in the truth? The answer is as follows. The soul carries out its proper motion—that is, the roving of reflection—so as to attain the truth it pursues. But for its pursuit, it would not move, and but for the motion it carries out, it would not be alive and impart life to the body. The soul is alive through this perpetual, essential motion. We are immediately made aware of this by the fact that we are incapable of making it halt reflection and thought for a single moment. For it is always either reflecting on and roving over sensory things, or reflecting on and roving over intelligible things, without ever ceasing. It is thus perpetually in motion, and this motion is directed toward a certain object, that is, the attainment of the truth. Once it attains it, it finds rest from that aspect. It never ceases moving until it has attained the truth from all the aspects from which it is possible to attain it. Once it attains it, it finds rest; for the end of every moving thing is to come to rest once it has reached the end it was moving toward. These allusive remarks may open up a very wide vista to you. May God help you in this through His grace.

On a question put by Aḥmad ibn ʿAbd al-Wahhāb concerning why animals are generated inside plants but plants are not generated inside animals

150.1 Aḥmad ibn ʿAbd al-Wahhāb confronted al-Jāḥiẓ with the following abstruse question:[112] Why are animals generated inside plants, whereas plants are not generated inside animals? That is, a worm might be generated inside a tree, whereas no tree grows inside an animal. Why did he not reply?

Miskawayh's response

Animals need plants for their existence, whereas plants do not need animals for their existence. The reason is that animals are more composite than plants, because they are composed from the latter and from other substances, that is, the animal soul. This is why at the first stage of their formation animals are plants, the movement of animals emerging at a subsequent stage. The effect of the soul emerges in human beings after the vegetative form has been completed within the womb. While they are there, they draw their nourishment by means of roots that are connected to the womb of their mother and that resemble the roots of plants. Once the animal form is perfected as well and the animal soul emerges in them, those roots are sundered, which is what produces the labor pains that the mother experiences and that move the child out of the womb. Once the child emerges from the womb and breathes in the open air, he opens his mouth and receives nourishment through it. The animal form continues to be perfected within him until he receives the effect of the rational soul, and then he is perfected through it and he becomes a human being through the power of God and through the grace of His wisdom. 150.2

As we have mentioned, plants are simpler than animals and prior to them in existence; that is, they do not need animals for their existence. The earth, the air, the water, and the heat they receive from the sun are all the material substance they need in order to be completed and to enter existence. For animals, by contrast, those elements are not enough unless they are supplemented by another type of material substance that serves to nourish them. For the simple elements—water, earth, and air—are not enough, and they need plants to nourish them, to perfect their existence, and to preserve them in their proper state. Since they depend on plants in 150.3

order to exist and be sustained, it is possible for them to be generated inside them; and since plants achieve their existence through other means and do not need them, they are not generated inside them. Were plants to be generated inside animals—even though they are not nourished by the latter and do not need them, and even though nature does nothing in vain or in error—this would expose animals to destruction, and they themselves would be destroyed in their own being. It would expose animals to destruction because of the need plants have for a base in which they may distribute their roots, through which they absorb the material substance that preserves them in their being and that replaces those of their parts that dissolve. Were they to strike their roots inside the bodies of animals, the latter would disintegrate, and when the body of a living being disintegrates, it perishes. The plants themselves would also perish because they would not find the simple water, earth, and air that sustain them and provide them with their material substance. For these simple elements are not actually to be found within animals. This amount of discussion suffices for the present question.

On the Nature of Alchemy and Why People Are So Enamoured of It

151.1 Why does everyone converge on the pursuit of alchemy? We that find the rich, the poor, and those neither rich nor poor share the same disposition irrespective of their level of material comfort. What is alchemy in the first place? Does it have any real substance? Long have inquiries into the topic been pursued, and people have said much about it; it is a battleground for truth and falsehood, errors, sound views, and incoherencies. Those who affirm it seem to lack conviction, and those who reject it seem unassured of their dismissal. What's more, it has been used to deceive. To lay this question bare is to lay bare truths about a noble domain hidden from view and a topic subtle to grasp. Is there truth in what is ascribed to Jābir ibn Ḥayyān, and is there a basis for what is attributed to Khālid ibn Yazīd? Can such a thing be conceded with respect to something fabricated and contrived, concocted and wrought by guile? And if matters are so ambiguous, how can we arrive at a position that removes doubt and guarantees certainty? I have known, as have we both, people who have changed and shifted their position as to whether they give or deny credence to this field. Its most curious aspect, it seems to me, is how sweet it is to speak about, how much it captivates speakers to touch upon, and how strongly people's souls incline to it, so that even those who deny its credibility give it their undivided attention, lend a listening ear, and devote their minds to it, with no hope of benefit or profit.

Miskawayh's response

The reason why people pursue alchemy is manifest and clear— 151.2
namely, that they have a keen desire for all the various pleasures and appetites to do with food, drink, sexual relations, and other sensual amusements. The love of obtaining ever larger amounts and of having exclusive possession of things and the insatiable desire to amass and hoard are rooted in nature. Silver and gold are the only means to do this, for they are equivalent to any of the various objects of desire. Every person knows that when he acquires both, or one of them, he can acquire any of the countless possible objects of desire whenever he has a mind or will to do so. At the same time, he views them as provisions laid up for his children and for times of hardship when he is visited by the misfortunes and trials of the world. By means of these precious metals one gains access to all we have mentioned, and one repels every evil and tribulation. This is the reason why people seek and desire them keenly. One can only obtain them by facing many hazards, venturing on frightful undertakings, and braving arduous deeds, among other things—and even then, they are vulnerable to damage and to the brute force and depredations of others. By contrast, obtaining them in this way,

through alchemy—supposing it stands up to scrutiny—would be the simplest and easiest thing in the world.

151.3 The proper way to inquire into your questions "What is it?" and "Does it have a real substance?" is, first, to begin by asking whether something exists, and only afterward to ask what it is. If we inquire into whether it exists, we find that the matter is riddled with obscurities and requires one to draw on a large number of premises related both to nature and to craft. Therefore, before we proceed to examine them ourselves, we must adduce the doubts directed by detractors against those premises and the arguments offered by supporters of the craft who have sought to counter them—for they have had much to say on the subject. Ancient and modern philosophers have differed over this topic. Al-Kindī was the most recent scholar to have spoken against the validity of alchemy and refuted the claims of its practitioners; his book on the subject is familiar to all. Muḥammad ibn Zakariyyā al-Rāzī countered him, and his book is also well-known.[113] Among the people of our times, we have observed a number of people affirming the soundness of this craft, whereas the majority deny its validity. The dialectical theologians, for all the different types who belong to their classes, are unanimous in denying its validity, alleging that this would nullify the miracles of the prophets, given that what the alchemists claim to be doing is changing one specific object into another. This is something that they believe can only be accomplished by a prophet; and it is God and not His creatures who has the exclusive power to change one specific object into another.

151.4 Each party has arguments in support of its case, and we will provide a satisfactory examination of them and adduce the views of all parties. We will approach our inquiry into the topic with the aim to discover the truth rather than to reap the benefit one hopes alchemy will provide. That is the end pursued by those who philosophize when they examine and inquire; beyond that we care not whether it proves valid or invalid, so that we do not let the soul be deceived by blind desire and thus are led to affirm it by our wish and hope that it be valid or deny it for partisan reasons. This kind of examination would be lengthy, and, given the principle of concision we stipulated, the present book cannot accommodate it, but we shall devote a separate treatise to the topic as we did with the topic of justice when the discussion grew somewhat lengthy.[114] Once we have carried out this task in the treatise we have promised, we may then go on to consider the question further. If the question of whether it exists has been answered affirmatively, we will continue by examining the question of what its nature is. If the first question is declared null, the second will inevitably be declared null as well.

On a question put by Aḥmad ibn ʿAbd al-Wahhāb concerning the difference between the words "indeterminable" and "impenetrable"

Aḥmad ibn ʿAbd al-Wahhāb said in response to Abū ʿUthmān al-Jāḥiẓ's book *The Square and the Round*: What is the difference between the term "indeterminable" and the term "impenetrable"? The answer to this is plain, but I have adduced it here for such and such a reason. 152.1

Miskawayh's response

Things that are termed "indeterminable" are one level above those that are termed "impenetrable."[115] This is shown by their etymological derivations. Etymological derivation occurs in a way conformable with meanings, for the one who performs it derives a word for every meaning from a term that necessarily agrees with it; otherwise, there would be no point in performing the derivation and no benefit in taking this trouble. We would not impute pointless activity like this to discerning adults, let alone to the institutor of language. Since the root term refers to the closing of a door, and since one may hope that a door that is closed can be opened, the 152.2

same thing will apply to that which has been compared to it and has had its name or inflection derived from it. As for "indeterminable," the root verb is only used to say that one has closed the door if one has not merely closed it but blocked it and the like, so the prospects are dimmer. This is how things stand with regard to questions and matters referred to as "impenetrable" and "indeterminable" by comparison with doors.

On the disagreements between jurists

153.1 I once attended a social gathering of some eminent figures. The conversation raged back and forth over topics alternately grave and jovial, and then the attendees were challenged with the question: By God, it is beyond me how it is possible for one jurist to state that a particular pudendum is unlawful while another states that the selfsame pudendum is lawful. Yet a pudendum is a pudendum, just as money is money. Likewise with the taking of life and the topics that follow; one person says things that make it out to be obligatory to put a given person to death, whereas his colleague prohibits it. They are divided by such troubling differences and pass rulings with odious willfulness, following their blind desires and appetites and wandering far and wide in their interpretations. This is not the way devout and God-fearing people should behave, nor is this the character one expects of people endowed with intelligence and learning. This is how they carry on, even as they assert that God made the rulings manifest, set up their indications, separated the particular from the general, and left "not a thing, fresh or withered"[116] that He failed to deposit in His book and incorporate into His address of mankind.

153.2 This epistle is not the proper place for this question, as it directs itself to the jurists or the dialectical theologians who defend our religion. But it was my wish that this book should contain something that points to the principles of the religious Law, even if the bulk of it is taken from nature and draws on philosophers of distinction, masters of empirical knowledge, and people of excellence of every type and creed. It is for God to bring what we will to fruition and to preserve us from envious backstabbing.

Miskawayh's response

The jurists speak with the utmost truth and the greatest soundness when they say that God made the rulings manifest, set up their indications, and left not a thing, fresh or withered, «but in a Book manifest». How could it be otherwise? For we are incapable of coming up with a single ruling that has no basis in the Qur'an, whether by recourse to interpretation or by the categorical affirmation of an evident text; the Qur'an also informs us about the transcendent realm, apprises us of events that took place centuries ago, offers us similitudes regarding the future life we have been promised, indicates the outcome awaiting us, and alerts us to the way we should act, whether in administering the present world or achieving our welfare in the next. It is possible for jurists to say that a single thing is both lawful and unlawful because this issue was left to the interpretive effort of human beings, in order to realize another advantage that accrues to human beings thereby, for interpretive efforts to determine the rulings are never alike, that is, they never lead to a single result, as is the case with other rulings that relate to necessary matters. 153.3

To explain the point: In the interpretive effort to arrive at the truth concerning God, there is only one route for the interpreter to follow, and he will inevitably find it if he gives rational inquiry its due. If he veers from sound inquiry, he goes astray and loses his way, failing to find what he is looking for, and, if he stubbornly clings to his error, he merits instruction or punishment. This is not how things stand with the interpretive effort that relates to rulings, because some rulings change depending on the time, the custom, or considerations of human welfare. For rulings are posited on the 153.4

basis of conventional justice, and welfare may be vested in one thing one day and in another the next, or something may serve the welfare of Zayd but undermine the welfare of ʿAmr. Yet insofar as interpretive effort has the status of a devotional exercise and is an act of obedience, or insofar as general welfare is served by inquiry and interpretive effort itself as against the object of pursuit, there is no harm if mistakes are made once the interpretive effort has been properly carried out. By way of analogy, the aim in hitting a ball in polo is to exercise by moving, and there is no harm done if one misses the ball, and there is nothing gained if one hits it, even if the umpire's orders are to hit the ball, for the purpose in engaging in the activity is exercise through movement. Similarly, suppose a sage were to bury a treasure in the desert and say to people, "Search for it. He who finds it will get such and such a reward," the purpose being that people should make an effort and that he should observe how much effort they expend, in order that this search, and not the discovery of the treasure, should benefit them. In that case, likewise, no harm would be done if the treasure were not found, and no gain if found. The benefit lies in the effort of searching, and both parties would realize that—that is, both those who found it and those who did not.

153.5 Many kinds of interpretive efforts and inquiry follow this principle. This includes questions of arithmetic, geometry, and many other subjects. The philosophers' purpose in pursuing these is not to achieve the utmost results. Their intention, rather, is that the soul should be trained through inquiry and should become accustomed to persevering in properly conducted deliberation and thought, so that it acquire a disposition and settled aptitude for prolonged thought and for separating itself from the senses and from corporeal things. The ultimate purpose of inquiry has been achieved if this benefit is realized. Those aspects of the Law left undetermined and not fully elucidated answer to the same principle; the purpose they achieve and the welfare they serve lie in the inquiry and interpretive effort alone. Beyond that, every conclusion that the disagreements of jurists lead to is correct and judicious. People should not be amazed that one and the same thing could be deemed lawful by al-Shāfiʿī and unlawful by Mālik and Abū Ḥanīfah. For "lawful" and "unlawful," as these pertain to rulings and legal matters, do not have the status of contraries or contradictories as when they pertain to natural matters and the like. It is not impossible that one and the same thing belonging to the former class should be lawful or unlawful depending on the circumstances or the persons involved, or in the way we illustrated through the examples of hitting a ball with a stick or of discovering the sage's buried treasure.

If this is correct, then when an intelligent person examines any 153.6
of the rulings of the Law—assuming that he is capable of making an interpretive effort and has the competence to conduct such examination, which is to say that he has knowledge of the Qurʾan and its rulings, and of sound hadith, of transmitted prophetic practices, and correct instances of scholarly consensus—he must make an effort to examine matters and then act on the basis of that interpretive effort. Other people with a similar level of learning can make an interpretive effort and act on the basis of whatever conclusion their interpretive effort leads them to, even if this conflicts with the conclusion of the first party, in the confident knowledge that interpretive effort is what is required of them and that there is no harm in disagreement. The only possible exception is if the matter under examination does not fall in the class we mentioned and illustrated through different examples—for instance, when it concerns principles with regard to which the end of examination is to arrive at the truth and nothing else, for that forms a different object and involves a kind of examination which must necessarily lead to it. Just as the exercise of swinging the stick and hitting the ball is done for the sake of our health, and, once health-inducing exercise has been carried out, it does not matter what happens to the ball—whether one hits it or whether one misses it—so it is with this second aspect, that is, the one in which it is necessary specifically to arrive at the truth itself. It resembles bloodletting, which one must specifically get right and let the blood, as opposed to any

other treatment, if health is to be achieved, and bloodletting alone can help. Once you have grasped these two modes of examination and discriminated between them appropriately, you will no longer be amazed by what you reported in your question, and you will perceive the soundness of my response, God willing.

On why people despise kings who are governed by pleasure and fear kings governed by reason

154.1 Why is it that if the common people know the king to be fond of pleasures, engrossed in his appetites, and given over to the caprices of his soul, they make light of him, even if he is a murderer, a killer, a wrongdoer, and a ravager, whereas if they know him to be a man of reason, merit, and gravity, they stand in awe of him and take care not to cross him? What evidence do present circumstances give on this question? For to answer it is to elucidate a piece of knowledge that far exceeds the measure of the question.

Miskawayh's response

154.2 Kingship is a craft that effects political order; induces people, by choice or force, to conform to the religious laws and governing policies that serve their welfare; and preserves people's stations and livelihoods so that they might follow the best possible course. Since this craft occupies such a lofty rank, it is necessary that its practitioner have acquired all of the excellences within himself. For he who has not put himself in order cannot put others in order, but it is possible for him to refine others, if he himself has been refined through the realization of the excellences. The way the soul realizes the excellences is, first, by realizing temperance, which consists in putting the appetitive power in order so that it not incline to the wrong objects and that it move toward the things it ought, in the manner it ought, and under the circumstances it ought. Second, it does this by putting the irascible power in order, so that the movement of this power might also be balanced, and that it be exercised in the right manner, toward the right people, and under the right circumstances, and so that it be adjusted properly in seeking honor, tolerating harm, and enduring disdain as the case requires, and in desiring honor in the right measure and according to the conditions described in books of ethics. That person has realized the quality of justice, the fruit of all of the excellences, if these two powers come into balance within him, and their movement is balanced as it ought to be, neither running to excess nor falling short. Through the realization of these excellences, the rational soul is fortified and a person comes to stably possess the perfected form that makes him fit to be the governor of a city or the ruler of a region. A person who has not realized these excellences needs to be governed by others and to be ruled by people who put him to order and set him straight. So could there be anything worse than for this situation to be inverted and to pursue the wrong course? Human nature loathes crookedness, so how could it fare otherwise when things are turned upside down and transposed from their proper places?

You remark that this is so even if the king acts with extreme 154.3
oppression and much tyranny, shedding blood and profaning things that ought to be inviolable. This is something that detracts from, rather than adding to, the conditions of kingship, and such a king is more likely to fall in his subjects' regard, for it is a condition of kingship that these things be applied in the right manner and according to all the conditions we mentioned earlier. Isn't this like the case of a doctor who claims he can cure people of all ailments, and who pledges to sustain the health of bodies and preserve their balanced states whatever their various humoral mixtures, yet who, upon inquiry, is found to be prone to illness and to have an irregular humoral mixture as a result of his bad regime? When he is questioned and his condition is probed, he is found to have such poor insight and to be so defective in self-management that he could

not be expected to rectify the humoral mixture of his own body. How could such a person avoid ridicule and mockery, and not be disdained by people who are not doctors and who do not pretend to be practitioners of this craft, yet who follow a fine bodily regime and govern themselves well? If this pretender should happen to gain ascendancy and power and demand that people submit to his regime, how could people not find him all the more repugnant and ridicule him all the more? This is a sound comparison adequate to its target, so it should be considered carefully, for it meets the purpose of your question, God willing.

On the physical reactions people exhibit when listening to music

155.1 Why do people in a transport at singing and delighted by a musical performance stretch out their hands, move their heads, and sometimes get up and drift about—dancing, making impassioned sounds, crying out, and sometimes even running and wandering here and there distractedly—whereas people who are afraid do not act like this; rather, they shudder and shrink, conceal their presence and obliterate their traces, lower their voices and say as little as possible?

Miskawayh's response

155.2 We answered this question in our earlier discussion of the causes of joy and grief, where we said that when the soul experiences joy it expands the blood in the veins toward the exterior of the body, and when it experiences grief it constricts it. The constriction of the heat into the interior of the body and into its point of origin in the heart makes the smoky vapor increase and cools the exterior of the body. The meaning of "grief" (*ghamm*) is revealed in its etymological derivation, for what happens to the heart is what happens to something hot when it is "covered" (*ghumma*), preventing the heat from spreading and reaching the surface of the body. That is why people breathe very heavily when they are aggrieved, on account of the heart's need for air to expel the smoky excess it contains and allow in pure air to increase and aerate the heat, as is the case with fire in the external world.

These two aspects—the mixture of the heart and the movement 155.3
of the soul—are inseparably linked, for if the soul experiences a contraction, the heat sinks from the various regions of the body toward its interior; and if in the mixture of the body the heat happens to sink and constrict itself in the area of the heart, the soul undergoes contraction, because the one is inseparably linked to, and follows upon, the other. This is why some people have thought that the soul consists in a particular mixture, and why others have thought that it is a state that depends upon the mixture of the body. Wine and similar drinks, and medicines that expand the body's heat through their fine qualities, increasing it and spreading it toward the body's exterior, produce joy and delight, whereas medicines that make the body cold and contract the heat produce the opposite. A melancholic mixture is always accompanied by grief, whereas a sanguine mixture is always accompanied by joy. Just as medicines and foods produce this kind of effect in the mixture, which is followed by a movement of the soul, so too words, melodies, and the sound of instruments, such as strings and woodwinds, move the soul, and that is followed by a movement in the mixture of the body, since the mixture is connected to the soul. As the two are inseparably linked, one has an impact on the other, and the action of one is followed by the action of the other.

On why liars often tell the truth but not the reverse, and on whether habits can change

156.1 Why do liars often speak the truth, whereas truth tellers rarely lie? Can a habit of telling the truth change to a habit of lying? Can a habit of lying transform into a habit of telling the truth, or is that impossible?

Miskawayh's response

156.2 Telling the truth and lying are as health and illness to the soul, for telling the truth represents a form of health for the soul, whereas lying represents a form of illness. Furthermore, telling the truth relates to informative statements as to their state of health, and lying relates to them as representations of their illness. Just as health outweighs illness in the body—illness being confined to one or two or three bodily members—similarly, health outweighs illness in the soul, illness being confined to one or two powers or one or two character traits. And just as the body would be annihilated if the illnesses affecting its members became numerous or if a certain member was affected by numerous, successive illnesses, similarly the soul would perish if the illnesses affecting its powers became numerous or if a single power was affected by numerous, successive illnesses. The balanced state appointed for the body and the soul is that which preserves the existence of each. If in certain circumstances one of these is struck by an illness and dislodged from its balanced state, this is confined to one particular part and one particular power, and moreover it only lasts for a short amount of time, after which it returns to the balanced state appointed for it. The supposition that illnesses might take control over all members of the body so that not a single part remained healthy, or that a large number of successive illnesses might affect a single member without interruption over a long period of time, would be false, for were it true, the body in question or the member that formed the subject of the supposition would be destroyed. This is demonstrated by the fact that the heart, as the source of life from which life flows out to the entire body, enjoys the utmost degree of protection against illness, for were it to be affected by illness, that illness would quickly extend to all parts of the body, and this would soon lead to a speedy death.

This is how things stand with the soul as regards its balanced state 156.3
or its illness. Since lying imparts a disfigured form to the soul—that is to say, a form of the object that conflicts with the way it really is—the one who imparts it and the one to whom it is imparted fall ill on its account. That is why nobody undertakes to lie or intentionally pursues lying unless he is driven by some necessity or unless he believes that act of lying is beneficial to him, the way poison might be beneficial to the body in certain circumstances, so that he brings himself to engage in this distasteful action despite the repugnance he feels toward it. He might do this a number of times, and it might then become a habit, the way all other foul deeds become traits of character and habits, and the way harmful foods become a bad habit for some people. Furthermore, the person who habitually lies can only lie with success if he mingles his lies with a bit of truth and if he is also heard to be telling the truth on other occasions. Otherwise, he would not be able to lie successfully, for falsehood can only stand if mixed with the truth.

You ask, can a person who habitually tells the truth change into 156.4
a liar, or can a person accustomed to lying change into a teller of the truth. Were this not possible and attested among people, there would not be norms of behavior, the young would not be corrected, the education of children would not be a matter for concern, and there would be no censure. Yet these things are widespread and manifest among people. This matter has been clarified in books of ethics, so if you wish to probe it in depth you can consult such works, God willing.

On certain popular sayings

157.1 Here you mentioned—God grace you with His support—questions that merit no reply, questions that derive from opinions of the common people and from ignorant notions they have conceived, such as their saying, "When a fly enters a person's clothing he falls ill," "The blood money of an ant is a fruit," and "If a person's ears buzz, people are gossiping about him." These questions and their like should be viewed with derision and only brought up facetiously and in jest. But to solicit replies to them—I believe there is hardly an intelligent person who accepts them, so how could we possibly reply to them? May God grant you forgiveness and guide you to goodness.

On the distinction between different forms of divination

158.1 What is the distinction between the types of divination referred to as *ʿirāfah* and *kihānah*, divination by means of the stars, divination by means of pebbles, and the two types of divination by means of birds? Do the Arabs share these practices with any other nation or not?

Miskawayh's response

158.2 The distinction between the forms of divination termed *ʿirāfah* and *kihānah* consists in the fact that the practitioner of *ʿirāfah* gives information about things that lie in the past, whereas the practitioner of *kihānah* gives information about things that lie in the future. *ʿIrāfah* consists in the knowledge of physical traces and in their use for determining their cause, but *kihānah* is a power of the soul that, by abandoning the senses, discloses things that will be in the future. It occupies a higher rank than *ʿirāfah*. We discussed this in our book *The Triumph*, when considering the distinction between a prophet and someone who claims to be a prophet, the power through which inspiration is achieved, and how that happens, so you can consult that work for this purpose.[117]

The distinction between divination on the basis of the stars and that which resembles divination on the basis of random occurrence is plain. Astrology is a craft by means of which one acquires knowledge of the movements of the higher bodies and their effects on the lower bodies. It is a natural craft, even though more has been referred to it than it can accommodate; that is, astrologists sometimes claim to have knowledge of particulars and minutiae that cannot be gained through this craft. Astrologists thus give information about future events based on the effect something has on its like. When the sun carries out one of its rotations, it exercises a variety of effects on this world, as does every planet through its movement, its rotation, and the rays it emits, which reach the world we live in. What the astrologist might say, for example, is that in the coming year, the indicators of the sun and of Saturn will both be present, and they will have an effect on our world that will be a composite of the natures of these movements, so the condition of the air will be such and such, and likewise with the condition of the four elements. Since animals and plants are composed from these natures, everything that has an effect on their basic elements must also have an effect on the things composed from them. Thus, the effect the stars have on our world is a natural one. Astrologists give information based on the calculations they make concerning their movements and their rays, whose effects reach us through natural force, though astrologists might sometimes make mistakes, depending on how accurate their examination is, how large the aggregate of movements and relations yielded by the ensemble of celestial bodies and planets is, and how receptive the parts of the world of generation and corruption that receive those various effects are. 158.3

158.4 The practices of augury by means of animals, birds, pebbles, and the like are all groundless speculations. They only happen to come true fortuitously and on rare occasions. They do not rest on any foundation, nor can any proof be given to support them, for they are neither natural, nor derived from the soul, nor divine. They are, rather, willful choices based on fancies and groundless speculations, and they often turn out to be false and seldom come true, as happens when someone without any proof or persuasive grounds for his claim states that tomorrow it will rain or the emir will ride out. He simply produces his statement and makes free with his judgment; occasionally it turns out to be correct and correspond with the truth, but most often it proves to be invalid and incorrect. Other nations share these practices with the Arabs, but, compared with other nations, Arabs have a greater number of forms of the kind of divination known as *ʿirāfah* and of bird augury exclusive to them.

On why there are four categories for inquiry: whether, what, which, and why

159.1 Why do the categories for inquiring about any existing object come down to four—namely, whether, what, which, and why?

Miskawayh's response

159.2 These four aspects form the principles and first causes of all existents, and any doubts that arise direct themselves to these; so once they have been fully grasped, all occasions for doubt have been removed. For the first principle regarding the existence of a given thing is that its being should be established—that is to say, the fact that it is, which we inquire about using the interrogative "whether." If a person has doubts about the fact that something is—that is, that its being exists—he makes no further inquiries about it. Once his doubts about its existence have been eliminated and he has established that it has being and that it is, he may then inquire about the second principle of its existence, which is its form—that is, its species, which constitutes it and makes it what it is. This is the inquiry that uses the interrogative "what"; for "what" poses a question about the entity's species and its constitutive form. Once a person has determined these two aspects about the thing that is unclear to him—namely, the first existence, the fact that it is, which we inquire with the interrogative "whether"; and the second existence, which is its species, that is, its constitutive form, which we inquire about with the interrogative "what"—he may inquire about the aspect that distinguishes it from other entities, that is to say, its specific difference. That is the third principle; for what distinguishes it from other entities is what we inquire with the interrogative "which," that is to say, the specific difference essential to it.

Once these three principles have been determined regarding the 159.3
object of inquiry, there is nothing left to arouse doubt, and sound knowledge of the object has been obtained except as regards the state that constitutes its perfection and that for the sake of which it exists. This is the final cause that is designated as "perfectional," the noblest of the causes. Aristotle was the first to call attention to it and expound upon it. For all the other three causes are subservient to and conducive to this final cause; it is as though they all existed on its account and for its sake. This is the cause that we inquire about using the interrogative "why." Inquiry comes to an end, once why the thing exists and what its final purpose is—that is, that for the sake of which it exists—have been understood: Complete knowledge of it has been achieved, every doubt eliminated, and no aspect remains that the soul yearns to attain through reflection and longs to know, for its causes and principles have been grasped fully and in their entirety, and there is no aspect to which doubt can adhere. This is why there are four forms of inquiry, no more and no less.

On the nonexistent

160.1 What is the nonexistent, and how can it be investigated? What is the benefit of disputing about it? What has occupied the dialectical theologians to such an extent that they have gone on debating its name and meaning at length? Do their views deliver anything of value? It is the only question I have ever seen that grants the inquirer no leverage over itself.

Miskawayh's response

160.2 The nonexistent specifically referred to by dialectical theologians possesses existence of some kind; this is why it is possible to refer to it and speak about it. For example, if Zayd is imagined to be nonexistent, his form obtains in the imagination of the person speaking about his nonexistence, and this form found in the imagination constitutes a kind of existence for him. The same applies to everything else they imagine to be nonexistent, be it body, accident, or state: its state is not nonexistent; rather, it is an object of consideration. The proof of this is that whenever we imagine a nonexistent thing, we envisage a state in which it existed or in which it exists. That envisaged form obtains in our imagination, and constitutes a kind of existence. The imagination cannot grasp the absolute nonexistent—the one that cannot be referred to any individual entity, to any accident that inheres in it, or to any state that pertains to it—it cannot be discussed, and no one can possibly ask about it, for it is nothing in the absolute sense. We can only ask questions about things on which certain states either supervene at present or are expected to supervene. That is why the majority of dialectical theologians asserted that the nonexistent is a thing, whereas some asserted that it is not a thing, that is, that they do not designate it as a "thing." The reason they fell into this dispute is that some of them considered it from the perspective of the imagination, whereas others considered it from the perspective of the senses. Those who considered it with regard to the imagination affirmed it to be a thing, whereas those who considered it from the perspective of the senses did not affirm it to be a thing.

The proof that the nonexistent they refer to is what we have mentioned and as we have described is that when these people make their successive forays on the topic of the nonexistent, they ask, "Is an atom an atom when it is nonexistent?" and "Is black black when it is nonexistent?" In the same vein, all of their examples are drawn from sense-perceptible things, and the question asked is: What happens to them if they cease to be perceived by the senses? The answer they give to that question is then based on what can be envisaged by the soul and obtain in the imagination. Thus, they say about the color black—whose basic reality is that it is an effect produced on the visual sense by an object that creates a contraction—that it is the same when it is nonexistent. It is as though they imagined it to be acting upon vision when nonexistent in the same way it acted upon it while existent. The reason they were affected by this imaginary idea is that the power which the senses feed into receives effects that are similar to those of the senses; that is, the form occurs in it denuded of matter, which is what constitutes sensory knowledge. Had they been able to affirm and deny an intelligible form, they would have spoken about intelligible existents and intelligible nonexistents. And had they been able to do that, it would have been possible for them to also ask about the absolute nonexistent, "Can it be referred to, or can it not be referred to?" But these matters escaped their notice. However, you asked about their approaches and the questions they pose, and my answer has emerged and become plain, God willing. 160.3

On why a physician rejoices at the recovery of his patient

161.1 I heard an accomplished physician say: I rejoice when a sick person recovers under my stewardship; it makes me very happy. I asked him: Don't you know the cause of that? He replied: No. I shall mention to him what you say in reply, God willing.

Miskawayh's response

161.2 What the physician rejoices in is his soul and his sound understanding. When he sees a sick person, he first needs to ascertain the cause of his sickness and to gain a sound and correct understanding of it. Once he has gained an understanding of it, he addresses it using medicines and foods that oppose it, which brings about the sick person's recovery. When this happens, the physician has been successful in determining the cause and then addressing it using the medicine that opposes it. This success and right determination are what he seeks to achieve through his knowledge and what he strives for during the entire time he spends studying and reflecting. When the soul moves with vigor and ardent desire toward a particular end over a long period of time and then obtains it, it rejoices in it and experiences an extraordinary feeling of happiness and delight.

On why money is made of silver and gold and not other substances

162.1 Then you said, may God grace you with His support: Ibn al-ʿAmīd was asked, Why didn't people agree to use sapphires and jewels, or copper, iron, and lead, instead of silver and gold, as the basis of value for their transactions? What made them restrict themselves to these two, even though it was possible to replace them with others to serve the same role?

Miskawayh's response

It has been shown that human beings are not capable of living in isolation owing to their need for great amounts of assistance from people who supply them with agreeable foods, medicines, clothing, housing and shelter, and other items, some of which are necessary for people to live, while others are beneficial for improving and enhancing life, so that it may be pleasant, fine, or excellent. Human beings are not like other animals, whose impediments were removed regarding what they need to live and what naturally sustains their life, such as being able to procure food, being protected by their bodily coverings, and other corporeal needs. That is why they were equipped with reason and provided with its assistance, so as to put everything to their service and attain every desire through its power. 162.2

Since cooperation constitutes an unavoidable necessity and since it is natural for large groups to be formed in order for single individuals to survive, people must necessarily enter into a civic state; that is, they must form groups and distribute the different kinds of labor and occupations among themselves so that everyone may achieve the desired end—namely, to survive and live in the most excellent way possible. Once people have formed groups and cooperation has been established, the following situation arises: The carpenter who cuts the wood and prepares it for the blacksmith, the blacksmith who shapes the iron and prepares it for the plowman, or any other person in the group may need something from his fellow to whom he provides help, yet his fellow may not need anything from him at that particular time. If the blacksmith has a need for the craft of weaving yet the person who makes garments has no need for the blacksmith's craft, cooperation comes to a standstill, exchange has ceased to flow, and every person can only obtain the product of his own labor, which is of no use to him for his bodily necessities, 162.3

for the sake of which cooperation was established. That is why someone was needed to serve as a custodian for the group and as trustee capable of supervising their different kinds of labor and occupations—a person known for his honesty and fairness, so that his command might be accepted by everyone, his judgment stand, his orders be effective and enjoy credibility, and his trustworthiness be sound. His task was to exact in full and receive from every person the value of the help he has provided, and to give him his fair share of others' help. The way he was to accomplish this was by appraising and mustering the labor of every person, and then by giving him an amount of the labor of the other person whose help he seeks that corresponds to the amount of his own effort and labor.

162.4 Furthermore, the only way this action could be accomplished by the custodian who exacts the different kinds of labor carried out by people is by having everyone who has carried out some labor come to him, show it to him, and receive a mark from him, such as a stamp or some other such thing. The laborer would then hold on to this, and whenever he showed it to another, it would be accepted and its purport not forgotten, so his claim would be recognized as sound, and he would receive a corresponding amount of another person's effort in return. Upon consideration of the object that could satisfy this description, it was clear that the kind of objects that are always available and that anyone could get hold of could not be selected, for they could be acquired by people who do not carry out any labor or help anyone through their hard work, and they might then use them to gain access to the hard work and effort of others; thus, a measure designed to further political association and cooperation would have an effect contrary to that intended. Hence, it was necessary that the stamp in question be drawn from a rare and precious substance, so that it might be possible to preserve and protect it, and so that those who had a rightful claim to it and who could demonstrate their labor and effort should only be able to receive it from the custodian. At the same time, it was necessary that, in addition to being rare, it should not be susceptible to the kind of damage through water, fire, or air that is possible in our world. For were it the type of thing that could be soaked in water or burnt by fire or whose form could be damaged by one of the four elements, the person who had toiled greatly would not be insured against the possibility that, having acquired it, it might subsequently be damaged while in his possession; this would result in the loss of his labor and there would be no means of verifying the help he had provided and the hard work he had contributed. Thus, it was necessary that this stamp be capable of preserving its form, be light enough to carry, and remain impervious to damage by the four elements as well as to damage from handling, such as by being broken, crushed, and so on.

When the different kinds of existents were inspected, the only 162.5
objects found to unite these excellences were minerals, and among minerals only precious substances that melt in fire and solidify in air, and of these gold alone. For it is the most durable and rarest mineral, the most capable of retaining its form, and the most immune to the impact of fire, air, water, and earth. At the same time, it is impervious to breaking, cutting, and crushing, and can recover its form through smelting, preserving it from damage for a very long time. So it was chosen as a measure for the appraisal of crafts and as a distinguishing mark of the custodian, and was subsequently protected by having his seal and marks stamped upon it. All of this was done for fear that it might be obtained by evildoers, who help themselves to others' labor yet offer no help to others, for that is the type of injustice that nullifies cooperation, destroys order, and brings communal life and coexistence to ruin. Then, once the precious substance that combined all these excellences had been located and protected in a variety of ways against the prospect of falling into the hands of people with no rightful claim over it, another contingency arose—namely, that someone who had provided help to people and thereby acquired a rightful claim to a certain amount of it might happen to need some light help that was not equal to his original effort and did not come near its level. For example, a

person might put in several days' effort in order to operate, with toil and hard work and considerable skill, a mill for another person. If he was given an amount of this precious substance equivalent to his labor and he subsequently needed a few herbs or a pin or some other minor commodity, he would not be able to exchange any of the precious substance in his possession for it, not even the smallest fraction, as even the smallest fraction of it would be worth more than the labor he was soliciting from another. That is why another precious substance was needed, one with fewer excellent qualities than gold, which despite its inferiority could act as its deputy and perform its function. Silver was the only object found to unite the excellences that we have said gold possesses, so it was appointed as its representative, and one part of gold was assigned the value of ten parts of silver. Single units stop at ten, and therefore it was necessary that one part of the former precious substance be valued at ten similar parts of the latter.

162.6 As for the disparity between the conversion rate of gold dinars and silver dirhams—that is, the fact that one dinar is equivalent to fifteen or so dirhams, which was the question you next posed—this is due to the disparity between the weight of dinars and dirhams and also due to the debasement undergone by one of the two. Nevertheless, the principle is preserved insofar as one part of gold is equal to ten parts of silver, so long as neither has been subjected to adulteration or debasement.

On the Specific Time When the Soul Attaches Itself to the Body

163.1 When does the soul attach itself to the body, and when does it come to be present in it? Is it when the body is a fetus, or before or after that?

Miskawayh's response

To talk of the soul as "attaching" itself to the body and "becoming present" in it involves a loose usage of words. It is preferable to say: The effect of the soul is manifested in the body in accordance with its preparedness for and receptivity to it. The reason we are wary of those words is that they give the impression that the soul has an accidental or physical attachment, and neither of these notions can be unqualifiedly predicated of the soul. If we wish to convey this meaning, it is more appropriate to say: The soul is a simple substance such that, when a certain humoral mixture arises that is prepared to receive a certain effect from it, that effect is manifested in the measure of that preparedness. This expression may preserve us from the notion of those who have claimed that the soul changes and performs its acts intentionally and by choice—that is, that it acts at one time and restrains at another, for this gives rise to a great number of doubts unbefitting to the characteristics and actions of the soul. 163.2

Having established the correct expression, we may now respond as follows: When the drop of semen from which the fetus is produced arrives in a suitable womb, the first effect of nature to manifest itself in it is of the kind manifested in mineral objects. That is, the delicate heat ripens and agitates it, and if it is mixed with suitable water produced by the female's desire, it gives it a composite form such as one sees in milk when mixed with rennet. That is to say, it curdles and coagulates, and then the heat persists with it so that it acquires a reddish tinge and becomes a lump of flesh. After that it prepares to receive another effect, which is when the embryo draws nourishment, developing roots like the roots of trees and plants by means of which it derives nourishment from its mother's womb, just as tree roots get this from soil. The growing—that is, the vegetative—soul manifests its effect in it, and this effect grows stronger in it and takes firm hold until it is perfected over time. The next step is that it prepares itself to receive nourishment without the roots, which means reaching for its nourishment through its own movement, 163.3

and the animal effect manifests itself in it little by little. Once it has fully prepared itself to receive this effect, it leaves its location and receives the effect of the animal soul. It remains at the level of beasts until it develops the preparedness to receive the effect of rationality, that is, discrimination and reflection. At that point, the effect of the intellect manifests itself within us, and this effect continues to grow strong within us in the measure of our preparedness and receptivity, until we reach the highest grade and perfection possible for us with regard to humanity. We then come within view of the grade above the grade of human beings, and we prepare to receive the effect of the angels. At that point, we must rise up in the next realm in a stronger state than the earlier preceding state.

163.4 This form of words does not allow for the question, "When does the soul attach or detach itself?" The person who holds to that view should rather ask, "When is there preparedness and receptivity?" The soul essentially gives to everything that receives its effect in accordance with its receptivity, preparedness, and readiness. It has been established that it imparts a variety of states and disparate forms to the body before it becomes an embryo. Once the human form is complete, the soul never wholly ceases to exercise its effect on the body throughout its manifold states until it completes its manifold cycles and reaches its ultimate perfection. It must not be said that it is ever without it in any of its states; rather, the effect grows stronger and weaker depending on its receptivity. That is all there is to say.

On whether souls can recollect what they used to know after leaving the body

164.1 A thinker was asked: When the soul leaves the body, does it recollect any of the things it used to know, or not? He answered that it recollects all intelligible but not sensible things. The questioner followed up by pointing to the forgetfulness that ill people are prone to. That is, how can the soul recollect intelligible things when it leaves the body, when it does not recollect any of them when the body, or some parts of the body, fall ill? He gave the reply that you shall see.

Miskawayh's response

The effect of the soul manifests itself in the body in accordance with the body's need and relative to its progression from one state to the next, as we have explained above. Recollection consists in summoning the forms of sensible objects from the power of memory to the power of imagination. Both these powers first acquire the forms of sensible objects from the senses out of the natural bodies that bear them, and then acquire them simply, not in a corporeal carrier but in the power of the soul that is called memory. This power is needed because of the purposes of the body and its successive needs for different things. When the body is transformed and the need for the senses is eliminated, the need for memory also falls away, and the soul comes to require nothing outside itself and outside the forms of the intellect it contains, that is, outside those that are termed first principles. For those constitute the intellect itself and in order to exist do not need any matter or any body. That is, the things found in the intellect are what the intellect consists in, and they are the ones we now term first principles, which are not found in matter nor need it. All of the powers of the soul that are realized through the body and physical organs cease with the cessation of the body, that is, the soul ceases to require them insofar as it is a soul and simple substance. It needed them on account of the needs of the body that was partnered to the soul and that used them to derive the continued existence that was suitable to it, depending on whether it was plant, animal, or human. 164.2

Insofar as it is a simple substance, by contrast, the soul needs none of these physical organs. The reason you succumbed to this confusion was that you inquired about a simple entity while 164.3

fancying it to be composite, and composite entities do not have the same qualities as simple ones. That is, all bodily organs also have a composite character oriented to particular ends, in order that something composite be in turn perfected through them. The five senses and the powers that fall in with them—such as imagination, fancy, and thought—are realized through appropriate organs and humoral mixtures, through which composite acts are accomplished. When substances revert to their simple elements, the composite acts also cease to exist with the cessation of the composite organs, and the self-subsisting simple substance dispenses with the needs and necessities of the body, through which its existence was realized insofar as it was composite on account of them.

On why mountains exist

165.1 Here a question was posed about the purpose served by the existence of mountains.

Miskawayh's response

165.2 There are very many benefits to mountains and to their presence on the surface of the earth. Were it not for mountains, there would be no plants or animals on the surface of the earth. For what enables plants and animals to come into existence and to continue in existence thereafter is the fresh water that flows over the face of the earth. Fresh, running water is caused by the thickening of vapor in the air—I am referring to clouds and to the compression they undergo through cold, producing rain, snow, or hail. Were we to suppose that mountains were removed from the face of the earth and to imagine the earth as a round sphere with no protuberances or cavities, the vapor that rises from this sphere would not thicken in the air or become compressed, nor would fresh water be produced by it. All that would come of the vapor is that it would dissolve and turn into air before it had the chance to bring about that which causes the face of the earth to be filled with life. The vapor that rises from the earth accumulates in the cavities of the earth and among the mountains, which prevent it from drifting and from submitting to the movement of the celestial sphere and to the factors that produce the wind, which constitutes the movement of the air. That is, the high summits of mountains preserve the air that has concentrated itself among their cavities from the movement necessarily caused in it by the whole of the celestial sphere, along with its stars and their effective, emollient rays, which necessarily cause it to drift. If the air finds itself among the mountains, likewise, the vapor that rises in it is also preserved against dispersion and against movement produced by the motion of the air; the cold of the mountains the vapor is exposed to—retained during wintertime—causes it to freeze and thicken and then be pressed out, transformed into water or suchlike.

Were it not for mountains, the water produced in this manner 165.3
with the characteristics we have mentioned would only run on the face of the earth while rains are falling, and the earth would absorb it. The result would be that plants and animals would not have access to it at the height of summer and at times when they urgently need it to survive, so that access to it would only be gained as happens in desert areas located far from mountains, that is, by digging wells that run one hundred or two hundred cubits deep. Under current circumstances, by contrast—with mountains in existence—the rains and the snow remain there, and if they absorb them straightaway or after some time, springs of water well up at the feet of the mountains and streams and rivers gush forth and run over the face of the earth in the direction of the seas, from north to south. When the rains they have collected are depleted in the course of the summer, the next bout of wintry weather and rainfall comes along and restores things to their former state.

The proof that springs of water, streams, and rivers all stem from 165.4
mountains is that when we follow a stream or a river to its source, it

always leads us to a mountain. Springs of water are only ever found close to mountains. The same applies to the water canals we come upon and the like. Thus, in causing water to flow over the earth, mountains relate to the earth like sponges or pieces of wool that are soaked in water and take in a large amount of it, and are then placed in a position where the water can seep out of them bit by bit. When dry, they are soaked and filled with water anew, so that the moisture may continue to seep out of them over the face of the earth. This arrangement makes it possible for life to flourish in the world and for plants and animals to exist in it. Mountains provide many benefits, but what we have mentioned is one of their greatest benefits, so that is enough. Thābit[118] wrote a treatise about the benefits of mountains, and whoever wishes to probe this topic in depth may read about it there, God willing.

On why there are three souls

166.1 Why are the souls three in number? Is it possible that they be two? Or is it impossible that they be four?

Miskawayh's response

166.2 In reality the soul is one, but as we said earlier, its effect is manifested according to the receptivity of that which receives it. The reason it has been described as threefold is that it is natural for something whose effect is initially weak and then reaches its fullest strength to divide into three parts—namely, beginning, middle, and end. As the effect of the soul first arises in plants—which is to say that a certain element manifests itself in them that accepts suitable nourishment, expels what is superfluous and unsuitable, and preserves the form of their species—this first stage was called the vegetative soul. When this aspect grew stronger and the ensouled being began to move in order to take its nourishment and acquired senses and a will, this level was called the intermediate or the animal soul. When this effect grew stronger, and along with these conditions it began to judge, think, and exercise discrimination by laying down premises and deriving conclusions and then acting on the basis of the latter, it was called rational, intelligent, and the like.

Each of these levels could be divided into a large number of further levels, yet the most proper approach with everything of this sort is to divide it into beginning, middle, and end, as has been done with the powers of nature. For heat, cold, and the like are divided into three levels—namely, beginning, middle, and end, even though each of these levels is in turn subject to further division. If you dwell on all of the different powers, you will find that they answer to the same pattern. You ask, "Is it possible that they be two?" It is first one, then two, and then it is perfected and becomes three; this has been explained. 166.3

On why the sea is located on a particular side of the earth

Why is the sea located on one particular side of the earth?[119] 167.1

Miskawayh's response

Were it not for the momentous wisdom that demanded water be withdrawn from the face of the earth, the natural course of things would necessarily be that water cover the entire face of the earth, such that the earth would stand in the middle like the yolk of an egg, water would encircle it like the white of an egg, air would surround the two as it does now, and fire would surround the whole ensemble. The heaviest object, which is the one closest to the center—namely, the earth—would thus stand at its proper place 167.2

relative to the center, followed by water, which is lighter than earth and heavier than air, followed by air and then by fire, according to the natural inclination of the elements. Yet, had these things been left to their natural inclinations, no life would have flourished on the face of the earth, such as plants, animals, human beings, beasts, and birds, and this wonderful wisdom and good order would have been thwarted. That is the reason why the center of the sun's orbit and the center of the highest celestial sphere were made to diverge. As a consequence, the sun rotates around a distinctive orbital center of its own other than the earth. In other words, the center of its orbit lies outside the earth.

167.3 When the sun follows its orbit, it approaches closer to one side of the earth and draws farther away from the other, and as a consequence the side it is near to becomes heated. When water is heated, it tends to be drawn in the direction in which it is being heated by vapor. When drawn up, it withdraws from the surface of the opposite end of the earth, the half from which the sun is distant. When withdrawn from the surface of the earth, the two combined—that is, the water and the earth—form a single sphere, yet the southern part of the sphere, the one close to the sun, is where water is located—that is, the sea—whereas the northern half of the sphere, the one distant from the sun, is dry, and land is visible. Then it was necessary that mountains be erected, so that the wise purpose should be properly executed and the state of the world be ordered as its existence requires. Mighty is the one who originated and created all of this, who ordered and determined it. May His name be blessed, His glory extolled, and His names be sanctified, and may He be exalted far above the claims of the iniquitous.

On why seawater is salty

Why is seawater salty? 168.1

Miskawayh's response

This is because the sun, being close to the surface of the water, is able to cook it. The nature of water is such that, when heat is applied to it through cooking, its finer parts dissolve into vapor and the remainder receives an effect of saltiness. If the heat increases and is sustained for a long time, the water becomes extremely salty, and eventually turns bitter. Alchemists prepare with fire a particular sort of water they use, repeatedly exposing it to fire, so that the water becomes hot and salty with a touch of bitterness. 168.2

On how we can see things in our sleep without an organ of sense perception

If the only way to perceive objects of sight is by means of an organ, and it—that is, the eye—is the relevant sense, then what can one say about what we see in our sleep? Do we perceive this without employing a sense, without the emission of rays, and without the use of an organ? 169.1

Miskawayh's response

The exposition we provided to the question about dreams and the response there make it unnecessary for us to undertake a response to this question, yet we will outline some general points.[120] All of the senses feed into a power called the common sense, which receives different effects from the senses and preserves them in the 169.2

power known as the imagination. If the sensible object is absent, this power produces the form of that object from the imagination, regardless of whether it is an object of sight or hearing or some other sensible form. No forms can arise in this power unless it has received them and taken them from the senses. These matters were discussed in detail in the place we mentioned, along with a definition of the objects of sight and subsidiary topics.

On a puzzle concerning the possibility of seeking something we do not know

170.1 When we seek to know something, one of two possibilities obtain: either we know the object we seek, or we do not. If we know it, there is no reason for us to seek it and to apply ourselves to pursuing it. If we do not know it, it is impossible to seek something we do not know. In that case we resemble a person looking for a runaway slave whom he does not know.

Miskawayh's response

170.2 Matters would be as you describe if we only ever sought something from a single aspect and that aspect was unknown, yet we have already explained that one can inquire into any given object under four concerns: first, its existence—that is, the inquiry conducted through the interrogative "whether," then through "what," then through "which," and then through "why."[121] These considerations pertain to every object. One may be familiar with one consideration but ignorant of another, and knowledge of one does not relieve us of the need to know another. For example, if we inquire whether the existence of the body of the ninth celestial sphere exists and reach a clear view on this topic, the other consideration persists, namely, what it is; for we have established "whether," yet remain ignorant of "what." If we establish this consideration, the third persists, namely, "which."

These considerations were explained earlier in the discussion. Once this has been secured, the consideration of the ultimate cause remains open, namely, "why": this involves inquiring why it exists in its specific nature and modality. If we establish this consideration, the only thing about the object that we are ignorant of is the particulars, which are infinite in number. These yield little advantage, so we do not inquire into them, that is, by seeking to know their extent, the total number of parts they extend over, the relation of each part to every other part, its position, and the like. These concerns constitute the inquiry into "how" and other categories pertaining to their species and individuals. If we have established the high-level genus, then we do not seek its parts, for we have secured the highest consideration. Thus, it has been established that what we seek is not the known but the unknown consideration, and that a single thing may both be known from one consideration and unknown from another; so the point of doubt has been removed, God willing.

On why it does not snow in the summer

Why doesn't snow come during summer, as rain sometimes does? 171.1

Miskawayh's response

The difference between snow and rain is as follows. When vapor 171.2
rises from the earth, it carries an earthly part with it. The quantity of this earthly part is such that it grows light with the vapor, moves with it, and ascends along with it, like the motes we always see in the air, for it is so light that it moves with the air and ascends with the water's vapor. If it so happens that while this vapor is ascending, it is exposed in the air to severe cold so that it freezes, the earthly part freezes along with it and becomes heavier because of how the different elements aggregate together through the cold, and

it inclines downward. This is snow. If it happens that the cold is slight and not severe enough to freeze it, the vapor is pressed out and water comes out in drops. This is rain. The fact that we are able to hold snow in our hands proves that it contains an earthly part, whereas rain is not amenable to that. Moreover, snow contains the body of vapor itself, that is, the condition that is neither water nor air. If this condition freezes, the nature of vapor is established. Rain, by contrast, does not contain any of the nature of vapor, and it is water itself. This is why a person who eats snow experiences bloating and the kinds of effects produced by vapor, but a person who drinks rainwater does not. Now that the difference between rain and snow has become clear, we respond to your question as follows. During winter, the coldness of the air intensifies, with the result that the vapor ascending to it from the earth freezes and turns into snow. In summer, by contrast, the coldness of the air does not intensify, but, depending on the amount of cold that affects it, the vapor thickens and is then pressed out, and rain is produced from it.

On the proof for the existence of angels

172.1 What is the proof that angels exist?

Miskawayh's response

172.2 The Qur'an and prophetic practice are filled with references to the angels, noting that they are noble beings created by God and occupy ranks of varying excellence. Reason also judges their existence to be necessary, based on the fact that when the intellect produces a division in something, that thing must necessarily exist unless something renders it impossible. For the divisions produced by the intellect represent the first existence and the pure truth, which is not affected by any impediments or thwarted by matter. So, if the intellect produces a division, it possesses an intelligible existence, and if this existence is realized, it is followed by existence in the soul and by natural existence; for these two emulate the intellect, imitate it, and follow it, without wearying or falling short. Yet nature needs movement for this imitation owing to its inability to effect existence completely. That is why nature has been defined as the principle of movement. When the intellect divides substance into living and nonliving, subdividing the living into rational and nonrational and subdividing the rational into mortal and non-mortal, the result of this division is fourfold: living, rational, mortal; living, nonrational, non-mortal; living, rational, non-mortal; and living, nonrational, mortal.

The third subdivision represents the beings designated as angels, 172.3
which have in common the fact that they are not mortal and have varying degrees of excellence with regard to rationality. This variance is what makes some of them closer to God than others, and also what makes us human beings vary with respect to how close we come to God and how distant we are from Him. This is why we say, "He's like an angel" and "He's like a devil," and also, "He's an enemy of God" and "He's a friend of God." As abuse we say, "May God drive him far away and damn him," and then there's "May God draw him close and bring him near." We could also establish the existence of angels on the basis of the acts and effects they manifest in this world, but in order to do that I would need to lay down a number of premises and to expand on the topic in such a way that I would breach the terms you set at the start of your questions, so I have restricted myself to these points. That is sufficient, God willing.

On what justifies the suffering of children and non-rational animals

You asked—may God grace you with his support—about the pains 173.1
suffered by children and animals lacking reason, and about the wise purpose behind this.

Miskawayh's response

173.2 This question addresses itself to those who affirm that all acts not performed by people are to be ascribed to God, and who do not acknowledge the acts of nature or the acts of the things that serve as intermediaries between us and God. For dialectical theologians appear to be united in believing that heat and burning and all the other acts of the elements and the things that we ourselves ascribe to the intermediaries to which God has delegated the governance of our world—such as the celestial spheres and the stars—are all acts of God, which He performs without intermediary and undertakes in His own person. Refuting these people is a lengthy task; if you wish me to devote a separate treatise or book to the topic I will be happy to do so. Now, there are those who have asserted that when fire approaches naphtha it makes it burst into flame, and when it approaches water it heats it, and similarly with every element and principle and every ray and effect extending from the higher to the lower region—for it produces different effects in everything it encounters, either because of differences in the acting elements or because of differences in the receiving elements—however, these topics are not necessarily connected to the question you have asked. The question would have had to be posed under a different aspect, which you did not inquire about, so I have not gone to the trouble of responding to it. The indications I have provided make the response to your question clear, God willing.

On why it takes us longer to hear thunder than to see lightning

174.1 Why does it take longer for us to hear the sound of thunder than to see lightning, and why is it farther away?

Miskawayh's response

Lightning arises when air changes into a state of luminance. Air is quick to receive light—indeed, it becomes illuminated in no time, for when the sun rises in the east, the air in the west is illuminated in no time. The same applies to everything that illuminates, such as fire and the like; when it meets air it receives illumination in no time. Moreover, air is connected to our eyes with no intermediary. Consequently, our perception of it must also happen in no time. This is also why the moment we open our eyes we perceive Saturn and the rest of the luminous fixed stars, so long as there is nothing in the air to screen or conceal them. The effect of thunder on the air, by contrast, occurs through motion and undulation rather than through a change of state, so how it reaches our ears must depend on the speed or slowness with which it moves. For sound, which consists in an impaction in the air, causes the air adjoining it to undulate, just as a stone causes that part of the water adjoining it to undulate if it strikes it. This results in different parts of the water and different parts of the air causing each other to undulate, by way of mutual propulsion among the parts if connected. 174.2

When one side of a pond undulates, it moves the part next to it within a certain interval of time, then the next part moves the part next to it, until it finally reaches the far side; the two sides are separated by an amount and interval of time commensurate to the extent of the water's surface. It is similar with air; when a firm body is impacted in it, it moves the adjoining air and causes it to undulate, and this part then moves the air that adjoins it over successive moments in time, until it finally reaches the part that adjoins our ears and we sense it. This is why the sound of a stone falling on another stone, when we glimpse the agent producing this movement from a distance, reaches our ears some time after our seeing it. Something similar happens when we see a clothes washer on a riverbank from a distance, for we see the movement of his hand and the way he waves the garment about as he raises it and beats it against the stone some time before we hear the sound of 174.3

the blow. This is exactly what happens with lightning and thunder; for clouds clash against each other, and the clashing sparks off the same thing that is sparked off whenever two bodies clash against each other with great force, and sound also emerges from them. Both of these—I mean lightning and thunder—occur together at a single time, as the cause of both is clashing and striking, that is, the movement of the firm body and the way part of it strikes against the other, as happens with a fire steel and flint. Air is illuminated by lightning through a change of state, which occurs in no time and which we thus sense immediately. Thunder, by contrast, causes the air that adjoins the cloud where the clashing happens to undulate, and then the air adjoining it undulates, and this moves from one part to the next until over a certain interval of time it reaches the air that adjoins our ears, and only then do we sense it.

On the possibility that a person may abandon every belief he adopts ad infinitum

175.1 If a person adheres to a certain doctrine and then abandons it after noticing that it contains an error, can you deny the possibility that he might abandon the second doctrine as he did the first and do the same with all doctrines, so that he ends up considering no doctrine to be sound and reaching no conclusions about what is true?

Miskawayh's response

175.2 If the different forms and levels of persuasion involved in all views were equal, I would not deny the possibility that what you mention should happen. Yet I have found the levels of proofs and persuasions involved to be subject to variation. They include that which is termed certainty, that which is termed a persuasive proof and syllogism in accordance with the premises of that syllogism, that which is termed supposition and imagination, and the like. Thus, I deny the possibility that different views should be equal despite the variation in the syllogisms used to support them. For example, if a syllogism is demonstrative—which means that its premises derive from necessary matters and are soundly combined—it produces a conclusion that is insusceptible to doubt, impossible to abandon, and impervious to error. Likewise . . . .[122] through which it is extended, so heat has a weak effect in the beginning because there is an abundance of matter that presents resistance. When the heat grows progressively stronger and reaches its highest level, this is the time of youth. It is as though it were an ascent and a state that develops until it reaches its end point, upon which it pauses—as happens with all natural movements—and then enters decline, this being the time of middle age. It continues to diminish until it naturally succumbs to destruction, as we have described; this is the time of old age and decrepitude. There was a person in Galen's time who entertained the same notion as you and whose view Galen reported, mentioning that he was afflicted with a long illness that provoked laughter among those who remembered his view.

This was the last question you posed in your "Wandering Herd." 176.1
In responding to them, I have followed the course chosen and recommended by you, keeping my exposition concise and allusively indicating subtler points, and, for anything that requires explanation, referring to the books where proper discussions can be found. May God make you profit from them and may He, through His bounty and grace, teach you that in which is vested the happiness of both abodes. Praise be to God, Lord of all being, and His blessings be upon His messenger Muḥammad and all his family.

Notes

1 This echoes Aristotle's references to a friend as another or second self in the *Nicomachean Ethics* (e.g., 1166a31–32, 1169b6–7, 1170b6–7).

2 Miskawayh must here be referring respectively to the verses by the second/eighth-century poet Bashshār ibn Burd that read, "If you reproach your friends in all things, you will find none who do not provoke your reproach / So live alone or be joined to your brother in amity, for at one time he does wrong and at another abstains from it / If you do not accept your drink despite its impurities you will go thirsty, for who is ever so lucky to drink from crystal-pure springs?" (al-Iṣfahānī, *Kitāb al-Aghānī*, 3:137); and to the verse by the pre-Islamic poet al-Nābighah that reads, "You would have no brothers left who do not need to have their defects corrected—what man is pure beyond reproach?" (*al-Aghānī*, 11:6).

3 This is partly a reference to Aristotle's discussion in *Categories* 1a1–16, though the specific five-fold scheme Miskawayh outlines was developed by later commentators. See, e.g., Simplicius, *On Aristotle Categories 1–4*, 22, 20–23, 5. Several commentators in the Arabic tradition deploy this scheme; see for example al-Fārābī, *Kitāb al-Ḥurūf*, 71, §19, and al-Ḥasan ibn Suwār's commentary in Aristotle, *Manṭiq Arisṭū*, 1:80–82.

4 Q Ibrāhīm 14:51.

5 The verbs discussed are *ʿaṭā, yaʿṭū* ("to receive") and *ʾaʿṭā* ("to give"), both derived from the root *ʿ-ṭ-w*; they are compared with *qāma* ("to rise") and *ʾaqāma* ("to make someone rise"). In Arabic grammar, the

verbal paradigm referred to is *fāʿala*, in the context of *nāwala* ("to hand over") and *ḥāwala* ("to strive").

6 The verse is by the first/seventh-century poet Miskīn al-Dārimī (d. 89/708).

7 The poet is Abū Miḥjan al-Thaqafī (d. ca. 16/637).

8 Miskawayh may have in mind the kind of ideas discussed by al-Fārābī in *Kitāb al-Mūsīqā al-kabīr*, 188–94.

9 The association of the soul with numbers is a standard Neoplatonic idea. See Adamson, *Al-Kindī*, 178–79.

10 Q Baqarah 2:255.

11 Q Muddaththir 74:56.

12 Elsewhere, Miskawayh attributes this description to Plato: *al-Fawz al-aṣghar*, 12.

13 This point evokes Miskawayh's broader understanding of the ethical life as a transcendence of nature to the metaphysical realm through an actualization of the "divine" (*ilahī*) element of one's being, reason. The best kind of life represents an assimilation to the angelic order and an imitation of God (*al-iqtidāʾ bi-l-bārī*). See, indicatively, the remarks in *Tahdhīb al-akhlāq*, 87–90.

14 This view goes back to Aristotle, and was adopted in different forms by a number of Miskawayh's predecessors, including the Ikhwān al-Ṣafāʾ and al-Fārābī. See Nader El-Bizri's helpful overview in "Time, concepts of."

15 This definition again has Aristotelian roots. Miskawayh's specific formulation echoes the one given by Abū Bakr al-Rāzī in *Rasāʾil falsafiyya*, 198. Yet al-Rāzī's phrase was *al-saṭḥ al-mushtarak bayna al-ḥāwī wa-l-maḥwī*: "the surface common to . . ." Miskawayh's expression seems to invert the relevant relationship.

16 Q Baqarah 2:62.

17 The reference is to Bryson, the obscure neo-Pythagorean philosopher who authored the influential treatise *Management of the Estate*. The passage Miskawayh has in mind can be found in Swain, *Economy, Family, and Society*, 18 (§113).

18 See Aristotle's remarks in the *Nicomachean Ethics*, Book IV.9.

19 The source for this saying is unclear.

20 The manuscript continues in the margin: "I say, how could it not be remarkable that he claims this falsely when he is lying and lying is necessarily evil?"

21 As Miskawayh's response in §13.3 indicates, this question segues into a second one relating to old men who act like juveniles. This continuation does not appear in the text of the question itself in the manuscript.

22 The term *khalāʿah* ("wantonness") is derived from *khalaʿa* ("to throw off the bridle"). The verb *ḥajara* means "to hinder" or "prohibit."

23 This is a celebrated Platonic idea set out in the *Phaedo* and other dialogues.

24 In framing his question, al-Tawḥīdī used the verb *taʿallama*—translated here as "to acquire knowledge," but which strictly means "to learn"—in connection with both knowledge and ignorance. This term has the same morphological pattern as *taṣawwara*, which is the term that focuses Miskawayh's philosophical view of knowledge.

25 This view is expressed in *Metaphysics* 982b–983a, but the remarks here also echo passages from Greco-Arabic gnomologia. See, e.g., Gutas, *Greek Wisdom Literature*, 161 (§2).

26 This is one of a handful of places where Miskawayh slightly alters the wording (and inevitably the meaning) of al-Tawḥīdī's question in quoting it.

27 Q Anbiyāʾ 21:22.

28 This may be a reference to a common philosophical conception of the hierarchical relationship between the different powers of the soul, with the rational power seen as the ruling or kingly (*malakiyyah*) power to which all others must be subordinated. See, e.g., *Tahdhīb al-akhlāq*, 16 (cf. the reference to the archetypal virtue of this power, knowledge or wisdom, as "kingly" on p. 17). Compare the remarks about the soul's governance of the body in *al-Fawz al-aṣghar*, 49.

29 This saying appears in Greco-Arabic collections of wisdom literature; see, e.g., Gutas, *Greek Wisdom Literature*, 173–74 (§35).

30 Q Ṭā Hā 20:84.

31 The poet is al-Mutanabbī (d. 354/965). See *Dīwān al-Mutanabbī*, 371, using variant wording (*min shiyam al-nufūsi*).

32 The reference is to the short treatise *Risālah fī māhiyyat al-ʿadl*, edited by M. S. Khan under the title *An Unpublished Treatise of Miskawaih on Justice*. The Arabic terms discussed in the next sentences are *jawr* ("inequity") and the verb *jāra, yajūru* ("to be inequitable"); and *ʿadl* ("justice") and the verbal noun *iʿtidāl* ("moderation").

33 This is likely a reference to Galen's synopsis of Plato's *Republic*, which we know to have been translated into Arabic.

34 See the discussion of commercial exchange in Aristotle, *Nicomachean Ethics*, Book V.5.

35 The two words derive from the same triliteral root, *w-f-q*.

36 The term for luck, *bakht*, is a Persian loanword.

37 As in many such passages in the book, the discussion hinges on Arabic morphology, which we have tried to convey in English without cluttering the argument with too much transliteration. We offer the following, less free, rendering, for those who are interested in the specific morphologies under discussion: "*Tamkīn* is the verbal noun of the verb *makkana*. The principal parts of the verb are thus *makkana tamkīnan*; compare *karrama takrīman* and *kallama taklīman*. *Imkān* is the verbal noun of the verb *ʾamkana*. The principal parts of the verb are thus *ʾamkana imkānan*; compare *ʾakrama ikrāman*. The term *mumkin* adopts the morphological pattern *mufʿil*; compare *mukrim*. The noun from which the verb theoretically derives is not used in the Arabic lexicon, nor does it come from it. For the thing has no verb connected with it other than the transitive verb expressed with the prefix *ʾa-*. So if you say that a certain thing is possible, it is as though you were saying that this thing which exists *in potentia*—for which there is no ordinary noun in use, but which exists virtually, and its virtual meaning is 'that which is possible'—has given itself to you, and has put you in the position to make it actual through your voluntary choice. *Imkān* is the verbal noun from *ʾamkana*. *Tamkīn* is an action performed on someone by something else, whereby it puts him in the position to make that thing actual through voluntary choice. It is

the verbal noun of *makkana*, and the geminate verb form appears at this kind of lexical juncture to signify iteration and intensity of action, the way one says *ḍaraba* and *ḍarraba, shadda* and *shaddada.* The term *tamkīn* can also carry another sense, namely, as a verbal noun of the form *tafʿīl* deriving from the term *makān*, the way we say 'I established (*makkantu*) the stone in its position' when we give it the amount of space it requires so that it sticks firmly to the spot. In the same sense we speak of a horseman as being 'firmly fixed' (*tamakkun*) in the saddle, and of a person as being 'firmly established' (*tamakkun*) in his seat. Talk of a person 'establishing himself' (*tamakkun*) with an emir falls in the same class by way of comparative and figurative use. As you can see, there is a vast difference between this meaning and the first."

38 Q Maryam 19:62.

39 Q Ḥashr 59:7. The discussion involves permutations of the root *d-w-l.*

40 The reference is to a proverb that has different interpretations, in one referring to a man who found a wife comparable to him in intelligence, in another to two tribes that were evenly matched in force. See al-Maydānī, *Majmaʿ al-amthāl*, 2:359–60 (#4340).

41 At this point, Miskawayh notes that "the original form of the verb is **iwtafaqa.*"

42 Fully: "This is *tawfīq*, which derives from the term *wafq*, with the morphological pattern *tafʿīl.*"

43 The Arabic terms are *maḥdūd*, *ḥadd*, and *ḥaddād*, respectively.

44 The Arabic terms are *wilāyah* and *mawlā.*

45 Miskawayh must be referring to Question 14, where al-Tawḥīdī used the term *laʾīm* in framing his question. Miskawayh reframed it using the term *bakhīl*, without, however, spelling out the distinction between the two.

46 *Masīk* ("stingy") comes from the verb *masaka*, "to clutch, to grasp"; cf. *amsaka*, "to withhold, to retain." *Manūʿ* ("ungiving") comes from the verb *manaʿa*, "to refuse, to deny, to withhold."

47 *Jaʿd* ("tightfisted") can also have the literal meaning "contracted" or "short." *Kazz* ("skinflint") can also mean "dry," "stiff," "rigid," "contracted."

48 The Arabic terms are *ʿādah*, *ʿāda yaʿūdu*, and *iʿtādā yaʿtādu*, respectively.

49 For the broader metaphysical picture that underlies this point, see *al-Fawz al-aṣghar*, 55 ff., where Miskawayh discusses the twofold movement of the soul: upward toward the intellect and downward toward matter.

50 The notion of "muddled dreams" has Qur'anic overtones: see Q Yūsuf 12:44.

51 The Arabic terms are *abṣara, istabṣara, baṣar*, and *baṣīrah.*

52 See al-Maydānī, *Majmaʿ al-amthāl*, 1:249 (#1336) and 2:43 (#2595).

53 No fourth view seems to have been mentioned. Combined with the elliptic character of these passages, this suggests this may be another instance of editorial intervention on the part of Miskawayh.

54 There seems to be a lacuna in the text here.

55 See Wakelnig, *A Philosophy Reader*, 137, for a similar statement attributed to the "Greek sage."

56 Q Qiyāmah 75:20.

57 The verse is by the Umayyad poet Jarīr (d. ca. 110/728–29): see *Dīwān Jarīr*, 1: 737.

58 Miskawayh appears to be splicing a number of loosely quoted passages from the New Testament, including Matthew 6:25 and 7:21.

59 The text seems to be corrupt here and it is difficult to discern alternative readings.

60 Miskawayh here echoes ideas articulated by al-Kindī, for example in *Risālat al-Kindī fī l-luḥūn wa-l-nagham*. For further discussion, see Adamson, *Al-Kindī*, 173–80.

61 *Urghan* (Greek *organon*) could refer to either a wind-blown or stringed instrument, though Miskawayh must have the latter in mind. This organ was reported to be capable of inducing extreme rapture, as al-Iṣbahānī reports in *al-Aghānī*, 10:146.

62 Q Zumar 39:15.

63 This oft-cited incident—which was transposed from an anecdote featuring the physiognomist Zopyrus and Socrates—is reported in different versions. See Hoyland, "The Islamic Background to

Polemon's Treatise," in *Seeing the Face*, ed. Swain, 237–38, and Ghersetti, "The Semiotic Paradigm: Physiognomy and Medicine in Islamic Culture," section II, in the same volume.

64 In *Al-Baṣāʾir wa-l-dhakhāʾir*, al-Tawḥīdī attributes this saying (in slightly altered wording) to a certain al-Kindī [?] as reported by the ʿAlid supporter Ibrāhīm ibn al-Ashtar: *Al-Baṣāʾir wa-l-dhakhāʾir*, 7:16 (#16).

65 The line is by the third/ninth-century poet Ibn al-Rūmī but does not seem to be included in the extant recension of his diwan.

66 In one report, the verse is by the poet Abān al-Lāḥiqī, a court poet of the Barmakids. See al-Suyūṭī, *al-Muzhir*, 1:180.

67 Miskawayh has in mind Aristotle's remarks in *De Anima* Book III.4, 429a27–29.

68 The verse is by the sixth-century Christian Arab poet ʿAdī ibn Zayd. See *Dīwān ʿAdī ibn Zayd*, 106, using variant wording.

69 This is a loose reference to Aristotle's remarks in *Nicomachean Ethics* 1115b7–9.

70 This example is discussed by Galen, as Miskawayh goes on to mention. See Galen, "The Diagnosis and Treatment of the Affections and Errors Peculiar to Each Person's Soul," in *Psychological Writings*, 252, 257. Miskawayh brings it up again in *Tahdhīb*, 203.

71 Miskawayh is referring here to §24.1.

72 The term "materialists" refers loosely to different groups with irreligious views, including the denial of a future life. They often featured in theological discussions about the nature of ethical value and moral motivation, and in arguments against the dependence of ethical value on revealed scripture.

73 Abū Dāwūd, *Sunan Abī Dāwūd*, 6:586 (#4530); Aḥmad ibn Ḥanbal, *Musnad al-Imām Aḥmad ibn Ḥanbal*, 2:286 (#993).

74 Abū Dāwūd, *Sunan Abī Dāwūd*, 6:59 (#3916); Aḥmad ibn Ḥanbal, *Musnad al-Imām Aḥmad ibn Ḥanbal*, 8:392–93 (#4775).

75 Miskawayh is evidently omitting part of the text of al-Tawḥīdī's original question here. It is unclear what story this is a reference to.

76 This hadith doesn't appear in the main collections, but see for example Ibn Abī Shaybah, *al-Muṣannaf*, 17:521 (#33679).

77 The Arab terms are respectively: *ghurāb*, *ghurbah*, *bān*, *bayn*, *nawan* ("date pits" and "distance"), and *buʿd*.

78 The verse is by the pre-Islamic poet Zabbān ibn Sayyār al-Fazārī, who was related by marriage to the renowned poet al-Nābighah al-Dhubyānī—the poem's "Ziyād."

79 The verse is by Ibn al-Rūmī: see *Dīwān Ibn al-Rūmī*, 1:335 (#237).

80 The term translated as "fair skinned" is *aḥmar*, which also means "red," giving an extra lexicographical context for this point.

81 A broad reference to a constellation of heterodox religious groups, which most notably included the Manicheans. They featured prominently in theological polemics as challengers of key tenets of the Muslim faith.

82 Q Zumar 39:15.

83 See §§33.1–34.17, especially the response at §§34.11–15.

84 Miskawayh touches on both these points at various stages of his responses: see, e.g., §§63.1–11, especially §63.8; §§71.1–2; and §§93.1–4, especially §93.4.

85 The verse is by the poet and anthologist Abū Tammām (d. 231/845 or 232/846).

86 Miskawayh no doubt has Galen's work in mind here, particularly his immensely influential *De usu partium* (*Fī manāfiʿ al-aʿḍāʾ*).

87 A reference to Q Muʾminūn 23:14: «. . . then We created of the drop a clot then We created of the clot a tissue then We created of the tissue bones then We garmented the bones in flesh; thereafter We produced him as another creature.»

88 It is not completely clear which response Miskawayh refers to here. Perhaps he means §22.2?

89 It is difficult to determine who is speaking here because the comment seems opaque: How could al-Tawḥīdī be telling Miskawayh "you will hear your own response"? Some odd editing hand seems to have been at work in the text at this point.

90 The poet is Isḥāq al-Mawṣilī (d. 235/850).

91 Abū Bishr Mattā was at the heart of a culturally important controversy regarding the claims of philosophical logic, which found its best-known

expression in an exchange between him and the grammarian Abū Saʿīd al-Sīrāfī reported by al-Tawḥīdī in his *Imtāʿ* (1:107–28). The question posed is: "Isn't *manṭiq*, 'logic,' simply a derivation from the term 'speech,' *nuṭq*, on the morphological pattern *mafʿil*?"

92 "Abū Ḥafṣ" was the patronymic of the second caliph, ʿUmar, whom Shiʿah have historically regarded with animosity for having undermined the claims of ʿAlī and the House of the Prophet.

93 The former view had been expressed by several Ashʿarite theologians, among others, and fiercely opposed by Muʿtazilite thinkers. The latter view found a number of expressions in the Greek philosophical tradition, notably in Plato's *Cratylus*, as contrasted with Aristotle's conventionalist approach to language. In Islamic theological circles it is perhaps most strongly associated with the Muʿtazilite ʿAbbād ibn Sulaymān (d. 250/864).

94 See, e.g., §§3.1–7 and §§93.1–4.

95 The reference is to the Muʿtazilites, and to the distinctive doctrine about God's attributes that divided them from Ashʿarites and other theologians, as outlined in the continuation.

96 The text is clearly corrupt.

97 The discussion of God's existence and attributes takes up the entire first question in the *Fawz*. See *Fawz*, 3–32, and especially the programmatic remarks at 25–27.

98 The term *muwalladūn* is a loose category that can indicate more broadly poets who belong to the post-Umayyad, early Abbasid era.

99 The translation of these lines draws in part on Jones, *Early Arabic Poetry*, 2:114. See *Mufaḍḍaliyyāt*, 247 (#57), with slightly altered wording.

100 That is, effecting changes in the syllables, e.g., by reducing a long syllable to a short one, or two short syllables to one. For further detail, see Stoetzer, "Ziḥāf."

101 This line has been attributed to different poets, including al-Shanfarā and Taʾabbaṭa Sharran. See Ibn Manẓūr, *Lisān al-ʿarab*, 8:161 (s.v. *s-l-ʿ*).

102 The distinction between types of argument—demonstrative, dialectical, rhetorical, sophistical, and poetic—carrying different epistemic

credentials is key to Aristotle's *Organon* as a whole. See al-Fārābī, "Kitāb al-Burhān," in *Al-Manṭiq ʿinda al-Fārābī*, 20–22, for a discussion that provides some context for Miskawayh's remarks.

103 The term *Kānūn* could strictly refer to either December (Kānūn I) or January (Kānūn II).

104 Al-Tawḥīdī's term here is *al-shawāmil*, which is the second half of the book's title.

105 Miskawayh has in mind Aristotle's discussion of future contingents in *De Interpretatione* Chapter 9, though his ensuing remarks also draw on ideas developed by later commentators in both the ancient and Arabic tradition. See Adamson, "The Arabic Sea Battle," for some helpful context. Miskawayh's remarks echo the terminology used by al-Fārābī in his related discussion in "Kitāb Bārī Armīniyās ay al-ʿIbārah," *Al-Manṭiq ʿinda al-Fārābī*, 1:160–162; cf. at greater length, *Al-Fārābī's Commentary*, trans. Zimmermann, 76–96.

106 Q Furqān 25:23.

107 The reference is to the fifth caliph, Hārūn al-Rashīd (d. 193/809) and to the two brothers, al-Faḍl (d. 193/808) and Jaʿfar (d. 190/805), members of the influential Barmakid family.

108 The reference is probably to ʿAbd Allāh Muḥammad ibn Sālim al-Baṣrī (d. 297/909), the disciple of the Sufi Sahl al-Tustarī.

109 Our translation of this obscure passage is tentative. One would have expected the opposite: "what is unknown is as good as nonexistent/might as well not exist."

110 Miskawayh makes this point in the course of his response to question §101.1: see §101.2.

111 Peter Adamson, in a private communication, suggests that *aʿrāḍ* (accidents) should be read for *amrāḍ* (illnesses).

112 As mentioned in the Introduction, Aḥmad ibn ʿAbd al-Wahhāb was the addressee of al-Jāḥiẓ's *Kitāb al-Tarbīʿ wa-l-tadwīr*, whose objective was partly to lampoon him and expose his ignorance through a fusillade of challenging questions. The phrasing of both the present question and Question 152 seems to suggest that al-Jāḥiẓ's victim responded in kind by issuing his own counter-fusillade of

questions (in this regard, responding to al-Jāḥiẓ's apparent invitation in *Tarbīʿ*, 88, §166). Yet, perplexingly, the topic of Question 152 is brought up by al-Jāḥiẓ himself on p. 38, §67.

113 Al-Kindī's works included an *Epistle on the Deceptions of the Alchemists* (*Risāla fī-l-tanbīh ʿalā khudaʿ al-kīmiyāʾiyyīn*) according to Ibn al-Nadīm, *Fihrist*, 320. Al-Rāzī's response is mentioned by al-Masʿūdī, *Murūj al-dhahab*, 5:159–60 (#3312). Neither work has survived. Note that in the Arabic Miskawayh gives al-Kindī's name as Yūsuf ibn Isḥāq rather than Abū Yūsuf ibn Isḥāq.

114 It is unclear whether Miskawayh went on to compose the promised epistle, though a broad reference in the overview of his output in the *Muntakhab Ṣīwān al-ḥikmah* allows us to speculate that he may have: al-Sijistānī, *Muntakhab Ṣīwān al-ḥikmah*, 347. In any case, no such work has come down to us.

115 The Arabic terms are *mustabham* and *mustaghlaq*, respectively. As Miskawayh goes on to explain, the latter term derives from *ghalaqa*, meaning "to close a door," and the former from *abhama*, to close a door in such a way as "to block" it.

116 A reference to Q Anʿām 6:59.

117 The discussion of prophecy, which touches on the themes just mentioned, takes up the whole of the third question in the *Fawz*: see *Fawz*, 85–120.

118 The reference must be to a treatise titled *Kitāb fī sabab kawn al-jibāl*, which is mentioned by the biographer Ibn Abī Uṣaybiʿah, *ʿUyūn al-anbāʾ*, 1:218.

119 This may be a reference to the common assumption that the inhabitable landmass was encompassed on all sides by an "Encircling Sea" (*al-baḥr al-muḥīṭ*).

120 See §§48.1–5.

121 See §§159.1–3.

122 Here there is a lacuna in the manuscript, and when the text resumes it is clear that Miskawayh has moved on to a new question. It seems difficult to speculate about the exact question al-Tawḥīdī had posed.

Glossary

Abū Ayyūb al-Anṣārī (d. ca. 52/672) companion of the Prophet and participant in many of the military operations of the early Islamic period.

Abū Bakr (r. 11–13/632–34) the first caliph and Muḥammad's father-in-law.

Abū Bakr Muḥammad ibn Zakariyyā al-Rāzī (d. ca. 313/925 or 323/935) prominent philosopher, physician, and alchemist. His best-known philosophical works include *Spiritual Medicine* (*Kitāb al-ṭibb al-rūḥānī*) and *The Philosophical Life* (*Kitāb al-Sīrah al-falsafiyyah*).

Abū Bishr Mattā ibn Yūnus (d. 328/940) Nestorian Christian who translated and commented on Aristotle's works and played an important role in the translation of Peripatetic philosophy from Syriac into Arabic.

Abū l-Fatḥ ibn al-ʿAmīd (d. 366/976) son of Abū l-Faḍl ibn al-ʿAmīd and one-time vizier of the Buyid emir Rukn al-Dawlah.

Abū Ḥanīfah (d. 150/767) theologian and jurist who founded an eponymous school of law.

Abū Hāshim al-Jubbāʾī (d. 321/933) theologian who was one of the foundational figures of the school of Baṣran Muʿtazilites, best known for his theory of modes or *aḥwāl*.

Abū l-ʿIbar (d. 252/866) a poet and relative of the Abbasid caliphs who was known for composing humorous and frivolous verse.

Abū ʿĪsā l-Warrāq independent Shiʿi thinker and religious skeptic of the third/ninth century, said to have been Ibn al-Rāwandī's teacher, author of well-informed reports and refutations of non-Muslim religions, including Christianity.

Abū Saʿīd al-Ḥaṣīrī Sufi theologian and heresiographer with skeptic tendencies, also referred to in other sources as al-Ḥuṣrī, al-Ḥaḍrī, or even al-Ḥaḍramī.

Abū Tammām (d. 231/845 or 232/846) poet and anthologist who achieved fame during the rule of the caliph al-Muʿtaṣim.

Abū ʿUthmān al-Jāḥiẓ (d. 255/868–69) eminent Muʿtazilite theologian and belletrist from Baṣra whose works inspired many generations of prose writers, including al-Tawḥīdī.

Abū ʿUthmān al-Nahdī (d. ca. 95/714) first-century transmitter of prophetic traditions.

Abū Yūsuf al-Kindī (d. after 256/870) philosopher and scholar who played a paramount role in the reception, translation, and dissemination of Greek philosophical thought and authored multiple works across a broad range of philosophical sciences.

Abū Zayd al-Balkhī (d. 322/934) prolific author of philosophical, scientific, and religious works in the Kindian tradition, possibly a teacher of the philosopher Abū Bakr al-Rāzī.

ʿAlī ibn Abī Ṭālib (d. 41/661) the Prophet's son-in-law and fourth caliph, and the first Imam of the Shiʿah.

Allāt the name of a pre-Islamic goddess, given to many goddesses worshipped in the ancient Near East.

ʿAlwah name given to the beloved in many poems by al-Buḥturī.

ʿĀmir ibn al-Ẓarib sage of the pre-Islamic era.

Aristotle (d. 322) Greek philosopher who authored an influential series of works on logic, ethics, metaphysics, and scientific and other subjects. Many of these works, including the *Organon* and the *Nicomachean Ethics* to which Miskawayh refers in this book, were translated into Arabic during the Abbasid era. Reflecting his stature, many writers refer to him simply as "the Philosopher."

Baghdad capital city of the Abbasid caliphate, founded along the Tigris river in 762 by the second Abbasid caliph, al-Manṣūr. In Tawḥīdī and Miskawayh's day, the capital of the Buyid principality of Iraq, with Rayy (now a suburb of present-day Tehran) being the capital of the principality of the Jibal and Shiraz the capital of Fars.

Bāqil a figure proverbial for a lack of eloquence, often mentioned in the same breath as Saḥbān Wā'il.

Bashshār ibn Burd (d. ca. 167/783) renowned poet of Persian origin of the late Umayyad and early Abbasid period.

Bryson (fl. before the second century CE) obscure neo-Pythagorean philosopher who authored the treatise *Management of the Estate*, which was highly influential for Arabic approaches to economics.

al-Buḥturī (d. 284/897) prominent court poet of the Abbasid era.

Da'd woman's name, given to the beloved in some Arabic poems.

al-Faḍl ibn Yaḥyā (d. 193/808) member of the powerful Barmakid family and eldest son of Yaḥyā ibn Khālid al-Barmakī. He served as vizier to Hārūn al-Rashīd.

Farghānah valley in present-day eastern Uzbekistan and parts of Kyrgyzstan and Tajikistan, surrounded on three sides by the Tianshan Mountains and traversed by the Syr Darya river, which flows out of the western end of the valley to the Aral Sea. In the third/tenth century, it represented a remote eastern outpost of the Muslim world.

Fartanā woman's name, given to the beloved in some Arabic poems.

Galen (d. ca. AD 216) medical writer and physician from Pergamon whose translated works played a critical role for the development of the medical tradition in the Islamic world. Though more limited in extent, his ethical writings (notably the *Peri Ethon*) were also highly influential.

Hārūn al-Rashīd (d. 193/809) fifth ʿAbbasid caliph, whose rule was enmeshed with the Barmakid family and whose court formed a lodestone of poets, scholars, and entertainers.

Hind woman's name, given to the beloved in many Arabic poems.

Ibn al-Khalīl unidentified individual.

Ibn Mujāhid (d. 324/936) religious scholar best known for his role in establishing the seven canonical variants or readings of the Qur'an.

Ibn al-Rāwandī prominent heterodox figure of the third/ninth century, notorious for his polemics against religious (including Muslim) belief, and his attacks on prophecy, the credibility of miracles, and the compatibility of religious claims with reason.

Ibn Sālim al-Baṣrī, ʿAbd Allāh Muḥammad (d. 297/909) Sufi thinker who was a disciple and companion of Sahl al-Tustarī.

Imruʾ al-Qays (fl. sixth century) renowned pre-Islamic poet who was the author of one of the most famous of the pre-Islamic poems known as the *Suspended Odes* (*al-Muʿallaqāt*).

Isḥāq al-Mawṣilī (d. 235/850) musician, poet, and composer associated with the court of several Abbasid caliphs.

Jābir ibn Ḥayyān (d. ca. 193/812) linchpin figure in the early development of alchemy in the Islamic world and putative (though disputed) author of a vast corpus of alchemical writings.

Jaʿfar ibn Yaḥyā (d. 190/805) member of the powerful Barmakid family and youngest son of Yaḥyā ibn Khālid al-Barmakī, vizier to Hārūn al-Rashīd.

Khālid ibn Yazīd (d. ca. 85/704) Umayyad prince who, according to a disputed tradition, commissioned translations that first introduced alchemy into Arabic culture.

al-Khalīl (d. ca. 175/791) celebrated Baṣran grammarian and lexicographer who laid the foundations for Arabic phonetics and prosody.

Kharijites hardline Islamic sect that arose in the first Islamic century in connection with a dispute about the caliphate and that remained a source of political and theological unrest during the Umayyad period.

Khurasan region comprising present-day northeastern Iran, Afghanistan, and parts of Central Asia.

Luqmān ibn ʿĀd a figure from pre-Islamic times, proverbial for his wisdom.

Mālik ibn Anas (d. 179/796) Medinan jurist who founded an eponymous school of law.

al-Maʾmūn (d. 218/833) seventh Abbasid caliph, whose rule was punctuated by theological upheavals but also by a flowering of intellectual activity, including the large-scale translation of Greek philosophical and scientific texts.

Maʿrūf al-Karkhī (d. 200/815–16) prominent early ascetic and mystic of the Baghdad school.

al-Muraqqish al-aṣghar (fl. sixth century CE) poet from the predominantly Christian town of Ḥīrah in southwestern Iraq.

al-Mutanabbī (d. 354/965) renowned poet and panegyrist who flourished under the patronage of the ruler of Syria, Sayf al-Dawlah.

Muʿtazilites theological school that emerged in the second/eighth century, distinguished by its rationalistic methods and austere emphasis on theological tenets relating to divine unity and justice.

al-Nābighah (fl. sixth century CE) celebrated poet of the pre-Islamic era famous for his panegyrics of the rulers of the predominantly Christian town of Ḥīrah in southwestern Iraq.

The Philosopher *See* Aristotle.

Plato (d. 347) Greek thinker who played a seminal role in the development of ancient philosophy and whose ethical and metaphysical views, especially in their Neoplatonic reworkings, were highly influential in the Islamic world.

Polemon of Laodicea (d. ca. AD 144) politician and intellectual who authored an influential treatise on physiognomy, the science of discerning character from external appearance. The work was translated into Arabic in Abbasid times.

al-Rūdakī (d. ca. 329/940–41) prominent Persian poet who flourished in the first half of the fourth/tenth century.

Saḥbān Wāʾil a figure of proverbial eloquence, often mentioned in the same breath as Bāqil.

Salmā woman's name, given to the beloved in many Arabic poems.

al-Shāfiʿī (d. 204/820) jurist and legal theoretician who founded an eponymous school of law.

Tāhart city in northwest Algeria founded by the Rustamid dynasty in the late second/eighth century.

al-Ṭarmī an obscure poet about whom little is known.

Thābit ibn Qurrah (d. 288/901) eminent mathematician and scientist known both for his original scientific work and his translations of Greek texts.

Bibliography

Abū Dāwūd Sulaymān ibn al-Ash'ath. *Sunan Abī Dāwūd*. Edited by Shu'ayb al-Arna'ūṭ et al. 7 vols. Damascus: Dār al-Risālah al-'Ālamiyyah, 2009.

Adamson, Peter. "The Arabic Sea Battle: Al-Fārābī on the Problem of Future Contingents." *Archiv für Geschichte der Philosophie*, 88 (2006): 163–88.

———. *Al-Kindī*. Oxford: Oxford University Press, 2007.

'Adī ibn Zayd. *Dīwān 'Adī ibn Zayd al-'Ibādī*. Edited by Muḥammad Jabbār al-Mu'aybid. Baghdad: Sharikat Dār al-Jumhūriyyah li-l-Nashr wa-l-Ṭab', 1965.

Amīn, Aḥmad. *Fajr al-Islām*. 3 vols. Cairo: Lajnat al-Ta'līf wa-l-Tarjamah wa-l-Nashr, 1928.

———. *Ḍuḥā al-Islām*. 3 vols. Cairo: Lajnat al-Ta'līf wa-l-Tarjamah wa-l-Nashr, 1936.

———. *Ẓuhr al-Islām*. 4 vols. Cairo: Lajnat al-Ta'līf wa-l-Tarjamah wa-l-Nashr, 1955.

Aristotle. *Manṭiq Arisṭū*. Edited by 'Abd al-Raḥmān Badawī. 3 vols. Kuwait: Wakālat al-Maṭbū'āt; Beirut: Dār al-Qalam, 1980.

———. *Aristotle's Ars Rhetorica: The Arabic Version*. Edited by M. C. Lyons. Cambridge: Pembroke Arabic Texts, 1982.

Arkoun, Mohammed. "Deux épîtres de Miskawayh (mort en 421/1030)." *Bulletin d'études orientales*, 17 (1961–62): 7–74.

———. "L'humanisme arabe au IVe/Xe siècle, d'après le *Kitâb al-Hawâmil wal-Šawâmil*." *Studia Islamica*, 14 (1961): 73–108, and 15 (1961): 63–87.

———. *L'humanisme arabe au IVe/Xe siècle: Miskawayh, philosophe et historien*. Paris: Vrin, 1982.

Daiber, Hans. "Masā'il wa-Adjwiba." *Encyclopaedia of Islam, Second Edition*. Edited by P. Bearman, Th. Bianquis, C. E. Bosworth, E. van Donzel, and W. P. Heinrichs. Brill Online.

El-Bizri, Nader. "Time, Concepts of." In *Medieval Islamic Civilization: An Encyclopedia*, vol. 2, edited by Josef W. Meri, 810–12. New York: Routledge, 2006.

Al-Fārābī, Abū Naṣr. *Kitāb al-Mūsīqā al-kabīr*. Edited by Ghaṭṭās ʿAbd al-Malik Khashabah. Cairo: Dār al-Kātib al-ʿArabī li-l-Ṭibāʿah wa-l-Nashr, 1967.

———. *Al-Fārābī's Commentary and Short Treatise on Aristotle's De Interpretatione*. Translated by Franz W. Zimmermann. London: Published for the British Academy by Oxford University Press, 1981.

———. *Al-Manṭiq ʿinda al-Fārābī*. Edited by Rafīq al-ʿAjam. 3 vols. Beirut: Dār al-Mashriq, 1985–87.

———. *Al-Manṭiq ʿinda al-Fārābī*. Edited by Mājid Fakhrī. Beirut: Dār al-Mashriq, 1987.

———. *Kitāb al-Ḥurūf*. Edited by Muḥsin Mahdī. 2nd ed. Beirut: Dār al-Mashriq, 1990.

Filius, Lou S. "The Genre *Problemata* in Arabic: Its Motions and Changes." In *Aristotle's* Problemata *in Different Times and Tongues*, edited by Pieter De Leemans and Michèle Goyens, 33–54. Leuven: Leuven University Press, 2006.

———. *La tradition orientale des Problemata Physica*. In *Dictionnaire des philosophes antiques, Supplément*, edited by Richard Goulet with Jean-Marie Flamand and Maroun Aouad, 593–98. Paris: CNRS, 2003.

Galen. *Psychological Writings*. Edited by P. N. Singer and translated by Vivian Nutton, Daniel Davies, and P. N. Singer. Cambridge: Cambridge University Press, 2013.

Ghersetti, Antonella. "The Semiotic Paradigm: Physiognomy and Medicine in Islamic Culture." In *Seeing the Face, Seeing the Soul: Polemon's Physiognomy from Classical Antiquity to Medieval Islam*, edited by Simon Swain, 281–308. Oxford: Oxford University Press, 2007.

Gutas, Dimitri. *Greek Wisdom Literature in Arabic Translation*. New Haven: American Oriental Society, 1975.

Hoyland, Robert. "The Islamic Background to Polemon's Treatise." In *Seeing the Face, Seeing the Soul: Polemon's Physiognomy from Classical Antiquity to Medieval Islam*, edited by Simon Swain, 227–80. Oxford: Oxford University Press, 2007.

Ibn Abī Shaybah, ʿAbd Allāh ibn Muḥammad. *Al-Muṣannaf*. Edited by Muḥammad ʿAwwāmah. 26 vols. Jeddah: Dār al-Qiblah li-l-Thaqāfah al-Islāmiyyah; Damascus: Muʾassasat ʿUlūm al-Qurʾān, 2006.

Ibn Abī Uṣaybiʿah, Aḥmad ibn Qāsim. *ʿUyūn al-anbāʾ fī ṭabaqāt al-aṭibbāʾ*. Edited by August Müller. 2 vols. Frankfurt: Institute for the History of Arabic-Islamic Science, Johann Wolfgang Goethe University. Reprint of 1882 Cairo edition.

Ibn Ḥanbal, Aḥmad ibn Muḥammad. *Musnad al-Imām Aḥmad ibn Ḥanbal*. Edited by Shuʿayb al-Arnaʾūṭ et al. 50 vols. Beirut: Muʾassasat al-Risālah, 1993–2001.

Ibn Manẓūr, Muḥammad ibn Mukarram. *Lisān al-ʿarab*. 15 vols. Beirut: Dār Ṣādir, 1997.

Ibn al-Nadīm, Muḥammad ibn Isḥāq. *Al-Fihrist*. Edited by Riḍā Tajaddud. Tehran: Maṭbaʿat Dānishgāh, 1971.

Ibn al-Rūmī, Abū-l-Ḥusayn ʿAlī. *Dīwān Ibn al-Rūmī*. Edited by Ḥusayn Naṣṣār. 6 vols. 3rd ed. Cairo: Maṭbaʿat Dār al-Kutub wa-l-Wathāʾiq al-Qawmiyyah, 2003.

Irwin, Robert. *The Penguin Anthology of Classical Arabic Literature*. London: Penguin, 2006.

Al-Iṣfahānī, Abū l-Faraj. *Maqātil al-ṭālibiyyīn*. Edited by Aḥmad Ṣaqr. Cairo: Dār Iḥyāʾ al-Kutub al-ʿArabiyyah, 1949.

———. *Kitāb al-Aghānī*. Edited by Iḥsān ʿAbbās, Ibrāhīm al-Saʿāfīn, and Bakr ʿAbbās. 25 vols. 3rd ed. Beirut: Dār Ṣādir, 2008.

Al-Jāḥiẓ, Abū ʿUthmān. *Al-Tarbīʿ wa-l-tadwīr*. Edited by Charles Pellat. Damascus: Institut Français de Damas, 1955.

Jarīr ibn ʿAṭiyyah. *Dīwān Jarīr*. Edited by Nuʿmān Muḥammad Amīn Ṭāhā. 2 vols. Cairo: Dār al-Maʿārif, 1969–71.

Jones, Alan. *Early Arabic Poetry*. 2 vols. Reading: Ithaca Press, 1992–96.

Al-Kindi, Abū Isḥāq. *Risālat al-Kindī fī l-luḥūn wa-l-nagham*. Edited by Zakariyyā Yūsuf. Baghdad: Maṭbaʿat Shafīq, 1965.

Kraemer, Joel L. *Humanism in the Renaissance of Islam: The Cultural Revival during the Buyid Age*. Leiden: Brill, 1992.

Al-Masʿūdī, Abū-l-Ḥasan. *Murūj al-dhahab wa-maʿādin al-jawhar*. Edited by Charles Pellat. 7 vols. Beirut: al-Jāmiʿah al-Lubnāniyyah, 1966–79.

Al-Maydānī, Aḥmad ibn Muḥammad. *Majmaʿ al-amthāl*. Edited by Muḥammad Muḥyī l-Dīn ʿAbd al-Ḥamīd. 2 vols. Cairo: Maṭbaʿat al-Sunnah al-Muḥammadiyyah, 1955.

Mez, Adam. *Die Renaissance des Islams*. Heidelberg: Carl Winter, 1922.

Miskawayh, Abū ʿAlī. *Tahdhīb al-akhlāq*. Edited by Constantine Zurayk. Beirut: American University of Beirut, 1966.

———. *Al-Fawz al-aṣghar*. Beirut: n.p., 1319 AH [1901].

———. *An Unpublished Treatise of Miskawaih on Justice*. Edited by M. S. Khan. Leiden: Brill, 1964.

Montgomery, James E. “Al-Ǧāḥiẓ and Hellenizing Philosophy.” In *The Libraries of the Neoplatonists*, edited by Cristina d’Ancona, 443–56. Leiden: Brill, 2007.

Mufaḍḍal ibn Muḥammad. *Al-Mufaḍḍaliyyāt*. Edited by Aḥmad Muḥammad Shākir and ʿAbd al-Salām Muḥammad Hārūn. 6th ed. Cairo: Dār al-Maʿārif, 1979.

Muhanna, Elias. “The Scattered and the Gathered: Abū Ḥayyān al-Tawḥīdī’s Infrequently Asked Questions.” In *Essays in Islamic Philology, History, and Philosophy*, edited by Alireza Korangy, Wheeler M. Thackston, Roy P. Mottahedeh, and William Granara, 248–80. Berlin: De Gruyter, 2016.

Al-Mutanabbī, Abū l-Ṭayyib. *Dīwān al-Mutanabbī*. Beirut: Dār Bayrūt, 1983.

Naaman, Erez. *Literature and the Islamic Court: Cultural Life under al-Ṣāḥib Ibn ʿAbbād*. London; New York: Routledge, 2016.

Pines, Shlomo. "A Tenth Century Philosophical Correspondence." *Proceedings of the American Academy for Jewish Research*, 24 (1955): 103–36.

Pomerantz, Maurice A. "An Epic Hero in the *Maqāmāt*?: Popular and Elite Literature in the 8th/14th Century," *Annales Islamologiques* 49 (2015): 99–114.

Al-Rāzī, Abū Bakr. *Rasā'il falsafiyya*. Edited by Paul Kraus. Cairo: Jāmiʿat Fu'ād al-Awwal, Kullīyyat al-Ādāb, 1939.

Al-Ṣafadī, Ṣalāḥ al-Dīn ibn Aybak. *Al-Wāfī bi-l-wafayāt*. 30 vols. Beirut; Wiesbaden; Berlin: Franz Steiner; Klaus Schwarz, 1931–2010.

Ṣaqr, Sayyid Aḥmad. *Sharḥ dīwān ʿAlqamat al-faḥl*. Cairo: al-Maṭbaʿah al-Maḥmūdiyyah, 1935.

Sayyid, Ayman Fu'ād. "Les marques de possession sur les manuscrits et la reconstitution des anciens fonds de manuscrits arabes." *Manuscripta Orientalia* 9 (2003): 14–23.

Al-Sijistānī, Abū Sulaymān. *Muntakhab Ṣīwān al-ḥikmah wa-thalāth rasā'il*. Edited by ʿAbd al-Raḥmān Badawī. Tehran: Bunyād-i Farhang-i Īrān, 1974.

Simplicius. *On Aristotle Categories 1–4*. Translated by Michael Chase. Ithaca, NY: Cornell University Press, 2003.

Stoetzer, W. "Ziḥāf." In *Encyclopedia of Islam, Second Edition*. Edited by P. Bearman, Th. Bianquis, C. E. Bosworth, E. van Donzel, W. P. Heinrichs. Brill Online.

Al-Suyūṭī, Jalāl al-Dīn. *Al-Muzhir fī ʿulūm al-lughah wa-anwāʿihā*. Edited by Muḥammad Aḥmad Jād al-Mawlā, Muḥammad Abū l-Faḍl Ibrāhīm, and ʿAlī Muḥammad al-Bajāwī. 2 vols. Saida: al-Maktabah al-ʿAṣrīyyah, 1986.

Swain, Simon, ed. *Seeing the Face, Seeing the Soul: Polemon's Physiognomy from Classical Antiquity to Medieval Islam*. Oxford: Oxford University Press, 2007.

Swain, Simon. *Economy, Family, and Society from Rome to Islam: A Critical Edition, English Translation, and Study of Bryson's Management of the Estate*. Cambridge: Cambridge University Press, 2013.

Swanton, Christine. *Virtue Ethics: A Pluralistic View*. Oxford: Oxford University Press, 2003.

Talib, Adam. "Caricature and Obscenity in *Mujūn* Poetry and African-American Women's Hip Hop." In *The Rude, the Bad and the Bawdy : Essays in Honour of Professor Geert Jan van Gelder*. Edited by Adam Talib, Marlé Hammond, and Arie Schippers, 276–98. Cambridge: E. J. W. Gibb Memorial Trust, 2014.

Al-Tawḥīdī, Abū Ḥāyyan. *Al-Imtāʿ wa-l-muʾānasah*. Edited by Aḥmad Amīn and Aḥmad al-Zayn. 3 vols. Cairo: Lajnat al-Taʾlīf wa-l-Tarjamah wa-l-Nashr, 1939–44.

———. *Al-Baṣāʾir wa-l-dhakhāʾir*. Edited by Wadād al-Qāḍī. 10 vols. Beirut: Dār Ṣādir, 1988.

Al-Tawḥīdī, Abū Ḥāyyan, and Abū ʿAlī Miskawayh. *Al-Hawāmil wa-l-shawāmil*. Edited by Aḥmad Amīn and al-Sayyid Aḥmad Ṣaqr. Cairo: Lajnat al-Taʾlīf wa-l-Tarjamah wa-l-Nashr, 1951.

———. *Il libro dei cammelli errabondi e di quelli che li radunano*. Translated by Lidia Bettini. Venice: Ca' Foscari, 2017.

Wakelnig, Elvira, ed. and trans. *A Philosophy Reader from the Circle of Miskawayh*. Cambridge: Cambridge University Press, 2014.

Yāqūt ibn ʿAbd Allāh al-Ḥamawī. *Muʿjam al-udabāʾ: Irshād al-arīb ilā maʿrifat al-adīb*. Edited by Iḥsān ʿAbbās. 7 vols. Beirut: Dār al-Gharb al-Islāmī, 1993.

Further Reading

ʿAbbās, Iḥsān. *Abū Ḥayyān al-Tawḥīdī*. Beirut: Dār Bayrūt, 1956.

Bergé, Marc. *Pour un humanisme vécu: Essai sur la personnalité morale et intellectuelle d'Abū Ḥayyān al-Tawḥīdī*. Damascus: Institut francais de Damas, 1979.

———. "Abū Ḥayyān al-Tawḥīdī." In *ʿAbbāsid Belles-Lettres*, edited by Julia Ashtiany, T. M. Johnstone, J. D. Latham, R. B. Serjeant, and G. Rex Smith, 112–24. Cambridge: Cambridge University Press, 1990.

Endress, Gerhard. "The Integration of Philosophical Traditions in Islamic Society in the 4th/10th Century: Tawḥīdī and al-Siǧistānī." In *Philosophy in the Islamic World, Vol. 1: 8th–10th Centuries*, translated by Rotraud Hansberger, edited by Ulrich Rudolph, Rotraud Hansberger, and Peter Adamson, 272–304. Leiden: Brill, 2017.

———. "Ancient Ethical Traditions for Islamic Society: Abū ʿAlī Miskawayh." In *Philosophy in the Islamic World, Vol. 1: 8th–10th Centuries*, translated by Rotraud Hansberger, edited by Ulrich Rudolph, Rotraud Hansberger, and Peter Adamson, 304–44. Leiden: Brill, 2017.

Fakhry, Majid. "Aḥmad ibn Muḥammad Miskawayh (d. 1030), Chief Moral Philosopher of Islam." In *Ethical Theories in Islam*. 2nd ed. Leiden: Brill, 1994.

Al-Kīlānī, Ibrāhīm. *Abū Ḥayyān al-Tawḥīdī*. Cairo: Dār al-Maʿārif, 1957.

Kraemer, Joel L. *Philosophy in the Renaissance of Islam*. Leiden: Brill, 1986.

Leaman, Oliver. "Islamic Humanism in the Fourth/Tenth Century." In *History of Islamic Philosophy*, edited by Seyyed Hossein Nasr and Oliver Leaman, 155–61. London: Routledge, 1996.

———. "Ibn Miskawayh." In *History of Islamic Philosophy*, edited by Seyyed Hossein Nasr and Oliver Leaman, 252–57. London: Routledge, 1996.

Rowson, Everett K. "The Philosopher as Litterateur: Al-Tawḥīdī and His Predecessors." *Zeitschrift für Geschichte der arabisch-islamischen Wissenschaften*, 6 (1990): 50–92.

Stern, Samuel M. "Abū Ḥayyān al-Tawḥīdī." In *Encyclopaedia of Islam, Second Edition*. Edited by P. Bearman, Th. Bianquis, C. E. Bosworth, E. van Donzel, and W. P. Heinrichs. Brill Online.

ʿUmar, Fāʾiz Ṭāhā. *Al-Ẓamaʾ: Dirāsah fī asʾilat al-Tawḥīdī, al-Ḥawāmil.* Baghdad: Dār al-Shuʾūn al-Thaqāfiyyah al-ʿĀmmah, 2007.

Index

About the NYU Abu Dhabi Institute

The Library of Arabic Literature is supported by a grant from the NYU Abu Dhabi Institute, a major hub of intellectual and creative activity and advanced research. The Institute hosts academic conferences, workshops, lectures, film series, performances, and other public programs directed both to audiences within the UAE and to the worldwide academic and research community. It is a center of the scholarly community for Abu Dhabi, bringing together faculty and researchers from institutions of higher learning throughout the region.

NYU Abu Dhabi, through the NYU Abu Dhabi Institute, is a world-class center of cutting-edge research, scholarship, and cultural activity. The Institute creates singular opportunities for leading researchers from across the arts, humanities, social sciences, sciences, engineering, and the professions to carry out creative scholarship and conduct research on issues of major disciplinary, multidisciplinary, and global significance.

About the Translators

Sophia Vasalou is Senior Lecturer and Birmingham Fellow in Philosophical Theology at the University of Birmingham. Her books include *Moral Agents and their Deserts: The Character of Mu'tazilite Ethics*, *Wonder: A Grammar*, and *Ibn Taymiyya's Theological Ethics*.

James E. Montgomery is Sir Thomas Adams's Professor of Arabic, Fellow of Trinity Hall at the University of Cambridge, and an Executive Editor of the Library of Arabic Literature. His latest publications are *Loss Sings*, a collaboration with the celebrated Scottish artist Alison Watt, and *Dīwān 'Antarah ibn Shaddād: A Literary-Historical Study*. He is preparing a translation of poems by al-Mutanabbī for Archipelago Books.

The Library of Arabic Literature

For more details on individual titles, visit www.libraryofarabicliterature.org

Classical Arabic Literature: A Library of Arabic Literature Anthology
Selected and translated by Geert Jan van Gelder (2012)

A Treasury of Virtues: Sayings, Sermons, and Teachings of ʿAlī, by al-Qāḍī al-Quḍāʿī, with the *One Hundred Proverbs* attributed to al-Jāḥiẓ
Edited and translated by Tahera Qutbuddin (2013)

The Epistle on Legal Theory, by al-Shāfiʿī
Edited and translated by Joseph E. Lowry (2013)

Leg over Leg, by Aḥmad Fāris al-Shidyāq
Edited and translated by Humphrey Davies (4 volumes; 2013–14)

Virtues of the Imām Aḥmad ibn Ḥanbal, by Ibn al-Jawzī
Edited and translated by Michael Cooperson (2 volumes; 2013–15)

The Epistle of Forgiveness, by Abū l-ʿAlāʾ al-Maʿarrī
Edited and translated by Geert Jan van Gelder and Gregor Schoeler (2 volumes; 2013–14)

The Principles of Sufism, by ʿĀʾishah al-Bāʿūniyyah
Edited and translated by Th. Emil Homerin (2014)

The Expeditions: An Early Biography of Muḥammad, by Maʿmar ibn Rāshid
Edited and translated by Sean W. Anthony (2014)

Two Arabic Travel Books

Accounts of China and India, by Abū Zayd al-Sīrāfī

Edited and translated by Tim Mackintosh-Smith (2014)

Mission to the Volga, by Aḥmad ibn Faḍlān

Edited and translated by James Montgomery (2014)

Disagreements of the Jurists: A Manual of Islamic Legal Theory, by al-Qāḍī al-Nuʿmān

Edited and translated by Devin J. Stewart (2015)

Consorts of the Caliphs: Women and the Court of Baghdad, by Ibn al-Sāʿī

Edited by Shawkat M. Toorawa and translated by the Editors of the Library of Arabic Literature (2015)

What ʿĪsā ibn Hishām Told Us, by Muḥammad al-Muwayliḥī

Edited and translated by Roger Allen (2 volumes; 2015)

The Life and Times of Abū Tammām, by Abū Bakr Muḥammad ibn Yaḥyā al-Ṣūlī

Edited and translated by Beatrice Gruendler (2015)

The Sword of Ambition: Bureaucratic Rivalry in Medieval Egypt, by ʿUthmān ibn Ibrāhīm al-Nābulusī

Edited and translated by Luke Yarbrough (2016)

Brains Confounded by the Ode of Abū Shādūf Expounded, by Yūsuf al-Shirbīnī

Edited and translated by Humphrey Davies (2 volumes; 2016)

Light in the Heavens: Sayings of the Prophet Muḥammad, by al-Qāḍī al-Quḍāʿī

Edited and translated by Tahera Qutbuddin (2016)

Risible Rhymes, by Muḥammad ibn Maḥfūẓ al-Sanhūrī

Edited and translated by Humphrey Davies (2016)

A Hundred and One Nights

Edited and translated by Bruce Fudge (2016)

The Excellence of the Arabs, by Ibn Qutaybah
Edited by James E. Montgomery and Peter Webb
Translated by Sarah Bowen Savant and Peter Webb (2017)

Scents and Flavors: A Syrian Cookbook
Edited and translated by Charles Perry (2017)

Arabian Satire: Poetry from 18th-Century Najd, by Ḥmēdān al-Shwēʿir
Edited and translated by Marcel Kurpershoek (2017)

In Darfur: An Account of the Sultanate and Its People, by Muḥammad ibn ʿUmar al-Tūnisī
Edited and translated by Humphrey Davies (2 volumes; 2018)

War Songs, by ʿAntarah ibn Shaddād
Edited by James E. Montgomery
Translated by James E. Montgomery with Richard Sieburth (2018)

Arabian Romantic: Poems on Bedouin Life and Love, by ʿAbdallah ibn Sbayyil
Edited and translated by Marcel Kurpershoek (2018)

Dīwān ʿAntarah ibn Shaddād: A Literary-Historical Study, by James E. Montgomery (2018)

Stories of Piety and Prayer: Deliverance Follows Adversity, by al-Muḥassin ibn ʿAlī al-Tanūkhī
Edited and translated by Julia Bray (2019)

Tajrīd sayf al-himmah li-stikhrāj mā fī dhimmat al-dhimmah: A Scholarly Edition of ʿUthmān ibn Ibrāhīm al-Nābulusī's Text, by Luke Yarbrough (2019)

The Philosopher Responds: An Intellectual Correspondence from the Tenth Century, by Abū Ḥayyān al-Tawḥīdī and Abū ʿAlī Miskawayh
Edited by Bilal Orfali and Maurice A. Pomerantz
Translated by Sophia Vasalou and James E. Montgomery (2 volumes; 2019)

The Discourses: Reflections on History, Sufism, Theology, and Literature—Volume One, by al-Ḥasan al-Yūsī
Edited and translated by Justin Stearns (2020)

Impostures, by al-Ḥarīrī
Translated by Michael Cooperson (2020)

Maqāmāt Abī Zayd al-Sarūjī, by al-Ḥarīrī
Edited by Michael Cooperson (2020)

The Yoga Sutras of Patañjali, by Abū Rayḥān al-Bīrūnī
Edited and translated by Mario Kozah (2020)

The Book of Charlatans, by Jamāl al-Dīn ʿAbd al-Raḥīm al-Jawbarī
Edited by Manuela Dengler
Translated by Humphrey Davies (2020)

A Physician on the Nile: A Description of Egypt and Journal of a Plague Year, by ʿAbd al-Laṭīf al-Baghdādī
Edited and translated by Tim Mackintosh-Smith (2021)

The Book of Travels, by Ḥannā Diyāb
Edited by Johannes Stephan
Translated by Elias Muhanna (2 volumes; 2021)

English-only Paperbacks

Leg over Leg, by Aḥmad Fāris al-Shidyāq (2 volumes; 2015)

The Expeditions: An Early Biography of Muḥammad, by Maʿmar ibn Rāshid (2015)

The Epistle on Legal Theory: A Translation of al-Shāfiʿī's Risālah, by al-Shāfiʿī (2015)

The Epistle of Forgiveness, by Abū l-ʿAlāʾ al-Maʿarrī (2016)

The Principles of Sufism, by ʿĀʾishah al-Bāʿūniyyah (2016)

A Treasury of Virtues: Sayings, Sermons, and Teachings of ʿAlī, by al-Qāḍī al-Quḍāʿī with the *One Hundred Proverbs* attributed to al-Jāḥiẓ (2016)

The Life of Ibn Ḥanbal, by Ibn al-Jawzī (2016)

Mission to the Volga, by Ibn Faḍlān (2017)

Accounts of China and India, by Abū Zayd al-Sīrāfī (2017)

Consorts of the Caliphs: Women and the Court of Baghdad, by Ibn al-Sāʿī (2017)

A Hundred and One Nights (2017)

Disagreements of the Jurists: A Manual of Islamic Legal Theory, by al-Qāḍī al-Nuʿmān (2017)

What ʿĪsā ibn Hishām Told Us, by Muḥammad al-Muwayliḥī (2018)

War Songs, by ʿAntarah ibn Shaddād (2018)

The Life and Times of Abū Tammām, by Abū Bakr Muḥammad ibn Yaḥyā al-Ṣūlī (2018)

The Sword of Ambition, by ʿUthmān ibn Ibrāhīm al-Nābulusī (2019)

Brains Confounded by the Ode of Abū Shādūf Expounded: Volume One, by Yūsuf al-Shirbīnī (2019)

Brains Confounded by the Ode of Abū Shādūf Expounded: Volume Two, by Yūsuf al-Shirbīnī and *Risible Rhymes*, by Muḥammad ibn Maḥfūẓ al-Sanhūrī (2019)

The Excellence of the Arabs, by Ibn Qutaybah (2019)

Light in the Heavens: Sayings of the Prophet Muḥammad, by al-Qāḍī al-Quḍāʿī (2019)

Scents and Flavors: A Syrian Cookbook (2020)

Arabian Satire: Poetry from 18th-Century Najd, by Ḥmēdān al-Shwēʿir (2020)

In Darfur: An Account of the Sultanate and Its People, by Muḥammad al-Tūnisī (2020)

Arabian Romantic: Poems on Bedouin Life and Love, by Ibn Sbayyil (2020)

The Philosopher Responds: An Intellectual Correspondence from the Tenth Century, by Abū Ḥayyān al-Tawḥīdī and Abū ʿAlī Miskawayh (2021)

Printed and bound by CPI Group (UK) Ltd, Croydon, CR0 4YY

25/03/2025

14647335-0001